The FBI and
Martin Luther King, Jr.

The FBI and Martin Luther King, Jr.
From "Solo" to Memphis

DAVID J. GARROW

W·W·NORTON & COMPANY

NEW YORK   LONDON

W. W. Norton & Company, Inc. 500 Fifth Avenue, New York, N.Y. 10110
W. W. Norton & Company Ltd. 25 New Street Square, London EC4A 3NT

ISBN 0 393 01509 2

2 3 4 5 6 7 8 9 0

087955

The most important things are not always to be found in the files.

Goethe

Contents

Preface

This book explains why the Federal Bureau of Investigation pursued Martin Luther King, Jr., throughout the 1960s. It argues that the Bureau's probe of King went through three different periods of development, and that distinctly dissimilar motives underlay the FBI's behavior in each of these phases. It further argues that the Bureau's conduct in the King investigation was indicative of more than just its attitude toward one man, and that a careful analysis of why the FBI went after King can point toward a broader understanding of why the FBI acted as it did toward a whole range of individuals and organizations.

This work began as part of a much larger study of Dr. King's public career from 1955 to 1968. For that work, which remains in progress and is scheduled to appear in 1983, I examined reports produced by two well publicized inquiries into the Federal Bureau of Investigation's activities concerning Dr. King—the 1975–76 review by the Senate Select Committee on Intelligence Activities, commonly known as the Church Committee,[1] and the 1978–79 investigation conducted by the House Select Committee on Assassinations.[2] In doing so, I was struck again and again by a very large omission. While both committees detailed a host of unpleasant Bureau activities concerning King, and the House committee's work convincingly revealed no connection between the Bureau's hostility toward King and his assassination,[3] neither body had made any meaningful attempt to account for the *why* of it; *why* had the FBI developed such a viciously negative attitude toward King in the six

9

years before his death? Why would the United States's major police agency devote so much energy and resources to an intense pursuit of one man and his organization, the Southern Christian Leadership Conference?

Unsatisfied and puzzled by the lack of attention to that question, I examined two other major studies of the Bureau's activities concerning Dr. King, those of the Justice Department in 1975–76 and 1976–77. While the latter of these, which reviewed both the FBI "security" probe of King and the Bureau's assassination investigation, was publicly available,[4] the earlier, more detailed one was classified "Top Secret" and was obtained only by a Freedom of Information Act (FOIA) request.[5] Here again, however, I discovered that both teams of investigators had failed to appreciate the importance of asking that question, "why?," and my disappointment with this blindness remained acute.

The value of pursuing that question was further impressed upon me when I first examined some of the FBI's own documents pertaining to the King case. Many of the most crucial items had crossed the desk of FBI Director J. Edgar Hoover himself, and Hoover had retained copies of some of them in his personal "Official and Confidential" file on Dr. King. This file of Hoover's, along with several other "O & C" folders, was released in 1978 in response to an FOIA request filed by the Center for National Security Studies, and that sample of sensitive documents was a fascinating trove. Coupled with additional important items published by the House Assassinations Committee early in 1979, those "O & C" documents convinced me that that question of "why" the Bureau had pursued Dr. King so intensively was not only important to ask, but possible to answer. Thus I decided in mid-1979 to request all of the relevant FBI files on King and the Southern Christian Leadership Conference (SCLC), and to couple an analysis of that material with critical interviewing of those directly involved who were willing to talk.

Understanding the FBI's extensive and complicated filing system is no easy task. Quite probably no one outside the Bureau fully grasps its intricacies.[6] When I initially applied to the Bureau for its material on Dr. King and SCLC, they quickly informed me that processing of the main files on both King and his organization already had begun, and that the files might be ready for release before the end of 1979. While that estimate proved overly optimistic—for release actually began only in the summer of 1980—it soon also became apparent that those two main files were only the tip of the iceberg.

First, FBI *headquarters'* files actually contain only a part of the paperwork and documentation that a Bureau investigation generates. Most of the actual work, of course, takes place not at headquarters, but in Bureau field offices around the country. Only one-third or so of the material produced there is ever forwarded to Washington. The Bureau is very reluctant to process these voluminous field-office files for release under the Freedom of Information Act. To date I have received no assurance that my request for the Atlanta, New York, and Birmingham field-office files on King and SCLC will be processed anytime soon.[7]

Second, the FOIA allows the Bureau to make major deletions in files that it does choose to release. Most deletions occur under two particular exemptions, one known as (b)(1), which is designed to remove classified information about "the national defense or foreign policy," and the second called (b)(7)(d), which is aimed at protecting the identities of "confidential sources," i.e., human informants.[8] The Bureau makes liberal use of these two major exemptions, especially (b)(1), and much information that has absolutely no possible relationship to "national defense" or even the most inclusive conceptions of the widely abused idea of "national security" is deleted.

While the FOIA is seen as a dangerous and even "un-American" weapon by some, few would view the FOIA as any threat to the country if they had an opportunity to witness firsthand the way the Bureau and other agencies employ it. The FOIA is widely abused, but in exactly the opposite fashion from what its many detractors charge.

Deletions under the (b)(1) rubric are surely nettlesome for anyone seeking to obtain FBI files under the FOIA, but there are two even more serious deletion problems that plague the King and SCLC files. One is that most material gathered by the FBI on King and SCLC from mid-1966 to the time of King's death came from one human informant. In a futile attempt to protect this person's identity the Bureau has adopted a policy, as it often does, of releasing none of the information furnished by that individual, under the theory that the content itself will indicate who supplied it. While this book reveals that man's identity and discusses his role in chapter 5, the Bureau's extensive deletions greatly inhibit a fully informed analysis of this man's behavior in the FBI's investigation of King and SCLC.

A second serious problem concerns the material that the FBI garnered from its extensive telephone wiretapping of Dr. King's Atlanta home and SCLC headquarters between late 1963 and mid-1966. Though in theory this material would be eligible for release under the FOIA, all of the "fruits" of those wiretaps, along with the products of the many microphone surveillances or "buggings" of Dr. King in hotel rooms across the United States, were removed from the FBI's possession early in 1977 by an order from the Federal District Court in Washington. All FBI recordings, transcripts, logs, and quotations from both the bugs and the wiretaps on King's home and the SCLC offices were transferred to the National Archives, where they are to remain sealed for fifty years—until 2027.[9]

One might think that with a series of obstacles like the Bureau's abuse of subsections (b)(1) and (b)(7)(d) and the results of that court order, there would be little left to analyze. That turns out not to be the case largely for two very different reasons.

First, throughout the 1962–68 period, and especially in 1962–63, an extremely heavy portion of the Bureau's investigation of King was based on extensive electronic surveillance of two of his closest friends, New York attorneys Stanley D. Levison and Clarence B. Jones. The conversations, including King's, overheard by those surveillances are still within reach of the FOIA, and neither (b)(1) nor (b)(7)(d) have blocked release of Bureau memoranda concerning that material. Second, intelligent interviewing can and has filled in almost all of the gaps created by the restrictions on the files. I have had what I regard as striking success in digging out the essentials of the still highly classified information involved in the Bureau's probe of King. This experience has impressed upon me the truth of Goethe's statement that I used to open this book—that many of the most important items of knowledge are not to be found in the files.

A healthy skepticism toward what one does find in the files is essential to any intelligent use of the Bureau's own records. One must appreciate the warning, well articulated by Frank J. Donner, that "the clandestine character of [the] intelligence process tends . . . to legitimize it. Information derived from clandestine sources is assumed to be intrinsically valuable. . . . In the same way, the fact that the information is obtained secretly invites the inference that it is accurate."[10] Simply because the Bureau holds certain data tightly does not mean that that information is accurate, and one must constantly guard against accepting as fact every statement contained in a once highly classified document. Bureau files contain countless obvious errors, such as one striking memo from Associate Director Clyde Tolson to Director Hoover about the head of the NAACP, "Clarence Wilkins,"[11] and no doubt many less easily recognizable ones as well.

An excellent example of this problem and the attendant dangers occurred in 1978. One Bureau memo released as part of Hoover's "Official and Confidential" file on Dr. King indicated that NAACP Executive Secretary Roy Wilkins supposedly had told one Bureau executive in 1964 that he would be willing to assist the FBI in removing Dr. King from any position of leadership in the civil rights movement. The accuracy of the memo is questionable, but the manner in which its contents initially were reported was a disservice to Wilkins no matter what the case.[12] A similar example, different only in that the man in question, Washington CORE President Julius Hobson, is deceased and cannot comment on the claim, is a statement in one 1963 memo from one high-ranking FBI executive to another that Hobson "has been a most effective source for this Bureau and has furnished a great deal of information concerning the planned activities of CORE."[13] I do not know whether this is true or false, but the matter deserves skeptical inquiry by people who know the history of CORE before anyone writes a story saying that Hobson *was* an FBI informant.

Detailed conversations with a number of people cleared up many confusing issues and most substantive gaps in the withheld files. Even that, however, does not convey a full grasp of so extensive a subject as the Bureau's investigation of Dr. King. On a number of points I wish my own understanding was somewhat more complete. A good example is the question of break-ins or "black bag jobs" in the King and SCLC investigations. At least five such entries occurred, and those initial five apparently were carried out not on

King's own home or office, but against one or more of his closest friends and advisers, apparently Stanley Levison but perhaps also Clarence Jones or Harry Wachtel. I have not learned the specifics of these activities, or determined where the documents underlying these efforts may (or may not) be filed.[14]

Just as some questions are unresolved by extensive interviewing, the interviews themselves raise questions that the available files do not answer. Most commonly, of course, one person's memory of the chronology is in conflict with the available documentation. I have been able to resolve most of these conflicts to a passable degree of satisfaction, but I certainly believe that in time, as additional materials are extracted from the Bureau, greater precision and certainty will ensue.

Even as I gained extensive knowledge from these conversations with actors in the investigation, I reaped an unintended dividend. Early in September, 1980, the FBI discovered that I knew about two highly placed double agents, sources of the information that had stirred the FBI's interest in Martin King and his close adviser, Stanley Levison. The Bureau had had an active interest in my research since December, 1979, when they had been alerted to my inquiries by a former official of the Central Intelligence Agency. But only when I tried hard to contact one of the still concealed double agents did the Bureau suspect just how much I knew. The double agent himself warned the Bureau and the Bureau immediately interviewed a retired FBI executive who had a good understanding of my research. From him they learned that I had uncovered not only the identities of these two crucial and still active double agents, but also the name of another international agent connected to the Levison-King story, a man whose true allegiance long has been a matter of debate. This retired FBI official himself notified me of what was developing. Within two days I was called by the chief of the Bureau's foreign counterintelligence unit. Might he fly to North Carolina the next day to speak with me? I consented.

After two days of verbal fencing with this chief of foreign counterintelligence, I concluded he had come for essentially two reasons. First, he wanted to find out exactly what I did know about both operations, "Solo" and "Fedora," and whether I could be persuaded not to reveal it. The further implication was that if I was not cooperative, the Bureau might ask the Department of Justice to take legal action against publication of this material. Second, my visitor was extremely interested in how and from whom I had learned what I knew. He presupposed that I could know these tightly held real-life names only through one of a very small number of former Bureau executives. Implicit here was that the FBI might move legally against the Bureau veterans who it believed were my sources.

I told my visitor that I would not withhold from publication any of the information I had acquired, nor would I say anything about the identities of my sources. One week after his return to Washington, and in the aftermath of a Bureau conference to discuss what to do about me, my visitor phoned again. He wanted to confirm several other matters that he believed I knew, such as the identity of the SCLC employee whom the Bureau had hired as an informant in 1965.

In two subsequent encounters in Washington and New York, this same counterintelligence officer unsuccessfully tried to dissuade me from interviewing people who had been victimized by but were not yet aware of the Bureau's double agents. He also renewed his attempts to identify my sources, and made further hints about the legal difficulties that might follow publication of my material.

Given the FBI's pointed interest in my work, I have decided not to reveal the identities of any former Bureau employees with whom I have spoken. Though this means that some passages lack suitable footnotes, I think those deletions are a small price to pay in order to save a number of people possible legal difficulty.

A few non-FBI people have asked that I not reveal their names. Many more who have no such hesitancy have been most kind and generous with their time to me. I want to thank them all for their willingness to discuss a subject that often is not a pleasant one. I also want to exculpate all of them from association with any of my views or conclusions they do not share.

My greatest regret is that I was unable to have an extended conversation with Stanley Levison, one of the most crucial people in this story, who was extremely ill throughout the last year of his life and who died in September, 1979. That misfortune has been remedied in part by the willingness of many of Stanley's closest relatives and acquaintances to speak with me, often on multiple occasions. I want to thank Stanley's widow, Beatrice Levison, his son, Andrew Levison, and his twin brother, Roy Bennett, as well as Joseph H. Filner and Moe Foner. Under circumstances that could have been most trying, both Jay Richard Kennedy and Dr. Janet Kennedy also were most kind to me. I also benefited from conversations with Mrs. Eileen Newman, Roger W. Loewi, Mrs. Nancy Rabson, Paul Cowan, Lem Harris, and Victor Lessiovski, among others.

I would have been unable to unravel many crucial aspects of this story had it not been for the repeated willingness of Harry Wachtel and Clarence B. Jones, two others of Dr. King's closest advisers, to respond frankly to my queries. I also am indebted to Reverend Wyatt Tee Walker, Reverend Ralph David Abernathy, Reverend C. T. Vivian, Randolph T. Blackwell, Mrs. Dorothy F. Cotton, and Mrs. Marian Logan, among others, for sometimes lengthy conversations. I also had the pleasure of speaking with Herbert T. Jenkins and Howard Baugh in Atlanta, and with James Farmer in Washington.

A number of former officials of the Kennedy and/or Johnson administrations willingly shared with me their perspectives on this story, and especially the stance of Robert F. Kennedy. These included Harris Wofford, Nicholas deB. Katzenbach, Burke Marshall, Edwin Guthman, John Seigenthaler, Arthur Schlesinger, Jr., Bill Moyers, and John Doar.

Professor Schlesinger, Jean Stein vanden Heuvel, Professor David L. Lewis, Harold Weisberg, Victor S. Navasky, Scott J. Rafferty, Jim Bishop, Ladislas Farago, and Professor Arvil V. Adams, among others, all gave me great help by making available the fruits of their own interviews and research, some of which were extremely valuable. I also am very deeply indebted to Professor Lucy M. Keele and Joan Daves for allowing me to see material not previously available to any students of Dr. King, and to Bill Stein for his incisive comment on it.

I owe perhaps my deepest debt to Professor Harvey Klehr, who at a crucial moment was able to answer a most pressing riddle. Professor Klehr and many other people who share his interest but whom I cannot name here gave me the most kind assistance on a query whose full meaning I could not explain to them at the time.

A great source of assistance in my FOIA dealings with the FBI has been Marvin Whiting, Robert Corley, and the other good people in the Archives Division of the Birmingham Public Library. They are building an invaluable collection of materials related to civil rights events in Alabama, and police surveillance—both local and federal—of them. Their eagerness to contribute toward my FOIA requests has been valuable.

Staff members at other archives also have given me helpful assistance. Dr. Elinor D. Sinnette, Esme Bhan, Thomas C. Battle, and Denise D. Harbin at Howard University's Moorland-Spingarn Research Center, Eleanor McKay, Louisa Bowen, and Marcy Kinkennon at Memphis State University's Mississippi Valley Collection, Clifton H. Johnson and Florence E. Borders at New Orleans's Amistad Research Center, Father Irenaeus Herscher at St. Bonaventure University, Dr. Henry Gwiazda, William Johnson, and Deborah Greene at the John F. Kennedy Library in Boston, Linda Hanson, Martin Elzy, Nancy Smith, Claudia Anderson, Tina Lawson, and Gary Gallagher at the Lyndon B. Johnson Library in Austin, Howard B. Gotlieb and his staff at Boston University's Special Collections Department, Faye Gamel at the Southern Historical Collection at the University of North Carolina, Chapel Hill, Arthur A. Charpentier at the Yale Law School Library, Eva Mosely at Radcliffe's Schlesinger Library, Nancy Breschler at Princeton's Mudd Library, and Monica Andres at the Center for National Security Studies all have been helpful. Also, Martin Wood and William Smith in the FBI's FOIA unit, Janet Blizard and Renee Holmes in the Civil Rights Division, and Gail B. Padgett at the Community Relations Service all have given me help with my many FOIA requests. I hope my thanking them causes them no troubles.

My research also has been helped by conversations or correspondence with Frank J. Donner, Christopher Pyle, Athan Theoharis, James Q. Wilson, Victor S. Navasky, Richard E. Morgan, Governor LeRoy Collins, George McMillan, James H. Lesar, Edward Jay Epstein, John T. Elliff, and Michael Epstein, among others.

For almost two years my work on this book and on the larger study of Dr. King has been supported by an individual grant from the Ford Foundation, and I am happy to thank Robert B. Goldmann and Carol Arnold of the foundation for their help. My research at the Johnson Library in Austin was assisted by a modest grant from the Johnson Foundation.

One of the greatest pleasures has been the opportunity to spend one entire year at the Institute for Advanced Study at Princeton, and I deeply want to thank Clifford Geertz and Harry Woolf for that incomparable opportunity. The institute is the most remarkable and pleasant place I ever have been, and I especially want to thank Peggy Clarke, Catherine Rhubart, Barbara Tucker, Franz Moehn, Barbara Paal, Amy Jackson, Portia Edwards, and Janis Agnew for all contributing to the enjoyment that I experienced there. Among the professors and members, I particularly benefited from conversations with Alex Field, Dennis Thompson, Albert O. Hirschman, Aram Yengoyan, Bill and Ellen Sewell, Margaret Gilbert, Alan Spitzer, Charles Rosenberg, Tim Breen, and, at the university, Nancy Weiss.

Marian Neal Ash of Yale University Press, Robert Cowley of Random House, and Walter Lippincott and Steve Fraser of Cambridge University Press have given me valuable counsel about how to proceed with this book. The manuscript itself has benefited from comments by Peter G. Fish, James David Barber, and David E. Price. In Boston and Atlanta Robert B. Shepler, Robert P. Hoyt, and Mary Hahn have been helpful friends, and in Chapel Hill Barry Nakell, James W. Prothro, Lou Lipsitz, Alan Stern, Jim White, Thad Beyle, Charles Phillips, and Catherine Hawes all have given me valuable advice. I also want to thank Jane and David Oliver, Jim and Selaine Neidel, Barbara Stearns, and my parents.

Before I began this undertaking, I always had been much impressed by Joseph Conrad's message in *The Heart of Darkness*. I have come to feel, however, that the true nature of evil is much more akin to that described by Hannah Arendt than to Conrad's horror.[15] The danger we all face is not the consequences of man unbound from the restraints of society. It is the surrender of independent and critical judgment by people who work in large organizations. Evil is far more the product of people in complex institutions acting without personal reflection than it is something inherent in individual man. Once again Reinhold Niebuhr may have been closer to the mark than anyone.[16]

The FBI and
Martin Luther King, Jr.

1

"Solo"—
The Mystery of
Stanley Levison

By May of 1961 Martin Luther King, Jr., had been a man of national stature for over five years. His name had first appeared in the headlines of March, 1956, when the Montgomery bus boycott was three months old. The novelty and courage of that effort made King the leading spokesman for the South's "new Negro" that he himself often spoke of. He had played prominent roles in the May, 1957, Prayer Pilgrimage for Freedom, organized to note the third anniversary of the Supreme Court decision in *Brown* v. *Board of Education of Topeka,* and in two other, less heralded Washington demonstrations, the 1958 and 1959 Youth Marches for Integrated Schools. When a deranged black woman stabbed King in a Harlem department store in September, 1958, King again was thrust into the public eye. Two years later, when King was jailed in Georgia on a trumped-up charge of violating parole conditions stemming from a minor traffic conviction, the successful efforts of Democratic presidential nominee John F. Kennedy and his brother Robert to free King were highly publicized.

Despite this notoriety, until May of 1961 the Federal Bureau of Investigation had not taken much notice of King. At that point, King stepped in to take a leading role in the "Freedom Rides" begun by the Congress of Racial Equality (CORE) to desegregate interstate bus transportation facilities across the Deep South. The Director's office requested information on a number of participants, including King. Bureau officials had little to offer.[1]

The Mobile, Alabama, field office had compiled a modest amount of information concerning King and the Montgomery bus boycott. Little of it had been forwarded to headquarters, and most of that was filed, without reference to King, under the name of the Montgomery Improvement Association, the organization that had led the boycott.[2] The Bureau had been unaware that King and several dozen other southern black ministers had established the Southern Christian Leadership Conference in 1957 until the bureau's clipping service came across an article on SCLC in the *Pittsburgh Courier* nearly seven months later.[3] In mid-September, 1957, Bureau headquarters' supervisor J. G. Kelly forwarded that clipping to the Atlanta field office, where SCLC was based, along with the following instructions:

> In the absence of any indication that the Communist Party has attempted, or is attempting, to infiltrate this organization, you should conduct no investigation in this matter. However, in view of the stated purpose of the organization you should remain alert for public source information concerning it in connection with the racial situation.[4]

Thus, the Atlanta office proceeded to collect routine public information about the SCLC, now one of a number of groups that received such attention. Occasional press clippings about SCLC attempts to organize voter registration drives were routinely noted at Bureau headquarters. In July, 1958, a headquarters' directive asking for field-office reports on possible "Communist infiltration" of any and all "mass organizations" led Atlanta to summarize its meager file on the SCLC. Atlanta reported "no infiltration known by CP [Communist party] members," but that SCLC "appears to be [a] target for infiltration." One Lonnie Cross, allegedly a member of the Socialist Workers party, had sought to work with SCLC in the fall of 1957. Nevertheless, Atlanta agent Al F. Miller concluded, "It is not believed that . . . [SCLC] warrants active investigation at this time as nature of group's activities are open and subject to coverage by press. Their prime objective is through public gatherings and meetings to induce Negro qualified citizens to register for voting purposes."[5]

In September, 1958, the Bureau's New York field office opened a file on King when prominent black Communist Benjamin J. Davis, Jr., approached King outside a New York church. Six months later, Bureau headquarters took routine note of a State Department memo announcing an upcoming trip by King to India. In April, 1960, the FBI also noted King's appearance on "Meet the Press," and one month later a field office reported that King and black singer Harry Belafonte had met with Benjamin Davis, the black Communist. Late in September, 1960, just after King's Georgia conviction on a minor driving charge, a low-ranking Bureau headquarters' official put together a summary of all information the FBI possessed on King. It described the histories of the Montgomery Improvement Association and the Southern Christian Leadership Conference, noted King's reported contacts with Ben Davis, and detailed the assistance that a number of supposed leftists had provided during the Montgomery bus boycott. Nearly forty percent of the seventy-one-page report consisted simply of press clippings on Montgomery or the SCLC.[6]

The Bureau's muted interest in King and SCLC continued throughout 1960 and 1961. In October, 1960, the New Orleans field office notified headquarters that one of its informants had attended a three-day SCLC conference in Shreveport. The source reported, "The raising of money appeared to be one of the most important matters at the various meetings. . . . it appeared the money was all they were after." Two months later, in December, 1960, U.S. District Judge Irving Kaufman of New York advised the Bureau that both King and the NAACP were supporting the "Committee to Secure Justice for Morton Sobell," a convicted espionage figure. The information was filed routinely.[7]

The first high-level Bureau interest in King occurred immediately after publication of an article in the *Nation* in February, 1961. In it,

King made a passing reference to the FBI, calling for the elimination of racial discrimination in federal employment and greater representation of blacks in federal police agencies. Headquarters' supervisors assigned to monitor just such references reported it to Assistant Director Cartha D. "Deke" DeLoach, adding, "Although King is in error in his comments relating to the FBI, it is believed inadvisable to call his hand on this matter as he obviously would only welcome any controversy or resulting publicity that might ensue." Two months later, when the State Department notified the Bureau that King was under consideration for membership on its Advisory Council on African Affairs, the FBI responded with a negative evaluation.[8]

That apparently was all that the Bureau thought it knew about King when the Freedom Rides burst upon the nation in May, 1961. The Director's office immediately asked for information on King and four other leading figures in the rides. A memo resulted, sent first to Assistant Director Alex Rosen and then to J. Edgar Hoover himself. It stated that "King has not been investigated by the FBI," and went on to detail the few innocuous contacts King was known to have had with supposedly "subversive" groups and individuals. He had thanked the Socialist Workers party for supporting the Montgomery bus boycott and black Communist Ben Davis, now a member of New York's city council, for giving blood after his 1958 stabbing. King's name also had been used in public appeals by the Young Socialist League and by the committee seeking justice for Morton Sobell. It also was said that King had attended meetings of the Progressive party—apparently while an undergraduate at Atlanta's Morehouse College in 1948—and "in 1957 attended [a] Communist Party training school seminar and reportedly gave [the] closing speech." Next to the statement that King had not been investigated, Director Hoover wrote, "Why not?" Beside the "training school" allegation he added, "Let me have more details."[9]

Regarding the "Communist Party training school," the author of the memo was repeating a canard that had circulated among right-wingers for over three years. The story stemmed from a speech King had given on September 2, 1957, at the twenty-fifth anniversary celebration of the Highlander Folk School in Monteagle, Tennessee. In attendance that day had been a photographer for a Georgia state segregation commission, Ed Friend. By concealing his identity, Friend had managed to photograph King and others in attendance, including *Daily Worker* correspondent Abner Berry. Segregationist leaders in Tennessee had been harassing the school for years, since it featured integrated facilities. This 1957 incident was merely one more in a series. Not even the FBI, however, was willing to take this "Communist Party training school" claim seriously. Bureau veterans report that the supervisor who had been so sloppy as to draw Hoover's interest to this story came to an unhappy end. He was transferred out of headquarters when a more thorough examination showed that the Highlander characterization was clearly erroneous.[10]

This internal flap may have distracted Bureau supervisors from Hoover's other question—why King never had been investigated. As the files reveal, and as a Justice Department investigation in 1976 concluded, "FBI personnel did not pursue the King matter at this time. Thus, FBI personnel did not have nor did they assume a personal interest in the activities of Dr. King through May, 1961."[11]

Bureau field offices, however, were beginning to pay more attention to the activities of the SCLC. Indeed, SCLC had taken a more energetic role in the burgeoning civil rights movement with the July, 1960, appointment of talented Reverend Wyatt Tee Walker as executive director. A July, 1961, Atlanta field-office report on Walker, written by agent Robert R. Nichols, alleged that Walker subscribed to the *Worker,* the newly renamed Communist party newspaper. It also said that he and King had taken an active role in seeking clemency for Carl Braden. Braden, convicted of contempt of Congress for refusing to answer questions before the House Un-American Activities Committee, was also once named by a Bureau informant as a Communist party member. No other sources, Nichols reported, knew anything "subversive" or unfavorable about Walker.[12]

The Bureau's Memphis office kept headquarters informed of plans for SCLC's annual convention, to be held in Nashville in late September. This news was furnished by a Nashville pastor associated with SCLC. When the convention ended, Memphis was able to report that its source "knew of no Communist Party (CP) influence at the Conference" and that SCLC had resolved to concentrate on voter registration activities in 1962.[13] The Miami office was instructed to look into word that SCLC might organize a door-to-door canvassing effort in that city. Miami reported that no confirmation of the rumor could be obtained.[14] In late November, 1961, in line with this innocuous field traffic, Atlanta agent Nichols reported to headquarters, "There is no information on which to base a Security Matter inquiry or Racial Matters investigation of the SCLC at this time."[15]

Within barely five weeks of that conclusion, however, Bureau headquarters reported a startling piece of information to Attorney General Robert F. Kennedy. A January 8, 1962 letter from Director Hoover stated the Bureau had learned that Stanley D. Levison, "a member of the Communist Party, USA. . . . is allegedly a close advisor to the Reverend Martin Luther King, Jr." A reliable informant, Hoover said, had reported on January 4 that Isadore Wofsy, a high-ranking communist leader, had said that Levison had written a major speech that King delivered to the AFL-CIO convention in Miami Beach on December 11, 1961. From all indications, this was the first time that the FBI had realized King and Levison were close friends. In fact, the two men had known each other extremely well for over four years.[16]

Levison, a white attorney from New York City, had first become involved in the southern civil rights struggle as one of the most active sponsors of a New York group named In Friendship. Organized in 1955 and 1956, In Friendship provided financial assistance to southern blacks who had suffered white retaliation because of their political activity. In Friendship had sponsored a large May, 1956, rally at Madison Square Garden to salute such southern activists, and a good percentage of the funds raised went to King's Montgomery Improvement Association. Through Bayard Rustin, a black pacifist and civil rights figure who was active in "In Friendship" and who had been the first outside adviser to come and volunteer assistance to King in the early weeks of the Montgomery boycott, Levison was introduced to King in the summer of 1956.[17]

Levison was eager to be of service to the young and nationally inexperienced leader of the Montgomery protest. His skills lay in exactly those areas where King's were weak: complicated financial matters, evaluating labor and other liberal leaders who sought to be of assistance, and careful, precise writing about fine points of legal change and social reform programs.[18] On this last point Levison's talents often were combined with Rustin's. Levison tackled the programmatic sections and Rustin spelled out the detailed analyses of nonviolent direct action. Nowhere was this collaboration and assistance, especially from Levison, of greater help to King than in the drafting and publication of his first book, *Stride Toward Freedom,* [19] an autobiographical portrait centered on the Montgomery protest. Throughout the fall of 1957 Levison shepherded King through the contract negotiations for the book with Harper & Brothers. In early 1958 he turned his attention to the preparation of King's 1957 income-tax returns. [20]

By late March, 1958, Levison was carefully reviewing the book manuscript itself, counseling King against including a segment on black self-improvement and urging that he add a section on registration and voting, which King had not touched upon. Levison also told King that the manuscript left an impression that in the Montgomery protest "everything depended on you. This could create unnecessary charges of an ego-centric presentation of the situation and is important to avoid even if it were the fact." Levison in particular concentrated on the concluding chapter of the book, telling King that it was repetitious and poorly organized. Levison drafted new passages, which were incorporated verbatim into the published text. [21]

By late summer Levison was informing King of Harper's promotion plans, and advising that he had been contacted by Civil Rights Commission attorney Harris Wofford. Another contributor to King's book, Wofford wanted Levison to know that the newly established commission had not received a single voting-discrimination complaint. Levison, as recommended by Wofford, suggested that King find and submit some. [22] When King was stabbed at a Harlem department store on September 20 while promoting his new book, it was Levison, accompanied by Rustin, Ella Baker, and Reverend Thomas Kilgore, who met Coretta King at the airport. As King's recovery proceeded slowly, Levison took charge of administering the flow of contributions that were coming in. He also advised King that SCLC needed to establish a systematic fund-raising mechanism to secure money for a large-scale national program for whenever King chose to launch one. Levison felt King should approach labor leaders such as Walter Reuther for support. He urged, as he had in manuscripts drafted for King, that labor and civil rights join forces to attain their goals. [23]

King valued the assistance that Levison was giving him on so many fronts. He offered several times to pay Levison for his work and each time Levison strongly refused. "It is out of the question. . . . My skills," he explained to King, "were acquired not only in a cloistered academic environment, but also in the commercial jungle. . . . Although our culture approves, and even honors, these practices, to me they were always abhorrent. Hence, I looked forward to the time when I could use these skills not for myself but for socially constructive ends. The liberation struggle is the most positive and rewarding area of work anyone could experience."[24]

Levison's counsel and assistance, sometimes coupled with Bayard Rustin's, continued throughout 1959 and 1960. In November, 1959, King asked Levison and Rustin to draft a press release announcing King's decision to resign as pastor of Montgomery's Dexter Avenue Baptist Church. King wished to move to Atlanta where SCLC's offices were located, and where he could share a church with his father. Three months later, when the state of Alabama indicted King on baseless charges of income-tax evasion, Levison again stepped into the breach.[25] Levison had been disappointed by SCLC's and King's relative quiescence in 1958 and 1959, and when the spontaneous college student sit-ins began in Greensboro on February 1, 1960, he welcomed them with special relish. "This," he wrote to King, "is a new stage in the struggle. It begins at the higher point where Montgomery left off. The students are taking on the strongest state power and demonstrating real will and determination. By their actions they are making the shadow boxing in Congress clear as a farce. They are by contrast exposing the lack of real fight that exists among allegedly friendly congressmen and presidential aspirants. And by example they are demonstrating the bankruptcy of the policy of relying upon courts and legislation to achieve real results."[26]

King also came to trust Levison's judgment regarding SCLC employees. Levison and Rustin had sent Ella Baker to Atlanta to oversee the SCLC office, and King repeatedly enlisted Levison in his attempts to bring Bayard Rustin into a more formal role in the organization.[27] Levison and Rustin interviewed Wyatt Walker before Walker was named executive director, and in early 1961 King asked Levison to evaluate a young man who had written seeking advice about a job with the Highlander School's citizenship education program. King could not recall having met the man—Andrew J.

Young. As a result, Young did take a citizenship education job, but one affiliated with SCLC as well as Highlander. In time he moved exclusively onto the SCLC staff and payroll.[28] By fall 1961 Levison also had brought onto the staff another young black man, Jack O'Dell, to assist with SCLC administrative work in New York.[29]

This, then, was a long, close, and selfless friendship that the FBI learned of only at the beginning of 1962. What lay behind this initial FBI allegation that Levison was a member of the Communist party?

Levison himself knew that the FBI had tracked him long before he met Dr. King. In 1954, the superintendent of the Levison apartment building had warned that the family phone was wiretapped, and both Levison and his wife had noticed that Bureau agents sometimes followed them. Unbeknownst to Levison, Bureau agents also attempted to interview Levison's first wife, divorced from him for more than a decade, as well as other associates he had known in the 1940s. He would rarely mention the incident in later years, but Bureau agents on one occasion confronted Levison himself, reading to him a list of names—mainly other New York attorneys—and asking if he knew any of them. Levison told the Bureau representatives that all except perhaps one of the names were unfamiliar to him.[30]

When close friends queried Levison about this marked federal interest, Levison stated that the difficulty stemmed from a 1940s business relationship that had ended badly. The former associate, Levison said, apparently had had his own problems with the FBI. In an attempt to improve his standing, as well as settle an intense grudge, he had made accusations against Levison. Levison himself rarely mentioned the man's name, telling one persistent questioner years later that the former associate was "clinically sick." Revealing his identity would only rekindle the man's hostility toward Levison. The animosity was deeply mutual.[31]

There actually was a good deal more to the story than Levison chose to reveal. Levison and this man had been more than business acquaintances, and the other's story had many touches of mystery.

Levison was born in May of 1912 in New York, and had grown up on Long Island. After high school, he had attended the University of Michigan, while his identical twin brother, Roy, who soon was to change his surname from Levison to Bennett, went off to Ohio State. Also at Ohio State was Stanley's high-school sweetheart, Janet

Alterman. Stanley returned to New York in the mid-1930s, receiving an LL.B. from St. John's University law school in 1938 and an LL.M. the following year. At that time Janet graduated from medical school, and on June 8, 1939, Stanley and Janet were married. Stanley's and Roy's father, Harry Levison, was working as an accountant for a Brooklyn tool-and-die firm, Unique Specialties Corporation.

By mid-1940 both Stanley and Roy had taken jobs with the firm, Roy as a manager in the plant and Stanley as general troubleshooter and counsel. One of the owners of Unique Specialties also operated a real-estate management firm, where Stanley's and Roy's mother, Esther, was employed. That man went by the name Jay Richard Kennedy.[32]

Actually, as Janet in particular and the rest of the Levison family less directly knew, Jay Richard Kennedy had been Jay Richard Kennedy only since mid-1939. For twenty-eight years prior to that, he had been Samuel Richard Solomonick. Solomonick had been born in a tough area of the East Bronx in 1911. He had left school in the seventh grade, and had gone on to work a variety of jobs, including one stretch on a German-speaking farm in the state of Kansas. By 1929 he was the eighteen-year-old manager of a successful Bronx movie theater. Early the following year he quit that job, and worked intermittently as a bricklayer, before working in a printing plant. Not long after, he attended an organizational meeting of the Industrial Printing Employees Union. A forceful speaker, Solomonick almost immediately became an officer of the union, and took part in a successful strike against a Polish-language fascist paper. The fight against fascism strongly attracted him. By 1935 he had left the printing job to become a full-time organizer for an umbrella group known as the American League against War and Fascism, while also working for the People's Committee against Hearst.

Through these two organizations Solomonick met a number of dedicated antifascists who were active in the Communist party. In 1938 Solomonick became circulation manager for the party paper, the *Daily Worker*. Solomonick, now married, stayed at the paper until the shock of the Hitler-Stalin Pact struck in the late summer of 1939. When that hit, he walked out, but soon found that it was impossible to get new work, apparently because of strong party efforts to punish him for quitting. As his concern about employment mounted, so did the attraction of a pseudonym. One afternoon Solomonick raised the question with a close friend, Andrew Loewi, as they walked down a New York street. On a billboard up ahead was the name Kennedy. Solomonick saw it, liked it, and tried it out on Loewi. Within a few moments the decision had been made: Samuel Richard Solomonick became Jay Richard Kennedy.

With a new identity, and now on his own, Kennedy's luck changed. He and another acquaintance, Charles Newman, put together some $50,000 and bought into Unique Specialties. In a year or two, Kennedy's success grew further, and he established Kennedy Management Corporation, a real-estate management business. Soon Stanley Levison, with his law degree, moved from Unique Specialties to the management firm. At the same time, however, some personal matters had not been going well, and in December of 1941 Stanley and Janet divorced, though with no animosity or recrimination. Within several years time, Janet and Jay Kennedy married, and subsequently moved to California. Kennedy maintained the successful management firm nonetheless, with Stanley and Roy administering it in New York. Stanley himself soon remarried, to Beatrice Merkin, and the entire group remained on friendly terms.[33]

Kennedy's attention now turned to writing and producing a radio program entitled "El Mysterioso," which, with some State Department assistance, was beamed into Central and South America throughout the mid-1940s for the purpose of disseminating strong antifascist themes. An English-language version of the same basic story was developed for American radio, and achieved striking popularity as "A Man Called X," featuring Herbert Marshall. Kennedy's success in this work led him to a movie project on international drug trafficking, entitled "To the Ends of the Earth," produced with assistance from the Bureau of Narcotics. Then, relying on contacts that both he and Stanley had made in 1944 as active members of "Business Men for Roosevelt," Kennedy in 1946–47 made an unsuccessful attempt to organize a major motion picture on the life of Franklin Roosevelt, with Roosevelt-family endorsement.[34]

Janet Kennedy wanted to return to New York, and after the failure of the Roosevelt venture, Jay too was ready for something new. Stanley had continued to look after Kennedy's New York interests during these years, and had grown close to the Loewi family, whose substantial realty holdings he helped managed and one of whose sons, before his death in World War II, had been both Kennedy's and Levison's close friend. During the war years Stanley and Roy had maintained an interest in Unique Specialties' manufacture of artillery fuse parts, but as defense production slackened in 1945, each brother cast an eye toward new opportunities. Roy took the lead in acquiring a Ford dealership in Essex County, New Jersey, in which Stanley also held an interest. Stanley himself in 1946 traveled to Warsaw, Poland, for two weeks in what he and Roy said was an unsuccessful effort to acquire the American import franchise for Polish ham.[35]

Upon Jay Kennedy's return to New York in late 1948, the relationship between him and Stanley, which had survived marital developments and six years of geographical separation, deteriorated rapidly. Whether this schism stemmed from money that Kennedy owed Levison for work in the management firm and was unable to pay, or from Levison's alleged errors in administering Kennedy's interests, cannot be determined from evidence both incomplete and more than thirty years old. At any rate, in early April of 1949 Kennedy and Levison signed a letter of agreement that cancelled all debts Kennedy owed Levison and assigned all stock and obligations in the Kennedy Management Corporation to Levison. All that the agreement provided Kennedy was temporary office space in the firm's Madison Avenue quarters. Though the agreement itself is a document of spare legal prose, the emotions underlying it were still intense more than a quarter century later.[36]

Stanley's role with the Loewi family realty firm, Park Management Corporation, the increasingly successful Ford dealership operated by Roy, and several trading ventures all served to give Stanley a solid financial base as the 1950s began. He also became active in other endeavors. He became especially involved in the American Jewish Congress, heading up its West Side Manhattan organization. In the early 1950s, through his friendship with another of the Loewi family offspring, Nancy Loewi Newman Rabson, who, with her second husband, Mortimer Rabson, had moved to Guayaquil, Ecuador, Stanley became part-owner of a Guayaquil wholesale laundry firm named Secomatico. This investment afforded him the opportunity to travel to South America at least once a year.[37]

Jay Kennedy now turned his efforts to writing a novel, while Janet, whose medical interests had shifted, began psychiatric training. The publication of Kennedy's novel *Prince Bart* in 1953 was a major success. It even brought a congratulatory phone call from Levison, the last time the two men spoke. The success of the novel also greatly enhanced Kennedy's efforts to promote himself as an agent for authors and entertainers and soon thereafter Kennedy became the agent for the promising young black entertainer Harry Belafonte. After less than two years' association, however, the Kennedy-Belafonte relationship ended angrily with a flurry of charges and countercharges concerning financial misconduct and exploitation that made the earlier Levison-Kennedy one seem tame by comparison.[38]

The Kennedy-Belafonte animosity came to have greater import when Belafonte began to work with Dr. King in 1956–57 and through King met Levison. The two men discovered that they shared similar experiences with, and similar feelings toward, Jay Kennedy.[39] Five years later, in 1962, when the FBI renewed its watch on Levison, Stanley again cited Kennedy as the source of the problem, a suspicion that Belafonte heartily seconded. Within a few months, as news of the FBI's activity spread within King's circle of New York friends, a third person, young black attorney Clarence B. Jones, endorsed this view. Jones had first come on board to assist the defense team in King's 1960 Alabama tax case, and he provided further information that pointed toward Jay Kennedy. Jones, who had been associated with the Young Progressives of America while a Columbia undergraduate in the mid-1950s, said that he recalled hearing a number of leading Communist party figures, such as Louis Burnham, Elizabeth Gurley Flynn, and Alan Max, voice strong suspicion that Kennedy was an FBI informant. Indeed, they speculated, could not the government assistance to Kennedy in the mid- and late-1940s have been a form of reimbursement?[40] There did indeed seem to be plausible grounds for suspecting Kennedy as the source of Levison's problem.

This suspicion was a false trail, however. Jay Richard Kennedy, despite his intriguing life history—a history that certainly did not end in 1957—was not the source of the FBI's allegations against Stanley Levison. Kennedy's forthright statements that he never had friendly contact with the FBI are true.[41] Wherever fault may lie in the business antagonisms between Kennedy on the one hand and Levison and Belafonte on the other, Kennedy is innocent of any nefarious role relating to Levison's problems with the Bureau. If Kennedy had not named Levison to the FBI, then who did?

Another possible accuser, one often mentioned in the past several years, is "Fedora," a Soviet employee of the United Nations who volunteered his services to the FBI in early 1962.[42] "Fedora," who has not been publicly identified, is Victor M. Lessiovski, a KGB agent and long-time special assistant to the UN secretary general. But he also was not the source of the allegations against Levison.

Lessiovski's cooperation with the Bureau, stemming ostensibly from disappointment that the KGB was not letting him keep his entire UN salary, did not begin until March of 1962. This was two months after the Levison matter was raised. Lessiovski had been sent to New York because the new secretary general, U Thant of Burma, had known Lessiovski when Lessiovski had been stationed in Rangoon in 1951–54. Although by 1963 Lessiovski had met Stanley's brother Roy, then serving as UN correspondent for the British Labour party weekly, the *London Tribune,* as well as a national officer of the Americans for Democratic Action, the familiarity, though ironic, was evidently innocent.

Sometime around 1965 Roy introduced Stanley to Lessiovski, and over the next decade the two men occasionally met for lunch. Stanley did not doubt that Lessiovski worked for the KGB. He told relatives that he viewed Victor as a comical figure, interesting to talk to but difficult to take seriously.[43] Although by the time Stanley and Victor met, Lessiovski's true status—whether he was a U.S.-controlled double agent, or a Soviet-controlled source of disinformation—had become a matter of great controversy within the American intelligence community, Levison never knew anything about Victor's supposed double role or the debate concerning him. That debate about Lessiovski has never been settled authoritatively, and Lessiovski in early 1981 still held an important job in the UN secretariat. Nonetheless, the story of "Fedora" and the story of Stanley Levison are essentially separate matters.[44]

Suspicion that the charges against Levison did stem from some Bureau informant with Soviet contacts is correct, however. The true source was an operation that has been one of the most carefully guarded secrets in FBI history. It is an operation that has lasted for more than a quarter century and one the Bureau leadership regards as a great accomplishment. The operation began in the early 1950s and lasted until the eve of the publication of this account in 1981.

Its code name is "Solo." "Solo" stands not for one person, but for a team of two brothers whose accomplishments over some twenty-eight years of activity may well make them the most success-ful double agents in American history. Although the full details of "Solo" are not known, its initial roots go back to a meeting of the American Communist party's national committee on June 27, 1947. One member of the national committee, *Daily Worker* editor Morris Childs, had just returned from a trip to Moscow, where he had met with high Communist officials. Childs often had traveled to Mos-cow, and this time on his way back he stopped in Paris to meet with French Communist party leader Jacques Duclos. Back in New York, however, Childs became aware that an aspect of his trip had not set well with some interested parties. His persistent heart trouble was back once again, and he considered asking for a brief leave of absence from his editor's job. Childs was allied with the majority group on the national committee, but he was a particular target of the hard-line minority faction composed of party leaders William Z. Foster, Robert Thompson, and Benjamin Davis. The majority group, led by Eugene Dennis, was seeking to ameliorate some of the inter-nal dissension being created by this minority. With this goal in mind, as one member of the majority faction recalled it, "the grouping around Dennis decided to throw Childs to the wolves," to make a sacrificial offering of one of its own. The unlucky Childs "was not even informed of the move to replace him until the proposal was put forward at the meeting." Eugene Dennis stood and proposed that Childs be given an indefinite leave of absence from his job, and that he be replaced as *Daily Worker* editor by Spanish Civil War veteran John Gates, a young, highly touted party figure. One eyewitness reported that "Childs's face turned white as a sheet." William Fos-ter spoke up in support of Dennis's recommendation, and the com-mittee approved it without opposition. Childs himself and one other member abstained. As Childs's replacement John Gates, later described it, Childs "was rightly indignant. It was an inhuman way to treat a person, but it was also a common practice in the party."[45]

The move should not have come as a shock to Morris Childs. He was no novice in the cold-blooded ways of the party, which he had joined in the early 1920s in Chicago. Born Morris Chilofsky in 1902 near the Polish-Russian border, Morris had come with his brother Jack, a few years younger, to the United States when both were children. The Chilofsky surname was subsequently Americanized, and by the late 1920s Morris, while supporting himself as a draftsman and milk-truck driver, had emerged as one of the Chicago party's most promising youngsters. In 1926 the Comintern had established in Moscow a training facility known as the Lenin School where just such young workers from Communist parties around the world could receive intensive training in doctrine and practice. At the start of the new decade Morris Childs was one of the select few American Communists chosen to attend the Lenin School.

In Moscow Morris Childs met others of his generation from all over the world, acquaintances that decades later would prove useful to Childs and his true employers. Upon his return to the United States after this extended stay in Moscow, Childs first worked as the CP's district organizer in Milwaukee. Soon he was transferred to Chicago and named Communist party state secretary for Illinois and district organizer for the Chicago region. At the May, 1938, party convention in New York City, Childs was elected to the national committee, though he remained based in Chicago until mid-1945, when he took over the party's political action work and moved to New York. He remained in that position until early 1946. At that time he was named editor of the *Daily Worker,* a job he held for little more than one year.[46]

Morris's younger brother Jack was no less a party stalwart, but of quite a different style. Morris was a public figure. His name appeared in major newspapers, in the party's own tabloids, and in the publications of government bodies obsessed with investigating American communism. Jack was essentially an invisible member. He played an important role in party finances and the movement of money, but he never left a public mark as an official of the organization.

How Jack felt about his brother's fall from power in 1947 is not directly known, but, given the closeness of the two, is easily surmised. No details are yet available concerning exactly what the two brothers did in the aftermath of Morris's dismissal. Some witnesses believe they drifted away from the party. Some say they quietly quit outright. Others doubt that Jack Childs entirely ceased his activities. Few people were in a position to know for certain, and many of them are now dead, while the rest are silent. In any case, both Morris and Jack underwent in the late 1940s a sea change of political sentiment. It was a shift that by 1952 made them both willing, even eager, to work with all of their energy, and at great personal risk, against those individuals and beliefs to which they previously had dedicated twenty-five years. For the next twenty-five years they would be working for the Federal Bureau of Investigation. Stanley Levison and Martin King were only two of thousands of Americans whose lives would be forever changed by Jack and Morris Childs.

The full story of that shift in thought, and of the brothers' recruitment by the FBI, can be told only by Morris Childs, who at age seventy-nine is in precarious health in Chicago. His younger brother Jack died on August 12, 1980, in Hampton Bays, New York, leaving behind a widow, Rosalyn, and two sons, Robert and Philip. None of Jack's family apparently knew of the remarkable life he and Morris had led.[47]

Reportedly the brothers' work for the Bureau began when Bureau agents, as part of a routine program of contacting inactive or former CP members, visited the two men and found them strongly opposed to communism and the Soviet Union. The Bureau representatives broached the idea of the brothers' reactivating themselves within the party network, passing along to the FBI all the information they could acquire. The brothers accepted the idea eagerly, and immediately began to renew their activities within the upper reaches of the American CP.

Within a surprisingly brief time of their recruitment by the Bureau—sometime between 1951 and 1954—both Jack and Morris came to be the crucial link by which Soviet funds approximating one million dollars a year were channeled secretly to the American Communist party. As such the brothers not only came to know the most confidential details of the Soviet-CP connection, details of course passed on to the FBI, but also to have substantial entrée with those in Moscow who supplied this cash. Most of the "business" was transacted in New York, with Jack Childs receiving the Soviet money in American bills. But at least once a year one of the brothers, usually Morris, who spoke Russian, would travel to Moscow.

Over the years Morris Childs traveled all over the world. In these travels he served as the concealed representative of American party leader Gus Hall, with whom both brothers became extremely close. From Hall Jack and Morris learned virtually everything that was occurring within the American Communist party. Thus the FBI and the U.S. executive branch knew the full activity of the American party and witnessed firsthand the contacts of the domestic party with foreign powers. In fact, as one American official remarked, for years the FBI practically had been paying Gus Hall's salary, and with Soviet money. The American government could not have asked for more. "Solo" was indeed a remarkable accomplishment.

Morris Childs reportedly did not meet simply with low-ranking foreign bureaucrats when he made his trips abroad. In Moscow Childs was well acquainted with Boris Ponomarev, now a candidate member of the Soviet Politburo. A photograph showing Childs with a Soviet leader, reportedly party chief Leonid I. Brezhnev, is said to be in the hands of the U.S. government. That picture was shown to at least one U.S. senator in the mid-1970s. Current officials in a position to know state that Childs also met with Mao Tse-tung. There are also suggestive but far from conclusive indications that Childs briefed President Richard M. Nixon on some of his foreign travels and contacts.

A full and accurate account of what Childs did, and how fully informed American presidents and other officials have been of Childs's activities, awaits a full public discussion of this remarkable operation. All three American presidents of the 1970s, as well as other top-rank figures, have been aware of the "Solo" project, if not of Childs's real name.

Managing "Solo" was no small task for the FBI. Headquarters' executives often discussed closing the project down and making known to all the Soviet Union's funding of the American CP. Each time the decision went the other way. Entrée to Moscow and the virtual control of the American CP that "Solo" afforded the FBI were too valuable to be sacrificed for a public relations coup. The Soviet subsidy, most Bureau officials felt, made the American CP relatively lazy and content, and less of a domestic threat than if it had to support itself rather than merely "launder" the Soviet funds that Jack Childs administered. The most serious discussion occurred when "Fedora" notified the Bureau of the time and place of an upcoming Soviet rendezvous with Jack Childs. FBI officials worried that the warning might represent a KGB effort to determine whether the Bureau knew about the "Solo" payments. After some agonizing, the hint was ignored and the meeting took place, with no aftereffects. The inference was that in this instance "Fedora" had not acted as a Soviet loyalist. Another debate occurred when Jack Childs notified the Bureau that Hall had asked for a lump sum of $300,000 from the Soviet funds, a far larger amount than usually conveyed at any one time. Was Hall planning to abscond with the cash? Should the payment be refused and the entire "Solo" project terminated? The FBI let it proceed because Jack Childs said Hall probably intended to use the money to buy a printing plant for the party. Once again no ill consequences occurred, and "Solo" went forward as before.

These were not the only problems or issues that came up as part of "Solo." Handling so difficult a project was made more burdensome by the fact that both Jack and Morris Childs were demanding employees, employees who soon gained more control over their handlers than the handlers had over them. Perhaps it could have evolved in no other way. As a practical matter, the brothers were so valuable to the Bureau, and the American government, that no price could be too high to pay for their extraordinary information. No one with any firsthand experience of "Solo" doubted it: the tail was wagging the dog, and quite vigorously at that.

By the late 1960s some officials were coming to feel that the Childs brothers had been coddled too much and too long. Morris Childs was a worldly, sophisticated man whom Bureau and other officials found a congenial and interesting companion. Christmas cards sometimes were exchanged. Jack Childs, though, was more sly, indeed a crafty figure whose life experiences had not imparted the polish of his brother. When in the late 1960s the brothers requested that the Bureau block a federal banking investigation focused on family relatives, things had gone far enough. For the first time, a request was denied. The denial, however, represented no permanent change in the dynamics of the Childs-FBI relationship.

By the late 1970s the health of both brothers was deteriorating. An increasing number of government officials knew something of the "Solo" story because of the many probes of Bureau intelligence activities. Some FBI executives were firmly convinced that it was time for the operation to be closed down and both Jack and Morris Childs given mandatory retirement. Other people were now involved—the brothers had at least eight witting associates, including one female, providing them with assorted types of assistance. Chances of the operation being compromised had increased drastically. Morris Childs in particular, however, would hear no talk of ending his role. He had enjoyed his contacts, both with Hall and abroad, far too much and far too long to want to exchange them for solitude and quiet. While some Bureau officials privately believed that Morris should turn to writing his memoirs, Childs himself insisted that never would he acknowledge his double role. Other Bureau officials, including long-time Chicago case agent Walter Boyle, sided with Childs. "Solo" also had highly placed executive endorsement. Thus the operation remained active.

What had the Childs brothers said in the early years of "Solo" that had implicated Stanley Levison and, indirectly, Martin King in Communist activities? The allegations came from Jack Childs, who had regular personal contact with Levison in the 1953–55 period. He gave to the FBI an account of Levison's activities that was very different from Stanley's own, or that of his relatives and closest friends.

The FBI first took note of Stanley Levison in June, 1952, perhaps in the immediate aftermath of the recruitment of the Childs brothers. The Bureau focused its attention on Levison's financial affairs and business dealings, particularly those that related to his and the Loewi family's realty interests. Levison did not become the subject of intensive interest until the summer of 1953, when the Bureau began examining both his recent tax returns and his long-distance telephone call records.[48] According to some former FBI agents, Jack Childs told the Bureau that Levison reportedly had been an important secret financial benefactor of the Communist party since perhaps 1945 or 1946. Levison was reputed to have played a central role in establishing businesses whose real purpose was to earn or perhaps launder money needed by the Communist party. Ventures as innocent as Roy's New Jersey Ford dealership, and as mysterious as Stanley's trip to Poland and his more recent role in the Ecuadorian laundry, may all have had a darker underlying purpose, the Bureau was told.

In creating the "front" businesses, Levison allegedly had worked with another New York attorney, Isidore G. "Gibby" Needleman, who represented Amtorg Trading Corporation, the Soviet purchasing commission, and other party or Soviet interests. Needleman had been active in lend-lease negotiations during World War II and, like Stanley, had earned his law degree at St. Johns. He supposedly was implicated in activities ranging beyond legal representation, but the Bureau's information, even from the Childs brothers, was incomplete. Furthermore, even in the present day there is no independent confirmation that Needleman, who died in 1975, and Levison were acquainted; both Stanley's widow Bea and his brother Roy deny any familiarity with the name.[49]

Beginning in 1953 or early 1954, however, Jack Childs also told the FBI that Levison was assisting Communist party financial chiefs William Weiner, Lem Harris, Jack Kling, and Isadore Wofsy in acquiring and managing the CP's secret monies, including the so-called reserve fund. In this period Levison supposedly was directing some $50,000 per year into the party's coffers. Throughout the late summer and fall of 1953, the FBI busied itself with further inquiries about Levison's business activities. Then, in February, 1954, party treasurer Weiner died, and Levison's reported role in CP financial affairs became even more important. Stanley, Jack Childs told the Bureau, was now the interim chief administrator of the party's most secret funds, and Childs's nominal boss. The FBI's interest in Levison heightened even further. Physical surveillance was instituted on a regular basis, and when Levison traveled to Chicago in late April, his room at the Conrad Hilton Hotel was bugged. The transcript of a meeting between Levison and another individual, perhaps Jack Kling, a Chicagoan who also had inherited some of Weiner's responsibilities, was rushed to Bureau headquarters.

Levison's activities remained under extremely close surveillance throughout the remainder of 1954 and into the summer of 1955. Then, apparently at some point between June and November of 1955, Levison's central role in secret CP financial dealings declined greatly. Jack Childs's direct contact with Levison came to an end. The Bureau's interest in his activities noticeably slackened. From all appearances Levison had decided to reduce and perhaps terminate his involvement in the CP's secret financial dealings.[50]

From mid-1955 on all that Jack Childs could tell the Bureau about

Levison was what he himself was told by other important party figures who said they still had some occasional contact with Levison, such as Lem Harris. The FBI's New York office continued to pay some attention to Levison's activities, and his 1956 and 1957 work on behalf of In Friendship, the civil rights fund-raising group, was reported to Bureau headquarters. In March, 1957, Levison's lack of continued CP activity led the New York office to delete him from its list of "key figures" in Communist doings.[51] Some former Bureau officials also recall hearing that CP leaders such as Gus Hall and Harris were extremely disappointed by the termination of Levison's involvement and contributions. All indications are that while the Bureau knew of Levison's interest in assisting the nascent civil rights movement, it was generally unaware of his growing friendship with Martin Luther King, Jr.

Levison's termination of his direct dealings with the CP, and the reports from Jack Childs that the CP hierarchy was very unhappy about Levison's loss of interest, led the Bureau to consider the same sort of approach to Levison that the FBI had made to the Childs brothers six or seven years earlier. On November 27, 1959, the New York office recommended to headquarters that Levison be considered for recruitment as an informant. If Levison were willing, then perhaps he too could reactivate himself within the netherworld of CP financial activities. On December 9, 1959, FBI headquarters told New York to go ahead and approach Levison when an opportunity presented itself.

The New York office did not act until eight weeks later. On February 9, 1960, two Bureau agents approached Levison. Although the details of the conversation are not available, Levison agreed to talk with them further at some later date. That second approach took place on March 4, and—although the specifics again are lacking— Levison made it clear to the agents that he had absolutely no interest in accepting the suggestion they gently put forward. Although headquarters authorized another attempt, New York apparently did not pursue it. From that time forward until the warning conveyed to Robert Kennedy in early January, 1962, Stanley Levison received very little attention from the FBI.[52]

All available evidence indicates that Levison had been closely involved in CP financial activities between 1952 and 1955, but that he ended that association sometime in 1955 and that he had no active ties to the CP once he became associated with Dr. King in 1956. Levison's closest relatives confirm that in the years prior to his friendship with Dr. King, Stanley had been well-acquainted with important Communist party figures such as Lem Harris. Harris himself acknowledges that he and Levison knew each other, that Levison also had been associated with William Weiner, and, most importantly, that Levison was personally acquainted with Jack Childs.[53] Hence the reports from Childs to the FBI that Levison was deeply involved in secret CP financial affairs between 1952 and 1955 in all likelihood were quite accurate. However, from late 1955 on, the FBI had no direct or convincing evidence that Levison had continued to work with the party. Childs apparently did hear from Harris and from party leader Gus Hall on occasion about conversations that they said they had had with Levison, but those hearsay reports clearly indicated that Levison no longer was active on behalf of the party. The Bureau's own attempted recruitment of Levison in 1959–60 testifies to that, and Levison's relatives recall that he ended a number of his previous associations once he began to grow close to Dr. King in 1956–57. In short, the FBI's information tied Levison to the CP only for the years before 1956, and not for those after. While Jack Childs could supply firsthand testimony that Levison had been directly involved in secret Communist activity in 1954, activity that almost certainly made Levison privy to the party's financial link to the Soviet Union, the FBI possessed no evidence that connected Levison to any CP activity in the years after he and Martin Luther King, Jr., first became acquainted.

The FBI's lack of interest in Levison between early 1960 and late 1961 ended suddenly when it learned in very early 1962 that Levison and King were close friends rather than just casual acquaintances. If the Bureau previously had assumed, even after Levison's rebuff of its recruitment offer in March, 1960, that he had largely disassociated himself from the CP, the discovery of his close relationship with King made the FBI reconsider the question. Was it not quite possible that Levison's disassociation from the CP's secret work had been merely a cover, and that his close relationship with King was motivated by a more sinister purpose than sincere support of civil rights? Would someone who in 1954 had been intimately involved in the CP's most sensitive work, and who had not made an open break with the party, turn up at the side of an important, emerging leader like King in 1957 simply by accident?

The Bureau's first report of Levison's close relationship with King to Robert Kennedy on January 8, 1962, produced a flurry of activity. Justice Department officials close to Kennedy discussed whether to warn King of this apparent danger. Robert Kennedy himself made the decision. King should be warned, and Kennedy asked his administrative assistant, John Seigenthaler, and Assistant Attorney General Burke Marshall to see that it was done.

One day soon after, King came to Washington to see Robert Kennedy and to attend a meeting of civil rights leaders and Justice Department officials. The subject was voter registration efforts in the South. After meeting with the Attorney General, King and Seigenthaler went downstairs and onto the sidewalk in front of the attorney general's entrance to the building. Without naming anyone, Seigenthaler told King of word that several people close to King had Communist backgrounds. These backgrounds could be used to smear King himself. King listened quietly, looking Seigenthaler directly in the eye. He gave no indication of familiarity with the subject. He thanked Seigenthaler for his interest, and said that he didn't question the motives of people who sought to assist him, and that absent some clear evidence, he took people at face value. The men shook hands and parted. Seigenthaler went back upstairs, and described the conversation to Robert Kennedy. The Attorney General felt they had done what they could.[54]

Burke Marshall also had acted. Not knowing of Seigenthaler's conversation, and not well acquainted with King, Marshall asked his good friend, White House civil rights adviser Harris Wofford, to intercede. Wofford had known King for several years and he was extremely skeptical when Marshall raised the matter.

Indeed, Wofford had had a foreshadowing experience a year earlier. Kennedy in-law Sargent Shriver had questioned Wofford about an FBI report detailing Wofford's own contacts with Levison at a time when both men were providing assistance to King. Wofford was amazed then at FBI suggestions of deviltry on Levison's part and, he told Marshall, he was no more inclined to think them accurate now. He pressed Marshall. Just what did the Bureau claim to possess on Levison? Marshall replied that he knew only that Levison was secretly a Communist party member. The Bureau's liaison with the Justice Department, Courtney A. Evans, had forbidden Marshall to pass along any more than that, for fear of endangering the Bureau's source. Even that characterization was not to be given to King, for fear of alerting Levison or others.

Wofford was extremely unhappy. Even so, his respect for Marshall led him, very reluctantly, to mention the issue to King, perhaps the same day or the day after Seigenthaler's warning. Wofford delivered the message to King, explicitly stating Levison's name but stressing his own doubts about the accuracy of the information. King, Wofford wrote many years later, "seemed depressed and dumbfounded when I talked with him about Levison; he could not believe it and said he had far more reason to trust Levison" than the Bureau. Wofford agreed.[55]

That day or the next the voter registration meeting took place at a downtown Washington hotel. Dr. King was accompanied by Andrew Young and Stanley Levison; the Kennedy administration was represented by Wofford, Marshall, Seigenthaler, Louis Martin, and Robert Kennedy. The Attorney General arrived somewhat late, and took a seat next to a man he did not recognize. It was, of course, Levison, who said nothing during the meeting. Later, Wofford asked Robert Kennedy if he had been aware of whom he had been sitting next to. Kennedy said no, and Wofford told him it was Levison, the man they were so concerned about. The Attorney General indicated that he appreciated the irony of it.[56]

Deputy Attorney General Byron White had also seen the Bureau letter of January 8. Like Marshall and Kennedy, he spoke to Bureau liaison man Evans about whether a warning should be given King. Evans brought back a simple answer from the Bureau's domestic intelligence division. No details about Levison were to be conveyed to King. Doing so, it said, "would definitely endanger our informant and the national security." Director Hoover forcefully endorsed that order, noting "King is no good anyway. Under no circumstances should our informant be endangered." After a further conversation with Evans, White was persuaded not to pursue the matter at all.[57]

A further Bureau report on the Levison-King relationship went to the Attorney General, and to key White House aide Kenneth

O'Donnell, on February 14. It also pointed out that Jack O'Dell, the young man whom Levison had hired for SCLC's New York office, had a long public record of Communist party ties. In late February supervisors in the Bureau's domestic intelligence division recommended that electronic surveillance of Levison be instituted. On February 27 headquarters ordered the Atlanta and New York field offices to review all of their files and report "all information of a security nature plus complete background data" on King. Three days later the domestic intelligence division formally proposed that a telephone wiretap and a microphone "bug" be installed in Levison's New York office. On March 6 the formal authorization memo requesting approval for the wiretap was sent by the Director's office to the Attorney General; several days later it was returned with Robert F. Kennedy's signature in the lower-left-hand corner authorizing the tap. Headquarters notified the New York office that it could proceed with both items; microphone surveillances did not require the Attorney General's express authorization. On the night of March 15–16, Bureau agents broke into Levison's office and implanted the microphone. The wiretap followed four days later.[58]

Installation of the tap and mike dramatically increased the Bureau's flow of information on Levison. None of the overheard conversations, however, lent any support, even indirectly, to "Solo's" characterization of Levison. Most of the intercepted dialogue was of no real value, but the Bureau did pay particular attention to the Levison-King phone conversations that were picked up. Summaries of those calls were sent to Attorney General Kennedy, to Vice President Lyndon B. Johnson, and to White House aide Kenneth O'Donnell. They proved only that Levison was an influential adviser to King. Typical of these reports was the following Hoover memorandum of April 20 to Robert Kennedy:

> This Bureau has recently received additional information showing the influence of Stanley David Levison, a secret member of the Communist Party, upon Martin Luther King, Jr. You will recall that I have furnished you during the past few months substantial information concerning the close relationship between King and Levison.
>
> A confidential source who has furnished reliable infor-

mation in the past [the wiretap on Levison's office phone] advised on April 16, 1962, that he had learned that Levison is forming in King's name an organization to be known as the Ghandi [sic] Society for Human Rights. Levison contemplates sending invitations signed by King to approximately 20 prominent people to attend a luncheon on May 17, 1962, in Washington. . . . You as well as the President, Senator Clifford Case, Senator Eugene McCarthy and former Attorney General William P. Rogers, are among those being considered to be invited. . . . The informant said that he is under the impression that Theodore Kheel . . . Harry Belafonte . . . and A. Philip Randolph . . . are involved in the formation of the organization.[59]

Unfortunately, no one questioned the presumption on which this sort of reporting was based—the belief that Levison still represented, in his dealings with King, the same interests with which he had been associated in 1954. The lack of any direct, confirming evidence of any present-day contacts of Levison's was ignored.

It was common knowledge among Bureau headquarters' personnel that "the old man," Director Hoover, oftentimes spoke too openly about the Bureau's secrets to his conservative friends on Capitol Hill. In one conversation, apparently with Mississippi Senator James O. Eastland, chairman of the Internal Security Subcommittee, Hoover mentioned the Bureau's strong new interest in Levison, and may even have given Eastland a copy of a Bureau report on Levison. Before Bureau executives knew it, Eastland's staff director, J. G. Sourwine, on April 25 issued a subpoena to Levison. He was to appear before the subcommittee in an unpublicized executive session five days hence. Levison's first reaction, he told friends, was that the session would be the beginning of a conservative attack on King. Levison asked a friend, attorney Arthur Kinoy, to recommend someone as his counsel for the Senate appearance. Kinoy strongly recommended one of his own law partners, a man whom Levison—and, at that time, most everyone else—was unfamiliar with: William M. Kunstler. Accompanied by Kunstler, Levison went to Washington for the April 30 appearance.

The secret session itself was attended by a small number of people: senators Eastland and McClellan, Sourwine and several other subcommittee staffers, Levison and Kunstler, and, presumably, a representative of the Bureau. Levison began by saying, "To dispose of a question causing current apprehension, I am a loyal American and I am not now and never have been a member of the Communist Party." Eastland and Sourwine then moved to question Levison, but Levison supplied only his name and address, invoking the Fifth Amendment in response to all other queries. Attorney Kunstler took out a statement defending the use of the Fifth Amendment, and read it to the subcommittee, erring only when he gave the name of his client as something not at all resembling "Levison." Apparently the statement had been used before in similar circumstances. Sourwine attempted to provoke Levison into some substantive responses, saying, "The Committee . . . has received information that you have been a party to and are aware of certain financial dealings of the Communist Party." Levison again took the Fifth, and an irritated Eastland asked, "Isn't it true that you are a spy for the Communist apparatus in this country? . . . Isn't it true that you have gotten funds from the Soviet Union and given them to the Communist Party, USA?" Levison continued to refuse to answer, and the session concluded with an exasperated Senator McClellan remarking, "I think this is one of the shabbiest performances I have ever heard before a Senate congressional committee by any witness."

Levison himself felt considerably better about the hearing. Much to his surprise, King's name had never come up. He had taken the Fifth, he later told friends and relatives, partly to avoid an interrogation concerning King, and partly at Kunstler's strong recommendation. That Kunstler had not been an impressive counsel was a thought that grew in Levison's mind as the years passed. But all told, he believed it had gone as well as it could. Not even a hint of the session appeared in the public press. The FBI, however, immediately informed both Attorney General Robert Kennedy and White House aide Kenneth O'Donnell of Levison's refusal to respond.[60]

Sourwine had issued the subpoena on April 25. On the same day, the Atlanta field office sent headquarters a thirty-seven-page report stating that no significant Communist influence was being exerted on King or the SCLC. Headquarters' supervisors, steeped in the Levison allegations, notified Atlanta in early May that its statement was incorrect. It ordered a revised report.

Headquarters at that same time ordered the New York office to intensify its coverage of both Levison and Jack O'Dell. Two days later, on May 11, Dr. King's name was added to the Bureau's number-two "enemies list," Section A of the "Reserve Index," only one step below the top-ranked "Security Index," where Levison was categorized. Inclusion in the Security Index was reserved for individuals whom the Bureau believed to be actual members of the Communist party or "similar ideological groups," such as the Socialist Workers party. The Security Index held some twelve thousand names in the early 1960s. But inclusion in Section A of the Reserve Index required only that the person be "in a position to influence others against the national interests or . . . likely to furnish financial or other material aid to subversive elements due to their subversive associations and ideology." The real purpose of both lists was to make detention of allegedly dangerous individuals as easy as possible in the event of a presidentially declared national emergency. The Atlanta office was advised that King should be added to its pick-up list.[61]

Throughout May and June of 1962 the Atlanta office maintained a close watch on the activities of King and the SCLC. Headquarters was told of SCLC's intent to conduct an extensive voter registration effort in Shreveport, Louisiana.[62] Plans were afoot for a June 6 benefit show in Atlanta starring Harry Belafonte.[63] In New York the electronic surveillance of Levison's office continued to supply nothing of note.

In mid-June, however, a nugget seemed to appear. On June 20 the wiretap intercepted a phone conversation between Levison and Jack O'Dell. Levison told O'Dell that he and King recently had discussed King's need for an executive assistant to supplement Wyatt Tee Walker, and that Levison had recommended to King that he shift O'Dell from New York to Atlanta to fill that role. Levison said he had warned King that O'Dell had a public record of past ties to the Communist party, but that King had said that would not pose a problem. "No matter what a man was, if he could stand up now and say he is not connected, then as far as I am concerned, he is eligible to work for me," Levison quoted King as saying. The Bureau's path seemed clear. O'Dell might be quite important within SCLC. The initiative behind his rise was coming from the supposedly malevolent Levison. The FBI immediately notified Robert Kennedy of the conversation, and also told him it now had a report that O'Dell had been elected to the Communist party's national committee in December, 1959, under the pseudonym "Cornelius James." The Bureau greatly increased its interest in O'Dell's tie to SCLC.[64]

No one, including O'Dell, denied his work with the Communist party from the late 1940s to at least the late 1950s. O'Dell had been for a number of years a party organizer based in New Orleans. He had appeared before the Senate Internal Security Subcommittee in April, 1956, and before HUAC in July, 1958. O'Dell had first become involved with the party while working as a merchant marine seaman and as a member of the National Maritime Union. The union had expelled him in the summer of 1950, apparently because of his work for the party. Unbeknownst to the Bureau, O'Dell had first met King at the 1959 Youth March for Integrated Schools. Once in 1959 and twice in 1960 O'Dell sent King unsolicited letters giving assorted political advice and recommendations, emphasizing his belief that black voter registration was *the* thing to stress, both north and south. King replied to the first of these; the second was acknowledged by his secretary and the third apparently ignored.[65]

Despite King's lack of interest in O'Dell's advice, by early 1961 O'Dell was working out of the New York SCLC office overseen by Levison. This was discovered by the Bureau's New York agents on April 27, 1961, when a New York agent posing as a potential SCLC contributor made a pretext phone call to the office and spoke at length with O'Dell. O'Dell patiently explained that the office was two things—SCLC *and* the Committee to Aid the Southern Freedom Struggle, a fund-raising group founded by Levison and Belafonte to assist in King's defense against the Alabama tax charges. Contributions, O'Dell said, could be made to either organization. Financially speaking, they were one and the same. Six months later, on October 27, 1961, Bureau agents secretly watched O'Dell enter the SCLC office and then made another pretext phone call to him. All of this information was filed routinely, for the New York agents were still ignorant of Levison's relationship with King and, presumably, O'Dell. In late January, 1962, soon after the Levison issue arose, a third pretext phone call was made to the New York SCLC office.[66]

O'Dell remained of only moderate interest to the Bureau until Levison recommended him as King's executive assistant. O'Dell did begin traveling to Atlanta a good deal in mid-1962, working not so much as an executive assistant to King as a voter registration adviser and tactician. King's message and appointment books for the summer and early fall show a number of calls and apparent meetings with O'Dell. Several SCLC brochures included O'Dell's name as a ranking employee of the organization.[67]

The Bureau was very much aware of all this. Headquarters' supervisors were inclined to view O'Dell's role, and Levison's part in setting it up, as the first new evidence supporting the subversive allegations against Levison. Hence, on July 20 headquarters' supervisor R. J. Rampton directed the New York office to send Atlanta all of its information on O'Dell and Levison. The Atlanta office was to examine that material as well as its own, and recommend to headquarters "whether a communist infiltration investigation is warranted" for SCLC. Rampton made no secret of what Atlanta was expected to recommend. He noted Atlanta's previous conclusion that "no information has been developed on which to base a security investigation of SCLC," and observed, "In view of the continued activity of Levison and O'Dell and the fact they exert influence on King, it is deemed advisable to again ask for a review of the appropriate field office files to determine if any CP direction and infiltration of the SCLC has developed." Copies of the instructions to Atlanta were sent to New York and Mobile. Those offices were asked to volunteer comments.[68]

The Atlanta office still had none of the eagerness for a formal "Communist infiltration" (COMINFIL) investigation that New York and headquarters did. Two months—from July 20 to September 20—passed without Atlanta making any response.

The New York office was much quicker. In fact, New York was reprimanded by headquarters for using the "COMINFIL" caption on two of its communications in the absence of headquarters' approval for beginning such a case on SCLC. Headquarters, Rampton told New York on August 7, was waiting to hear from Atlanta. Until it did so, the formal stance remained that SCLC's "activities are in the racial field and as yet we have not received evidence of communist infiltration." New York shrugged that one off. On August 21 it reported that "a COMINFIL investigation of the NY

Chapter of the SCLC is warranted, due to the dominant CP influence on the executives of the NY Chapter of the SCLC." Headquarters acknowledged New York's comments on August 29—ignoring New York's confusion over whether SCLC had an office or a "chapter" there—and noted that it was still waiting to hear from Atlanta. A copy of the communication to New York pointedly was sent to Atlanta.[69]

After several more weeks, Rampton supplied a prod. On September 17 he brought to Atlanta's attention an August 29 report by the Savannah field office that SCLC was using the Dorchester Community Center in McIntosh County as some sort of training center. Savannah had suggested that demonstrators in the August protests in Albany, Georgia, "were all trained" at Dorchester and asked that headquarters approve an active Savannah office probe of Dorchester. Rampton then asked Atlanta for comment. On September 20 Atlanta agent Nichols made the office's first response to headquarters on SCLC in two months. He and many other Atlanta agents had been preoccupied with investigating the arson of five black churches in the Albany area, burnings that were in retaliation for the civil rights upsurge in the area. This was why Atlanta had taken no action on the COMINFIL SCLC matter. Atlanta would make its recommendation as soon as possible.[70]

Rampton waited ten more days and heard nothing further from Atlanta. On October 1 the Atlanta special agent in charge (SAC) was told that headquarter's patience was at an end. Rampton noted that the request dated from July 20, and that "it is not readily apparent why there should be continued delay in furnishing the information that has been requested. Atlanta is instructed to immediately commence the necessary file reviews and furnish the Bureau a letter including the recommendations requested heretofore to reach the Bureau not later than 10–15–62. In the event this deadline cannot be met, a communication should be furnished to the Bureau which includes the explanations of personnel responsible for the failure to meet the deadline and your [the Atlanta SAC's] recommendations concerning administrative action," or, in other words, disciplinary measures.[71]

Atlanta could hold out no longer. On October 11 agent Nichols sent north a ten-page memo summarizing all possible subversive information related to SCLC, and making what he viewed as the most modest recommendation headquarters would accept. Nichols summarized the public source information on King's and Wyatt Walker's support of Carl Braden and Morton Sobell. He detailed the highlights of New York's information on Levison and O'Dell. He noted that Atlanta's own sources "had no information regarding any Communist Infiltration of the SCLC." He closed by saying that as recently as two weeks ago O'Dell had registered as an SCLC staff member at an Atlanta motel and apartment complex, the Waluhaje, whose desk clerk was a Bureau source. Thus, Nichols concluded, "It is recommended that a COMINFIL investigation be authorized by the Bureau in view of the information furnished by the New York Office" in its letter to headquarters of August 21. A full-scale, formal investigation of King and SCLC now could begin.[72]

On October 22 headquarters' supervisor Rampton sent a formal recommendation, in the name of his superior, Internal Security Section Chief Fred J. Baumgardner, to the FBI's assistant director in charge of the domestic intelligence division, William C. Sullivan. A COMINFIL probe of SCLC should be authorized. Both Atlanta and New York, Rampton stated, had recommended such an investigation, and files revealed that the Communist party "has been attempting to exert influence on" King and his organization. Not only was there the matter of Levison's presence. There also was the allegation that O'Dell had been a secret member of the Communist party's national committee since 1959. Rampton attached for approval orders to Atlanta and New York formally initiating the COMINFIL SCLC probe. His recommendation was approved by Sullivan and by other Bureau executives, including Director Hoover. On October 23 the letters to Atlanta and New York were dispatched and each office was ordered to submit an initial report within forty-five days.[73]

One day later, headquarters undertook another initiative. The Bureau's counterintelligence program (COINTELPRO) against the Communist party often used friendly newspapers to plant embarrassing stories. On October 24 the Crime Records Division disseminated to five of these—the *Augusta* (Ga.) *Chronicle,* the *Birmingham* (Ala.) *News,* the *St. Louis Globe-Democrat,* the *New Orleans Times-Picayune,* and the *Long Island Star-Journal*—a story on O'Dell's association with SCLC and his ties to the Communist party. Not surprisingly, the stories were virtually identical to each other. Each stated that O'Dell was "acting executive director" of SCLC, which was incorrect, and that he was "a concealed member of the national committee of the Communist Party." Each paper also precisely agreed on how it had obtained this information: "a highly authoritative source." The stories went on to give some biographical data on O'Dell, highlighting his expulsion from the National Maritime Union and his two appearances before Red-hunting congressional committees.[74]

King's phone records fail to indicate his own first response to this media barrage. The story, however, was not picked up by larger papers. On November 1 King issued a statement. He denied that O'Dell had been acting executive director, and added, with much overstatement and some inaccuracy, that "Mr. O'Dell has functioned purely as a technician, with 90 per cent of his work taking place in the North, where he resides, and involving the mechanization of our mailing procedures. He was briefly and temporarily filling in in some areas of voter registration, but ceased functioning there long before this publicity appeared. . . . While Mr. O'Dell advises us that he rejects the implications of the charges made against him, in order to avoid embarrassment to SCLC, he has tendered his resignation. We have accepted it pending further inquiry and clarification."[75] The resignation, however, was more fiction than fact, as King's own message and appointment books for late 1962 and the first half of 1963 reflect. In mid-1963 the O'Dell matter would erupt again.[76]

Several weeks after this initial flurry, however, there occurred an incident whose importance would grow with the passage of time. On Sunday, November 18, Dr. King preached at New York's Riverside Church. After the service, a reporter for the *New York Times* asked King if he agreed with the substance of a report on the Albany protests of the past summer issued by the Southern Regional Council. One of the statements in the report, written by historian Howard Zinn, was, "There is a considerable amount of distrust among Albany Negroes for local members of the Federal Bureau of Investigation. . . . FBI men appear to Albany Negroes as vaguely-interested observers of injustice, who diffidently write down complaints and do no more. With all of the clear violations by local police of constitutional rights, . . . the FBI has not made a single arrest on behalf of Negro citizens."[77]

King said he agreed with the report, and particularly with its characterization of the FBI's role. "One of the great problems we face with the FBI in the South," King told the reporter, "is that the agents are white Southerners who have been influenced by the mores of the community. To maintain their status, they have to be friendly with the local police and people who are promoting segregation. Every time I saw FBI men in Albany, they were with the local police force." King went on to recommend that the Bureau assign non-southerners to its Deep South offices. "If an FBI man agrees with segregation," King added, "he can't honestly and objectively investigate." A prominent account of King's comments, headlined "Dr. King Says F.B.I. in Albany, Ga., Favors Segregationists," appeared in Monday morning's *Times,* as well as in many other papers.[78]

The Bureau's reaction was sharp and swift. The Atlanta office immediately sent to headquarters a copy of the Monday morning story in the *Atlanta Constitution.* An attached memo added that the five-man Albany office, which reported to Atlanta, had only one man who was a native southerner—the other four were from Boston, Minneapolis, Indiana, and Kingston, New York. Assistant Director Alex Rosen, whose general investigative division contained the Bureau's civil rights section, reported King's criticisms in a memo to the Bureau's number-three man, Assistant to the Director Alan H. Belmont. Rosen observed how this attitude towards the Bureau tied in with the information "that King's advisors are Communist Party (CP) members and he is under the domination of the CP." Rosen's memo recommended that King be contacted and his erroneous statements pointed out to him. Belmont approved that suggestion, and several days later passed the recommendation on to Associate Director Clyde Tolson. The idea was approved by Tolson and Director Hoover, and both Assistant Director Cartha D. DeLoach and the Atlanta office were instructed to call King and arrange such a meeting.[79]

King's phone message book for Friday, November 30 reflects two calls that did not reach him: "DeLoatch Wash DC cancelled" [*sic*] and "Chuck Harding FBI JA1–3900." Harding was an agent on the Atlanta office's security and racial matters squad who had had a number of past contacts with King. Apparently both he and DeLoach assumed that if they left their names, King would get back to them. King's review of his phone messages was often perfunctory. He did not return the calls and neither FBI man, King's message book shows, called again.[80]

To King, the entire event seemed minor and of no continuing concern. The Bureau had, strictly speaking, been correct that most of the Albany agents were not native southerners. That was the full extent of the Bureau's accuracy, however. It was obvious to any independent observer that the Albany agents were not a distinguished group. The five resident agents were divided by a host of personal quarrels, and the dominant one of the group was the one native southerner, Marion Cheeks.

Albany blacks, and even some Bureau agents, agreed that Cheeks hated black people with a passion. As former Atlanta agent Arthur L. Murtagh, a well-known Bureau dissenter who spent considerable time working out of the Albany office, described Cheeks, "Marion was a nice guy, [but] he was a racist, and he had very strong feelings and he made them known to everybody around him." Cheeks's sentiments also strongly affected his handling of civil rights cases. He was known to advise other agents to pay little heed to blacks' complaints of misconduct by local law enforcement officers. Cheeks also reviewed all investigatory reports that were sent to headquarters from Albany, and he was known to edit them in such a way that allegations against local officers were heavily watered down. Since investigations were not pursued without express FBI headquarters *and* Justice Department approval, the biased reports meant that Washington superiors received a very incomplete picture of police misconduct in the Albany area.[81] On that larger issue Professor Zinn and Dr. King were wholly correct, though that of course meant nothing to FBI executives. Their most pointed memory of the incident, as Assistant Director DeLoach would recall years later, was that "Dr. King would not return my calls."[82] Little did King know how his comments about the Albany agents, and his supposed slighting of the easily offended DeLoach, would affect the events of the next three years.

As the Bureau was reacting to King's comments concerning Albany, it also was moving forward with additional electronic surveillance of Stanley Levison. The wiretap on Levison's office phone had been in place for eight months, and throughout the fall the Bureau had continued to send Attorney General Robert Kennedy regular reports of the many pedestrian activities that Levison, "a secret Communist Party member," was carrying out on behalf of King and SCLC. In mid-November the Bureau moved to get Kennedy's approval for a tap on Levison's home phone as well. Kennedy authorized it on November 20, and the order to install it was transmitted to the New York office on November 23. Adding this additional coverage brought about no change in the character of the conversations that the Bureau could overhear; Levison's conversations with King and with others remained as innocuous as they had been from the outset.[83]

In early December both the Atlanta and New York offices submitted the comprehensive forty-five-day reports specified when the COMINFIL investigation formally was begun in late October. Atlanta agent Nichols's report on SCLC activities made the organization seem all but harmless. He quoted extensively from SCLC brochures detailing the organization's purposes and goals, noted the newspaper articles on Jack O'Dell, and stressed, "This investigation has been instituted solely to determine the extent of Communist Party infiltration of SCLC and does not involve investigation of the legitimate activities of the organization." The New York office's report, written by agent Patrick J. Stokes, sounded a different theme. Unlike Nichols, Stokes began by observing that Communists "have infiltrated" SCLC. He went on to detail the activities of Levison and O'Dell and the SCLC's most tangential associations with anyone who ever had had a supposed connection with the Communist party, the Young Socialist League, and so forth.

Headquarter's response to these contradictory field office reports was predictable: New York was ordered to take over direction of the COMINFIL probe from the reluctant Atlanta office. Headquarters' supervisor Rampton explained it this way: "Although the SCLC is headquartered in Atlanta and the bulk of its legitimate activities are centered in the South, the main subversive influences and activities are taking place in New York City."[84]

The Bureau remained aware that Jack O'Dell was still working full-time for SCLC despite his supposed resignation. The New York office notified headquarters, and Hoover promptly advised Attorney General Kennedy, that both O'Dell and Levison would be attending a major two-day SCLC planning session to be held at the Dorchester Center in southeast Georgia on January 10 and 11, 1963. On the tenth Atlanta agents watched King and nearly a dozen aides and advisers board a plane for Savannah. When they arrived, Savannah agents covertly observed them, and two days later, when the group departed, the Savannah agents used a movie camera to film King, O'Dell, and others walking through the airport terminal.

The Bureau had no clear idea of the purpose of the meeting, and was thus unable to tell Kennedy and Marshall what transpired—namely the planning of SCLC's secret upcoming protest campaign in Birmingham.[85] In later years Levison would recall the retreat as having been perhaps the most dramatic and touching experience of his twelve-year association with Dr. King. "I thought," Levison said in recalling his comments to the group, that "it would be useful to point out that Bull Connor," Birmingham's public safety commissioner, "had an ugly history with the labor movement and had fought it for years to keep it out of Birmingham . . . and the use of forced brutality and all kinds of devices were employed to defeat what was then a powerful movement; that we were not *as* powerful as the labor movement had been in its organizing days; and consequently, we had to realize that we were facing a rough adversary with much less power than the earlier movements. After this generalized observation was made, Martin said, 'I want to make a point that I think everyone here should consider very carefully and decide if he wants to be with this campaign.' He said, 'There are something like eight people here assessing the type of enemy we're going to face. I have to tell you that in my judgment, some of the people sitting here today will not come back alive from this campaign. And I want you to think about it.' " On this note, Levison said, the sessions ended and the decision was made to go ahead with the Birmingham campaign.[86]

Even lacking substantive information on the meeting, Robert Kennedy was greatly worried by the continued presence of Levison and O'Dell in the King entourage. On one Bureau report, which he passed on to Marshall, the Attorney General scribbled, "Burke—this is not getting any better." Bureau executives were fully aware of Kennedy's attention, and the flow of memoranda to him on Levison and King was stepped up. On January 18 he was notified of King's supposed refusal to speak with Bureau representatives, a grossly exaggerated version of the two unreturned phone calls of more than six weeks earlier. That perceived snub had left DeLoach boiling. DeLoach also told the assistant to the Director, John Mohr, that King "does not desire to be told the true facts" about the Bureau's role in the South. King, DeLoach claimed, "obviously used deceit, lies and treachery as propaganda to further his own causes. . . . he obviously does not desire to be given the truth. The fact that he is a vicious liar is amply demonstrated in the fact he constantly associates with and takes instructions from Stanley Levison who is a hidden member of the Communist Party." Hoover concurred with DeLoach's recommendation that no further attempts be made to contact King.[87]

Sometime in late January, again at Robert Kennedy's behest, Marshall once more suggested to King that continued association with O'Dell and Levison was not wise. King seemed somewhat receptive concerning O'Dell, but Marshall had had to be extremely vague with King about the allegations against the two men because of the Bureau's concern about protecting its sources. He did tell King that O'Dell had maintained his ties to the Communist party, which O'Dell had denied to King. King paid little heed to Marshall's undocumented assertions.

Also in late January both the Bureau and the Justice Department's internal security division considered the idea of prosecuting Levison under the membership provisions of the Internal Security Act of 1950. FBI headquarters asked its New York office for all available information on Levison. Assistant Attorney General J. Walter Yeagley requested a prosecutive summary report from the Bureau. The idea of filing charges was dropped, however, apparently because exposing and ending "Solo" was judged too high a price to pay for Levison's scalp.[88]

In mid-March the Bureau informed Marshall, Robert Kennedy, and White House aide Kenneth O'Donnell that the wiretaps indicated that Levison and O'Dell were writing an article under King's name that soon would appear in the *Nation* magazine. Not reported to Kennedy or the White House was information from Jack Childs that his colleagues in the upper reaches of the Communist party recently had changed their tune about Levison. While throughout 1962 and early 1963 Childs had heard numerous second- or third-hand boasts about Levison's supposed sympathy to the party, in mid-March he had to report that his acquaintances now were saying that Levison was "disenchanted" with the CP. The FBI kept this news strictly to itself.

Throughout April, May, and June of 1963 the Bureau kept both Robert Kennedy and the White House posted on the substance of King-Levison conversations about SCLC's protest campaign in Birmingham, Alabama. The two men spoke on numerous occasions concerning the Kennedy administration's response to the events in Birmingham, and King's hope that the developments there would force President Kennedy to pay greater heed to King's recommendations, such as one that an executive order be issued banning all segregation. They also discussed King's desire to meet with both of the Kennedys. When New York's report of that conversation arrived at headquarters, Hoover himself personally called Robert Kennedy to relay the information. On June 3 a nine-page memorandum summarizing the highlights of Levison's advice to and influence on King was sent to the Attorney General. It was followed several days later by two additional reports on more recent phone conversations in which King had discussed the idea of a mass "march on Washington" later in the summer. One week after those discussions, and in the immediate aftermath of President Kennedy's major civil rights address to the nation, the Bureau furnished both the Attorney General and the White House an account of a King-Levison conversation in which both men expressed their great happiness over the President's remarks.[89]

The Bureau's stepped-up flow of reports on the King-Levison association coincided with the Kennedy administration's decision to press for a comprehensive civil rights bill. The initiative behind that step was almost wholly Robert Kennedy's. Fast upon the heels of that decision came yet higher concern about the O'Dell-Levison-King ties. Robert Kennedy knew that King and other civil rights leaders were scheduled to see him, Marshall, and the President on June 22. On June 17 the Attorney General called Hoover to discuss the King matter. Should not Marshall give King more specific information about Levison and O'Dell? Hoover, according to his own account of the conversation, said yes. Thus, when King arrived at the Justice Department on the twenty-second, Marshall once again spoke to him strongly; any and all ties and contact with Levison and O'Dell should be ended. Later in the morning Robert Kennedy repeated the message, and that afternoon, after a meeting of the assembled civil rights leadership with the President, John Kennedy himself took King out into the Rose Garden.[90]

Kennedy, according to an account that King later gave three close friends, asked King, "You've read about Profumo in the papers?" King had. Kennedy went on, "That was an example of friendship and loyalty carried too far. Macmillan is likely to lose his government because he has been loyal to his friend. You must take care not to lose your cause for the same reason." Kennedy then named Levison and O'Dell. "They're Communists. You've got to get rid of them." He pointed out that public exposure of the Levison and O'Dell allegations would affect not only King, but the entire civil rights effort and the administration's civil rights bill as well. "If they shoot *you* down, they'll shoot us down too—so we're asking you to be careful." The President went on to warn King that these opponents of civil rights would have him under very close surveillance. King should keep this in mind. King indicated that he appreciated that, and he did not quarrel with the President about O'Dell. But about Levison he felt differently. "I know Stanley," he told John Kennedy, "and I can't believe this. You will have to prove it." The President paused, and then said that he would arrange for Burke Marshall to give proof of the matter to King. With that, the brief stroll and conversation ended.

King had found the experiences of that day both troubling and amusing. He joked to Andrew Young that the President must be worried about someone bugging him as well. Why else would he have taken King into the Rose Garden to talk? The conversations had not created doubt within him about Levison, or, for that matter, O'Dell. But King was troubled by the great consternation that the Kennedy brothers and Marshall were exhibiting.[91] He made no move to sever ties with either O'Dell or Levison, however.

The Bureau was aware of that. On June 29 the Crime Records Division again went into action. The *Birmingham News* of June 30 carried a front-page headline: "King's SCLC Pays O'Dell Despite Denial." The story noted O'Dell's reported resignation in late 1962, and King's assertion that very week that O'Dell had not been associated with SCLC since December 1, 1962. But, the story went on, O'Dell was still working out of SCLC's New York office. In January he had traveled with King, at SCLC's expense, from Atlanta to Savannah—for the Dorchester strategy sessions. The story further reported on O'Dell's background of party ties and the allegation that even now he was a secret member of the CP's national committee. [92]

This revelation brought matters to a head once more. Marshall again pressed King, reminding him of his promise to sever ties with O'Dell as well as Levison. King responded that there were no continuing ties with O'Dell, but on July 3 King sent a formal letter to O'Dell, with copies to Marshall and Robert Kennedy. O'Dell's earlier "temporary resignation" was now unfortunately being made permanent. Although King had been "unable to discover any present connections with the Communist party on your part, . . . in these critical times we cannot afford to risk any such impressions." O'Dell would have to end all association with SCLC. [93] That satisfied Marshall and the Kennedys with respect to O'Dell, but there remained the question of Levison, and the President's promise that King would be shown convincing evidence. Again the task fell to Burke Marshall.

Marshall arranged to meet with Andrew Young at the federal courthouse in New Orleans, where the Civil Rights Division was arguing a case before the Fifth Circuit Court of Appeals. Marshall, as Young has recalled it, once again did not have the requested evidence. Of course, the Bureau would not give it even to Marshall himself, much less allow him to share it with Young or King. What Marshall did say as they walked the courthouse corridors, Young recalled, was that "I can't give you any proof, but, if you know Colonel Rudolph Abel of the Soviet secret intelligence, then you know Stanley Levison." Marshall went on to stress again, as he had with King, that Levison must separate from the civil rights effort. Young reported that conversation to King and Levison, and King again dismissed the allegations in the absence of supporting evidence.

Now, however, Levison stepped in. It was early July. Hearings on the administration's civil rights bill were about to begin. Levison told King that for the good of the movement they should separate. As Levison later recounted, "I induced him to break. The movement needed the Kennedys too much. I said it would not be in the interests of the movement to hold on to me if the Kennedys had doubts."[94] King was still reluctant to cut off relations, but an added twist provided a solution—although they would not speak directly to each other, or meet in person, Levison and King would each speak regularly to a third person who could serve as a channel of communication between them. That person would be the young New York attorney who had been managing the affairs of the Gandhi Society and who had proved invaluable at the height of the Birmingham campaign two months earlier, Clarence B. Jones.

Until July of 1963 Clarence Jones had been an extremely helpful but admittedly junior member of the informal team of advisers around Dr. King. Jones had attended Columbia University in the early 1950s, and had been drafted into the army, where his left political views and firm resistance to any symptoms of racial discrimination had placed him in hot water a number of times. After leaving the military Jones attended Boston University Law School, graduating in 1959. Then he had helped perform legal research for King's 1960 defense against the Alabama tax charges, a job that Levison had interviewed and hired him for. In 1962, working closely with Harry Wachtel, Jones had played a major role in the administration of the Gandhi Society's fund-raising efforts. In 1963 he had carried the northern bail money to Birmingham, where he also had served as the conduit to the imprisoned Dr. King.[95]

On July 15 or 16, in the wake of King's decision to break off direct contact with Levison, Jones dropped by the Justice Department to see Burke Marshall. The previous few days had been busy ones, highlighted by the appearance of segregationist governors Ross Barnett of Mississippi and George Wallace of Alabama at Senate hearings on the civil rights bill. Both governors had claimed that the civil rights movement was infested with if not controlled by Communists. Further, King himself was undoubtedly a Communist pawn, as the much-used photo of him at Highlander supposedly showed. Two senators, Monroney of Oklahoma and Magnuson of Washington, announced they had written letters to Hoover asking for comment on these claims.

Thus the subject of Communists and civil rights was quite visible just as Jones made his first notable appearance on the scene. Marshall apparently wrote no memorandum describing his own meeting with Jones. But he did immediately describe it to Robert Kennedy. Somehow Jones's appearance gave Marshall and Kennedy the idea that he would become a link between Levison and King. A memo written late on the sixteenth by the Bureau's liaison to Kennedy and Marshall, Courtney Evans, appears to supply some understanding of what had occurred. The Attorney General, Evans wrote to his superior, Alan Belmont,

> was contacted at his request late this afternoon. He said that Clarence Benjamin Jones, a NY attorney who has had close association with Martin Luther King, and with Stanley David Levison [deletion], had been in to see Burke Marshall about the racial situation. According to the AG, Jones had indicated he had some reservations about talking with Levison on the phone. Marshall thought he might have been referring to a possible telephone tap, and passed it off by telling Jones this was something he would have to take up with [deletion].
>
> The purpose of the AG's contact was that this brought to his attention the possibility of effecting technical coverage on both Jones and Martin Luther King. I told the AG that I was not at all acquainted with Jones, but that, in so far as King was concerned, it was obvious from the reports that he was in a travel status practically all the time, and it was, therefore, doubtful that a technical surveillance on his office or home would be very productive. I also raised the question as to the repercussions if it should ever become known that such a surveillance had been put on King.
>
> The AG said this did not concern him at all; that in view of the racial situation, he thought it advisable to have as complete coverage as possible. I told him, under the circumstances, that we would check into the matter to see if coverage was feasible and, if so, would submit an appropriate recommendation to him.
>
> If you approve, we will have a preliminary survey made to see if technical coverage is feasible with full security.

Belmont passed Evans's memo along to Tolson and Hoover, and Hoover noted next to the last paragraph, "Yes." He added, "What do our files show" about Jones?[96]

Jones's appearance, and Kennedy's reaction to it, moved the entire King-SCLC-Levison case into a higher gear. On July 17 and 18, Hoover wrote to Senators Monroney and Magnuson that a response to their inquiries would soon be forthcoming, but from the Attorney General, not the Bureau. Hoover sent the senators' letters to Kennedy, along with a memorandum on Levison that stated Levison was still a "secret member of the Communist Party" who "retains his strong communist convictions and still acts as an effective Party advisor to King." Although conceding that Levison supposedly had become critical of the CP in recent months, Hoover emphasized that the party was trying hard to influence the civil rights movement. It had had little success to date, and now was pinning all its hopes on Levison.

Five days later, on Monday, July 22, the Bureau forwarded to Kennedy an initial report on Jones and a formal request for wiretaps on his home and office. Only one basis for the intercepts was cited— an allegation that Jones had been a member of the Labor Youth League nine years earlier. Even so, Kennedy approved the request.

The Atlanta office, meanwhile, had been ordered to look into the question of tapping King's home and the SCLC office. On the twenty-fourth it informed headquarters that taps would be "feasible with full security" at both locations. The Atlanta communication added, in a change of stance, the "installations [are] recommended. Advise if desired and if so forward Atlanta four dial recorders complete, three tape recorders and one playback unit."

With Atlanta's assurance in hand, Courtney Evans went to see the Attorney General the following day. Kennedy told Evans, so Evans wrote in a memo to Belmont later that day, that he had been pondering their conversation of the sixteenth about wiretapping King. He "was now of the opinion that this would be ill advised." Kennedy handed back to Evans the Bureau's formal request for the taps on King, dated July 23, which had cited King's close association with Levison as the sole basis for the national security surveillance. Kennedy, Evans reported, had decided that King's peripatetic life style, plus the degree of embarrassment that would be risked, both made the idea of the Atlanta taps inadvisable. Evans ended his memo on the conversation by telling Belmont, "We will take no further action to effect technical coverage on Martin Luther King, either at his home or at his office . . . in the absence of a further request from the Attorney General."[97]

The same day that Evans had that conversation with Kennedy, Kennedy's own letter of response to senators Monroney and Magnuson, dated July 23, was released to the press. Worded with the greatest of care, the letter told the senators that no civil rights leaders, and specifically King, were "Communists or Communist-controlled." That last word had been very carefully chosen, to avoid saying that no such leaders were Communist *influenced,* as Kennedy and Marshall did believe was the case with King. Lest they mislead the senators with even that language, Kennedy sent Marshall and Deputy Attorney General Nicholas deB. Katzenbach up to the Hill to brief Monroney and several other senators.[98]

Also on the twenty-fifth the O'Dell matter reappeared in the press, again at the Bureau's instigation, for a third time. The Bureau's New York office had been aware that O'Dell had maintained a presence at SCLC's Manhattan office even after his "permanent" and public resignation of July 3, and it alerted Bill Shipp of the *Atlanta Constitution* to that fact. Shipp's story, headlined "Onetime Communist Organizer Heads Rev. King's Office in N.Y.," was a virtual reprint of the Bureau's assorted facts on O'Dell. Matters were made considerably worse, though, when the New York SCLC office, ignorant of the Atlanta story, told an inquiring UPI reporter on the morning of the twenty-fifth that yes, O'Dell still was the "administrator" of that office. That report, immediately given wide circulation, led King to hold an early afternoon press conference in Atlanta, where he again denied that O'Dell had any remaining link to SCLC. King said that after O'Dell's "temporary" resignation had been accepted in late 1962, SCLC had determined that he had no present connection with the Communist party, and, "On the basis of this, we brought him back on the staff and continued his employment for a few months on a temporary basis." Then, King asserted, he and O'Dell mutually had agreed on June 26—*before* the *Birmingham News* story of the thirtieth appeared, and well before King's letter to O'Dell of July 3—that O'Dell would leave SCLC for good on July 15. By the time this press conference was complete, SCLC's New York office was saying, in contrast to its earlier acknowledgement, that O'Dell was not with the organization and that it had no idea as to his whereabouts.[99]

King's handling of the O'Dell matter did not sit well with Robert Kennedy and Burke Marshall. On July 29 Evans met again with Kennedy and Marshall. He gave the Attorney General an eighteen-page report prepared by the Bureau's New York field office on July 22 entitled, "Martin Luther King, Jr.: Affiliation with the Communist Movement." Kennedy was extremely displeased. The document emphasized King's ties with Levison, the "Solo" information on Levison, and a further report, apparently also from "Solo," that Levison had told someone that King once had told him, "I am a Marxist." Kennedy forcefully complained to Evans about the timing of the report. Kennedy had just gone on record in defense of King, and the Senate hearings were in full swing. Kennedy also said the report's contents were disappointing—no hard evidence or documentation was presented to back up the assorted claims and characterizations. On August 2 Hoover resubmitted the report to Kennedy, adding only further characterizations of Levison drawn from the July 17 and February 14, 1962 memos on him.[100] Kennedy apparently protested no further, though as the August 28 March on Washington neared, the flow of Bureau memos detailing Communist party efforts to infiltrate or join the march swelled.

In that flow were the first fruits of the new wiretaps on Clarence Jones. By chance, King and his family stayed at Jones's suburban New York home for several days in early August. This visit afforded the FBI its first comprehensive coverage of King's phone calls. On August 13 Hoover's office sent a two-page memo to Deputy Attorney General Katzenbach that dealt only with King's personal life and sexual activities. Copies of that memo went to Marshall and the Attorney General as well. On August 20 Robert Kennedy sent a copy to his brother at the White House, with a cover note stating, "I thought you would be interested in the attached memorandum." Evans saw Robert Kennedy that same day. He reported to Belmont that the Attorney General remained keenly interested in the O'Dell—SCLC connection in addition to the Levison-Jones-King path of indirect communication.[101]

Immediately before the March on Washington the Bureau's domestic intelligence division prepared a comprehensive sixty-eight page report. It laid out all Communist party efforts to influence or join in civil rights movement efforts, and noted the tiny—4,453 active members, the report said—party's total failure in such attempts. The report would have been of little note without the response it provoked from Director Hoover. Hoover was totally unwilling to accept domestic intelligence's implicit conclusion that the Communist party was of no relevance to the American racial scene. "This memo reminds me vividly," Hoover scribbled on the covering letter of the lengthy report, "of those I received when Castro took over Cuba. You contended then that Castro & his cohorts were not Communists & not influenced by Communists. Time alone has proved you wrong. I for one can't ignore the memos re King, [deletion] et al. as having only an infinitesimal effect on the efforts to exploit the American Negro by the Communists."[102]

The domestic intelligence officials who had prepared the report, and especially Assistant Director William C. Sullivan, were extremely concerned over Hoover's unhappiness. Two days after the march itself, Sullivan submitted a new memo to his direct superior, Belmont. This one totally reversed his division's position from that presented in the lengthy report of a week earlier. Noting Hoover's criticism, Sullivan wrote, "The Director is correct. We were completely wrong about believing the evidence was not sufficient to determine some years ago that Fidel Castro was not a communist or under communist influence. [Why the FBI's domestic intelligence division should have been so concerned with Castro is a question no one seems to have posed so far.] On investigating and writing about communism and the American Negro, we had better remember this and profit by the lesson it should teach us." Sullivan went on to discuss the difficulties of defining and measuring "influence," and characterized King's August 28 "I Have a Dream" oration as a "powerful demagogic speech." After that address, Sullivan said, "We must mark [King] now, if we have not done so before, as the most dangerous Negro of the future in this Nation from the standpoint of communism, the Negro and national security." In pursuing its future investigations of King and Communist influence, Sullivan added, "it may be unrealistic to limit ourselves as we have been doing to legalistic proofs or definitely conclusive evidence that would stand up in testimony in court or before Congressional Committees.'' [103]

In the immediate aftermath of this exchange, the Bureau made another report to Robert Kennedy: the wiretap on Levison indicated that he still was in touch with King; furthermore, Jack O'Dell had spent approximately one hour in the New York SCLC office on August 30. The day after that information was passed to the Attorney General and Marshall, the domestic intelligence division requested, and received, Bureau approval that the New York and Atlanta field offices examine possible arrangements for effectuating wiretaps on the SCLC offices in both cities as well as on King's Atlanta home. The continued presence of Levison and O'Dell was the reason cited. The instructions were dispatched that day. [104]

Several days later, on September 11, the Bureau's New York office reported to headquarters the substance of a King-Jones conversation, and several others, that had been overheard on the Jones wiretap the day before. King had called Jones to discuss what action should be taken to market a record album of his "I Have A Dream" speech. He wondered whether the proceeds from such an album should be divided among all the major groups that had participated in the March on Washington, or go entirely to the SCLC. Jones advised King to seek A. Philip Randolph's opinion. After further discussion it was agreed that Jones rather than King would approach Randolph with the question.

King went on. They must consider hiring a replacement for "Jack" [O'Dell] as head of SCLC's New York office. King thought perhaps Bayard Rustin would do. Rustin had won widespread praise for his impressive performance in organizing and overseeing the March on Washington. He could rejoin SCLC. Jones and King then discussed the problem of Rustin's widely known homosexuality. Racists and right-wingers had often used it to impugn his reputation, and it had played no small role in Rustin's departure from SCLC in 1960. King finally said, according to the Bureau transcript, "I just don't know—maybe you ought to talk with our friend about it because he knows the problem very well." Jones responded, "Well, let me reflect upon it and I'll discuss it with our friend and get his feelings about it." King: "He understands why I haven't called him?'' Jones: ''Yes, absolutely. In fact, he would be a little upset if you did.'' King: ''I'm trying to wait until things cool off—until this civil rights debate is over—as long as they may be tapping these phones, you know—but you can discuss that with him.''

Subsequently, Jones called Levison and asked him if Rustin could be named head of SCLC's New York office without harming the organization. Levison told Jones he wanted to give the question some thought before responding. But he vetoed Jones's further suggestion that Ted Brown of the AFL–CIO be considered for the post.[105]

The taps were doing their work. Substantial evidence of continuing ties between King and Levison, and O'Dell and SCLC was being generated. Most of it was being passed on to Robert Kennedy. The FBI's Courtney Evans discussed the problem with Marshall on September 18, and several days later Hoover sent a further report directly to the Attorney General.[106]

Meanwhile, the rift between Hoover and Division Five, as domestic intelligence was called, continued to boil. On September 16, a memorandum drafted by one of the supervisors in Baumgardner's internal security section, Seymor F. Phillips, was approved by Sullivan and sent on to Belmont, Tolson, and Hoover. It spoke of some two hundred alleged Communist party members present at the August 28 March on Washington, and claimed that blacks were obviously now the CP's ''favorite target.'' Hence, ''increased coverage of communist influence on the Negro'' should be instituted. Key field offices should be instructed to work harder at tracking such CP efforts. Hoover, however, again rejected domestic intelligence's effort to mollify his anger over the initial report on the CP's relevance to the racial situation. On the memo, which reached him on September 18, he wrote:

> No. I can't understand how you can so agilely switch your thinking and evaluation. Just a few weeks ago you contended that the Communist influence in the racial movement was ineffective and infinitesimal. This notwithstanding many memos of specific instances of infiltration. Now you want to load the Field down with more coverage in spite of your recent memo deprecating C.P. influence in

racial movement. I don't intend to waste time and money until you can make up your minds what the situation really is.

On the attached transmittal slip from Tolson, Hoover added:

I have certainly been misled by previous memos which clearly showed communist penetration of the racial movement. The attached is contradictory of all that. We are wasting manpower and money investigating C.P. effort in racial matters if the attached is correct.[107]

Sullivan had been on vacation when the memo of the sixteenth came back down through channels with Hoover's angry marginalia. On returning, he made yet another effort to repair the breach, in a five-page memo sent first to Belmont on September 25. The overarching theme of the memo was that the gap between Division Five's first report and its follow-up memos was not wide. Sullivan quoted at length from earlier statements made by Hoover—statements drafted for him by Sullivan or Sullivan assistant Charles D. Brennan—that made essentially the same point as had the initial report: that while the CP had made extensive efforts to influence blacks, those efforts to date had been largely unsuccessful and had "not reached the point of control or domination." Next to that comment Hoover scribbled, "Certainly this is not true with respect to the Levison-King connection."

The crux of the issue to Sullivan was not a disagreement over facts, but over interpretation. One example, Sullivan said, was the importance of realizing that Martin Luther King, Jr., is "the most dangerous and effective Negro leader in the country." King's ability was a particular threat, Sullivan said, because "we are right now in this nation engaged in a form of social revolution." Sullivan renewed his September 16 request that field offices give even more attention to uncovering CP efforts to influence the racial struggle. The weeks since the March on Washington had witnessed "stepped-up activities" by the party in this connection; "communist officials have been doing all possible to exploit the very troubled racial situation." Second, he wanted Division Five to "prepare a concise document setting forth clearly those attempts to penetrate, influence, and control the Negro movement. By setting these facts forth, succinctly and clearly, the reader cannot help but be impressed with the seriousness of the communist activities.'' When Hoover placed his ''O.K.'' next to each of these final points, the intra-Bureau rift seemed on its way to repair.[108]

Several days later both the New York and Atlanta offices reported back. Wiretaps would be wholly feasible at both SCLC's New York office and at King's Atlanta home. Its inquiries concerning the main SCLC office, Atlanta said, were not complete. On October 4 headquarters' supervisor William T. Forsyth, who handled the King case in the subversive control section, drafted a memo in the name of his section chief, James F. Bland, recommending that the Bureau apply to Robert Kennedy for authority to install the first two taps. The memo recounted Kennedy's initial interest in a King tap in July, and then his decision against proceeding. Forsyth emphasized how the Levison and Jones wiretaps ''have been extremely productive in showing the influence of Levison on King as well as Levison's behind-the-scenes influence in the racial movement. . . . In view of the Attorney General's request that our coverage be as complete as possible and because of the communist influence in the racial movement shown by activities of Stanley Levison as well as King's connection with him, it is believed desirable to put all possible coverage on the racial leaders in order to obtain full information.'' Hoover approved the recommendation. On October 7 the formal request for the taps was forwarded to the Attorney General's office. King's association with Levison, and Levison's supposed status as a secret member of the CP, was the basis cited for the surveillance.[109]

Thursday morning October 10 Robert Kennedy sent a message to Bureau liaison man Courtney Evans asking Evans to come see him. Evans went to Kennedy's office early that afternoon. ''The Attorney General said,'' Evans reported, ''that he recognized the importance of this coverage if substantial information is to be developed concerning the relationship between King and the Communist Party. He said there was no question in his mind as to the coverage in New York City but that he was worried about the security of an installation covering a residence in Atlanta, Georgia. He noted that the last thing we could afford to have would be a discovery of a wire tap on King's residence.'' Evans had assured Kennedy that the tap on

King's home phone was, from a security standpoint, no more risky than the tap on the New York office. "After this discussion," Evans wrote, "the Attorney General said he felt we should go ahead with the technical coverage on King on a trial basis, and to continue it if productive results were forthcoming. He said he was certain that all Bureau representatives involved would recognize the delicacy of this particular matter and would thus be even more cautious than ever in this assignment. He asked to be kept advised of any pertinent information developed regarding King's communist connections." Kennedy then signed the authorization and handed it to Evans.[110]

Concurrently, the research section of the domestic intelligence division was finishing the monograph on the CP and blacks that Sullivan had proposed in his memo of September 25. The writer was Charles D. Brennan, and he focused the eleven-page document on the Levison-King relationship. Brennan asserted in the introduction that Levison remained a "dedicated Communist" and that King "is knowingly, willingly, and regularly taking guidance from communists." Brennan reviewed in detail King's less than forthright handling of the O'Dell matter, and called King "an unprincipled man" both in his political dealings and in his private life. Brennan's conclusion stated,

> The current atmosphere in the Communist party is marked by a vigorous spirit of enthusiastic optimism and a determination to launch more open, aggressive action on the national scene. As the situation now stands, Martin Luther King is growing in stature daily as the leader among leaders of the Negro movement. Communist party officials visualize the possibility of creating a situation whereby it could be said that, as the Communist party goes, so goes Martin Luther King, and so also goes the Negro movement in the United States.

The monograph did not confront the fact that the Bureau had no direct evidence that Levison was still in touch with the CP hierarchy, or that his advice to King was based upon hidden motives.

The document, entitled "Communism and the Negro Movement—A Current Analysis," was completed on October 15. Sullivan sent it to Alan Belmont, recommending distribution of it throughout the governmentwide intelligence community. Two days later Belmont forwarded the monograph to Associate Director Tolson with a warning: "The attached analysis of Communism and the Negro movement is highly explosive. It can be regarded as a personal attack on Martin Luther King. There is no doubt it will have a heavy impact on the Attorney General and anyone else to whom we disseminate it. . . . We may well be charged . . . with expressing opinions and conclusions, particularly with reference to some of the statements about King." This content, he repeated, "may startle the Attorney General, particularly in view of his past association with King, and the fact that we are disseminating this outside the Department. He may resent this. Nevertheless, the memorandum is a powerful warning against Communist influence in the Negro movement, and we will be carrying out our responsibility by disseminating it. . . ." Tolson forwarded the report, and Belmont's memo, to Hoover, who wrote on it: "We must do our duty. I am glad you recognize at last that there exists such influence." The following day copies were dispatched to the Attorney General, the White House, the secretaries of state and defense, the CIA, and each branch of the military services.[111]

By October 18 the Atlanta office felt that the SCLC office there could also be wiretapped without undue risk. Bland's section then prepared another authorization request. It was virtually identical to the one for King's home and the New York office, and it too was approved by Bureau executives and sent on to the Attorney General. Kennedy spoke with the Bureau's Courtney Evans about the second request on Monday, October 21. "The Attorney General," Evans wrote in his account of the conversation, "is apparently still vacillating in his position as to technical coverage on Martin Luther King and his organization. . . . The Attorney General said that he is still uncertain in his own mind about this coverage." Kennedy did go ahead and approve the second request, but he "asked that this coverage and that on King's residence be evaluated at the end of 30 days in light of the results secured so that the continuance of these surveillances could be determined at that time. This will be done."[112]

Four days after that conversation Kennedy learned how widely the "Communism and the Negro Movement" monograph had been distributed within the government. He called Evans to inquire pointedly as to why copies had been sent to the various military services. The report was being widely discussed at the Pentagon, and Kennedy was particularly unhappy about this sort of dissemination of such a report just at the time that the administration's civil rights bill was at a crucial stage in the Congress. Kennedy then went to Hoover's office and voiced those concerns to the Director himself.

The Attorney General, as he himself recalled the conversation a year later, told Hoover that he considered the report "very, very unfair" to King, as it presented only one side of what Kennedy believed was a more complicated picture. He noted how circulation of the document, and the danger of it being leaked, could damage, perhaps fatally, the administration's efforts to win passage of the civil rights bill. "I said," Kennedy recalled, that "I was as concerned about this matter as he was or as anybody was, but that we wanted to obtain the passage of legislation, and we didn't want to fail in the passage of legislation by a document which gave only one side. He said, 'I think it should be recalled.' So I said, 'Fine.' . . . Then, I had another conversation with him, and he said, 'Now, I want you always to remember: I was the one who had this document recalled and that you didn't suggest it.' So I said, 'Fine.' "

Hoover's account of the first conversation differed from Kennedy's only on the question of who first suggested the recall:

> He stated that he was quite concerned about the contents because while it did not state that King was a Communist, nevertheless, one could quickly draw that conclusion. I told him that every statement made in the document was accurate and supported by facts.
>
> He stated he of course realized this but felt that it would be desirable to recall all of the documents because he did not know who else might see it other than those to whom we had distributed the document. I told the Attorney General that his request would be immediately acted upon. . . .

Bureau agents assigned to liaison work immediately were sent to retrieve the various copies from around the Washington area, telling their contacts that revisions needed to be made in the document. By early the following morning, Saturday, October 26, all copies of the monograph had been retrieved.[113] The threat of a damaging leak had been averted.

Several days later another threat of disclosure appeared. Georgia Senator Richard Russell, like Monroney and Magnuson earlier in the year, had queried Hoover about communist influence in the civil rights movement, and particularly Jack O'Dell's tie to SCLC. Hoover had referred Russell's letter to the Attorney General, but Kennedy's office had forgotten to respond. Now Russell was angry, and wanted to know why he had not heard anything.

On Thursday, October 31, Burke Marshall and Robert Kennedy sat down and drafted three different possible responses to Senator Russell. One said virtually nothing, the second detailed the FBI's information on O'Dell, and the third contained both the O'Dell material plus a summary of the Levison issue. The two men were uncertain about which version should be sent, and Robert Kennedy called his brother to explain the problem. John Kennedy stated that nothing about Levison should be volunteered, but Russell's query about O'Dell should be answered frankly.

The next morning Marshall took that draft of the letter to Courtney Evans. Did the FBI have any objections to telling Russell the detailed allegations that O'Dell continued to have active ties to the Communist party? Evans did not like the letter's several references to how the FBI knew about O'Dell's ties because of its own secret sources in the communist hierarchy. Evans wanted these remarks deleted, but Marshall pointed out that this version already had been approved by President Kennedy himself. Evans and Marshall then went to see Robert Kennedy. The Attorney General, Evans wrote later that day, was not certain the deletions could be made.

> He called the President and told him that I had come into his office with Burke Marshall about the letter and objected that it might result in the disclosure of a very valuable Bureau source. He read the revised letter to the President, who was not satisfied. The AG and Burke Marshall then redrafted the letter three times. As each draft was completed, the AG telephoned the President and read the proposal to him. None of the drafted letters were apparently acceptable. At the conclusion of the last telephone conver-

sation, the AG said the President had advised that an innocuous letter should be sent to Senator Russell which should be delivered by Assistant AG Marshall and me.

John Kennedy further instructed that Marshall and Evans were to tell Russell orally about the information on O'Dell, and about the administration's repeated efforts to convince King to sever his ties to people with communist backgrounds.

At 5 P.M. that afternoon Evans and Deputy Attorney General Katzenbach, in place of Marshall, went to Senator Russell's office to deliver the letter. Katzenbach explained the situation to Russell, who said that he had not intended to make a major incident out of the issue. He added that it should come as no surprise that communists would try to join the civil rights movement, but that even he, a conservative southerner, did not believe that Martin Luther King himself was a communist. Any such allegations, Russell assured Katzenbach, had no proper place in Congress's debate over the administration's civil rights bill. Another threat to the legislation had been averted.[114]

On November 1, the same day that Katzenbach and Evans briefed Senator Russell, the FBI's New York office reported that installation of wiretaps on three phone lines at the SCLC office had been completed on October 30. Coverage on two of the lines had begun as early as October 24. New York also asked that headquarters consider wiretapping both Bayard Rustin and Levison's brother, Roy Bennett, as well.

A few days later the Atlanta field office reported that installation of taps on the one line at King's home and the four lines at SCLC headquarters had been completed on November 8. The Atlanta office procured an apartment in a building at 300 West Peachtree Street, directly across from the Bureau office, for monitoring and recording the conversations on the five tapped lines. Bureau agents or clerks manned the listening post twenty-four hours a day, seven days a week. Intensive electronic surveillance of Dr. King had begun.[115]

2

Criticism, Communism, and Robert Kennedy

Before proceeding with the story of the Bureau's intensified investigation of Dr. King, its first phase deserves closer analysis. A number of questions are raised by the evidence in the preceding chapter. What was the primary reason for the Bureau's growing attention to King in 1962 and 1963? What was the motive underlying the request to wiretap him in the fall of 1963? Why did Attorney General Robert Kennedy approve those wiretaps? What is the likely truth about Stanley Levison?

From 1964 until the present day it has been widely accepted that the root cause of the Bureau's pronounced interest in Dr. King lay in King's well-publicized criticism of the FBI's handling of civil rights cases in the South, and the Bureau's, especially Hoover's, angry reactions to those complaints. This interpretation is not surprising. The most famous single incident in the FBI-King story, Hoover's November, 1964, characterization of King as "the most notorious liar" in the country, apparently supports it. It was portrayed then

78

and afterwards as a delayed rebuttal to King's 1962 charges concerning the FBI agents in Albany, Georgia.

This explanation of the Bureau's activity against King has been voiced by former Justice Department officials, several former Bureau executives and agents, a large number of journalists, and the two principal investigating bodies that have looked into the FBI's handling of the King security investigation—the Senate Select Committee on Intelligence Activities and the House Assassinations Committee. No matter how widely accepted, however, this belief is largely wrong.

Perceptive students of the FBI have often noted that for over forty years the Bureau always reacted in a most hostile fashion to any public criticisms made of it. Individuals who became identified as FBI critics were targeted by Bureau officials for special and unpleasant attention, and well before 1950 most Americans in public life realized that the FBI's enemies list was one that no self-concerned person wanted to be chosen for. Most explanations of this hostility, both then and now, attributed this development largely if not solely to the person of J. Edgar Hoover himself. Although a more sophisticated explanation of this pattern could be given in terms of the Bureau's more thoroughgoing desire to protect and defend itself as an organization, that theme has rarely if ever been sounded, and explanations of the Bureau's sensitivity and defensiveness always have portrayed it as but the larger reflection of Hoover's own personal inability to admit error or exhibit tolerance toward opinions different from his own.

This pattern of active hostility and retaliation toward public critics always was combined with stringent internal warnings that no employee was ever to take an action that might publicly embarrass the Bureau. Over and over again in the instructions that FBI headquarters issued to field offices, agents were reminded that "no action should be taken which could cause embarrassment to the Bureau."[1] That refrain was one important indication of the fear and dread that FBI executives had of seeing any Bureau error or miscue written up in public print. Here again most observers have interpreted this theme as one more reflection of Hoover's own sensitivities, rather than as an institutional manifestation of a wholly rational desire to achieve and maintain as positive a public image and reputation as possible. That the Bureau experienced incomparable success on this latter score for almost half a century does not need to be underscored.

Against this background and pattern it is wholly understandable that so many observers and investigators have taken (a) King's public criticism of the FBI, and (b) the hostility that the Bureau exhibited toward him, and reached the conclusion that the former is the proximate cause of the latter. Former Attorney General Nicholas deB. Katzenbach, who had direct exposure to the Bureau's hostility toward King for over four years, felt then and feels now that King's remarks about Albany had been the animating force in the conflict, and that King's "color didn't make a difference." Katzenbach had ample opportunity to witness Hoover's reaction to criticism almost at firsthand, and he stresses that it was "almost impossible to overestimate Mr. Hoover's sensitivity to criticism of himself or the FBI. . . . In a very real sense there was no greater crime in Mr. Hoover's eyes than public criticism of the Bureau. . . . All public critics of the Bureau, if they persisted," were treated as enemies. "The only thing unique about Dr. King was the intensity of the feeling and the apparent extremes to which the Bureau went in seeking to destroy the critic." [2]

Someone else who has voiced virtually identical sentiments is the very Bureau executive who played the predominant role in responding to King's remarks about Albany, Cartha D. "Deke" DeLoach. Called twice before congressional committees in the mid-1970s to explain his conduct a decade earlier, DeLoach pleaded a poor memory on many incidents but had precise recall of how King's 1962 criticism had made Hoover "very resentful" and "touched off a feud." The Director, DeLoach explained, "was incensed that Dr. King would cast aspersions upon the integrity of FBI agents and particularly an organization that he, himself, had devoted his life to." Hoover, DeLoach added, "had somewhat of a towering ego . . . [and] overreacted to any allegations that concerned the organization." [3]

DeLoach was not the only Bureau executive who, in looking back on the King case, attributed an important role to King's Albany remarks. William C. Sullivan, who had an even more central part in the King probe than DeLoach, wrote just before his death that Hoover greatly resented King's criticism of the FBI and never forgave him for it. He added that "at bottom Hoover was concerned about King's repeated criticism of the FBI and its alleged lack of interest in the civil rights movement."[4]

Not only headquarters' officials like Sullivan and DeLoach have voiced this opinion. Former Special Agent Arthur L. Murtagh, the well-known dissenter who spent considerable time in Albany, and over a decade on the Atlanta security squad that handled the King and SCLC cases, has argued strongly that King's criticisms of the Albany agents were both justified and a prime cause of the Bureau's hostility toward King. "It appeared to me," Murtagh has remarked, that there was "a 'get King' movement in the Bureau. It was triggered by Hoover's hatred of King as a result of King's criticism of the Bureau back in '62. . . ."[5]

The criticism theory was widely suggested as the explanation when news of the Bureau's electronic surveillance of Dr. King created a brief public uproar in June, 1969.[6] It emerged again six years later when the Church Committee held both public and executive session hearings on the Bureau's conduct toward Dr. King. A number of the committee's ranking staff members came to believe, as Minority Counsel Curtis R. Smothers expressed it, that "it appears that the Bureau's effort against Dr. King starts with a response to the perceived dissatisfaction or complaints raised by Dr. King against the Bureau."[7] That explanation immediately was picked up by a number of influential reporters, and accounts of the committee's investigation published in the *New York Times, Time,* and *Newsweek* all explained to their readers that the Bureau's anger at King's remarks had been the major motivating factor in the Bureau's behavior. The *Time* story quoted one source as saying, "If you criticized the FBI, Hoover took after you. He'd do anything to destroy the credibility of a critic."[8]

When the House Assassinations Committee covered some of the same ground three years after the Church Committee's work, the same argument emerged once more. The committee quickly became impressed with "the Bureau's preoccupation with its image and its enemies," and noted that "FBI files reflect a constant preoccupation with situations which threatened to embarrass the Bureau, or otherwise jeopardize the agency's public image." It cited the testimony of both DeLoach and Murtagh in concluding that King's criticism had been the basic cause of the Bureau's hostility toward him.[9] Once again some press reports made prominent note of this theme.[10]

With so long-standing and extensive a record of statements in support of the criticism theory, it is not surprising that even one of the most insightful of all observers of the Bureau, Frank J. Donner, has cited the criticism theory in his brief treatment of the Bureau's actions in the King case. Noting Hoover's half-century-long inability to admit either "a personal mistake or a Bureau failure," Donner observed that "it was King's criticism of the Bureau and the Director that explains the reckless, personalized quality of his pursuit."[11]

The best possible evidence to support the criticism theory comes in Hoover's own words. The impact of King's 1962 remarks is reflected not only in Hoover's 1964 attack on King, but also, in somewhat more comprehensible fashion, in a long letter that the Director sent to Attorney General Robert Kennedy on September 30, 1963.

The ostensible subject of the letter was the Bureau's progress in attempting to build a case against the two leading suspects in the fatal September 15 bombing of Birmingham's Sixteenth Street Baptist Church, Charles A. Cagle and Robert E. "Dynamite Bob" Chambliss. After noting how the Alabama Highway Patrol had chosen not to cooperate with the Bureau's efforts, Hoover launched into a long account of how he viewed the FBI's problems in the South. "There is a strong feeling upon the part of the Negro elements in the South that they cannot work with or report to the FBI any information because of our cooperation with the local authorities," because that cooperation supposedly "prejudices the FBI and results in no results begin obtained." Calling this "an absolute fallacy," the Director stated that "in order to minimize as much as possible the unwarranted criticism which the FBI has received, we have over the last year refrained from close contacts or connection with local authorities. This I have regretted because a gulf has gradually developed and we are not kept informed as we have been in the past of actions contemplated and developments in cases handled by the local authorities. . . . I personally do not approve of this policy."

Hoover then focused in on what he called "the constant complaint made by the Negro elements in the South that there was no use to report matters to the FBI because all of our Agents were Southerners. This complaint was untrue. Martin Luther King several months ago made a speech [*sic*] in which he claimed that all of our Agents in Albany, Georgia, where there had been violent racial demonstrations, were born in the deep South and Negroes should not report matters to that office [*sic*]." After noting how only one of the five resident agents was a southerner by birth, Hoover's letter went on in a DeLoach-like vein. "I made an effort to affect an appointment with Martin Luther King so as to correct his impression, assuming he had been misinformed, but he refused to make an appointment so I, therefore, have to conclude that he was deliberately lying when he made the statement he did." Hoover went on to tell Kennedy that the Bureau had since instituted a policy of transferring southern-born agents out of southern offices, even though he himself again did not favor it. [12]

This account reinforces two important points: one, that Hoover and DeLoach grossly misrepresented and exaggerated what in reality was King's failure to return a telephone call, and attributed that failure to the most hostile of possible motives, and, two, that the incident of King's criticism did have a profound, though seemingly irrational effect on the FBI hierarchy.

Given so widespread and apparently well supported a belief in the criticism theory, one would think that an analysis of the "paper trail" and chronology of the King and SCLC investigations would support it. That is not the case. A closer and more critical look must be taken at the "criticism theory" itself.

Most examinations of this question begin with Hoover's November, 1964, outburst against King and then refer for explanation back to King's remarks of two years earlier. When one approaches the King case chronologically, however, much of the air goes out of the criticism-theory balloon. One of the first FBI headquarters memos on Dr. King is Milton A. Jones's February, 1961, report on King's brief reference to the FBI in a *Nation* magazine article. It does show that the Bureau took early and unfavorable note of King's regret that blacks were unrepresented among the Bureau's special agents. However, as that memo indicates, and the whole file confirms, no action was taken concerning King following that report. More than eighteen months then passes—from February, 1961, to November, 1962—

until the issue of King's attitude toward the FBI reemerges. King endorses the complaints voiced in the Southern Regional Council report on Albany on November 18. The Bureau hierarchy quickly decides that King should be contacted, apparently with an eye toward persuading him to retract the comment, or at least not repeat it. DeLoach and Atlanta agent Harding each phone King's office once on November 30 and fail to reach him. As time passes without King returning the calls, DeLoach's anger increases. By early January, when DeLoach drafts a memo reporting on this subject, King's failure to return the Bureau's phone calls is portrayed as an even more offensive act than the critical remarks themselves. Only here, in January, 1963, does any Bureau document for the first time contain a personally hostile characterization of King—DeLoach's phrase "vicious liar."[13]

By the time this develops, however, the investigation of King has been moving forward for over a year. The flood of memos on Stanley Levison and his influence on King had begun in January, 1962; the electronic surveillance of Levison by tap and bug had been instituted in March, 1962; headquarters had started pressing the Atlanta and New York field offices to recommend a "COMINFIL" investigation of SCLC in July, 1962; such a probe formally had been initiated in mid-October, 1962; and the first "COINTEL" action against Jack O'Dell's tie to SCLC had occurred in late October, 1962—all *before* King voiced his first criticism of the FBI's performance in Albany. Clearly, the criticism theory fails to explain the initial Bureau decision to institute an investigation of Martin Luther King, Jr.

Even in the aftermath of DeLoach's January, 1963, characterization of King as a "vicious liar," references or allusion to King's November, 1962, remarks are almost wholly lacking from the many intra-Bureau communications that date from January through October, 1963. Hoover's September letter to Robert Kennedy is the one prominent exception. It indicates that King's remarks and the FBI's reaction to them does contribute to the antipathy that develops toward him within the FBI hierarchy, but it does not prove that King's criticisms are the reason for the Bureau's pursuit of the King case throughout 1962 and 1963. The contradictory evidence is far more extensive.

If the criticism theory fails to explain the FBI's handling of the first phase of the King investigation, what does account for these actions?

The FBI's stated reason for opening the investigations of Dr. King and the SCLC was the presence and influence of Stanley Levison. Much like the widespread acceptance of the "criticism theory," it also has become fairly common to dismiss the Bureau's ostensible concern about Levison as merely a sham established to supply a "national security" justification for a pursuit of Dr. King rooted in some other, concealed motives. The Church Committee's report on the King case articulated this theme: "it is highly questionable whether the FBI's stated motivation was valid."[14] The major reason for the growth of this belief has been the refusal of the Bureau itself to explain the origins of the Levison case in the "Solo" project, and the reticence of the various investigating bodies to press for a full understanding of this story themselves, or to supply even a suggestive account of it to the public.

The truth of the matter is that the origins of the King investigation lay in an honestly held FBI belief that Stanley Levison was a conscious and active agent of the Soviet Union, and that Levison's friendship with King was motivated by something other than a desire to advance the cause of civil rights in America. The Bureau did possess convincing information, supplied by Jack Childs, that Levison had been directly involved in the Communist party's most sensitive financial dealings in the years prior to 1955. This involvement almost certainly made Levison aware of the active links between the CP and the Soviet Union. However, there was no firsthand information that Levison had maintained an active role in the CP's secret dealings in the years after 1955, the period when his association with Martin King had begun. When the FBI first learned in early 1962 that Levison and King were close friends, it presumed not that Levison had changed his loyalties over the previous seven years, but that the shift in his activities in 1955–56 had represented a devious change to a "deeper" role, where his mission was to win King's friendship and trust. The lack of any supporting evidence for this theory was dismissed on the grounds that Levison's new task was too sensitive for him to continue many of his past activities. Thus between December, 1961, and October, 1963, as the Bureau's concern about Levison and King steadily mounted, inference increasingly outweighed evidence in Division Five's analyses of the Levison-King case. Why that progression from justified suspicion, to understandable belief, to unsupportable conclusion occurred is the real explanation of why the King case became what it did.

"Solo" was the best "confidential source" the FBI has ever had. As such, the information supplied by Jack and Morris Childs was deemed totally reliable and assigned the highest possible value by Division Five supervisors and executives privy to it. "Solo" did report that Stanley Levison was a secret member of the CP and one of the few men who allegedly knew of the American CP's Moscow connection. Nothing else could be a more damaging and dependable source for an allegation that someone was a concealed CP operative. The credibility assigned to "Solo" constantly was remembered while the secondhand nature of "Solo's" post-1955 information on Levison regularly was forgotten.

The Bureau's frantic concern about Levison in 1962 reflected both the great credibility given "Solo" and severe discomfort over the belated discovery of the Levison-King friendship. Even though the best evidence of Levison's direct involvement with the CP ended in about 1955, the men of Division Five were hard pressed to imagine that someone so important to the CP as recently as the early 1950s would devote so much energy to Martin King solely out of the goodness of his heart. When the microphone and wiretap were installed on Levison's office in March, 1962, the Bureau expected to gain confirming evidence of Levison's malevolent role. As the weeks passed no such indications appeared. Division Five concluded not that Levison no longer worked with the party, but rather that he must be a very smart operator indeed. Levison's June recommendation of O'Dell as administrative assistant to King was his first act to support the Bureau's belief. Headquarters' pressure on Atlanta and New York to recommend a "COMINFIL" probe began immediately in its wake. While O'Dell's increased role was carefully noted, still no damaging statements or contacts had been picked up by the electronic surveillance of Levison's office. Still assuming that more of Levison's role would emerge, the men of Division Five moved both to "expose" O'Dell and to add a wiretap on Levison's home. That in turn revealed nothing to confirm "Solo's" reports.

This paucity of supporting evidence from the electronic surveillance of Levison continued through the winter of 1962–63 and the ensuing spring. Developing, however, was a clear perception that King was lying in his public explanations of Jack O'Dell's association with SCLC. By early July, 1963, in the wake of President Kennedy's personal warning to King about Levison and O'Dell, the Bureau had no more to support its suspicion about Levison than it had had eighteen months earlier when the matter began. What it did have was a clear indication that despite the ''break'' with Levison, King still was in close touch with him through Clarence Jones. That, and the Jack O'Dell matter, generated honest concern that King was concealing something, even though all of the electronic surveillance of Levison had come up empty.

Then came Sullivan's September 25 request, which Hoover approved, for the research section to do a more extensive analysis of Communist influence in racial matters.[15] That report, written by Charles D. Brennan, focused heavily on the evidence of both Levison's past central role in CP financial matters and his powerful present-day influence on King. While the document conveniently skipped over the absence of any evidence that Levison in his relationship with King in any way represented the CP or its beliefs, the monograph's impact within the FBI was substantial. Levison's position next to King, should the Bureau's presumption about him be correct, represented a very grave threat.

The most important effect of the Brennan monograph was not the distribution and recall of the actual document, following Robert Kennedy's complaint, but the reinforcing effect it had on the intra-Division Five discussions about adding wiretaps on King himself. Those discussions had begun in early September in the wake of the discovery of King's continued connections with Levison and O'Dell, and they culminated during the first week of October when the favorable ''survey'' reports arrived from both the Atlanta and New York offices.[16] That first week of October was the same time that the conclusions of Brennan's review, not formally drafted until the following week, began to circulate throughout Division Five. Thus the request for the wiretaps on Dr. King's home and offices went to the Bureau hierarchy, and on to Attorney General Robert Kennedy, in the immediate aftermath of (a) continued evidence that King was remaining in touch with Levison despite his statements to Marshall and others that he would not, and that O'Dell remained associated with SCLC, and (b) Brennan's overstated conclusion that Levison no doubt remained a loyal follower of the dictates of Moscow and the American Communist party. Division Five thus recommended the electronic surveillance of Dr. King at least in large part out of an honestly held belief that there must be fire where there was so much apparent smoke.

There is perhaps another explanation for the decision to recommend surveillance of Dr. King himself. Though its applicability is more limited than the "criticism" or "communism" arguments, it may have particular explanatory power for the events of August through November, 1963, especially the Division Five initiative to add the wiretaps on Dr. King. It is an argument that can be labeled the "bureaucratic politics" hypothesis, and it was developed by the Church Committee staff during its investigation in 1975–76.

The argument rests on two major premises: (1) that William Sullivan was *the* key decision maker in the King case in the summer and fall of 1963, and (2) that Sullivan was an almost ideal example of what one scholar has termed the bureaucratic "climber"—someone whose principal or only goal in a job is to maximize the power of his position, the amount of resources under his control, and the prestige that accompanies such an expanding role. "Climbers" are particularly noted for telling their superiors only what they believe those superiors want to hear.[17]

The Church Committee was led to its bureaucratic politics hypothesis principally, and unintentionally, by the executive-session testimony of William Sullivan himself. To all investigators of his conduct in the King case, Sullivan stressed his claim that he had not played an influential role in determining the course and character of the investigation. All of the important decisions, he asserted, had been made by Belmont, Tolson, and Hoover above him. The influential day-to-day handling of the case had involved only the supervisors and unit chiefs who were several layers below him. Concerning the events from August through October of 1963, Sullivan emphasized that he and his associates in Division Five had shifted their position on the question of the extent of Communist influence in the civil rights movement only out of fear of Hoover's retributions.

Sullivan described the last week in August, between the initial report of the twenty-third, and Hoover's comments on it, and the first Division Five apology of August 30, as follows: "The men and I discussed how to get out of trouble. To be in trouble with Mr. Hoover was a serious matter. These men were trying to buy homes, mortgages on homes, children in school. They lived in fear of getting transferred, losing money on their homes. . . . so they wanted another memorandum written to get us out of this trouble we were in. I said I would write the memorandum." Sullivan's exaggerated and implausible denials of having any influential role in the King case, however, effectively backfired on him with the Church Committee. The committee staff came to view any explanation offered by Sullivan with the greatest suspicion and skepticism. Also, many other Bureau alumni were telling the committee that Sullivan and Sullivan alone, for whom few of them had any liking, had determined the course of the King investigation and indeed of all FBI domestic security activity in the 1960s. Faced with these contrasting portraits, and with Sullivan's flawed credibility, the Church Committee viewed Sullivan's very reasonable account of the fall 1963 conflict with mistrust.

The committee's own explanation attributed far more devious motives to Sullivan—that he purposefully had initiated the conflict over Communist influence, and then manipulated its course and the Director's reactions in such a way that the final outcome would be a sizable expansion in Division Five's mission to investigate and attack Communist influence in civil rights circles. Sullivan and his associates, the Church Committee suggested, prepared the August twenty-third report not so much as an honest estimation of Communists' virtually nil influence on racial matters, but as an intentional red flag for provoking the Communist-obsessed Director, whom they well knew would never accept such a conclusion. Once Hoover reacted as expected, Sullivan and his men had merely to admit error, apologize profusely, emphasize that the Director of course was correct, and that the Director was so correct that Division Five's previously inadequate efforts in this field must of course be expanded. This scenario, the Church Committee suggested, would account for Sullivan's memos of August 30 and September 16 and 25. They can be read, it stated, "as indicating that the Domestic Intelligence

Division was manipulating the Director in a subtle bureaucratic battle to gain approval for expanded programs,'' one of which would be an intensified probe, including electronic surveillance, of Dr. King and SCLC.[18]

The difficulty with this argument is not that any of its particulars are demonstrably incorrect, but that its presumptions about Sullivan's motives and predesigned strategy (a) lack any direct supporting evidence, such as testimony from Sullivan's former assistants, and (b) reflect the incorrect belief that human action generally is prearranged on the basis of strategically rational and self-serving desires. For example, how plausible is it that, in the week prior to the much-heralded March on Washington, domestic intelligence supervisors exhibited the craftiness and foresight to prepare a monograph intentionally designed not to report the best information available, but rather to trick and provoke Director Hoover into a position where he would be subject to yet further manipulation? Is it not many times more plausible that a conclusion that Communist influence in racial matters was virtually nonexistent was an honestly reached and reasonably accurate analysis, which had the unintended effect of upsetting someone who had only the weakest grip on the true facts involved? And then, subsequently, is it not also many times more plausible that Sullivan and his men honestly did fear what the upset Hoover might do to them, as a number of them have testified, and thus acted to mollify him, than that they were playing a high-stakes game of risking their careers in order to gain an expanded mandate to investigate a subject that they already had suggested required no additional attention?

In sum, the hypothesis that Sullivan was a supercalculating manipulator who could stand back from the events of the day, and design a successful month-long scenario for manipulating the explosive Director down a certain path, is far less persuasive than either (a) Sullivan's and his colleagues' own simple explanation of what happened in the aftermath of their uncalculated initial report, and (b) the more immediate, more parsimonious, and immensely better supported theory that the intensification of the King case stemmed from the continued surreptitious contact with Levison and the contemporaneous impact of Brennan's overstated conclusions about Levison. That Sullivan regularly exhibited a desire to work his way up in the

Bureau, and to eventually become director, does not mean that his own actions and those of his division in every substantive investigation were consciously designed so as to bring him increasingly closer to that goal.[19]

If this critical analysis leads to the conclusion that the Bureau's action was rooted in a sincerely held fear of Stanley Levison, what accounts for Robert Kennedy's approval of the King and SCLC wiretaps in Atlanta and New York?

Robert Kennedy's role in this story usually is explained not by the substance of the King investigation but by a purely political concern over the congressional fate of the Kennedy administration's civil rights bill. The starting point of these accounts is July, 1963. In that month the Senate hearings on the bill elicited segregationist claims that the civil rights movement was a Communist conspiracy. At the same time, the Bureau reported that King still took counsel from Stanley Levison despite the pleas of the Kennedys and King's promise that contact would be severed.

The conjunction of these two developments, this argument states, led Robert Kennedy to a large fear: that the Bureau's information on King and Levison could be used in support of the segregationists' outlandish claims. It could torpedo Dr. King, the civil rights movement, and the administration's legislation all at the same time. This fear of the political and congressional danger is said to explain Robert Kennedy's July conversations with Courtney Evans about wiretapping Clarence Jones and Dr. King. It also reportedly accounts for his anger over the New York field-office report on King's "Communist ties" prepared just after Kennedy's public defense of King.[20] Further, it explains Kennedy's effort to reassure concerned senators publicly, while having them privately briefed on the Levison-King relationship. Kennedy's worry reappears in October, when receipt of the Brennan monograph on Levison and King produced a heightened fear that the Bureau's information might well leak out and fatally damage both the civil rights movement and the Kennedy administration's bill.

Kennedy and the Bureau thus made an implicit, perhaps explicit, trade on this subject, proponents of this argument suggest. The Bureau would withdraw the Brennan monograph, thus lessening the danger to the civil rights bill. The Attorney General in turn would approve the Bureau's request for wiretaps on Dr. King. A number of Robert Kennedy's closest aides and friends believe that he authorized the surveillance solely to protect the administration's bill. A detailed statement of this argument was made in Victor S. Navasky's insightful study of Robert Kennedy as attorney general. After reviewing the events of June through October, Navasky concluded that "in the last analysis Robert Kennedy authorized the tap on Martin King's phone to avoid problems with the FBI." He added, "Rather than risk the FBI's surfacing its damaging document through a disgruntled Senator, and thereby torpedoing the Kennedy civil rights bill, Kennedy decided to grant the FBI its wish and approve the tap."[21]

This argument is badly flawed. First, and most obvious, is a simple matter of chronology. Robert Kennedy signed the two authorizations for the wiretaps on King's home and the SCLC's offices on October 10 and October 21; the Brennan monograph on Levison and King was not even completed until October 15, and Kennedy did not voice any complaints about it, and apparently did not even learn about it, until October 25. Only on October 25, after the taps had been authorized, did the matter of recalling the widely distributed Brennan monograph arise.[22] Thus the notion of an implicit or explicit trade fails to conform with the simple chronology.

More important, it fails to fit, and is partially refuted by, Robert Kennedy's private explanation of his actions in the King-Levison matter. The same is true of the recollections of the other person most directly involved in the decision, Kennedy assistant Burke Marshall.

A full and accurate account of Robert Kennedy's decision to approve the King wiretaps has proven elusive because many people have wanted to portray Kennedy's feelings toward King as far more positive than they actually were. Kennedy friends and allies have emphasized that the initiative for the surveillance came not from the Attorney General but from the Bureau. Often these friends also have suggested that Kennedy had no doubts or worries about Dr. King himself. These are separate issues, and the fact that the initiative for the taps did not come from Robert Kennedy does not necessarily imply that he had no doubts about King. In truth he did, and the time for that to be honestly admitted is long overdue.[23]

In December, 1964, after resigning as attorney general and winning election to the Senate from New York, Robert Kennedy, along with Burke Marshall, spent several days recording his recollections of the Kennedy administration for the John F. Kennedy Library. These conversations, with Anthony Lewis of the *New York Times,* included discussion of Dr. King and Stanley Levison. Although Kennedy and Marshall occasionally erred on important dates, the transcripts of those conversations paint a very different picture of Kennedy's attitudes toward King and the FBI.

King's name came up when reporter Lewis asked about the former Attorney General's relations with Director Hoover. Kennedy responded that "he's basically very conservative," but he added; "I don't agree with this sort of general criticism that's been made that the FBI doesn't do anything in civil rights." Marshall stated that Hoover was "probably not sympathetic to the civil rights groups for all sorts of reasons, including the fact that Communists are always hanging around them." Hoover's then very recent characterization of King as a "notorious liar" was mentioned, and Kennedy said that "King was in a very vulnerable position, first, because of his association with members of the Communist Party, about whom he had been warned," and, second, because of information the Bureau possessed about his private life. Some of this was totally new to reporter Lewis. Kennedy explained the background: "In 1961 [*sic*], to protect ourselves, when I heard that he was tied up, perhaps, with some Communists, I asked them to make an intensive investigation of him, to see who his companions were and, also, to see what other activities he was involved in. I think there were rumors about him before that; but they made that intensive investigation, and I gave them, also, permission to put a tap on his telephone."

That astounded Lewis even further, and both Kennedy and Marshall then ran down the allegations against Levison, who they said was a member of the Communist party's "Executive Committee," plus their own efforts to persuade King to break his ties with Levison. They explained that King had remained in contact with Levison, and that, as Marshall phrased it, "Levison planted a person in King's organization named O'Dell who was also a Communist." They described President Kennedy's own warning to King, King's promise to sever the connection with Levison, and how King nevertheless had remained in touch with Stanley through Clarence Jones.

Neither Kennedy nor Marshall had any simple explanation when the stunned Lewis asked why King had not severed the link to Levison, despite the many warnings. Kennedy said:

> this is also . . . the reason that President Kennedy and I and the Department of Justice were so reserved about him . . . which I'm sure he felt. I mean, I never really had any conversations with him over the period other than what he should be doing in connection with the Communists. We never wanted to get very close to him just because of these contacts and connections that he had, which we felt were damaging to the civil rights movement and because we were so intimately involved in the struggle for civil rights, it also damaged us. It damaged what we were trying to do. There was more than one individual that was involved. That was what was of such concern to us. When we were sending the legislation up or when we were so involved in the struggles of Birmingham, Alabama, if it also came out what he was doing, not only would it damage him, but it would also damage all of our efforts and damage any possible chance of the passage of legislation.[24]

Thus Kennedy did fear the political damage that any leak of the Levison-King information would cause. However, he also was greatly bothered by King's continued, surreptitious contact with Levison. Burke Marshall repeatedly has stressed that it was the evidence of this ongoing link, especially in the face of King's promise that he had severed it, that was the decisive factor in Robert Kennedy's approval of the wiretaps. Marshall explained the situation in a lengthy interview in 1970:

> The reason that he approved the tap [on King] . . . is that after the third time or the fourth time, or whatever it was, when the President had talked to him and I'd talked to him and Bob Kennedy had talked to him and I talked to him again, which was in June of '63, right after the legislation was introduced, and tried to impress upon him the seriousness of this . . . there was a report in that . . . they were back in touch with each other as if nothing had happened. And that's what decided him to do it, that there didn't

seem to be any other course of action then. If you really wanted to find out what was going on, that was the only way to do it. . . . I still don't know what other course he could have taken. I mean, if you accept the concept of national security, if you accept the concept that there is a Soviet Communist apparatus and it is trying to interfere with things here—which you have to accept—and that that's a national security issue and that taps are justified in that area, I don't know what could be more important than having the kind of Communist that this man was claimed to be by the Bureau directly influencing Dr. King.

Relating the same story to the Church Committee in 1975, Marshall noted that "King had made a commitment on a very important matter . . . [and] King had broken that commitment."[25]

Hence the primary reason behind the decision to wiretap Dr. King was, for Robert Kennedy and Burke Marshall, just as it was for the FBI, honestly held fears about just what Stanley Levison represented and why Martin King was remaining in contact with him despite numerous warnings not to and King's own promise that he would end the relationship. Robert Kennedy's own doubts about King never reached a point where he considered that King consciously might represent the same forces that Kennedy and his associates believed Levison spoke for. Kennedy did believe that King's conduct was naïve and foolish, and that it imperiled not only the civil rights movement but also the political prospects of an administration that had allied itself with that movement.[26]

Kennedy's and Marshall's unquestioning acceptance of the FBI's statements about Stanley Levison reflects several themes that previous public discussions of the Kennedy administration have slighted or ignored. First, Robert Kennedy and those around him, including Marshall, were thoroughgoing believers in the cold-war view of communism and the pressing danger of Communist subversion and espionage in America. People who had known Robert Kennedy in the 1950s would find that no surprise. But the importance of this point in relation to Kennedy's and Marshall's failure to press the FBI for whatever solid evidence lay behind the allegations against Levison often has been missed.[27]

The standard myth of communism was not the only one that Ken-

nedy and Marshall embraced. They also believed the myth of the
FBI—that the Bureau's expertise on communism in America was so
great that its accusations against Stanley Levison could not be
wrong. Marshall and other Kennedy assistants like John Seigenthaler
and Ed Guthman say that it never occurred to them to doubt the
Bureau's statements about Levison. Such admissions are true, and
also wholly unsurprising when the tenor of those times and the
decade that had gone before is remembered.[28] In truth those men are
less at fault for accepting the Bureau's conclusions about Levison
than is the FBI itself for preparing reports that were based more on
inference than on evidence.

There is a third, little-noted fact here too. The Kennedy Justice
Department had far fewer complaints about the FBI's civil rights
stance than generally is assumed. Kennedy's own words from 1964,
quoted above, make this point as clearly as any can. The doctrine of
"federalism" and executive restraint that Kennedy and Marshall
believed was of controlling importance on the issue of the federal
government's role vis-à-vis the civil rights movement in the South
differed only slightly from the explanations that Hoover and the FBI
put forward when asked why the Bureau could not respond more
aggressively to racial incidents in the South.[29] The belief that there
was substantive conflict between the Justice Department hierarchy
and the FBI leadership in the years 1961–63 over the stance the
federal government should take toward the civil rights movement is
almost as much a myth as the beliefs about communism and the
FBI's expertise that were held by the Kennedy Justice Department
itself.[30]

The conclusion that both the FBI and Robert Kennedy went ahead
with the wiretapping of Martin Luther King, Jr., primarily because
of sincerely held fears about Stanley Levison's true allegiance and
Dr. King's continued contact with him is of course not incompatible
with the parallel conclusion that the Bureau's own statements about
Levison reached well beyond what actually could be proved against
him and that the Kennedy's unquestioning acceptance of the
Bureau's reports was unfair to themselves as well as to King and
Levison. Furthermore, neither of these conclusions necessitates any
particular answer to the one question raised by this story that has not
yet been confronted fully—was or was not Stanley Levison at one

time or another involved in Communist party financial dealings that were connected to the Soviet Union, as the FBI stated?

The FBI's sincere belief about Levison's post-1955 role was perfectly reasonable and justifiable as a mere hypothesis. As a fact or conclusion that was to be distributed throughout the American intelligence community, it was a claim that could not have been supported had the Bureau's reluctance to talk about "Solo" not stymied every inquiry for a more complete explication of the information on Levison. Neither then nor subsequently did the Bureau ever acquire any firsthand information on Levison's post-1955 activities that supplied meaningful confirmation for the beliefs generated by Jack Childs's reports and by such purely circumstantial or coincidental events as Levison's recommendation of O'Dell. To say that the Bureau never has possessed any convincing evidence to prove its suspicions and beliefs, is only to say that its case against Levison for the time of his association with King is in legal terms so weak as to be virtually worthless. It is not to say that the Bureau was wrong about Levison's pre-1956 activities, or some of his post-1956 contacts. In purely historical terms it is more than likely that there was considerably more to Levison's past and his ties to the Communist party than he ever publicly conceded.

It is doubtful any positive answer ever will be possible in the mystery of Stanley Levison.[31] However, once the gross inadequacy of the Bureau's post-1955 evidence against him is admitted, a more critical examination of Levison's own story shows that he probably did at one time have the involvement in CP financial dealings that the Bureau believed he had had. Three different factors all point in this direction. First, and most obvious, Jack Childs had had some direct personal contact with Levison, and in all likelihood Childs did hear the comments about Levison by Communist party officials such as Gus Hall and Lem Harris that are reported in the FBI's files. The possibility that someone, either the people voicing them or the people reporting them, simply fabricated these comments about Levison for some other purpose is, on reflection, considerably less likely than the possibility that these statements had some reasonable relationship to the truth.

Second, and more important, some former Communist party officials, individuals who were in the highest ranks of the party in the

1940s and 1950s, say that they believe Levison *was* an important secret friend or ''angel'' of the party, one who provided important assistance and counsel on matters financial and political. Some suggest that Levison perjured himself in 1962 when he testified under oath that he was not then and had never been a member of the Communist party. They concede, however, that Levison may not ever have been a ''formal'' member, or considered himself such. At a purely practical level, though, they have no quarrel with the FBI's characterization of Levison as a ''secret member'' who almost certainly knew that the party received substantial financial support directly from the Soviet Union.[32] That long-time ranking members who remain in the party, such as Lem Harris, confirm that Levison was acquainted with central figures such as Harris, Jack Childs, and William Weiner adds further support to these statements and to ''Solo's'' own reports.

Third, Levison's own belief that Jay Richard Kennedy was the root of his problem should be examined. Levison's closest relatives and friends almost all agree that Stanley never indicated the slightest doubt that his troubles stemmed from anyone but Kennedy.[33] How believable is this? Levison was confronted with some extremely specific questions by Sourwine and Eastland at the secret April, 1962, Senate Internal Security Subcommittee session.[34] Could Levison honestly have thought that allegations that he currently or very recently had been involved in CP–Soviet Union financial ties stemmed from Kennedy, whom he had not seen in well over a decade and whose own CP ties had ended in 1939? Why did not Levison ever suggest to any questioners that he had considered other possible grounds for the allegations against him, such as his acknowledged friendship with Lem Harris, who was widely believed to have had an important hand in Communist party financial affairs? Levison regularly would admit that he had known people who were close to or actually members of the party, but why did he never voice some suspicion other than that about Jay Kennedy? When viewed critically and from this wider perspective, it seems incongruous and inherently incredible that someone with the astute judgment and political sagacity of Stanley Levison would never come up with a more likely explanation for such extremely serious allegations that were made against him than the 1940s story of his relationship with Jay Kennedy.

Finally, there is a fourth consideration to take into account. Did Stanley Levison give Martin King the same explanation of his troubles with the FBI, the story of Jay Kennedy, that, minus names, he gave everyone else? Some testimony suggests no, that Stanley Levison privately gave to King a different, more extensive explanation of his own past political ties, an account considerably more detailed and frank than his standard statement that of course he had known some Communists in New York in the 1930s and 1940s.[35] If, then, Stanley Levison had in some way been something of what the FBI alleged that he had been, Levison almost certainly did not mislead Martin King. True, King never pressed Stanley hard for any admission that Stanley did not volunteer; such questioning would have been foreign to King's own attitudes. But, if one wants to make the hard judgments on the issues for which direct evidence is almost totally lacking, it is unlikely that Stanley Levison concealed anything potentially damaging about his own past from Martin King. It is much more likely that he told his friend a frank account, that King accepted it without question, found his faith and trust in Stanley in no way lessened, and never mentioned the matter to those who passed on to him the allegations against Stanley. The bond of friendship was strong and honest.

Even if, of course, the Bureau was right about Stanley Levison's activities between 1945 and 1955, there simply is no evidence, even circumstantial or secondhand, that Levison's friendship and association with Martin King were motivated by anything other than sincere support for the cause of civil rights. The FBI never acquired any information that in any way supported its assumption that Levison had befriended King at the behest of the Soviet Union and the American Communist party. Six years of nonstop electronic surveillance of Levison never produced one hint that his advice and counsel to King were motivated by anything other than genuine desire to assist the civil rights movement. Even if the judgments of some, like Andrew Young, that Stanley was essentially a conservative influence on King and the movement, especially on the eventual question of the war in Vietnam, are in all truth rather wide of the mark,[36] there are no grounds for believing that once Stanley met Martin King his role was anything other than that of an individual friend who quietly did more to assist and advise King than virtually anyone else. In all likelihood Stanley Levison underwent a gradual change in the mid-

1950s that he was as reticent to discuss as he was to talk about his actual political activities both before and after that time.[37]

With the decision to wiretap King's home and office in October, 1963, the story of the government's concern about Stanley Levison and his relationship with Martin King comes almost to its end. This is not because the King-Levison relationship ever was terminated; in fact the regular phone calls to Clarence Jones continued until King in mid-1965 decided that the friendship should be resumed openly. This, of course, the Bureau knew by virtue of its wiretaps on all three men, but nonetheless the question of King's relationship to Levison never again became the subject of great concern that it was throughout 1962 and 1963. That happened even though the intercepts continued to provide extensive evidence of Levison's substantive influence on Dr. King, and even though the men of Division Five never gave up their belief that Levison's friendship with King had been initiated by the commands of others.

The great lessening of concern over Stanley Levison after October, 1963, in the Bureau's intensified investigation of Martin King came not because of anything that the FBI learned or did not learn about Stanley Levison. It came because the extensive wiretapping of Dr. King almost immediately revealed other information that the Bureau found far more interesting than anything it ever knew or hoped to know about Stanley Levison. That information made the King investigation of 1964–65 a totally different probe than the one of 1962–63. The Bureau's activities concerning King became even more intense, and the principal motive underlying them shifted markedly and abruptly. While the Bureau's conduct of the King case up through the fall of 1963, and the Kennedys' support of it, reflected sincerely believed fears about Stanley Levison, the motive that dominated the Bureau's intensified pursuit of King in 1964–65 was far less honest and far less pleasant. It is to that story—the surveillance of Martin King—that we now turn.

3

"They Are Out to Break Me"— The Surveillance of Martin King

In November of 1963 the King and SCLC wiretaps were activated in Atlanta and New York, moving the Bureau's investigation to a higher intensity. FBI headquarters was overjoyed by the amount and variety of information generated from the SCLC headquarters and King-home taps. In mid-December the domestic intelligence division enthusiastically recommended that the Atlanta intercepts be continued for at least another three months.

The wiretaps installed at the New York SCLC office generated no such enthusiasm at headquarters. They added almost nothing to that overheard on the Levison and Jones taps. The New York office told headquarters that King and his advisers still had not settled on someone to head the office. In the absence of an administrator, little was taking place there. The New York Telephone Company also was experiencing "technical difficulties" with the wiretaps, which on occasion put them out of service. In mid-November headquarters authorized extension of the surveillance on a month-to-month basis only.[1]

Reports flowed into headquarters from Atlanta and New York. Many of them were passed on to Robert Kennedy. There was information on continued contact with Levison, new details of SCLC finances, of differences among King's advisers, of arrangements for the writing of King's next book, and of SCLC protest plans for the coming year. Often the reports would be somewhat garbled, as with one December communication that SCLC owed $16,000 to the "Sixteenth Street Baptist Church of Atlanta." Many items contained useful information, however. New York reported serious disagreement over the use of Gandhi Society funds between Jones and Wachtel on one hand and increasingly active attorney William Kunstler on the other. There was also a warning from Jones to King that Justice Department officials were inquiring about whether attorney Arthur Kinoy, a friend of Kunstler's, had any link to SCLC. All of this paled, however, beside information concerning King's own personal life that was picked up on the taps.[2]

To be certain that the Atlanta office could make full use of this information, the domestic intelligence division called for a major planning session to be held at headquarters on Monday, December 23, 1963. Attending from Atlanta were agent Robert R. Nichols, who for several years had had responsibility for the King and SCLC cases in that office, and his immediate superior, security squad supervisor Henry Rowse. Representing Division Five were supervisors Larry T. Gurley and David Ryan and internal security section chief Fred J. Baumgardner. Assistant Director William Sullivan stepped in and out throughout the day-long session.

"The purpose of the conference," a memo sent to Alan Belmont the next day stated, "was to explore how best to carry on our investigation to produce the desired results without embarrassment to the Bureau." The "desired results," the memo indicated, included "neutralizing King as an effective Negro leader and developing evidence concerning King's continued dependence on communists for guidance and direction." Several courses of action had been approved: all SCLC employees should be investigated; SCLC's financial situation should be monitored more closely; SCLC contributors should be identified and investigated; and: "We must continue to keep close watch on King's personal activities." Sullivan himself had stressed to the group that "although King is a minister, we have already developed information concerning weakness in his character which is of such a nature as to make him unfit to serve as a minister of the gospel." Field offices thus "should continue to gather information concerning King's personal activities" including his use of liquor as well as involvement with women. The reason for this, Sullivan explained, was so that "we may consider using this information at an opportune time in a counterintelligence move to discredit" King. "We will," the memo to Belmont vowed, "at the proper time when it can be done without embarrassment to the Bureau, expose King as an immoral opportunist who is not a sincere person but is exploiting the racial situation for personal gain." The memo further promised to "expose King for the clerical fraud and Marxist he is at the first opportunity." Sullivan noted that the "technical coverage on King and the SCLC [is] producing excellent information," and that Division Five and the Atlanta office also "will explore the possibility of utilizing additional specialized investigative techniques at the SCLC office," or, in other words, surreptitious break-ins.[3]

The quality of the discussion at this planning conference is reflected in a list of twenty-one agenda items. Among the topics considered were:

(7) What do we know about King's housekeeper? In what manner can we use her?

(8) What are the possibilities of using Mrs. King?

(12) What are the possibilities of placing a good-looking female plant in King's office?

(13) Do we have any information concerning any shady financial dealings of King, which could be used to our advantage? Has this point ever been explored before?

"The whole object" of this, the agenda suggested, was "to expose King." It asserted that "we are attempting to expose King because of communist influence brought to bear on him. . . . We are most interested in exposing him in some manner or another in order to discredit him.'' There was no explicit and convincing statement of why this group so wanted to discredit King.[4]

The following week *Time* magazine announced that Dr. King was its "Man of the Year" for 1963. The New York office soon reported a conversation between Jones and King regarding the *Time* honor, as well as other developments. Jones had had a long talk with "our friend" the previous evening—in fact Bureau agents had seen Jones and Levison meet at 6 East Thirty-ninth Street in Manhattan from 3P.M. to 5P.M.—about the disheveled state of SCLC finances. King said that they would all meet in New York the following Wednesday, January 8, 1964, to discuss the problem. King asked what "our friend" had thought of the *Time* article. Jones replied, according to the FBI transcript, that the "friend" had said, "We are lucky *Time* didn't go into the communist issue or the financial issue.'' King reminded Jones that he would be staying at the Willard Hotel in Washington from Sunday, January 5, through Tuesday, January 7, so as to be present for the Supreme Court arguments in *Sullivan* v. *New York Times Co.,* a case that stemmed from an allegedly libelous ad placed by SCLC in the *Times* in 1960. Handling the paper's case, Jones earlier had told King, would be former Attorney General William P. Rogers and a talented black associate, Samuel R. Pierce, Jr.[5]

The news that King would be staying at the Willard reached William Sullivan the day before King was to arrive. Sullivan detailed his reaction in a Monday morning memo to Alan Belmont. "Because of the importance of our investigation of the communist influence in racial matters and the intelligence and counterintelligence possibilities which thorough coverage of King's activities might develop and because time was of the essence, I authorized Washington Field Office to make effort to secure microphone coverage of King provided full security would be assured.'' Early that morning security coordinating supervisor L. W. P. Cherndorf of the Washington office had notified Sullivan of the microphone installation. Sullivan informed Belmont that "trespass is involved" and that he would "be promptly advised of positive results achieved.''[6] This was the first time that a Bureau "bug" had been used against King.

By Tuesday morning the Washington office could tell Sullivan that the surveillance was a grand success. The bug had recorded a lively party involving King, several SCLC colleagues, and two black women who worked at the Philadelphia Naval Yard. Over a dozen large reels of tape had been garnered. Bureau employees immediately set to work transcribing the material.

As that work proceeded, Sullivan and his Division Five staff were busy examining other options suggested at the December twenty-third conference. Supervisor Seymor Phillips thought "an examination of recent income tax returns of King might well reveal information which could assist the Bureau in its efforts to discredit King or neutralize his effectiveness." Phillips proposed that the Bureau obtain the returns of King, the SCLC, and the Gandhi Society and examine them for possible violations of the law and for material that could be used to embarrass King publicly. The following day Phillips asked the New York office for any information on SCLC or Gandhi Society finances that could be passed on to the IRS. Four days later Phillips himself called the IRS to ask for copies of the returns.[7]

Sullivan himself, meanwhile, had concentrated on a grander mission. The discrediting of King, Sullivan argued in a long memo to Belmont on January 8, should be paralleled with a Bureau effort to promote a suitable black replacement. "King," Sullivan wrote,

> must, at some propitious point in the future, be revealed to the people of this country and to his Negro followers as being what he actually is—a fraud, demagogue and moral scoundrel. When the true facts concerning his activities are presented, such should be enough, if handled properly, to take him off his pedestal and to reduce him completely in influence so that he will no longer be a security problem and no longer will be deceiving and misleading the Negro people.
>
> When this is done. . . . The Negroes will be left without a national leader of sufficiently compelling personality to steer them in the proper direction. This is what could happen, but need not happen if the right kind of a national Negro leader could at this time be gradually developed so as to overshadow Dr. King and be in the position to assure

the role of leadership of the Negro people when King has
been completely discredited.

Sullivan had in mind a specific man who would be this "right kind"
of leader. It was in fact a man King had watched in the Supreme
Court earlier that week—New York attorney Samuel R. Pierce, Jr.
Sullivan summarized Pierce's career, and asked for approval to
begin quiet efforts to promote Pierce toward national leadership.
Belmont passed the recommendation on to Hoover, who gave it his
"O.K." and added a dig at Division Five's analysis of the Communist party and blacks. "I am glad," Hoover wrote, "that 'light' has
finally, though dismally delayed, come to the Domestic Int. Div. I
struggled for months to get over the fact the Communists were taking
over the racial movement but our experts here couldn't or wouldn't
see it." [8]

By Friday, January 10, the transcriptions of some of the Willard
recordings were complete. "Highlights" had been played for Director Hoover himself. Hoover's reaction, Sullivan told interviewers
years later, was, " 'They will destroy the burrhead,' " 'burrhead'
supposedly being Hoover's favorite term for King. At 5:36 P.M. that
Friday evening Hoover called Walter Jenkins, President Lyndon B.
Johnson's closest aide, and described the Willard material. A transcript would be sent to the White House as soon as possible. On
Tuesday, January 14, "Deke" DeLoach carried an eight-page "Top
Secret" account of the Willard activities to the White House. A note
made at that time by DeLoach read, "Handled 1/14/64 with Jenkins
and the President." Jenkins, DeLoach reported to Hoover, "was of
the opinion that the FBI could perform a good service to the country
if this matter could somehow be confidentially given to members of
the press. I told him the Director had this in mind."

Simultaneously, Division Five recommended that a copy of the
Willard "results" be given Attorney General Robert Kennedy. The
memo warned, however, that Kennedy might personally "repri-
mand" King concerning the matter, and noted, "If he does, it is not
likely we will develop any more such information through the means
employed. It is highly important that we do develop further information of this type in order that we may completely discredit King
as the leader of the Negro people." Hoover's decision was "No. A
copy need *not* be given A. G." [9]

With the excitement about the Willard material, a New York report that King, Levison, Jones, and three other SCLC officials had met at the New York Hilton on January 8 received surprisingly little attention. New York also continued to report on the problems of the SCLC office there, which was still without an administrator. The Levison and Jones wiretaps were providing a surfeit of information on this subject, as well as unfavorable comments by both men about SCLC Executive Director Wyatt Walker. By contrast, the SCLC office tap was revealing little, and on January 15 headquarters instructed New York to discontinue it. One week later New York agents burglarized the SCLC office, and two days after that, on January 24, the wiretap was terminated.[10]

Within Division Five the attention of both supervisor Phillips and Assistant Director Sullivan was focused on obtaining more surreptitious recordings of Dr. King's private activities. Headquarters was extremely interested in what might occur at a January 20–22 SCLC retreat at Black Mountain, North Carolina. It nevertheless instructed the Charlotte field office not to "cover" it for fear the Bureau's efforts would be exposed.[11]

On January 17 headquarters learned King would be staying at Milwaukee's Schroeder Hotel on January 27. Sullivan immediately recommended that a Bureau "bug" be installed in King's room there so that additional "entertainment," as the memo termed it, could be recorded. That suggestion was adopted, and on January 23 Milwaukee assistant special agent in charge (ASAC) J. Wallace LaPrade was given the go-ahead. On the twenty-seventh itself, however, Milwaukee SAC Baker called to say that King had arrived, but that local police were housed in a room near King's in order to afford him protection. "In view of this," Sullivan noted in a memo, "it was the conjecture of Baker that the likelihood of King's going ahead with any [deletion] plans is greatly minimized. I agree with this observation." When the memo reached Hoover's desk later that day, however, the Director registered a dissent: "I don't share the conjecture. King is a 'tom cat' with obsessive degenerate sexual urges." Baker and Sullivan turned out to be correct, however. "No activities of interest developed," the Milwaukee office reported by phone the next morning.[12]

Division Five next learned that King would be in Honolulu from February 18 to 25. Phillips promptly recommended microphone surveillance of King's lodgings there, so that further evidence of his "moral weakness" could be acquired and then used to see that King was "completely discredited . . . for the security of the nation." Phillips proposed that San Francisco supervisor Harry F. Clifford, Jr., be brought to headquarters for a planning session in advance of King's trip. Sullivan approved that suggestion, and on February 3 Clifford "was thoroughly briefed on all aspects of this matter, with emphasis being given to the fact that security is paramount and that the need for discrediting King is based upon the communist influences upon him." Clifford was instructed to assemble a team of San Francisco field-office agents for the Honolulu mission—the Bureau's Hawaiian office agents might well be recognized by local hotel employees. Clifford and his "soundman," Special Agent Fordyce G. Lyman, arrived in Honolulu on February 12 to conduct a "dry run," as recommended by the FBI Laboratory. The three other San Francisco agents chosen for the team—Robert U. Mann, a "bug" installer, Richard E. Stephens, a photographic specialist, and Albert P. Clark, apparently a talented lock picker—arrived on the fifteenth. Clifford had the task of explaining his team's mission to the local Bureau office, but reported that that had been no problem, for Honolulu already was aware "from the copies of communications in its file that the Bureau had an intense interest in the extracurricular activities of" King. The surveillance team, assisted by the Honolulu SAC, obtained rooms adjacent to those King and his companions would occupy at the Hilton Hawaiian Village for the first three days of their trip. Clifford and Lyman checked into the hotel, pretending to be tourists, and, for the two days prior to King's arrival, "unpacked and experimented with all of the Bureau equipment sent out or brought out to Honolulu" for the mission. They also cased the Kahala Hilton, where King was expected to spend the balance of the week.

King and his party—SCLC Executive Director Wyatt T. Walker, Reverend Logan Kearse of Baltimore's Cornerstone Baptist Church, and two women—checked into rooms 404 and 405 of the Hawaiian Village on Tuesday, February 18. The surveillance team was waiting for them in rooms 403 and 406. Even before the prior occupants of room 405 had checked out, the Bureau agents had entered and established "double wasp coverage" of the room, adding a "minimite" bug before King himself arrived. At the same time, other members of the team were busy installing no fewer than *nine* electronic devices in the four rooms that King and his party were expected to move to at the Kahala Hilton on Thursday morning. That effort proved to be for naught, however. The Hawaiian Village surveillances indicated that King and company were changing their plans and would leave Thursday for Los Angeles. Agents Clifford and Lyman quickly prepared to travel to Los Angeles. Headquarters notified the Bureau field office there to install microphones in the rooms King's party would occupy at the Ambassador Hotel. By 11:45 P.M. Thursday night the Los Angeles bugs were in place.

For the third time, however, the Bureau's efforts to acquire further damaging recordings of King proved unsuccessful. All of the work at the Kahala had been wasted, and in addition nothing headquarters considered significant had been recorded at either the Hawaiian Village or the Ambassador. A particular problem, supervisor Clifford told headquarters, was that King and his friends almost always had the television on at high volume. That, plus use of the room airconditioners, "presented a considerable problem which made some of the conversations almost, if not completely, unintelligible," Clifford complained. Use of a microphone "becomes almost ineffective no matter where it is placed if the TV is blasting away."

The Bureau's luck took a sudden turn for the better when King and his companions checked into the Los Angeles Hyatt House Motel on Saturday, February 22, after leaving the Ambassador. By 9:30 P.M. that evening the Bureau had a "bug" in King's suite and agents were monitoring it in the next room. The surveillance continued until King and his party left to return east on Monday evening. In that forty-eight hours the Bureau acquired what in retrospect would be its most prized recordings of Dr. King. The treasured highlight was a long and extremely funny storytelling session during which King (a) bestowed supposedly honorific titles or appointments of an explicitly sexual nature on some of his friends, (b) engaged in an extended dialogue of double-entendre phrases that had sexual as well as religious connotations, and (c) told an explicit joke about the rumored sexual practices of recently assassinated President John F. Kennedy, with reference to both Mrs. Kennedy, and the President's funeral. The tapes of King's remarks, along with some still photos and 16-mm. film of King and his companions, immediately were sent to Washington.[13]

FBI headquarters' officials moved quickly to make maximum use of this new material. By March 4 an eight-page "Top Secret" account of King's remarks had been drafted. Supervisor Phillips, in a memo prepared that day, recommended distribution to presidential aide Walter Jenkins and Attorney General Kennedy, since the report contained "excellent data indicting King as one of the most reprehensible [deletion] individuals on the American scene today."

Phillips noted that Director Hoover had vetoed giving an account of the Willard material to Kennedy. However, one of the Atlanta taps recently had indicated that King would soon participate in a Kennedy family sponsored memorial to the late President. To provide Robert Kennedy with a copy of the Hyatt House material, and especially what another memo termed "King's vilification of the late President and his wife," Phillips said, "should remove all doubt from the Attorney General's mind as to the type of person King is. It will probably also eliminate King from any participation in the memorial."[14]

Sullivan and Hoover thought all this was a good idea. DeLoach gave a copy of the report to Jenkins on March 6 and Courtney Evans gave one to Robert Kennedy on March 10. The Bureau had been sending at least weekly letters reporting the highlights of King's telephone conversations to the White House, and DeLoach and Hoover together spent the entire afternoon of March 9 with President Johnson, giving him yet another update on the phone intercepts. Several weeks later the Director was able to inform both Kennedy and Johnson that an inebriated King had threatened to go on a hunger strike and die if Congress did not pass the civil rights bill.

The Bureau hierarchy also was busy handling information from the King case on two other fronts. The first began with off-the-record and unpreserved comments about Dr. King's supposed association with Communists and sexual activities by Director Hoover himself in executive session testimony before a House Appropriations subcommittee on January 29. Hoover apparently had claimed that Communist influence was very much present in the civil rights movement. Word of that statement spread rapidly among segregationist and right-wing members of Congress. In early February news of the loose talk reached Robert Kennedy, who called Hoover to complain. Several weeks later Virginia Representative Howard Smith, the well-known chairman of the House Rules Committee, asked De Loach for information on Hoover's comments. He, Smith, wanted to make a speech on the House floor concerning King. Smith told DeLoach

> he was seriously disturbed about the fact that there appeared to be considerable derogatory information about King and apparently no one in Congress was taking steps to advise the general public of this matter. He stated he thought this should be done.

DeLoach told Smith

> that despite our desire to see this scoundrel exposed, it would be out of the question for us to furnish him information and then his expecting us to back it up later on. I told Judge Smith that this would disrupt certain operations which appeared to be more important than an exposure of King from a communistic standpoint.

DeLoach agreed with Smith "that obviously King needed to be exposed," and that perhaps this could be done sometime in the near future using only information about King's personal life. DeLoach recommended this idea to Hoover, but the Director rejected it: "I do *not* want anything on King given to Smith nor anyone else at this time."[15]

At the same time there were indications that the tightly held material concerning King's association with Levison might have been leaked to one or more members of the press. In early February both Burke Marshall and Robert Kennedy's press secretary, Edwin Guthman, learned that reporter Reese Cleghorn was making inquiries concerning Levison. Marshall and Guthman each spoke about this with Bureau officials Evans and DeLoach. They strongly hoped the Bureau was not seeking to bring the Levison issue into public view. The FBI officials denied any such strategy, and Hoover ordered his subordinates to tell Marshall that any accusation of a Bureau leak was a conscious lie. The controversy subsided when Cleghorn ended his inquiries.

Fear of a damaging leak led Marshall to take further action. On Monday, February 17, he called Johnson White House aide Bill Moyers to say that Robert Kennedy felt it highly advisable that President Johnson see the entire Justice Department file on Dr. King as soon as possible. Moyers asked what the rush was, and Marshall explained that he feared the FBI was trying to leak unfavorable information to the press. Within minutes a courier appeared in Moyers's office with the Justice Department file.

Moyers consulted Johnson's top aide, Walter Jenkins, and Jenkins immediately summoned the FBI's Cartha "Deke" DeLoach to the White House. The two assistants showed the file to DeLoach, and told him that they suspected Marshall and Kennedy feared the political consequences should the King information become public. Sending it to Lyndon Johnson, if not reducing their own vulnerability, at least put the President in the same boat as they were. Jenkins and Moyers told DeLoach they would return the file to Marshall the next morning, and not show it to the President.

DeLoach informed Hoover of the White House's suspicions about Marshall's and Kennedy's true motives. Jenkins and Moyers, DeLoach said, had sent the file back with the following note:

> Due note has been taken of the attached file. Your interest, and that of the Attorney General, in bringing this information to our attention is appreciated.
>
> While it is presumed that the Attorney General is cognizant of the contents of this file, you may wish to make certain that he is fully aware of the Reverend King's propensities, particularly in view of newspaper accounts in July, 1963, quoting the Attorney General as stating, "There is no evidence" that Reverend King, or any of the other top leaders of the civil rights groups is a communist, or communist controlled.

Though their political concern was transparent, Marshall and Kennedy may well have been unaware of how much the FBI already had told the Johnson White House about King. "The President and his closest aides," DeLoach told Hoover, "are well aware of King's background from reviewing memoranda we have sent over."[16]

The FBI also had notified both Kennedy and Johnson that King and Levison had been seen meeting on two more occasions, February 29 in New York and March 9 in Atlanta. The continued concern about this contact was reflected in a mid-April story by Washington columnist Joseph Alsop. The article was intended to convey a not-so-subtle warning to King from the administration. Alsop described King's indecisive handling of the O'Dell matter, but went on to say something more. "Official warnings have been given to King about another, even more important associate who is known to be a key figure in the covert apparatus of the Communist Party. After the warning, King broke off his open connections with this man, but a secondhand connection nonetheless continues."

Two days after the story appeared, King had a long phone conversation about it with Clarence Jones. Jones already had discussed it with Levison, and told King that Levison felt strongly that King should discuss the matter with the government, tell them how limited the contact was, and that it was occasioned only by the need for some continuity in SCLC affairs. Two days later Jones again discussed the matter with Levison, saying that King was uncertain of what to do. Levison responded, in the FBI's account, that King should tell the government that all the worry was based on "a misunderstanding and a misinterpretation of a few pieces of evidence." Shortly thereafter one of the Atlanta wiretaps intercepted a conversation between King and his Washington representative, Walter Fauntroy. King explained to Fauntroy that Alsop's second reference had been to Levison, that King felt both O'Dell and Levison had had "earlier CP connections," but that King no longer had any contact with either Levison or O'Dell and that Fauntroy should reassure Burke Marshall of that fact. Once again Bureau officials felt that King was being dishonest.[17]

Several days later the first public report of Hoover's January House testimony appeared. King immediately was asked for comment. He stated that Hoover was helping extremists smear the civil rights movement, and that he found it "difficult to accept the word of the FBI on communistic infiltration in the civil rights movement when it has been so completely ineffectual in protecting the Negro from brutality in the Deep South." In a wiretapped phone conversation, King stated his anger at Hoover's remarks more bluntly: "I want to hit him hard—he made me hot and I wanted to get him."[18]

Two weeks later, in a nationally broadcast television interview, King commented, "I would like for those who are saying that Communists are in the movement to let us know who they are, so we can get rid of them, because we certainly don't want them in this movement." He went on to say, "I think it was very unfortunate that such a great man as Mr. Hoover allowed himself to aid and abet the racists and the rightists in our nation by alleging that you have Communist infiltration in the movement." King added that Communist efforts to penetrate the movement should not be minimized, but that likewise their presence should not be assumed, for "this just isn't true."

Reporter Ben Bradlee pressed King. Had he been warned about anyone who had not been removed from the movement? King answered, "Not at all. Not at all." Bradlee pressed him further, and alluded to O'Dell. King said there had been "Nobody else. The only person that they identified that had any connection with the Southern Christian Leadership Conference was removed. He has been off of our staff a long, long time." A Bureau memorandum on the telecast the next day noted that "King lied about being warned of anyone else because he had been warned about Stanley Levison and has nevertheless maintained a close association with Levison."[19]

Division Five officials meanwhile were moving forward with a variety of actions targeted against Dr. King. Efforts were made to block honorary degrees to King by Marquette University and Springfield (Mass.) College by notifying school officials of both the personal material and Communist allegations concerning King. Another hotel-room bug was installed when King and aide Bernard Lee spent the night of March 19 at the Detroit Statler. Apparently the surveillance was "unproductive."[20] In mid-March the Internal Revenue Service reported that despite careful scrutiny it had been unable to locate any violations in either King's or SCLC's tax returns. Director Hoover scrawled "what a farce" when the disappointing memo reached his desk.

Several days later headquarters asked New York and Atlanta to suggest actions that could be taken against King and SCLC. Each office also was to "continue to gather information concerning King's personal activities . . . in order that we may consider using this information at an opportune time in a counterintelligence move to . . . neutralize or completely discredit the effectiveness of [King] as a Negro leader.'' New York responded to the first instruction with alacrity. An anonymous letter should be sent to an unhappy SCLC New York office worker, Ruth Bailey, warning her that she was about to be fired. Headquarters approved that, but it was much more pleased with the many ideas submitted by Atlanta: putting a "trash cover" on the SCLC office; investigating King's bank and charge accounts; instituting electronic surveillance on an Atlanta hideaway apartment often used by King; installing a bug in King's office; looking for personal weaknesses among SCLC employees that could be used to win their cooperation with the Bureau; sending a forged letter in King's name to SCLC contributors warning them that an IRS investigation was about to begin; and attempting to intensify the well-known mutual dislike of King and NAACP head Roy Wilkins.

While Atlanta was warmly praised for its imagination, the New York office got into some trouble with headquarters by reporting, after its initial suggestion of the one anonymous letter, that Bureau coverage of SCLC and those associated with it already was "adequate," and that nothing more was needed. New York also noted the lack of recent information to support Levison's alleged ties to the Communist party, plus the absence of any evidence that King associate Bayard Rustin was in any way subversive. Headquarters angrily responded that there was no evidence that Rustin was *anti*-Communist, and that Bureau coverage could in no way be "adequate" when it was learning anything less than one hundred percent of what was taking place.[21] The chastened New York agents replied with a suggestion that a wiretap be reinstalled on the SCLC office there in light of frequent contacts between Levison and office manager Adele Kanter. Headquarters approved and ordered New York to make the plans.[22]

Division Five wanted further microphone surveillances of King. They did manage one "bug" when King stayed at Sacramento's Senator Hotel on April 23–24 and another when King and Wyatt Walker spent April 24–26 at Los Angeles's Hyatt House, scene of the Bureau's great success in February. Neither of these was especially rewarding, however.[23]

Immediately after the stay in Los Angeles, King and Walker flew on to Las Vegas, where King had two speaking engagements before NAACP groups. The Bureau established no electronic surveillance of King there, and thus was astounded when, almost four weeks later, the special agent in charge of the Las Vegas office sent a three-page letter straight to Director Hoover, outside of normal Bureau channels. The letter enclosed a copy of a memorandum concerning King's visit prepared by a local law-enforcement agency. This local investigator, the SAC wrote, could hardly believe his own information, which had come from a Las Vegas prostitute who was a regular source. The woman claimed that she had spent the evening with Dr. King during his visit. In addition to other activities, King had been extremely forceful, if not downright violent with her. She asserted, so the local officer wrote, that never again would she have anything to do with someone like King. The Las Vegas SAC noted that records showed King had called the woman from Sacramento several days before his visit, and added that he did not share the local officer's disbelief of the allegations against King: "knowing what we know about this individual I am certain she is correct." Headquarters made no effort to corroborate or disprove this thirdhand story but it did send a four-page "Top Secret" account of it to the White House and Attorney General Robert Kennedy.[24]

The Atlanta and New York offices were now responding to headquarter's April instructions to broaden their probes of SCLC. Atlanta reported that someone once had named SCLC affiliates' director Reverend C. T. Vivian as a 1940s Communist party member in, of all places, Peoria, Illinois. King adviser Lawrence D. Reddick, a well-known black historian and Baltimore professor, had been called a "concealed member" of the party in the early 1950s by former CP official turned informant Louis F. Budenz. New York reported that the SCLC office there was still in confusion, and that Levison had been in touch with fund-raising consultant Saul Mills, whom informant Budenz also had labeled a "concealed Communist."[25]

New York took particular pleasure in detailing Levison's criticisms of King, Rustin, and others, as well as critical assessments of King made by Clarence Jones and Harry Wachtel. Headquarters was extremely interested in New York's report that a "research committee" of King's advisers was being established to coordinate their advice. The group planned to meet with King every few weeks at Wachtel's law office. Learning that the first meeting of this committee would take place on June 22, New York requested permission to bug Wachtel's meeting room. Someone with entrée to the office would be paid $50 for assisting with the installation. Headquarters rejected the request "because of the occupations of the individuals using the office," but encouraged New York to find out all it could about the meeting. Files indicate that New York learned nothing of what transpired.[26]

King now was spending much of his time in Saint Augustine, Florida, where an SCLC campaign was meeting with brutal opposition from local Klan elements. The Bureau's wiretaps kept headquarters, the Justice Department, and the White House all fully informed of King's pessimism about the Saint Augustine situation. He feared that problems there would prevent SCLC from launching a summer effort in Alabama. King was especially upset, the intercepts indicated, with the lack of any federal government intervention in Saint Augustine. On one occasion he told Jones that he might call for a protest march on the White House.[27]

In late May the Bureau's Atlanta office learned that SCLC headquarters had expanded its number of phone lines from four to seven. It requested and received headquarters' approval to install wiretaps on the new ones. As one headquarters' memo indicated, the existing office phone surveillances "are of inestimable value in gaining intelligence not only concerning SCLC affairs, but concerning" King as well, and that coverage of the additional lines certainly was desirable. At that same time the New York office finally proceeded with reinstallation of the wiretap on the SCLC quarters there that had been authorized by headquarters in early May. Two weeks later, however, SCLC shifted its office to a new location, and the tap again was discontinued. New York chose not to install one at the new location.[28]

After a two-month hiatus during May and June, in early July Division Five recommended that both a microphone and a wiretap be installed in King's hotel room when he again returned to the Los Angeles Hyatt House from July 7 to 9. "It would be most desirable," supervisor Phillips wrote, "to effect as much technical-type coverage as can be safely done to cover King's activities" in order "to gain further evidence of the activities of this moral degenerate." Only after the memo had been typed did someone think to add the phrase "in view of his association with Communists," in handwriting, to the explanation of why the surveillance was desired. Los Angeles agents installed the two devices and manned the tape recorders, but a July 15 headquarters' memo reported that the recordings were repetitive of and not as good as previous material. Although Division Five thus recommended against disseminating a report of the coverage, Hoover instructed "Send to Jenkins." On July 17 a three-page account was carried to the White House.[29]

By mid-July presidential aide Jenkins was requesting Bureau reports on the expected presence of a large delegation from the Mississippi Freedom Democratic Party, a civil rights movement sponsored alternative to the all-white "regular" Mississippi Democratic party, at the upcoming Democratic National Convention in Atlantic City, New Jersey, from August 22 to 28. Lyndon Johnson and his aides were worried about the MFDP's plan to challenge the seating of the "regular," all-white Mississippi delegation. Should the "regulars" be thrown out and the movement activists seated in their place, the White House feared a Deep South electoral backlash against Johnson.

Maneuvering on the upcoming vote of the convention's credentials committee was underway by the second week in August. Dr. King was playing an active role on behalf of the MFDP, and the Johnson administration was employing all its available resources in opposing the MFDP challenge. King and his family at this time were staying at the New York City apartment of Louis and Justine Smadbeck, long-time acquaintances of Coretta King. The Bureau, invoking the King wiretap authorization signed by Robert Kennedy ten months earlier, installed a phone intercept on the Smadbeck apartment on August 14. Eight days later, when King took a room at Atlantic City's Claridge Hotel for the duration of the convention, a wiretap was put in there as well.[30]

The Bureau's intensified coverage of King and others associated with the Mississippi challenge undoubtedly was prompted by Lyndon Johnson's insatiable interest in developments at Atlantic City. One Bureau memo concerning the new wiretaps stated: "We have been able to keep the White House and others very currently informed concerning King and these important [MFDP] matters. The recommended extension of coverage will enable us to continue to do so." Assistant Director DeLoach, whose job included liaison with

President Johnson, took personal charge of the "special squad" sent to Atlantic City at the White House's request. The Bureau's men monitored the electronic surveillances on King and other movement activists and used a variety of disguises to observe other developments at the convention.

DeLoach kept in almost continuous telephone contact with White House aides Bill Moyers and Jenkins, passing along detailed reports on the thinking and plans of those supporting the MFDP challenge. Assisted by this information, and playing no-nonsense hardball with those Democratic liberals who initially had supported the MFDP effort, Johnson's men greatly eroded the MFDP's support inside the crucial credentials committee. In the end not even enough votes existed to file a minority report in support of the MFDP. When the MFDP delegates ignored the advice of King and other leaders and rejected a Johnson offer to seat two preselected MFDP members as "at-large delegates," the struggle was over. The movement activists headed for home. Many of the white Mississippians who retained their delegate seats subsequently supported not Johnson but Republican Barry Goldwater. Even that apparently did not cause Johnson to reevaluate his Atlantic City strategy.

Both the Bureau and the White House were happy with the work of DeLoach's "special squad." DeLoach himself, summarizing its achievements to superior John Mohr, reported, "We were able to keep the White House fully apprised of all major developments during the Convention's course" and "to advise the President in advance regarding major plans of the MFDP delegates. The White House considered this of prime importance." In a note thanking Moyers for his praise of the operation, DeLoach added, "I'm certainly glad that we were able to come through with vital tidbits . . . which were of assistance to you and Walter [Jenkins]. You know you have only to call on us when a similar situation arises."[31]

In the wake of the Democratic Convention, new instructions went out from Bureau headquarters to field offices. Coverage of Communist influence in civil rights matters should again be intensified. The term "Communist," headquarters said, "should be interpreted in its broadest sense." The Communist party and other formal organizations were not enough. The enemy, headquarters suggested, was both more numerous and more difficult to identify than previously realized. "There are clear and unmistakable signs," the field offices were told, "that we are in the midst of a social revolution with the racial movement as its core."

These instructions produced another surge of effort in the King and SCLC probes. SCLC's own national convention was about to be held in Savannah. Plans were made to bug King once again during his stay there. Preparations for that coverage reflected a new and transparently disingenuous concern about King adviser Harry Wachtel. Wachtel had been on the scene for over two years but previously had not been named as a supposed subversive. Instructing Savannah to install the bugs in King's quarters, headquarters cited Wachtel's expected presence and the likelihood of strategy discussions between him and King as the reason for the coverage. Wachtel, Bureau files indicated, was "reported to be an active member of the National Lawyers' Guild in 1949" and his wife Lucy, someone had claimed, "was listed as an officer of the Bath Beach Club of the Kings County Communist Party in 1944."

The Savannah office, perhaps misunderstanding the real purpose of the bugs, took headquarters' statements about subversive influence to heart. It asked for permission to bug other leftists who would be in attendance, such as Carl Braden and United Packinghouse Workers official Ralph Helstein. Division Five officials vetoed that request, but the entire effort apparently went for naught when the bugs garnered no recordings considered damaging to King.[32]

Wachtel was not the only person around King who received new attention as a supposed subversive in the wake of headquarter's promulgation of its new, broader definition of communism. Another was newly named SCLC Program Director Randolph T. Blackwell, who had joined SCLC when Andrew Young stepped up to be executive director following the departure of Wyatt T. Walker. The Atlanta office labeled Blackwell "a former member of the Communist party" in Washington, D.C., and cited both an informant's claim from 1953 plus a report that Blackwell had attended a Labor Youth League convention in Durham, North Carolina, in 1950. Nor did the expansion stop with SCLC employees. On September 28 Atlanta notified headquarters that its files indicated that once upon a time one Verna Scott had alleged that King's father, Martin Luther King, Sr., was a Communist party member. The Atlanta agents— who knew something of Daddy King's conservative ways—were doubtful of this charge, but reported it along with a host of other supposed associations of King, Sr. Several weeks later headquarters supervisor Phillips told Atlanta that one of the characterizations of King's father—that he was "reportedly sympathetic" to a leftist organization that had folded in the 1930s—was too insubstantial for inclusion. The CP story, however, remained.[33]

In September Dr. King went to Europe. Bureau officials, hearing that he hoped to obtain an audience with the Pope, immediately moved to try to prevent one. New York SAC John Malone was instructed to inform Francis Cardinal Spellman of the Bureau's derogatory information on King, and to encourage the Cardinal to alert the Vatican. Malone reported back that Spellman had agreed to assist the Bureau, and had contacted the Vatican. King's meeting with the Pope took place anyway. Hoover was astounded. "I am amazed that the Pope gave an audience to such a degenerate," Hoover scribbled on one newsclipping.

In early October of 1964 a headquarters' review of the King and SCLC wiretaps concluded that the intercepts were valuable indeed. The King home tap had furnished substantial material that had been passed on to the White House, plus "a great amount of information concerning racial disorders in the South, racial riots in Northern cities, as well as racial activities at both major political party conventions." It would be continued "because of the large contribution that it has made to our intelligence in the racial movement." The internal security section, which oversaw the SCLC case, said that the taps on the Atlanta office provided "extremely valuable information. . . . An example of valuable information obtained was information indicating that King was to unleash a public attack upon the Director in April, 1964 [the statement issued in response to news of Hoover's testimony]. Another example is that information was obtained indicating that the SCLC was attempting to have a woman allegedly employed by President Johnson intercede with the President to have the Director issue a public statement to the effect that the SCLC and King were not influenced by communists." Of course continuation of these wiretaps was also strongly recommended.[34]

News of King's Nobel Peace Prize broke on Wednesday, October 14, 1964. Hoover was outraged. "King could well qualify for the 'top alley cat' prize," the Director wrote on one news story. Soon a flood of new FBI reports on King was headed to the White House, with copies of some going to Acting Attorney General Nicholas deB. Katzenbach and other executive branch officials. Several government offices would play a role in King's December trip to Oslo to accept the prize—the State Department, the U.S. Information Agency, and American embassies in Europe. The Bureau laid plans to give each of them the information it possessed on King.[35] This effort was well underway when remarks by Hoover himself to a group of women news reporters on Wednesday, November 18, brought the Bureau's antipathy toward King into the headlines for the first time. Hoover rarely met with reporters, but he warmed to this interview, using three hours to criticize a host of individuals and organizations that he held in disfavor.

Concerning King, Hoover harshly attacked his statements—made exactly two years earlier—about the Bureau's Albany agents. Hoover detailed for the women that the Albany men were not all southerners. He further claimed that King had advised blacks not to report civil rights violations to the FBI and had refused Hoover's invitations to meet with him. That showed, Hoover went on, that King was "the most notorious liar" in America. Hoover also volunteered: "He is one of the lowest characters in the country," and gave an affirmative response when one reporter asked if rumors that King had ties to Communists were true. DeLoach, one of two Hoover aides attending the session, handed three different notes to him advising him to put the "most notorious liar" phrase off the record, as Hoover had done with the "lowest characters" remark and the response about communism. Hoover ignored the first two missives, and told DeLoach to mind his own business when handed the third. Thus the next morning's headlines came as no surprise to Bureau executives.[36]

King was on the island of Bimini in the Bahamas when the story broke. By Thursday afternoon his Atlanta office had fired off a telegram to Hoover and issued a public statement, both in King's name. The telegram read as follows:

> I was appalled and surprised at your reported statement maligning my integrity. What motivated such an irresponsible accusation is a mystery to me.
>
> I have sincerely questioned the effectiveness of the FBI in racial incidents, particularly where bombings and bru-

talities against Negroes are at issue, but I have never attributed this merely to the presence of Southerners in the FBI.

This is a part of the broader question of federal involvement in the protection of Negroes in the South and the seeming inability to gain convictions in even the most heinous crimes perpetrated against civil rights workers.

It remains a fact that not a single arrest was made in Albany, Ga., during the many brutalities against Negroes. Neither has a single arrest been made in connection with the tragic murder of the four children in Birmingham, nor in the case of the three murdered civil rights workers in Mississippi.

Moreover, all FBI agents inevitably work with local law enforcement officers in car thefts, bank robberies and other interstate violations. This makes it difficult for them to function effectively in cases where the rights and safety of Negro citizens are being threatened by these same law enforcement officers.

I will be happy to discuss this question with you at length in the near future. Although your statement said that you have attempted to meet me, I have sought in vain for any record of such a request.

I have always made myself available to all FBI agents of the Atlanta office and encouraged our staff and affiliates to cooperate with them in spite of the fact that many of our people have suspicions and distrust of the FBI as a result of the slow pace of justice in the South.

King's brief public statement had a somewhat different tone.

I cannot conceive of Mr. Hoover making a statement like this without being under extreme pressure. He has apparently faltered under the awesome burden, complexities and responsibilities of his office. Therefore, I cannot engage in a public debate with him. I have nothing but sympathy for this man who has served his country so well.

In a telephone interview from Bimini with an Associated Press reporter, King elaborated on what he had said in the telegram. ''I never advised Negroes in Albany not to report to the FBI," King noted. "On the contrary, we reported every incident. But we were dismayed by the fact that nothing was ever done." He stated how discouraged he was at the lack of arrests in high-visibility cases, but added, "Rather than criticize the FBI, I have acted as a mediator, urging Negroes to keep faith with the FBI and to not lose hope. But you can't explain to a Negro why a plane can be bombed and its pieces scattered for miles and the crime can be solved, but they can't find out who bombed a church."

At the same time that King was making those comments, other civil rights leaders—Roy Wilkins of the NAACP, James Farmer of CORE, Whitney Young of the Urban League, and A. Philip Randolph, Dorothy Height, and Jack Greenburg—were attending a previously scheduled meeting with President Lyndon Johnson, Acting Attorney General Katzenbach, and civil rights chief Marshall. Wilkins volunteered to Johnson that the black community agreed with King's criticisms of the FBI, and strongly objected to Hoover's characterization of King. Johnson, Wilkins told reporters afterward, "simply listened and gave no comment and no opinion."[37]

That same afternoon FBI headquarters was notified of an intercepted phone conversation between King advisers Wachtel and Rustin. Both men were urging King to take a more aggressive stance in responding to Hoover than his initial telegram and statement had, and to call publicly for Hoover's replacement. A memo to Sullivan detailing the Wachtel-Rustin exchange asserted that "they are seizing the opportunity, in line with a long-held communist objective, to launch a campaign to oust the Director as head of the FBI." If "King follows their advice," it added, "we will then have further evidence of the extent to which King is being used by communist sympathizers in support of communist objectives."

Early Friday Atlanta informed headquarters of two intercepted phone conversations involving King himself. In one, King told his secretary, Dora McDonald, that Hoover was "too old and broken down" and instructed that his SCLC aides ask other public figures and organizations to issue statements criticizing Hoover's outburst and the Bureau's civil rights stance. King subsequently spoke to SCLC's C. T. Vivian, stating that Hoover "is old and getting senile" and should be "hit from all sides" in order to force President

Johnson to censure Hoover publicly. Immediately after that, Atlanta reported, SCLC staffers Andrew Young, Bernard Lee, and Vivian began to make the contacts that King had requested.

Friday afternoon Director Hoover was informed of an intercepted conversation in which King's wife had remarked that her husband possibly might meet with Hoover in the near future. Hoover wrote on the report: "I have no intention of seeing King. I gave him that opportunity once and he ignored it." Also late Friday domestic intelligence chief Sullivan recommended to Hoover that the Bureau neither respond to King's telegram and statement nor offer the civil rights leader a meeting with the Director. Hoover responded, "O.K. But I can't understand why we are unable to get the true facts before the public. We can't even get our accomplishments published. We are never taking the aggressive, but allow lies to remain unanswered." Perhaps in response to Hoover's complaint about "never taking the aggressive," Sullivan had supervisor Phillips give the tapes of the King microphone surveillances to John Matter of the FBI Laboratory, and instructed Matter to prepare a composite tape of the "highlights" of the various recordings. When Matter returned with the new tape, Sullivan obtained from Phillips some unwatermarked paper, and sat down to draft an anonymous letter. With the tape, it would be mailed to King at SCLC headquarters. In part the letter read:

> KING,
>
> In view of your low grade . . . I will not dignify your name with either a Mr. or a Reverend or a Dr. And, your last name calls to mind only the type of King such as King Henry the VIII. . . .
>
> King, look into your heart. You know you are a complete fraud and a great liability to all of us Negroes. White people in this country have enough frauds of their own but I am sure they don't have one at this time that is anywhere near your equal. You are no clergyman and you know it. I repeat you are a colossal fraud and an evil, vicious one at that. You could not believe in God. . . . Clearly you don't believe in any personal moral principles.
>
> King, like all frauds your end is approaching. You could

have been our greatest leader. You, even at an early age have turned out to be not a leader but a dissolute, abnormal moral imbecile. We will now have to depend on our older leaders like Wilkins a man of character and thank God we have others like him. But you are done. Your "honorary" degrees, your Nobel Prize (what a grim farce) and other awards will not save you. King, I repeat you are done.

No person can overcome facts, not even a fraud like yourself. . . . I repeat—no person can argue successfully against facts. You are finished. . . . And some of them to pretend to be ministers of the Gospel. Satan could not do more. What incredible evilness. . . . King you are done.

The American public, the church organizations that have been helping—Protestant, Catholic and Jews will know you for what you are—an evil, abnormal beast. So will others who have backed you. You are done.

King, there is only one thing left for you to do. You know what it is. You have just 34 days in which to do (this exact number has been selected for a specific reason, it has definite practical significant [sic]). You are done. There is but one way out for you. You better take it before your filthy, abnormal fraudulent self is bared to the nation.

On Saturday morning, November 21, thirty-four days before Christmas, Sullivan called in one of the oldest agents assigned to Division Five, Lish Whitsun. He instructed Whitsun to fly to Miami with the small, unmarked package that was handed him by supervisor Phillips. Once in Miami later that day, Whitsun called headquarters and Sullivan told him to address the package to King, at SCLC's Atlanta office address, and mail it from a Miami post office. Within minutes the tape and the accompanying letter were on their way to King.[38]

Bureau officials did not let up. Monday morning Atlanta submitted a fifty-one-page report on King. Later that day Hoover sent two letters concerning King to presidential aide Bill Moyers at the White House. They contained information on King's upcoming travel plans, plus derogatory information on King advisers Rustin and Wachtel. Tuesday evening Hoover delivered a speech in Chicago that included a line attacking "pressure groups" that are headed by "Communists and moral degenerates." Few people had any uncertainty about Hoover's target, and the following day CORE National Director James Farmer called for Hoover's resignation. On Thursday columnist Victor Riesel, a well-known friend of the Bureau, released a story explaining how Hoover for two years had nursed a grudge over King's criticism of the Bureau's performance in Albany. Hoover, Riesel wrote, "was affronted by charges that the FBI men were doing nothing when informed of violent acts against Negroes. The director felt that this reflected on the integrity of himself and the entire FBI." Riesel went on to say that Hoover carefully had chosen when to respond to King's two-year-old remarks, waiting for a "quiet moment in our national and international life to say publicly what he had had on his mind." With that now accomplished, Riesel said, Hoover "considers the controversy closed."[39]

If Hoover wanted to let bygones be bygones, none of his subordinates were aware of it. The Bureau's crime records division, headed by DeLoach, initiated a major effort to let newsmen know just what the Bureau had on King. DeLoach personally offered a copy of a King surveillance transcript to *Newsweek* Washington bureau chief Benjamin Bradlee. Bradlee refused it, and mentioned the approach to a *Newsweek* colleague, Jay Iselin. On Wednesday, November 25, Attorney General Katzenbach learned of Bradlee's experience, and discussed the matter with Burke Marshall. The two Justice Department officials were shocked by the story. They knew that such material existed, but were deeply angered that the Bureau was trying to leak it. The two men already were scheduled to fly to President Johnson's Texas ranch Saturday morning so that the chief executive could attempt to dissuade Marshall from his decision to resign. They resolved to speak to the President about the matter, and early Saturday afternoon they related Bradlee's experience to Lyndon Johnson. Both Marshall and Katzenbach recall that Johnson said very little in response to their warning. He was in fact so close-mouthed that Marshall suspected the President was being less than frank when he said that he would look into the matter. Johnson's actual response perfectly confirmed Marshall's suspicion: he instructed Moyers to warn the Bureau that Bradlee was unreliable and was telling the story all over Washington.[40]

Bradlee had not been the only journalist whom DeLoach had approached, and Katzenbach and Marshall were not the only public figures whom newsmen alerted to the Bureau's efforts. Roy Wilkins of the NAACP had heard the rumors, and further was alarmed at Hoover's remark in the Tuesday speech. On Friday the twenty-seventh he called the Bureau to request an immediate meeting with DeLoach. It took place later that day. Wilkins subsequently stated that he had warned DeLoach that the Bureau's hostility toward King could cripple the civil rights movement, and that he hoped its campaign of vilification would be halted. DeLoach, however, described the meeting differently to other Bureau officials—and to President Johnson in a November 30 letter sent over Hoover's signature. He asserted that Wilkins had offered actively to assist the Bureau's campaign to remove King from leadership in the civil rights movement. Wilkins, DeLoach claimed, feared that any public battle over King's character would cost the movement much of its white support. Thus he had offered to assist in having King "retire" from the movement without a public battle. DeLoach's probably exaggerated report set Sullivan and his aides to thinking. Division Five soon was recommending that DeLoach recontact Wilkins and ask him to arrange a meeting of the nation's black leadership at which the King "highlights" tape could be played and matching transcripts distributed. Doing this might well persuade the black leadership to remove King "from the scene" on their own. That DeLoach did not pursue this suggestion may indicate the true content of his initial discussion with Wilkins.[41]

Another person who heard rumors of the Bureau's smear efforts was CORE's James Farmer, alerted by a *New York Post* reporter. Farmer called DeLoach and made an appointment to see him the next day. Farmer then called King, who was in Chicago seeing Reverend Archibald Carey, a good friend of both the King family and Hoover. King was scheduled to pass through one of the New York airports that evening, and Farmer arranged to meet him at a lounge in the terminal. The two men spoke privately for forty minutes. Farmer told King the reporter said he had heard three different allegations against King: charges he had participated in group sex, claims of financial misconduct, and vague accusations about associating with communists. Farmer asked King about each of these. Concerning the sex story, Farmer recalls, King "of course denied it. He could not remember any such incidents that the FBI claimed to have, and so on. I said, 'I'll forget it.' And he said, 'Don't forget it. No, let's do what we can to stop it. If something like this comes out, even if it isn't true, it will damage all of us in the whole movement.' " King forcefully denied the other two charges as well. Farmer told King of his intention to see DeLoach and to ask that the smear campaign be halted. King endorsed his idea, and the next morning Farmer flew to Washington.[42]

That next day King, too, headed for Washington. Efforts by Reverend Carey and Attorney General Katzenbach to arrange a face-to-face meeting between King and Hoover had succeeded, and a noontime phone call from Andrew Young to DeLoach set the appointment for 3:30 P.M. that very afternoon. King was accompanied to the meeting by Ralph Abernathy, Walter Fauntroy, and Young. The ubiquitous DeLoach sat in with Hoover. After greetings were exchanged, King said that Abernathy would speak first, and Abernathy made some favorable comments about Hoover and the Bureau. Then, according to DeLoach's detailed account of the meeting—an account that King's aides have since termed largely accurate—"Reverend King spoke up. He stated it was vitally necessary to keep a working relationship with the FBI. He wanted to clear up any misunderstanding which might have occurred. He stated that some Negroes had told him that the FBI had been ineffective; however, he was inclined to discount such criticism. Reverend King asked that the Director please understand that any criticism of the Director and the FBI which had been attributed to King was either a misquote or an outright misrepresentation. He stated this particularly concerned Albany, Georgia. He stated that the only time he had ever criticized the FBI was because of instances in which Special Agents who had been given complaints in civil rights cases regarding brutality by police officers were seen the following day being friendly with those same police officers." Then, DeLoach recorded, "King denied that he had ever stated that Negroes should not report information to the FBI," and stated his dislike of communism and Communists.

After that brief statement of about two minutes duration, Hoover launched into a description of the FBI's activities in the South that

continued, almost uninterrupted, for over fifty minutes. He emphasized the Bureau's strenuous efforts to solve the Chaney-Schwerner-
Goodman murders in Mississippi, saying that arrests would be made
within a very few days. He also gave chapter and verse on FBI
efforts against the Ku Klux Klan dating back as far as the 1920s.
King mentioned to Hoover that SCLC planned to initiate demonstrations concerning voting rights in Selma, Alabama, in the near future,
and Hoover responded with an account of the Bureau's work in five
cases that the Justice Department had filed against election and law
enforcement officials in that county. By then the one hour scheduled
for the meeting had expired. As King and his aides rose to leave,
King asked DeLoach if the Bureau planned to issue any statement to
the press about the meeting. DeLoach said no. King asked Hoover if
the Director would object to King giving a brief statement to the
waiting reporters, and Hoover said that that was up to King. Then,
standing in Hoover's reception room, King told the newsmen that
the meeting had been "very friendly, very amicable" and that he
and Director Hoover had reached "new levels of understanding."
King added, "I sincerely hope we can forget the confusions of the
past and get on with the job."[43]

King's aides, however, were not so pleased. They had hoped for
an explicit resolution of the conflict. Instead, the session had been,
as Andrew Young later termed it, "a completely nonfunctional
meeting." They soon learned that the Bureau's efforts to peddle its
information on King to reporters had not ended. Indeed, one
reporter, James McCartney of the *Chicago Daily News,* had been
shown photographs of King and a woman leaving a motel by a crime
records division official while waiting outside Hoover's office during
King's meeting with the Director. McCartney also was offered transcripts of the King surveillances, which he refused. Despite this,
DeLoach that same day denied to James Farmer, as he had to Wilkins, that the Bureau was trying to leak such material. He did admit
that the Bureau possessed it. Farmer, to his later regret, did not press
DeLoach further.

Others who were offered transcripts, photos, or the recordings
themselves included David Kraslow of the *Los Angeles Times,* John
Herbers of the *New York Times,* Chicago columnist Mike Royko,
Eugene Patterson of the *Atlanta Constitution,* and Lou Harris of the

Augusta (Georgia) *Chronicle.* Word of this continued to reach Young and other people close to King. On one occasion Young and Fauntroy met with a number of reporters for the *New York Times* to try to learn who had approached them with the material, and what the transcripts or recordings contained. The newsmen were unwilling to respond fully to either query.[44]

Shortly after the meeting with Hoover, King, and a large group of friends and advisers left for Europe to attend the Nobel Prize ceremonies. The FBI's hierarchy remained busy, disseminating its material on King to public officials and private citizens far and wide. Division Five had completed a new and revised version of "Communism and the Negro Movement: A Current Analysis," on November 27. A copy was sent to the President, and the Bureau asked for Johnson's approval to disseminate the monograph throughout the executive branch. On Friday, December 4, White House aide Bill Moyers called DeLoach to discuss the FBI's request. Moyers, DeLoach told his superiors, said

> he and the President had read the Director's letter in connection with possible dissemination of [the] monograph. He stated it was both his and the President's opinion that the FBI should disseminate this monograph if it was felt that dissemination would be in the best interest of internal security. I told Moyers that under the circumstances he appeared to be telling me that we should go ahead and disseminate. He answered in the affirmative.

Three days later copies of the thirteen-page document were on their way to Secretary of State Dean Rusk, Defense Secretary Robert McNamara, CIA Director Richard Helms, Attorney General Katzenbach, U.S. Information Agency Director Carl Rowan, three military intelligence offices, and the National Science Foundation. Meanwhile, the FBI's London office reported that it had advised the American ambassador to Norway of the Bureau's derogatory information on King, who was about to arrive in Oslo to accept the Nobel Prize. Back in Washington both Bureau headquarters and the White House strongly denied rumors that the Hoover-King flap might lead to the retirement of the Director, who would turn seventy on January 1.[45]

While DeLoach's crime records division went on trying to interest the press in the King material, domestic intelligence chief Sullivan was busy spreading the word to others. Learning that Harry Wachtel had told King that New York Governor Nelson Rockefeller might give SCLC $250,000, Sullivan endorsed a recommendation by supervisor Phillips that Rockefeller be briefed on King. The briefer would be a former Bureau agent now heading up the New York State Police. Crime Records already had had agent C. B. Fulton brief his friend Dr. Robert S. Denny, an official of the Baptist World Alliance, on King's personal life. Hoover on November 27, however, had vetoed a recommendation that one of the tape recordings be played for Denny and another BWA leader, Dr. Josef Nordenhaug. In the wake of the Hoover-King meeting, however, Denny apparently requested more information from his friend Fulton, and on December 10, with Bureau approval, Fulton gave a fuller briefing to Denny, Nordenhaug, and Reverend E. H. Pruden of Washington's First Baptist Church. News of the King information apparently traveled fast among the Baptists. On December 14 White House staff member Brooks Hays, a former congressman and active Baptist layman, sent a note to Bill Moyers. He had heard a story about King and the FBI from his friend Theodore F. Adams, program committee chairman for the BWA. He thought Moyers should be aware of it. Hays could not know how much Moyers already knew concerning dissemination of the King material.

The Baptists were not alone in hearing about King, however. On the evening of December 15 Assistant Director Sullivan personally briefed Dr. R. H. Edwin Espy, general secretary of the National Council of Churches, about King's personal life. Sullivan previously had discussed the subject with Espy in June, 1964. Now, he claimed, Espy, like Wilkins, was eager to assist the Bureau in removing King from leadership in the civil rights movement. Sullivan's assertion was uncorroborated, and no more came of this exchange than of DeLoach's meeting with Wilkins.[46]

By mid-December the Bureau had learned from its New York wiretaps of several lively incidents that had occurred during King's trip to Europe to accept the Nobel Prize. These incidents had disturbed several members of the King entourage who had not been accustomed to the style in which King and his closest colleagues partied, and these individuals had related their concerns to others over wiretapped phone lines. The FBI again sprung into action. On December 21 a two-page report entitled "Martin Luther King, Jr.: His Personal Conduct," was dispatched to the White House, the secretaries of state and defense, the CIA, USIA Director Rowan, four military intelligence offices, and the National Science Foundation. Vice-President-elect Hubert Humphrey received a copy as well, plus the earlier monograph on "Communism and the Negro Movement." Attorney General Katzenbach was sent a further report that alleged King had a reputation as a heavy drinker.[47]

King had been quite exhausted even before the trip began, in part due to the controversy with Hoover. On his return he was in an even bleaker state of mind. On December 29 Atlanta reported two conversations of Coretta King. One was with King's secretary, Dora McDonald, and the second with Andrew Young. Both concerned "King's mental state, his rambling conversations in New York, an attempted fight with Abernathy in London and the Hoover conflict. They discussed how King might be relieved of some pressures." Another Atlanta report several days later advised headquarters that "King was becoming more and more upset."

King's state of mind worsened, however, when, on January 5, the anonymous tape and threatening letter that Sullivan had had mailed on November 21 were finally discovered. The Bureau's package had arrived at SCLC headquarters even before King met Hoover, but the box, obviously containing a reel of tape, was placed unopened with other similar packages. Many acquaintances knew that Coretta enjoyed receiving recordings of her husband's public speeches. Such parcels sent to the SCLC office were put aside for transfer to the King home, where Coretta cataloged them. Apparently on January 5 Mrs. King stumbled upon this tape of a different sort, listened to a brief portion of it, discovered the accompanying letter, and then called her husband. King, Abernathy, Young, and Reverend Joseph Lowery then joined Mrs. King in listening to the entire recording. Most of this composite tape was from the initial Willard surveillance and was, as Andrew Young has remarked, somewhat garbled.

King and his aides did not doubt the source of the tape. The recording had been made in Washington, and the package was postmarked Miami. The letter, however, was more frightening. King indicated in several phone conversations on January 6 that he was both greatly distraught and quite convinced that the FBI was behind it. "They are out to break me," he told one friend. To another he said, "They are out to get me, harass me, break my spirit." He or his aides, he indicated, had to see Hoover or DeLoach immediately, for there was no privacy. "What I do is only between me and my God," he remarked in one conversation.

The Atlanta agents, who overheard every word of this, knew nothing about Sullivan's package. They took two actions in response to what they heard. First, aware that King was resting at a private location, they turned in a false fire alarm sending trucks to that address. Second, the agent in charge of the Atlanta office phoned headquarters to report on what had been overheard. Headquarters in turn took two actions of its own. First, a letter describing King's emotional state, though of course making no reference to his anonymous package, went to the White House and the Attorney General. The one to Katzenbach stated that King was emotionally distraught and feared public exposure. Second, New York was ordered to install microphone surveillances when King and several aides stayed at the Park Sheraton from Friday, January 8 through Sunday, January 10.

That Friday morning Andrew Young called DeLoach and asked for a meeting with him and/or Hoover on Monday. DeLoach said that Hoover would be unavailable, but that he would see Young. Throughout the weekend the Bureau's microphones in the New York hotel room listened to King, Young, and aide Bernard Lee discuss how Young should handle the Monday meeting. The bugs, in the words of one summary, "recorded King characterizing the mailing of the tape as, 'God's out to get you,' and as a warning from God that King had not been living up to his responsibilities in relation to the role in which history had cast him." On Monday morning Young and Ralph Abernathy arrived in Washington to meet with DeLoach and his assistant, Harold P. "Bud" Leinbaugh. DeLoach subsequently reported that Young and especially Abernathy had had great difficulty in speaking openly about King's personal life, and that DeLoach had tried to maximize their discomfort. Young questioned DeLoach about the FBI's interest in Communists in SCLC, SCLC finances, and stories about King's sexual activities. DeLoach told Young to go to the House Un-American Activities Committee for information on Communists. He said that neither SCLC's finances nor King's personal life were of any interest to the Bureau or the subject of any activity by it. Young was extremely disappointed by DeLoach's stonewalling and patently inaccurate denials. He later remarked that the meeting's only benefit had been to make him realize that Bureau executives like DeLoach had "almost a kind of fascist mentality. It really kind of scared me. . . . There really wasn't any honest conversation." Unsatisfied, Young and Abernathy left and reported back to King their sense of frustration. The Bureau meanwhile moved right ahead.[48]

One newspaperman approached several times in December or early January by Bureau agents was the *Atlanta Constitution*'s Eugene Patterson. Patterson's visitor encouraged him to send a photographer to a Florida airport at a certain time in order to obtain pictures of King in the company of a woman not his wife. Patterson attempted to explain to the agent that that was not the sort of "news" the *Constitution* wanted to print. He sent the agent on his way. Several days later the agent returned and the same scenario occurred.

Patterson was not the Bureau's lone target at the *Constitution*. Assistant Director Sullivan contacted publisher Ralph McGill in mid-December, and on January 20, 1965, the two men spoke again and at length. Sullivan's immediate purpose was not only to persuade the *Constitution* to "expose" King, but also to enlist McGill in a Bureau effort to undercut a testimonial dinner planned by Atlanta notables to honor their home-town Nobel laureate.

The two available versions of Sullivan's conversation with McGill differ greatly. Sullivan reported to his Bureau superiors—and to the White House, in a letter Hoover sent to Moyers on January 22—that McGill "believes that the very best thing that could happen would be to have King step completely out of the civil rights movement and public life." In an account reminiscent of DeLoach's description of his meeting with Wilkins, Sullivan stated that "McGill believes that an exposure of King will do irreparable harm to the civil rights movement," and thus was willing to assist the Bureau in torpedoing the banquet. When that account was revealed in 1976, McGill had died, but the story was strongly attacked by McGill's colleague, Patterson, and by others who had worked to arrange the Atlanta banquet. McGill, Patterson stated, had been as outraged at the Bureau's approach as Patterson himself was. Only Patterson's arguments kept McGill from calling King's father to warn him about the Bureau's activity. McGill also spoke of informing the Justice Department. Patterson himself a short time later spoke with John Doar, Marshall's successor as head of the civil rights division, about the Bureau's efforts. Patterson was shocked when Doar evinced virtually no reaction to this account of being offered material on King's sexual activities. Patterson concluded that Doar and his superiors must have been aware of this pattern, and were either unable or unwilling to halt it. Doar has said that Patterson's description of their conversation is correct, but he argues with the final inference. Doar claims to have known nothing about the Bureau's efforts against King.[49]

If Daddy King did not learn of the Bureau's efforts from editor McGill, he was alerted to them by long-time friend and Atlanta Police Chief Herbert T. Jenkins. Chief Jenkins had had experience with Bureau agents. On numerous occasions he and his officers had been encouraged to "raid" locations where the agents claimed King was visiting a woman friend. All but one of those suggestions had been rejected. The one time an officer had been provoked into going, the raid revealed King and five other people earnestly holding a meeting. On January 18, however, just before Sullivan's chat with McGill, Jenkins traveled to Washington for the inauguration ceremonies. There he met with Director Hoover.

Hoover greeted Jenkins with a long monologue about the three men he most hated: former Attorney General Robert Kennedy, Dr. King, and former Bureau official Quinn Tamm, now executive director of the International Association of Chiefs of Police. Concerning King, however, Hoover gave Jenkins a reasonably detailed account of just what information the Bureau possessed on him. Jenkins, startled by the strength of Hoover's animus, promptly called King, Sr., when he returned to Atlanta. Daddy King apparently spoke to his son about it immediately. By January 22 the Atlanta office was reporting to headquarters that King had been overheard on the phone complaining to Abernathy about how the Bureau's information had reached his father.[50]

In late January Dr. King once more was scheduled to spend a weekend at a New York hotel. Division Five again instructed New York to install microphone surveillances in the appropriate rooms.

What the Bureau gathered that weekend is unclear, but the continuing electronic coverage on both Clarence Jones and Levison kept an uninterrupted flow of reports on their phone conversations moving from New York to headquarters. Many of them were forwarded to the White House. In February, Division Five learned of various speeches and press releases that Jones, Wachtel, and Bayard Rustin were writing for King. By late that month, and for a number of weeks to follow, New York's reports were preoccupied with the increasing influence of Harry Wachtel in SCLC affairs, and how King's other advisers were reacting to that development. One communication detailed these supposedly crucial events as follows:

> Clarence Jones and Stanley Levison during late February, 1965, gossiped about Martin Luther King and his relationship with Harry Wachtel. Jones said that gossip he had heard indicated that people were concerned over King's "over-dependence" on Harry Wachtel and that Wachtel had an "assertive and take-charge attitude." Jones said that he himself had promised to devote more time to King's business. Levison said that Wachtel found it difficult to work with other people and never consulted anyone except Bayard Rustin. . . .

Several days later, New York reported, the same subject came up between Jones and King, and then again between Jones and Andrew Young. Both Young and Jones, New York said, felt that both Rustin and Wachtel were too assertive.

While the Bureau may have been fully informed about all of this minor backbiting, it was wholly unaware of Jones's and Levison's expressions on another issue, the rapidly escalating fighting in Vietnam. Within a few weeks of each other both men had sent letters to President Johnson strongly protesting American conduct in Southeast Asia. "Our national interests," Levison stated, "are not critically involved in the jungles of Viet Nam. . . . Your election was characterized by the clearest mandate for peace since World War II. Please execute it. . . ." Jones's somewhat stronger letter expressed his "vigorous dissent and alarm" over what he characterized as the United States's "completely irrational, illegal and immoral policy in South Vietnam," where we had been supporting "a succession of undemocratic regimes which are opposed by a majority of the people of South Vietnam.'' The White House responded to neither letter, and there is no indication that anyone connected the two writers with the men close to King whom the Bureau was so interested in. What the Bureau would have done had it learned that King's two confidants held such strong critical opinions about so sensitive a foreign-policy question can only be surmised.[51]

Throughout the spring of 1965, while all of King's advisers, and much of the country, were absorbed in SCLC's protest campaign in Selma, Alabama, the Bureau continued its efforts to bug King's hotel rooms and to distribute reports on King's activities and phone conversations. Although DeLoach's office apparently had become so frustrated by its failure to gain the cooperation of newsmen in ''exposing'' King that it had stopped trying, Sullivan's division continued to have a wide range of Americans who had some contact with King—including Massachusetts Governor John Volpe, Community Relations Service Director LeRoy Collins, and a number of religious leaders—briefed about the Bureau's information.

In late March Attorney General Katzenbach ordered the Bureau to obtain his approval for microphone surveillances as well as telephone wiretaps. This new policy did not halt the FBI's buggings of King's hotel rooms. It did result in Katzenbach being sent Bureau memoranda asserting that the bugs were meant to overhear the supposedly subversive advice offered King by Levison, Jones, Wachtel, and Rustin. These claims were merely a cover for the Bureau's continued interest in King's personal life, as one New York report revealed. On April 5 a microphone implanted in King's room at the Americana Hotel had not been activated because King left without spending the night.[52]

In early April the Atlanta office learned of King's plans to change residence in several weeks. Headquarters was asked to approve a shift of the wiretap when the appropriate time came. On April 19 headquarters granted authority to ''survey'' the new house, which King already had occupied, but not until May 6 did Atlanta report that it was ready to proceed with the new tap. Later that same day, however, and for reasons that are not revealed in surviving documents, Sullivan himself called the Atlanta office and instructed them *not* to install the tap. With that decision a ''source,'' which one memo described as ''most prolific,'' came to an end.

The end of the wiretap on King's home did not signal any decrease in the Bureau's interest in his personal life. Microphone surveillances of his hotel rooms continued. One was installed in mid-May when King spent two days at the New York Sheraton Atlantic. In line with the new policy, Attorney General Katzenbach was advised of it, though only after the fact. The purpose of the coverage, Katzenbach was told, was to obtain evidence of Levison's, Jones's, and Rustin's "influences upon King as well as information concerning the tactics and plans of King and his organization in the civil rights movement." A report based on that bug was sent to the White House. It stated that Levison was urging King to speak out publicly against American military involvement in Vietnam. Another bug was installed in early June when King and Andrew Young spent one day at the Americana in New York. "No intelligence information was obtained," Bureau records show, and Katzenbach was not notified of this attempt.[53]

In the spring of 1965 a familiar figure reappeared in the King case: Jay Richard Kennedy. Over the previous decade Kennedy had continued to work as an entertainers' agent and novelist; he also had continued his active support of civil rights causes. He had served as moderator of a television special on August 28, 1963, featuring the leaders of the March on Washington; he had become a particular acquaintance of CORE Executive Director James Farmer. Jay Kennedy also had become an excellent and regular source of information for the Central Intelligence Agency.

Kennedy's assertions that he had never gone to the FBI in the 1940s and 1950s concerning Stanley Levison are correct. However, beginning in perhaps 1959 or 1960, Kennedy spoke regularly with an officer of the Liaison and External Operations Branch of the CIA's Security Research Staff. The two men spoke about a wide range of subjects; by early 1965 one of their major topics of conversation was the conflict between the FBI and Martin Luther King, Jr.

Jay Kennedy strongly believed that a number of Communist elements were seeking to take advantage of the civil rights movement. He also was well aware of the information about King's personal life, information that Kennedy felt could be used against King by either the FBI or a host of others. Kennedy feared the damage that either "red" influence or public exposure of King's personal life could do to the civil rights movement. Hence, Kennedy felt very strongly that it would be best for the movement if the other major black leaders would encourage King to step aside and relinquish his leadership position.[54]

Kennedy detailed his sentiments in a conversation with his CIA friend on May 11. The CIA officer described Kennedy's comments as follows:

> In summarizing Kennedy's point of view, the problem appears to be something like this. The Communist left is making an all out drive to get into the Negro movement. If through any mechanism they can link prominent Negro leaders to illegal activities and activity which is against President Johnson's policy, this may cause a serious break between Johnson and the Negro leadership which, in turn, may create a violent disruption in the Negro Civil Rights Movement which would give the Communists an opportunity to cause chaos and disruption.
>
> Furthermore, if the above is coupled with an exposure of Martin Luther King, Jr., by other than members of his own race, the damage to the Negro movement would be impossible to estimate. Kennedy is gravely concerned that King may be exposed by white sources, official or otherwise, which would have no good effect and would probably only make King a martyr. Kennedy was also concerned that King might possibly be assassinated before his exposure which would have the effect of making him a martyr and would not be at all helpful to the Negro movement. It is Kennedy's belief that somehow or other Martin Luther King must be removed from the leadership of the Negro movement, and his removal must come from within not from without. Kennedy feels that somewhere in the Negro movement, at the top, there must be a Negro leader who is 'clean' who could step into the vacuum and chaos if Martin Luther King were either exposed or assassinated.
>
> In summary, Kennedy feels that unless the Negro leaders, other than King, are informed and are capable of intelligent maneuvering, the Communists or Negro elements who will be directed by the Communists may be in a posi-

tion to, if not take over the Negro movement, completely disrupt it and hence cause extremely critical problems for the Government of the United States.[55]

All evidence suggests that the CIA treated Kennedy's remarks and analyses with the utmost seriousness. The following day the Agency alerted FBI headquarters to Kennedy's comments, and the Bureau immediately asked its New York office to obtain an interview with Kennedy. If Kennedy would readily provide his information to the CIA, why would he refuse the FBI?

Refuse the Bureau Kennedy did. He long had had an active dislike of the FBI's style and tactics. When agents from the New York office visited him on May 24, he declined to have a substantive conversation with them. Bureau headquarters was advised, and the New York agents were instructed to visit Kennedy once again. Although Kennedy offered a few comments when the agents made their second contact, he again declined to have any extensive conversations with Bureau representatives.[56]

On June 8 Kennedy met with his CIA friend at the Washington Hilton from 1:15 P.M. until 5 P.M. The two men began by discussing Kennedy's reluctance to deal with the FBI. The CIA officer described this discussion, and its background, as follows:

> Sometime back, Chief, SRS [Security Research Staff] decided that it would be advantageous to have Jay Kennedy give information, particularly regarding the Civil Rights Movement, to agents of the FBI in New York City, particularly if this information concerned domestic or local events and activities. Chief, SRS, felt that it would be a faster means of communication than heretofore used wherein Mr. Kennedy communicated with SRS officers who, in turn, passed the information to either the FBI or areas where it was useful.
>
> Jay Kennedy made it very clear that he did not wish to communicate with FBI agents, that the Civil Rights Movement should be regarded as an international situation because of the Communist directed infiltration into the movement, and that he felt in some respects that he was being downgraded by being used as a source by the FBI

and not in a higher echelon of Government. While Mr. Kennedy did not absolutely refuse to cooperate with the Bureau, he made it obvious that only if there was a matter which he felt was of interest directly to the Bureau locally, would he furnish this type of information; otherwise, he would furnish it as he has done previously or cease altogether. The writer attempted, more or less unsuccessfully, to discuss jurisdiction with Mr. Kennedy, but Mr. Kennedy maintained his position that the matter was not one of jurisdiction for the FBI or any single Government agency, but was one that the Government, including CIA, should be interested in; namely, the international Communist efforts at corrupting and seizing the Negro Civil Rights Movement.

Having resolved that subject, Kennedy proceeded to bring the CIA officer up to date on developments in the civil rights movement. The CIA man recounted this part of the conversation in a memo to his superiors as follows:

For background information, it is to be recalled that Jay Kennedy has long provided information on the Negro Civil Rights Movement and its various leaders. Mr. Kennedy's position is one of complete sympathy with the Negro and the Civil Rights Movement, but holds that only through legal means and peaceful means should the Negro aims be accomplished. Mr. Kennedy, who is a violent anti-Communist, has been alarmed at the Communist movement into the Negro Civil Rights field and the Communist penetration into the various Negro organizations. He has undeniably done everything in his capacity to help the Negro leaders, particularly [deletion]. It is worth noting that Mr. Kennedy has been involved with various Negro leaders since as early as 1934; and he has known a number of the leaders, on a very close personal basis, since that time.

Mr. Kennedy's main concern has been that the highly derogatory information, of which [sic] he is familiar, concerning Martin Luther King, Jr., will be exposed to the public by the wrong people and at the wrong time which, in Mr. Kennedy's opinion, will set the Civil Rights Movement back years and would perhaps give the Communists a chance to either further disrupt it or to seize control of the movement.

To make certain that this report reflects as accurately as possible the derogatory information on Martin Luther King, Jr., here are three main categories:

(a) Highly derogatory information on [deletion] which have taken place within the United States and overseas;

(b) A possible theft of money; and

(c) Association with identified Communist or pro-Soviet types on an intense personal basis, particularly [deletion].

The CIA officer went on to summarize the public eruption of the Hoover-King dispute, and how Jay Kennedy had reported that both he and James Farmer feared that the Bureau might succeed in publicly leaking the damaging personal information it possessed on King. Farmer and other black leaders had discussed among themselves what they might do to resolve the problem, but no action had been agreed upon.

Jay Kennedy also gave his CIA friend an extensive analysis of the strengths and shortcomings of the major black leaders. He went on to explain that he had attempted to persuade both Farmer and Urban League President Whitney Young to take some action to persuade King to step aside from his leadership role, but that neither man, especially Young, had endorsed this suggestion. Kennedy also related his knowledge that the editors of several publications, including a major black magazine, knew the details of the personal information concerning King, but had resolved not to publish it.

The CIA official then asked Kennedy whether the assorted "Communists" around King, including "both the Moscow and the Peking types," knew about King's private life. If so, what might they do with that information? Kennedy answered that the real danger lay with the "Peking-line Communists," who might use it either to blackmail and control King, or to expose and ruin him. King's public exposure, Kennedy theorized, would so disrupt the civil rights movement that the "Peking Communists" would have a substantial opportunity to increase their own influence in the aftermath of King's demise.

The CIA officer eagerly pressed Kennedy for more information about the supposed and unnamed "Peking-line Communists" who were eagerly moving to seize control of the movement. The two men discussed this subject extensively, citing the opposition of a number of movement activists to American involvement in Vietnam as evidence that "Peking-line Communists" were playing a growing role in the movement. Both men agreed that this posed an increasing danger for the future.

On that note Kennedy's long conversation with the CIA officer ended. Kennedy, the officer reported to his superiors, "stated that he would be continuously in touch with either Chief, SRS or the writer as he obtained information of interest." Twice in early July Kennedy called the CIA officer to pass along further observations on the subject of "Peking-line Communists" and the civil rights movement, especially as it related to movement opposition to the Vietnam war. Although the particular concern about the FBI-King flap gradually receded, Kennedy continued to provide information to his friend at the CIA throughout the balance of the decade.[57]

The fact that the CIA treated Kennedy's observations and analyses with the utmost seriousness is far more important than the issue of whether many of Kennedy's impressions bore any close resemblance to what actually was happening within the civil rights movement. The CIA officer was just as fascinated with "Peking-line Communists" as was Kennedy, and how many officials in the higher echelons of the Agency were as captivated with Kennedy's views as was his immediate friend remains unknown. Whether the CIA utilized Kennedy's information in its own briefings of even higher level government officials also is unknown at present.

While the CIA was busy talking with Jay Kennedy, Martin Luther King, Jr., himself was deciding that he had made a grievous error some twenty months earlier when he had severed most of his direct contact with Stanley Levison. Faced in the anonymous tape with a vicious attempt to intimidate him, King realized that he had in effect allowed the FBI to drive him and Levison apart. Now, in the late spring of 1965, he resolved to correct that mistake.

King described his feelings about the Levison matter to a meeting of the "research committee" at Harry Wachtel's law office, and asked Wachtel to speak with Levison about the vague allegations the government had made against him. Wachtel, the committee agreed, would question Stanley about his past, ask him again for his explanation of why he thought the government regarded him with such fright, and invite him back into regular participation in the circle of advisers. Wachtel did as King asked, listened to Levison relate his belief about the unnamed former business associate, and told him of King's feelings. Shortly King himself spoke to Levison, and dismissed Stanley's continuing fear that he could be used to smear King. "I have decided I am going to work completely in the open," King told him. "There's nothing to hide. And if anybody wants to make something of it, let them try." The Bureau soon became aware of the results of, if not the reasons for, this change of heart. Agents of the New York office watched King, Levison, Jones, and Young meet one day in March at a Manhattan hotel, and in early June several different groups of agents tailed Levison, Jones, and several others as they flew from New York to Washington and then drove to an SCLC retreat being held in Warrenton, Virginia. Although King and Levison continued to route much of their phone conversation through Jones in an unsuccessful effort to avoid wiretaps, the Bureau of course was fully aware, from its taps on Jones, of the advice Levison was giving. That counsel remained wholly innocuous, as it had from the beginning. This made no apparent difference to the men of Division Five.[58]

The summer of 1965 witnessed a further Bureau hunt for additional "subversives" associated with SCLC, a wild-goose chase to confirm a rumor that King had established a secret Swiss bank account, and a minor controversy about Bureau-SCLC relations stemming from a chance remark made to a group of reporters by SCLC Treasurer Ralph Abernathy. In May there was brief but intense interest in a New York report that Levison had recommended Lawrence R. Perkins of the United Negro College Fund to King, who was looking for an executive vice-president for SCLC. This was most significant, headquarters supervisor Phillips advised New York, for Perkins had been listed in the Security Index as recently as 1964 and was reported to have been a Communist party member as late as 1955. Nothing further developed, apparently because Perkins had no interest in joining SCLC. That was followed, several weeks later, by a report that one participant in the SCLC retreat at Warrenton had been Don "Slayman," [actually "Slaiman"], civil rights director of the AFL–CIO. Bureau files showed that he once had been associated with a group called the Independent Socialist League. Instructions immediately were issued to prepare a memorandum for intragovernment distribution, which should stress "the significant fact . . . that Slayman [*sic*], who has a subversive background, is going to participate in an SCLC meeting." Headquarters also instructed field offices to look for potential subversives among the hundreds of college-age volunteers taking part in SCLC's summer 1965 "SCOPE" program. Not surprisingly, agents could find very few twenty-year-olds who had past associations with "old left" organizations.[59]

The Bureau's fruitless search for Dr. King's "secret Swiss bank account"—one memo spoke of it as "unnumbered"—began on a golf course. One day in late June supervisor Phillips's golf partner told him that he had heard stories that King was accumulating an overseas treasure. Within days Division Five was busy trying to locate the secret account. Nearly six months of futile searching passed before Phillips learned from his golfing friend that the story had been some other acquaintance's idle speculation. The Bureau also devoted hundreds of hours of work to an ultimately successful effort to identify a major SCLC contributor, Anne Farnsworth. Indications that some SCLC funds were being "laundered" through King's Ebenezer Baptist Church oddly were not pursued.[60]

In early July SCLC's Abernathy, in response to a press-conference question, said there were no Communists in SCLC, and that the FBI warned them about anyone who was. Abernathy's imprecise comment—one version had him saying that SCLC checked with FBI agents about potential new employees to "screen" them—set off alarms at Bureau headquarters. The Atlanta office immediately was instructed to issue strong denials to all local media outlets. Within hours Atlanta reported that the Bureau's statement was receiving excellent publicity. An angry Hoover scribbled on one account, "Abernathy's as big a liar as King," and added on another: "I think he is a liar but if I find anyone furnishing information to SCLC he will be dismissed." The incident, though revealing in its own way, blew over quickly.[61]

By the middle of the summer FBI headquarters had transferred primary authority for handling the SCLC "COMINFIL" case from New York back to Atlanta, where it had originated three years earlier. What prompted that decision is unclear, but the memo ordering the transfer also acknowledged receipt of a seventy-three-page Atlanta office report on SCLC activities. The Atlanta document stated that:

> It was impossible to determine what activity was legitimate desegregation activities or racial matters and which activity reflected CP influence and direction. In view of the subversive connections it is considered that basically all activity of the organization is significant and justly reported in this security report.

Lengthy sections describing SCLC's SCOPE, Operation Breadbasket, "Vision," Voter Registration, and "Dialogue" programs showed that the statement was no exaggeration.

Headquarters supervisor Phillips, now forced to rely on information from only the SCLC headquarters' wiretaps, and no longer King's home, developed a stronger interest in Atlanta reports of low morale among SCLC employees, and that some ranking officials like program director Randolph T. Blackwell and affiliates' director C. T. Vivian were talking about resigning. Several times he instructed Atlanta to be attentive in this regard "for situations which might be exploited under the counterintelligence program." Atlanta apparently forwarded no such suggestions. [62]

SCLC's 1965 convention, held in Birmingham in mid-August, received the careful attention that all such SCLC gatherings had had since 1961. Agents observed Levison fly from New York to Birmingham to attend it, and wiretaps reported that Bayard Rustin had been assigned to handle the sensitive question of a convention resolution on Vietnam. King had proposed that he send personal letters of appeal calling for a negotiated settlement of the conflict to the Soviet, Chinese, American, and North Vietnamese heads of state. Bureau headquarters instructed the Birmingham office to report any comments King might make, "particularly concerning U.S. foreign policy." Birmingham did not find much to report on that subject, but New York sent in word for word the answers that Levison prepared for King in response to twelve specific questions about King's Vietnam position submitted by the *New York Times*. The Bureau promptly sent that information to President Johnson. During subsequent weeks additional reports on King's and his advisers' comments on the Watts riots, a planned reorganization of federal civil rights offices, and SCLC financial troubles, also were dispatched to the White House. The Bureau continued to take particular pleasure in relating unfavorable comments about King by others, such as Bayard Rustin and Roy Wilkins, plus any remarks that King or his advisers might make about executive branch officials.[63]

October witnessed a renewed Bureau effort to implant microphones in King's hotel rooms, after an unexplained four-month lull. King was in New York for two days in the middle of the month, and Bureau agents both bugged his room at the Astor Hotel and also witnessed King, Levison, Jones, and Rustin arrive for a meeting at Harry Wachtel's Madison Avenue law office. Several days later a memo notified Attorney General Katzenbach of the microphone surveillance, which "involved trespass" but also "developed information concerning King's involvement in the Vietnam situation." Two weeks later when King returned to New York and stayed at the Hilton, another microphone was installed. Apparently it overheard nothing of particular interest to the Bureau. On the second day of the surveillance New York called headquarters to report that so far "no unusual intelligence had been forthcoming nor was there any indication that there would be." King, it explained, was going to be away from the room for the evening.[64]

At the end of October, in line with the revised electronic surveillance guidelines Katzenbach had issued in late March, the Bureau requested another six-month authorization for the wiretaps on SCLC's Atlanta headquarters. The intercepts, the Bureau told the Attorney General, had "provided considerable valuable intelligence information concerning communist influence on the SCLC through King, as well as the communist influence evident in the outspoken position which King has taken in opposition to the United States foreign policy concerning Vietnam." Also cited was the association with SCLC of "individuals with communist backgrounds such as Stanley David Levison, Harry Wachtel, Bayard Rustin, Clarence Jones and Randolph T. Blackwell." "Unless you instruct to the contrary," the request continued, "this technical surveillance will be continued for an additional six months." The taps remained in place.[65]

Initial planning for the upcoming White House Conference on Civil Rights took place in November. The Bureau gladly provided presidential aides with derogatory information on several King advisers who wanted to attend. On November 16 the SCLC headquarters wiretap overheard King tell his Washington representative, Walter Fauntroy, that he was upset that six particular individuals had not been invited. "Of the six individuals named by King," supervisor Phillips crowed in a memo to William Sullivan, "four were individuals concerning whom we had furnished the White House derogatory information. . . . We may be overly optimistic, but perhaps this is a favorable trend. We will continue, as in the past, to furnish the White House derogatory information concerning King's people who indicate possible association with the White House." Director Hoover scrawled "Right" by that statement when the memo reached his desk.

At the end of November King made another trip to New York. Once again a microphone was installed in his hotel room at the Americana. Katzenbach was advised the following day that the bug had garnered "information concerning the tactics and plans of King and his organization in the civil rights movement," as well as "information concerning King's involvement in the Vietnam situation." Katzenbach acknowledged the memo in a handwritten note to Director Hoover several days later. "Obviously," the Attorney General wrote, "these are particularly delicate surveillances and we should be very cautious in terms of the non-FBI people who may from time to time necessarily be involved in some aspect of installation." Division Five officials shared his sentiments.[66]

Bureau efforts to eavesdrop on King at New York's Sheraton Atlantic in December were dropped when King altered his plans, but in mid-January, 1966, Division Five once more authorized a bug at the Americana. This time, however, Sullivan's approval of the surveillance was overturned. There had been a new development not related to King. Senator Edward V. Long of Missouri had begun an investigation of federal agencies' use of electronic surveillance techniques. The Bureau, represented by DeLoach, was on the verge of winning agreement from Long that no FBI representative would be called to testify before Long's subcommittee. Extremely fearful that the Senate probe might uncover the Bureau's electronic activities, both Hoover and Tolson had grown suddenly conservative. Thus when Division Five's memo on the King microphone reached Tolson's desk on January 21, 1966, the Associate Director wrote on it, "Remove this surveillance at once. No one here approved this. I have told Sullivan again not to institute a mike surveillance without the Director's approval." Hoover himself added, "Yes, Right," to Tolson's order, and late that afternoon Sullivan's chief assistant, Joseph A. Sizoo, called New York to order that the bug be removed as soon as possible. New York, however, waited until King and his party left three days later to deactivate the bug. In the interim it recorded much information on King's personal activities, which was duly transcribed. On this note of anticlimax the era of hotel room microphones directed against King came to an end. Never again in the remaining two years of King's life would the Bureau install a microphone surveillance against him.[67]

4

Puritans and Voyeurs— Sullivan, Hoover, and Johnson

Much as chapter 2 drew certain conclusions about the first phase of the FBI's investigation of Dr. King, this chapter will consider questions raised by the story of the second phase of the King case.

In December, 1963, and January, 1964, the Bureau totally redirected its investigation of Dr. King. Throughout 1962 and 1963 the FBI had mainly feared the close relationship between King and Stanley Levison. Beginning in the winter of 1963–64, however, a major transformation took place. Division Five's memoranda began to contain explicit statements about a new purpose. The object now was to "discredit," "neutralize," or "expose" King.[1] Within a few weeks time, the seeming intent of the Bureau's activities changed from a concern with Levison's influence on King to a conscious and explicit desire to destroy King as a public figure. Why does this change take place? Why does the Bureau become so strongly committed to destroying King publicly?

There are a number of possibilities. Extending two of the perspectives considered in chapter 2, some observers say that the Bureau's behavior in 1964 and 1965 was simply an intensification of hostility toward King based on either (1) his preceived role as a public critic of the FBI, or (2) his close friendship with the supposedly dangerous Stanley Levison. The problems with each of these suggestions are substantial.

First, the essential weaknesses of the "criticism" case were detailed in chapter 2. Furthermore, the matter of King's public comments about the FBI reemerged only in late April, 1964, more than three months after the marked intensification of the Bureau's activities against him in December and January. Second, the idea that the Bureau's effort to destroy King was in any meaningful way related to King's tie to Levison fails on two points. At no time up through the end of 1965 did the Bureau plot any efforts to destroy or discredit Levison himself. More important, none of the 1964 and 1965 documents expressing the strong wish to ruin King ever really related that desire to King's friendship with Stanley.

Two other hypotheses, each more widely held and better documented, have been put forward. The first of these focuses upon the question of racism; the second stresses the thoroughgoing conservatism of the FBI's political stance.

The racism explanation is quite straightforward. It argues that the Bureau began its investigation of King, added the wiretaps, and then further intensified its activities throughout 1964 and 1965 not because King was a Bureau critic, or because he was connected to Levison, but because he was a black leader, indeed *the* black leader, pure and simple. This explanation has been suggested by a number of former officials and assorted writers. It has gained much acceptance in the black community. Like the criticism argument, this racism thesis comes in two versions—one, that Director Hoover's personal racism was the major factor, and, two, that the Bureau as a whole was thoroughly racist, and that that pervasive attitude was more crucial than anything particular to Hoover.

The Hoover version of this argument has been made most strongly by David Wise, who has written a number of books on the American intelligence community. Wise was heavily influenced by information from none other than William Sullivan. In yet one more effort to minimize his own role in the King case, Sullivan successfully argued to Wise that Hoover's personal racism lay at the bottom of things. After detailing Sullivan's comments that the "real reason was that Hoover disliked blacks," and had excluded them from the FBI, Wise concluded that "the FBI sought to discredit King because J. Edgar Hoover was a racist. Ultimately, Hoover battled King because King was black, and powerful, and his power was growing."[2] Sullivan made similar arguments to others, including the Church Committee, but no one else, including Sullivan himself in his own posthumous book, stated the argument as clearly and strongly as did Wise.[3]

The second version of the racism theory, that a pervasive racism infested the entire FBI, has been promoted by several former Bureau agents who became critics of the FBI and by black writers and leaders. Former agents Jack Levine, Robert Wall, and Arthur L. Murtagh all have spoken of what Wall termed "the endemic racism of the Bureau."[4] Similar explanations for the Bureau's stance in the 1960s, and particularly for its activities against Dr. King, have been suggested by black writers such as John A. Williams[5] and by some of King's former associates, such as Jesse Jackson.[6]

Hoover's racism is so widely documented as to require no extended comment here.[7] Further, the fact that much of the Bureau was hostile to blacks and that very, very few blacks actually worked as FBI agents until the early 1970s is also well proven.[8] Here again, however, an analyst needs to avoid the same error of inference that led many observers to propound the criticism theory: just because the Bureau was hostile to critics, and King was a Bureau critic, does not necessarily mean that that explains the Bureau's hostility toward him. Likewise, the fact that the Bureau and its Director were openly racist, and King was black, and prominent, does not necessarily mean that the effort to destroy him was principally rooted in that matter of skin color and bigotry. A closer look will show that the question of race, like the status of critic, did contribute in a moderate way to the Bureau's antipathy toward King, but that it no more explains the Bureau's conduct against King in 1964–65 than does the criticism hypothesis make meaningful sense of the events of 1962–63.

One can find some evidence to support the proposition that the Bureau set out to destroy black leaders simply because they were black leaders. One example is the Bureau's conduct toward Elijah Muhammad and the Nation of Islam (NOI), better known as the Black Muslims. The Bureau began wiretap surveillance of Elijah Muhammed's Chicago residence in 1957, with the authorization of Attorney General Herbert Brownell, on the grounds that members of the NOI "disavow allegiance to the United States" and "are taught they need not obey the laws of the United States." Furthermore, the Bureau claimed, "Allegations have been received that its members may resort to acts of violence," and the wiretap "will furnish not only data concerning the fanatical and violent nature of the organization, but also data regarding the current plans of the MCI ["Muslim Cult of Islam"] to expand its activities throughout the United States." When Elijah Muhammad bought a winter home in Arizona in 1961, a wiretap and a microphone were installed there. Both forms of surveillance continued for several years. The bug apparently was removed in June, 1965, and the wiretap a year later. When the Chicago surveillance ended is unclear. Mid-1960s Bureau documents lay heavy stress on the "violently antiwhite" character of the NOI, and both the organization and Elijah Muhammad were targeted for special attention when the Bureau established a "Black Nationalist Hate Group" COINTEL program in 1967 and 1968. The Bureau also had a strong interest in other Muslim leaders, such as Malcolm X, and played assorted COINTEL tricks on the organization as early as the late 1950s.[9] Furthermore, the Muslims were by no means the only black group, nor was Elijah Muhammad the only black leader, who received such close attention. Though Bureau files on the subject have not been released, groups such as SNCC and the Black Panther party also were intensively investigated in the mid- and late-1960s[10] In earlier days the Bureau had spared no effort to uncover "Communist infiltration" of the NAACP.

The public record is not full enough for a complete appraisal of FBI conduct toward the full range of black organizations and leaders. Even so, it is quite apparent that no other black leader came in for the intensive and hostile attention that Dr. King was subjected to in the mid-1960s. While King certainly was not alone on the Bureau's enemies list, there are some striking indications that the FBI felt positively toward a number of prominent black leaders who were by no means "Toms." Among them were Roy Wilkins, Whitney Young, and James Farmer. Though additional files remain to be released, present indications are that none of these other civil rights leaders was viewed with *any* of the antipathy that regularly and strongly was expressed toward King. As the events immediately following Hoover's public attack on King reflect, Bureau executives in their private discussions of how to move against King dropped a number of favorable references to men such as Wilkins.[11] Additionally, another indication that the Bureau's hostility was based on something other than race alone was Sullivan's effort to promote "the right kind" of black leader, someone like the unheralded Sam Pierce.[12] The Bureau and its hierarchy clearly did not express strong hostility toward *all* prominent black leaders, or even toward all black leaders who were in the forefront of the civil rights movement.[13] The principle of target selection was obviously more complicated than simply race, and the Bureau's intensified effort to destroy King was rooted principally in something other than the fact King was black.

Liberal academics have sought an explanation of how the FBI chose its targets that is more comprehensive than either the criticism or racism arguments. Several have contended that the Bureau identified its enemies, including Dr. King, on purely ideological grounds. The Bureau was strongly conservative, peopled with many right-wingers, and thus it selected people and organizations on the left end of the political spectrum for special and unpleasant attention. This view has been voiced by former Attorney General Ramsey Clark,[14] and by lawyer Charles Morgan. Morgan has applied it to the King case, writing that "it had to be ideology that made King numbers one through ten on Hoover's personal enemies list."[15]

The principal proponent of this conservatism thesis, however, has been Athan Theoharis, a one-time Church Committee consultant and a student of FBI surveillance practices. For the entire period of Hoover's directorship, Theoharis argues, Bureau executives "acted purposefully to advance their own political interests and to curb the potential influence of individuals or organizations whose political views they found abhorrent." The "criteria governing FBI . . . investigations were ideological," and "King's major sin derived from his prominence, his ability to influence public opinion, and his holding political views to the left of the FBI director." Theoharis specifically contends that the attempt to discredit King was no mere "personal vendetta" on the part of Director Hoover, but a "bureau policy" that was the work of all major Bureau executives, whose "principal concern about King in fact stemmed from political conservatism."[16]

The conservatism thesis is a more successful depiction of Bureau conduct than either the criticism or racism hypotheses. Indeed, as chapter 6 will contend, the conservatism argument is one limited part of a broader perspective on the FBI, a perspective that will subsume all three narrower explanations of the three distinct phases of the King investigation. However, on the specific question of the Bureau's intensification of the King case in 1964 and 1965, the conservatism theory falls victim to the same fallacy that claimed the criticism and racism hypotheses. True, the Bureau was conservative, and looked with disfavor and suspicion upon those who were not, and true also that King as a political figure was far enough "left" to be deserving of Bureau concern. Here again, though, the assumption that King was targeted in the manner that he was because he was "left," and the Bureau hated leftists, impedes our understanding of why the King case developed as it did far more than it assists us. Much as chapter 2 was able to show that the criticism theory failed to account for the events of 1962–63 once all the relevant events were examined in rigorous chronological order, here again a careful examination of the events from late-1963 through 1965 will show that the motive in the King investigation after the wiretaps go on was different from both what it was prior to that time, and from the suggested explanations of criticism, racism, and conservatism.

Two great changes occur in Division Five's behavior after installation of the wiretaps on King's home. First, the concern about King's relationship with Stanley Levison declines greatly, almost to the point of vanishing. Second, a marked interest in King's personal life and sexual activities quickly emerges. The crucial event marking these changes is the December 23, 1963, headquarters "conference." The discussions there reflected both of these developments, plus the first appearance of another motif of the greatest importance—how King must be discredited, exposed, neutralized, or destroyed.

Few items on the conference's "agenda" had anything to do with the King-Levison relationship. Since most Bureau memos on King as late as eight weeks before the big meeting were full of references to Levison, that absence is a marked surprise. Replacing Levison was the very heavy, indeed predominant concern with personal information on King. How can the Bureau obtain such information? How can the Bureau use it to damage King publicly? Surviving documents about the conference do not explicitly reveal why there was this new focus on destroying King personally.[17]

The first indication that the Bureau was collecting and disseminating information on King's purely personal activities came in August, 1963. One memo on that subject was sent to Deputy Attorney General Katzenbach and Attorney General Robert Kennedy, and then on to President Kennedy by his brother. The material in that report apparently was culled from King's conversations that were overheard by the wiretaps placed on Clarence Jones in mid-July.[18] That memo is the only indication that the Bureau was aware of or interested in King's personal life prior to the taps on his home and office. Years later William Sullivan confessed that he had heard gossip about King's private activities from Georgia Senator Richard Russell, whose brother Henry was a prominent Montgomery, Alabama, pastor. Even so, there is no convincing evidence that a desire to obtain information on King's personal life was a prime reason for the Bureau's fall, 1963, request for the wiretaps.

All indications are that the focus of the December 23 conference was shaped by what the Bureau overheard and inferred from the first six weeks of the wiretaps on King's home and office in late 1963. That information itself, that very personal information, supplied both the predominant motive for the Bureau's new desire to destroy King, and the means by which Division Five believed it could accomplish that new goal. The transformation of the King case in the winter of 1963–64, then, and the new desire to discredit King personally, thus stemmed not from King's perceived role as Bureau critic, not from his tie to Levison, not from intra-Bureau politics, not from King's race and prominence, and not from King's adherence to left political views. It stemmed largely if not wholly from the reactions to and feelings about King's personal life that Sullivan and the other men of Division Five developed immediately after the King wiretaps began.

Just as the December 23 conference was the first significant event after the wiretaps went on, the initial important development after the conference was the installation of the first hotel-room bug on Dr. King at Washington's Willard Hotel in early January. As the pertinent documents reveal and he himself later admitted, the initiative and decision to install that bug came from William Sullivan. Exactly why that microphone was implanted tells much about why the character of the Bureau's activities changed so drastically over so short a period of time.

Sullivan's memo of Monday, January 6, to Belmont explaining the installation of the bug stressed the "counterintelligence possibilities which thorough coverage of King's activities might develop" and Sullivan's hope that "positive results" would be achieved.[19] Thus it is extremely difficult to imagine that installation of the bug was motivated by anything other than the desire to obtain damaging information on King's personal activities, which had dominated the conference held less than two weeks earlier.

Confronted with this evidence ten years later, Sullivan claimed that the personal angle had played absolutely no part in his decision to install the bug. Instead, he asserted, he had been visited on Saturday, January 4, by Jack Childs, who had told him of a meeting that he had had the previous day in New York with Levison, King, and several other people. The subject had been SCLC's need for money, and whether Levison, King, and SCLC would be interested in accepting $90,000 from "Solo" without any questions about the money's source. Childs told him, Sullivan claimed, that Levison and King had wanted to consider the offer for several days before deciding. It was this firsthand information, that King and SCLC might well be on the verge of accepting Soviet money, that had prompted Sullivan to bug King's room at the Willard in the hope of hearing further discussions about whether to accept the offer. As it turned out, Sullivan later contended, the bug overheard no such discussions and "Solo" subsequently reported that King had instructed Levison to reject the offer with thanks.

Sullivan's story is fanciful and unsupported by any evidence. It is contradicted by Bureau memos from that same week reporting on

SCLC finances,[20] by Bureau indications that neither of the Childs brothers ever had direct contact with King, by the recollections of other Bureau executives close to Sullivan at that time, and by the Bureau's own reports of King's travels. There is every indication that Sullivan's story was merely another game effort to set himself apart from the seamier aspects of the King investigation.

If further evidence of the true purpose of the first bug is needed, one has only to look at what the Bureau did with the recordings it obtained. They immediately were played for Hoover; transcripts were quickly prepared, and DeLoach was dispatched with them to the Johnson White House. Then, a week later, Sullivan instructed the Milwaukee field office to install a bug in King's hotel room there so that further "entertainment" could be recorded. Hoover's pernicious remark about King's supposedly "obsessive degenerate sexual urges" indicated that his understanding of what the surveillance was designed to overhear was exactly the same as Sullivan's.[21]

All of the important Bureau memoranda from January, 1964, clearly show that Sullivan, Hoover, and the men of Division Five quickly became obsessed with Dr. King's sexual behavior and the possibilities of recording more of it. Those same documents also indicate a strong desire to circulate the information obtained on King to the White House, and perhaps to reporters as well. The Bureau's fixation was further evidenced by the extensive efforts to monitor King's February trip to Hawaii and Los Angeles, by the disappointment over the lack of "developments" in Hawaii, and by the unconcealed joy at what finally was recorded in Los Angeles. The tasteless pleasure that supervisor Phillips and others expressed over the thought of Robert Kennedy reading the results of that surveillance was but one more powerful indication of the extreme hatred of King that had developed in Division Five over the winter of 1963–64.[22]

From the time of that first Hyatt House surveillance up through the November, 1964, mailing of the anonymous poison-pen letter and tape, the Bureau's entire handling of the King case continued to reflect a predominant interest in collecting personally damaging information on King. True, Bureau files from the period also indicated an ostensible concern about the number of supposed "subversives" around King, but the worry was little more than a transparent affectation. This was reflected most clearly in the half-hearted effort to paint Harry Wachtel as a dangerous figure, and in the cataloging of decades-old rumors about individuals such as Vivian, Reddick, Blackwell, and Daddy King. It became extremely visible in September, 1964, when the Savannah field office read headquarters' concern about subversives such as Wachtel literally, and proposed to bug the rooms of a number of leftists, only to have headquarters reply that no, that was not necessary. The true purpose of the microphone surveillances was repeatedly indicated in documents concerning them, with the multiple references to King's "personal activities" and the need to "expose" him. The handwritten afterthought, "in view of his association with Communists," inserted in Phillips's July, 1964, recommendation that more information on King's personal activities be gathered, was only the most sadly amusing example of this veneer.[23]

Most of the 1970s probes of the Bureau's handling of the King case have made some reference in their final reports to the fact that "the development of personal information that might be derogatory to Dr. King became a major objective of the surveillance effort."[24] Hardly any of these investigators, however, have chosen to ask precisely "why" this occurred. Although the Church Committee's final report remarked that "FBI officials believed that some of Dr. King's personal conduct was improper,"[25] no one has gone beyond this expression to state publicly the real reason why the Bureau's activities against Dr. King intensified in 1964–65. At bottom, the hostility of Sullivan, Hoover, and other Bureau officials toward King was motivated largely by their feelings about Dr. King's private life and especially his sexual activities.

This conclusion should not surprise anyone who has examined the excerpts from the Bureau's anonymous letter to King that have been made public.[26] It also will come as no surprise to anyone who knows much about the private attitudes of Hoover and especially Sullivan. Despite his disclaimers, it was principally Sullivan, even more than Hoover, whose animus was aroused by the information on King's private life. Sullivan led the way in transforming the King case from an investigation of Stanley Levison's influence to an all-out effort to destroy King. Sullivan's private feelings about King do not make pleasant reading, but an appreciation of them is necessary for any good understanding of *why* the Bureau moved against King as it did.

To the journalists and professors who visited his New Hampshire home throughout the years 1972–77, Sullivan portrayed himself as the only honest and liberal-minded man to have served in the top reaches of the FBI during the Hoover era. On the subject of King, Sullivan was consistent—and incorrect—in saying that the FBI had been investigating King even before Sullivan became head of the domestic intelligence division in June, 1961. Furthermore, Sullivan claimed that when he first took that post, "I was one hundred percent for King . . . because I saw him rising as an effective and badly needed leader for the black people in their desire for civil rights."[27] On top of that, Sullivan also told people that the Bureau never had had any solid evidence against Stanley Levison, and that he, Sullivan, had tried unsuccessfully to persuade Director Hoover that an investigation of King based on his contact with Levison was unjustified. Hoover, however, had been convinced that Levison was a Soviet agent and that King himself was either a conscious Communist or pro-Communist. True, Sullivan conceded, the Bureau did understand King to have said "I am a Marxist," but that meant very little, Sullivan argued.[28] The controversial Brennan monograph of October, 1963, which Sullivan had endorsed and supported at the time, was really a dishonest document that had been prepared only because Hoover had insisted on it, Sullivan claimed to interviewers in the 1970s. He himself had played no meaningful role in any of the activities against King, and what he had gone along with he had done only because he otherwise would have been fired. He told one close friend that he had never taken the initiative in expanding the King investigation, and that everything he had done had been in direct response to Hoover's orders. The truth was, Sullivan wrote on one occasion, "There was only one man at the bureau who made important decisions and the rest of us carried them out."[29]

Sullivan was especially vociferous in his denials that the mailing of the anonymous letter and tape to King had been his idea, or that he himself had either written or even known of the poison-pen letter. To the Church Committee and to other interviewers Sullivan repeatedly claimed that the initiative for the tape and letter had come from Hoover, that he had been instructed personally by Alan Belmont to have the composite tape prepared, and that Hoover himself had called to order that it be mailed to King from Florida. Sullivan asserted that he had argued against the anonymous package. He had done so on practical grounds, not idealistic ones, contending that instead of getting Mrs. King to leave her husband and publicly denounce him, it would only alert King and his family to the activities the Bureau had been undertaking against him. On the specific matter of the letter, Sullivan claimed that a draft or copy of it later found in his files at the Bureau had been planted there by his enemies, and that it actually had been prepared by three unnamed supervisors.[30] The only initiative he was willing to take credit for was the January, 1964, idea of promoting Samuel R. Pierce as the "right kind" of black leader.[31]

Were these assertions a full picture of Sullivan's stance in the King investigation? As Sullivan himself revealed to a number of people, they were far from it. Did Sullivan truly believe that the Bureau should not have been investigating King, and did he actually have a positive regard for the civil rights leader? In reality nothing could have been further from the truth. Did Sullivan's later emphasis on the inconclusive nature of the information on Levison really mean that he had opposed the Bureau's probe? No.

Sullivan told one friend that he had been forced to realize that King was a worthless charlatan. He had been particularly upset that many people contributed money to King without knowing that the real man bore little resemblance to his public image. King pocketed some contributions, Sullivan inaccurately claimed, and he and his associates wasted many thousands more on uninhibited revelry and high living. Even worse, in Sullivan's opinion, King on occasion had paid women to have sex with him, and also had carried on sexual affairs with a number of married women. Sullivan also thought that King had aspired to be secretary of labor, that King had considered funneling civil rights funds into secret foreign bank accounts, and that King had considered soliciting money from hostile foreign governments by claiming that he would use it to advance Soviet goals in America. King's opposition to the Vietnam War, Sullivan asserted, had merely been an effort to win such Soviet funding. In short, Sullivan had become convinced that King was an undesirable person who knowingly was doing harm to the United States of America.[32]

Sullivan often mixed fact and fantasy in his rambling recollections of the King investigation. Many times he avoided referring to King by his actual name. In letters to his close friend and lawyer, Joseph

E. Casey, in the mid-1970s, Sullivan claimed that the Levison tie had not been sufficient grounds for investigating King, but that there had been four other solid grounds for the probe: embezzlement, employing prostitutes, alienating wives' affections from their husbands, and violation of the Mann Act. Sullivan thought that King was an immoral person and that the investigation was appropriate. But he believed that Hoover and the Bureau had been wrong in using Levison as the basis for the investigation. To not have pursued King would have been, in Sullivan's view, a dereliction of the FBI's duty to the American taxpayer. On one occasion, Sullivan said, he explicitly had told Hoover there were several defensible reasons for probing King. King, for instance, had embezzled or misapplied substantial amounts of money contributed to the civil rights movement. King also had violated prostitution laws in numerous places. In particular, Sullivan said, King enjoyed a white woman in one midwestern city whose nightly fee was $100. Furthermore, there was the May, 1964, Bureau report about King in Las Vegas that had originated with a prostitute there. Finally, Sullivan believed King also had alienated the affections of numerous married women.

Did Sullivan imagine that an investigation of any of these supposed and much-exaggerated offenses would have led to federal criminal charges against King or others? Apparently not, for his conclusion revealed that deep-down he had no regret for any of the actions the Bureau had undertaken against King. Anyone like King, Sullivan believed, had to be exposed in a most ruthless manner to the American people.[33]

Sullivan's denial that he wrote or knew of the poison pen letter to King is effectively rebutted by many of his own later comments on King. The anonymous missive was particularly notable for the virulent characterizations it flung at King—"a colossal fraud," "an evil, abnormal beast," and "your filthy fraudulent self." Likewise, many intra-Bureau memos repeatedly characterized King as a "moral degenerate," one of Sullivan's, and Hoover's, favorite appellations. Sullivan's later statements closely mirrored these earlier ones. King, he told one person, was one of only seven people (and the only black) he had ever heard of during his thirty years in the Bureau who was such a total degenerate. King, Sullivan wrote in the mid-1970s, was on his way to exposure and ruin not because of the FBI's hostility or by virtue of his tie to Levison, but because of unwise personal conduct that was gross and animallike. The problem, Sullivan said in a 1976 letter to a Church Committee member, had been King's compulsive desire to lead the dual existence of a Dr. Jekyl and Mr. Hyde.[34]

At the root of Sullivan's hostility toward King were two key ingredients: a Puritanism on matters of personal conduct and sexual behavior that stemmed from his own rural New England background, and a subconscious racism that was more the paternalistic superiority of a false white liberal than the open hatred of a rabid bigot. For all his airs of being the Bureau's house intellectual, Sullivan's narrow-mindedness on anything concerning sex was well known to those who worked with him. All agreed that it took very little to offend his sensibilities. Most knew better than to tell a ribald joke in Sullivan's presence. His closest colleagues were nor surprised when Sullivan was so deeply upset by the material that was obtained on King's personal life. Such pure enjoyment of physical pleasure, and outside of marriage, was beyond the pale in Sullivan's mind. It took no time at all for him to conclude that King was not fit to be a national leader. The country had to be protected from someone whose values were so different from those that, in Sullivan's mind, every decent American cherished. When the anonymous tape and hate letter failed to drive Mrs. King away from her husband, Sullivan was stunned. As one of his colleagues later described it, Sullivan could not imagine any family surviving such a blow.[35]

Sullivan's puritanical inability to accept King's style of living was combined with, and magnified by, a largely hidden racism that saw black people as inferior beings. They required constant guidance from the great white fathers, men such as himself, if they were to progress on the road of self-improvement. Thus Sullivan desired to choose the "right kind" of leader for American blacks, who otherwise of course would be unable to find "the proper direction."[36] Sullivan's racism also showed in his repeatedly vicious characterizations of King, the labeling of King as a "beast" and "animal." This racist attitude toward black people, and especially the sexuality of black people, can be traced back for centuries in the writings of white Europeans and Americans. As Winthrop Jordan has pointed out, such perverse views reflect an underlying belief that blacks are really beasts and that sex itself is essentially bestial.[37]

Many others in the Bureau shared Sullivan's obsession with King's private conduct, but for somewhat different reasons. Sullivan was truly horrified by what he learned of King, and he had difficulty speaking openly about it. Many of those around him, however, were so fascinated by King's activities they could not stop talking about them in extensive detail. These voyeurs, of course, displayed no small element of racism in their own bizarre fascination with the minutiae of King's personal life. They, however, viewed his activities as entertaining rather than alarming. If Sullivan viewed King as a depraved animal, the voyeurs saw him as an animal too, but one in a circus, one to be watched in performance.

Sullivan later charged that the headquarters' case supervisor was such a voyeur, but the most important person within the Bureau so fixated was Director Hoover himself. Hoover's obsession with the sexual behavior of others is legend, and accurate. The King case was no exception to the rule.[38] Some remaining boosters of Hoover, such as former Deputy Associate Director W. Mark Felt, admit Hoover's preoccupation with things sexual, but have tried to argue that Hoover, like Sullivan, was a Puritan, a man offended by such material rather than a voyeur who took perverse pleasure from it.[39] Hoover, however, spared no effort to collect and view all possible information about the sexual activities of prominent Americans. Bureau tales about this predilection are numerous. While Hoover did utter denunciations of virtually every possible sort of sexual conduct, his relentless collecting of such material revealed that his professed offense, unlike Sullivan's, was rhetoric rather than fact. While Hoover's primary fascination was homosexuality,[40] activities that were interracial, or that involved more than two people, also captivated him.

From 1964 on, Hoover often blabbered about Dr. King's sex life. Former Attorney General Ramsey Clark has testified about his own repeated exposure to this phenomenon, and Clark was far from alone in the experience.[41] With Hoover too, like Sullivan, the presence of a strong racism magnified the obsession with King's private conduct even further. In Sullivan this combination produced an overpowering urge to see King publicly destroyed. Hoover, however, could not generate as intense a hatred because his attitude toward King was that of the voyeur rather than that of the Puritan. True, Hoover denounced King's behavior to anyone who would listen, and some who would not, but the performances always had an air of "isn't it awful; please show me more." Thus Hoover's voyeurism took place under the cover of an essentially false Puritanism, and his desire to disseminate the King information reflected a somewhat different motivation from that of Sullivan.[42]

While Sullivan's principal emphasis was on "exposing" King to the public, Hoover often seemed more interested in using the King material to entertain others whom he believed shared his desire for it than to destroy King himself. True, Hoover's instructions that the most damaging personal material on King be shown to Robert Kennedy and Lyndon Johnson could be read simply as one more means of destroying King as an influential public figure. As Burke Marshall later mused, Hoover's motive could have been that such information "was going to change the way we dealt with him or convince us that civil rights was a bad idea or that Negroes were all evil people or something."[43] Alternatively, it can be argued that the predominant motive for such intragovernment dissemination of the material was not a desire to destroy King, but a more calculated ploy to increase the FBI's bureaucratic status by impressing the organization's superiors with its thorough knowledge of the private lives of prominent citizens, including, by implication, the very people who were being shown such material on others. Such a purpose would be rooted in an organization's rational desire to maximize its own status with and value to those who are its bosses. However, while each of these hypotheses has substantial plausibility, it appears more likely that Hoover's desire to disseminate the information to others was based largely on the same attitude that his own interest in the material was rooted in. Hoover's primary purpose in conveying the information on King to others, such as Lyndon Johnson, seems to have been grounded more in a simple enjoyment of titillating others with that which titillated himself than it was in a consciously planned design to destroy King's reputation within the government or to win bureaucratic prestige for the FBI as an organization. No doubt some admixture of all three of these motives was present, but entertainment likely was predominant over destruction or bureaucratic self-promotion.

Hoover's attitude toward the King material was more complicated than Sullivan's, but there was not much complexity to the reactions of the two most important men to whom the Bureau disseminated its reports. Robert Kennedy was the offended Puritan. Lyndon Johnson was the entertained voyeur.

Kennedy was deeply shocked and surprised when he received the account of the February, 1964, microphone surveillance of King in Los Angeles and the summary of the earlier bugging at the Willard. Much as Division Five expected, Robert Kennedy saw no humor in King's joke about his recently assassinated brother. When the third-hand story of the Las Vegas incident was conveyed to him in early June, Robert Kennedy again was affronted. Although he never spoke about the subject even with some of his closest friends, Kennedy did discuss his reactions and feelings in the 1964 conversations with Burke Marshall and Anthony Lewis quoted in chapter 2. The passages where he detailed his thoughts about the personal information on King remain sealed, but Kennedy made his anger and resentment very clear. Burke Marshall, reflecting back on the matter several years later, commented that the material had affected Robert Kennedy's feelings toward King, "because Bob Kennedy just wasn't that kind of a person. He didn't understand that, you know, and he didn't like it. He wouldn't approve it." Despite that, Kennedy's overall evaluation of King, Marshall felt, had not been controlled by those reports. His bottom-line judgment had remained that King was a constructive leader.[44]

If Robert Kennedy had responded to the Bureau's information on King with offense and anger, Lyndon Johnson responded with a laugh and a grin. It had taken Hoover and DeLoach only a few weeks to learn that the new President greatly enjoyed the stories and tidbits about prominent people's private lives the FBI could convey to him. Within hardly any time at all Johnson was hooked.[45] By early 1964, when the material on King's private life was most voluminous, the flow of FBI reports to the White House far exceeded such transmissions during previous presidential administrations. King was not the only person who was the subject of such reports, but the hotel-room microphones that the Bureau used against him meant that Johnson received considerably more detailed accounts of King's private activities than of others.

Virtually all of Johnson's aides knew of his weakness for such material. Several will admit privately that he particularly enjoyed the information on King. More than with Robert Kennedy, the information also had a strong negative influence on Johnson's political feelings toward black America's foremost leader. As White House Counsel Harry C. McPherson, perhaps the most sensitive and intelligent member of the Johnson staff, has remarked, the President became "terribly disappointed in King for good reasons or not," especially after King came out strongly against Johnson's Vietnam policy in 1967. "Hoover had supplied the President with a vast amount of scurrilous . . . defaming information about King," and while Johnson "was contemptuous of the tape," he nonetheless "was affected by the information on it."[46] When one aide attempted to defend King's sincerity on the issue of the war, Johnson reportedly replied, "God damn it, if only you could hear what that hypocritical preacher does sexually."[47] As Johnson's last attorney general, Ramsey Clark, wrote in 1970 about the Bureau's dissemination of the personal material on King, "The course of the civil rights movement may have been altered by such a practice. The prejudice may have reached men who might otherwise have given great support—including even the President of the United States."[48]

Johnson, like the Kennedys before him, had feared political damage if he became closely linked with King in the public mind and the FBI's material leaked. Stories on either King's private life or his relationship to Levison, the supposed "Communist financier," could prove very embarrassing. Some aides also say that Johnson had an oftentimes pronounced personal fear of what Hoover could do to Johnson himself, but that fear did not keep Johnson from manipulating the Bureau at least as much as it manipulated him.[49] The stellar example of this was the intelligence activities of DeLoach's "special squad" at the 1964 Atlantic City Democratic National Convention. Of all the Bureau's electronic activities against King in 1964–65, only this one was motivated by a desire for political intelligence. The initiative for this project came directly from the White House. Although Johnson often claimed to be a truehearted opponent of electronic surveillance,[50] this sentiment was little in evidence when he was benefiting from the political information such FBI activities obtained for him, or when he was being entertained by the transcripts and recordings of King's personal life.

Whether Hoover's and DeLoach's intent in conveying such material to Johnson was rooted more in titillation and entertainment than in a desire to destroy King or promote the Bureau's organizational status, Johnson clearly viewed the information far more as entertainment than as anything else. King and his closest friends knew that the Bureau hoped to use that material against him, but they did not appreciate then, and have some difficulty accepting even now, the extent of Johnson's awareness of the Bureau's activities, the amount of material that was conveyed to him, and the injurious effect that it had upon Johnson's political regard for King and the civil rights effort. As Ralph Abernathy recalls, "We looked upon the President as our friend, and we really didn't hold him responsible" for what SCLC knew the Bureau was up to. "We didn't look upon him as involved."[51] Little did they know that the Bureau was running amok not on its own, but with the active support and participation of the President himself. How much the Bureau's dissemination of its reports to Johnson, to many other executive branch officials, and, of course, to a number of people not even in government, such as the assorted religious leaders, lowered the amount of support that King and SCLC otherwise would have received from those personages is impossible to calculate. That it did reduce it, however, is unquestionable, and many well informed observers privately echo the statement by Ramsey Clark quoted above.

The flow of the Bureau's highly valued reports on King's personal life to the White House continued through 1964, through the early winter flap over Hoover's public attack on King, and on into 1965. Throughout those same months, the Bureau was undertaking its various efforts to "warn" other notables about King, and in some cases the activity actually was motivated more by just such an odd desire to "protect" someone than a wish to damage King. The most notable case of this was the effort to block King's audience with the Pope, for, as Division Five veterans explain it, a number of staunchly Catholic officials truly did want to protect the Pontiff from what they imagined would be the "embarrassment" he would suffer should he meet King and then the damaging material on King appear in the public press. In most cases, however, such as Sullivan's efforts with the National Council of Churches and Crime Records' activity with the Baptists, the rationale was simply to damage King.[52]

By early 1965 the Bureau's leadership was extremely disappointed and surprised that no one had made available to the public any of the material believed damaging to King. This realization became especially pronounced in the wake of the December and January efforts to interest a substantial number of newsmen in the material, and in the aftermath of Sullivan's unsuccessful January talk with McGill.[53] All indications are that by the early spring of 1965 Sullivan had become so frustrated over the lack of success that he began to devote less and less personal attention to the efforts against King. Not only had no reporters printed anything, but none of the various attempts to persuade black leaders or church figures to undertake quiet efforts to replace or supplant King with someone else had shown any signs of success whatsoever.

Two important reflections of this disappointment and subsequent reduction of emphasis on the efforts against King were the late April, 1965, decision not to install a wiretap on King's new home, and a determination in May that nothing except public source information should be offered in response to a request from UPI reporter Al Kuettner for information on King.[54] Although the documentary record mirroring this great reduction in the intensity of the Bureau's desire to ''get'' King between January and May, 1965, is nowhere near as extensive as might be hoped, the extent of the reduction is easily visible both in the files themselves and in the decline in the number of overt activities being considered or undertaken against King.[55]

The continuing decline in the Bureau's interest in 1965 also was reflected in the four-month lull between June and October in efforts to acquire additional hotel-room recordings of King. Although the last months of 1965 witnessed a number of attempts to bug King's rooms, neither Sullivan nor any others protested in January, 1966, when the threat of Senator Long's probe caused Hoover and Tolson to order that no more microphones be used against King.[56]

From December of 1963 through the fall of 1965, however, the primary reason for the Bureau's intense pursuit of King was a virulent personal hostility toward him that was based upon the reactions of Bureau headquarters' personnel to the information obtained on King's private life, beginning in late 1963. Previous discussions and accounts of the Bureau's efforts against King have been understandably shy to voice this argument clearly. Most explanations that *have* noted the crucial role that this personal conduct played, however, also have committed the error of "blaming the victim." It was not really Hoover's or Sullivan's or the Bureau's fault that the FBI set out to destroy Dr. King, such arguments have implied. It really was King's own fault, because it was his supposedly reprehensible conduct that provoked decent, moral, and patriotic Americans like Hoover into concluding that he would have to be "discredited" or "neutralized" as an influential public figure if the good of the country was to be protected.[57] These implications have been almost as pernicious as the initial responses of the Bureau itself, for the fault and explanation of the matter lies not in anything that King did, but in the exceedingly puritanical and intolerant conceptions of personal conduct held by men such as William Sullivan and in the voyeuristic impulses of men like Hoover.

Secondly, with the one exception of a statement by Jesse Jackson in 1970, all comments on the King case that have admitted the central role that Bureau reactions to King's personal conduct played in the intensification of FBI activities against him have failed to appreciate that for most of the people involved the motives underlying the collection and dissemination of the personal information on King were more complicated than a solitary desire to destroy the civil rights leader.[58] If one were to look solely at the unfortunate William Sullivan, it would be correct to conclude that the one purpose of the hotel-room bugs, the transcripts, and the tapes was to destroy King. The extreme hatred and hostility was the product of combining an intolerant Puritanism with a paternalistic but nonetheless vicious racism.

With other crucial actors, however, such as supervisor Phillips and especially Director Hoover, the orientation toward the information about King was not a simple matter of abhorrence. The explicit accounts of sexual activities and remarks were more intriguing, titillating, and entertaining than they were displeasing or disgusting, and while King of course had to be denounced for what he did, his activities also amused and diverted most Bureau personnel more than anything else they dealt with in a day's work. The voyeur cannot generate the same strength of hatred as the Puritan, and because the Bureau's, and indeed the wider government's, reaction to the King material was much more that of the voyeur than that of the Sullivan-like Puritan, the story of the FBI's obsession with information on King's private life was necessarily more complicated than a single-minded interest in using it to destroy him. And even while Hoover himself represented the unconceded victory of the voyeuristic over puritanical, no such hypocrisy about the real value of the material was present in Lyndon Johnson. While no doubt both antipathy toward King and an organizationally rooted desire to promote the Bureau with the President each played a part in the concerted effort to furnish such information to Johnson, it also is clear on balance that Bureau executives correctly assumed that what appealed to their own earthy tastes would appeal to the unrefined sides of Lyndon Johnson as well.

In all likelihood the decline in the Bureau's efforts to gather and disseminate the damaging personal material on King in 1965 reflected both frustration at the inability to use the information publicly and a simple slackening of interest in something that no longer was as novel and intriguing as it had been in 1964. Throughout the summer and fall of 1965, even while occasional microphones continued to be installed, the files began to reflect an increasing interest in collecting information on SCLC's and King's plans not out of any honest fear of supposed Communists or out of a desire to gather material that could be used to embarrass or discredit King, but simply out of a desire to know ahead of time what events would be occurring in the civil rights movement. Why this focus was never present in the first three to four years of the investigations of King and the SCLC is a question that will be considered in chapter 6, but from the end of 1965 forward the FBI's investigation of King and SCLC entered a third distinctive stage, one where the collection of information largely for political intelligence purposes predominated. After the early focus on Stanley Levison, and then the two peak years of obsession with King's personal life, the third and concluding phase of the Bureau's probe focused on obtaining political information that could be disseminated to various offices of the federal government, including the White House. To aid in this effort, the Bureau took the initiative of acquiring a paid informant within SCLC. The story of that informant and the final phase of the King case is the subject of chapter 5.

5

Informant: Jim Harrison and the Road to Memphis

Recruitment of a live, human informant within SCLC had been discussed by the Bureau's Atlanta field office in 1963. The Atlanta agents viewed the talk about putting wiretaps on King's home and SCLC's office with more than a little ambivalence. They knew how burdensome an amount of paperwork a wiretap generated. A human informant, properly placed and coached, could supply the same information, and more, at a fraction of the cost and effort. Thus the Atlanta security squad several times had discussed with Division Five the pros and cons of making a recruitment pitch to someone already working for SCLC.

By the middle of 1963 the Atlanta agents had picked out the person in SCLC whom they thought the best candidate for recruitment as an informant—Andrew J. Young. Headquarters, however, rejected Atlanta's request to approach Young with an offer. The danger of Young telling the agents to get lost, and then informing the press and public about the contact, was too great a risk, Division Five stated. Once the taps went on in November, 1963, discussion about recruiting a live informant within SCLC all but stopped. Sifting the conversations overheard by the taps kept everyone more than busy.

In the fall of 1964 the Atlanta office by happenstance briefly acquired a source within SCLC. Within three to four weeks, however, the informant's active link to the Bureau was terminated, and the FBI remained without a human source in SCLC's large Atlanta office. Nine months later, in August, 1965, the FBI's Atlanta agents advised headquarters that Lillie Hunter, an SCLC bookkeeper, had been overheard on one of the tapped phone lines telling Ralph Abernathy's wife Juanita that she was unhappy with conditions at SCLC and was thinking about resigning. Atlanta suggested that Hunter's unhappiness might lead her to consider a recruitment offer from the Bureau. Could Atlanta approach her? Headquarters' supervisor Phillips granted permission, but the Atlanta agents changed their minds and decided not to pursue the matter. Thus as of September, 1965, the FBI still had no human source in SCLC.[1]

In early October supervisor Phillips moved to remedy that situation. He instructed the Atlanta, New York, and Chicago offices to encourage one or more of their established "security informants" to obtain employment with SCLC, preferably in Atlanta. The offices were told to keep in mind Atlanta's advice that any "penetration of SCLC headquarters to be practical should be at the level of an executive staff position." Neither New York nor Chicago had a black informant who could gain employment in the top reaches of SCLC and who was willing to move to Atlanta. New York explained, "Agents have noted a reluctance, primarily of Negro informants, to refer to Martin Luther King, Jr., and the SCLC in anything but favorable terms." Recruiting a black person to spy on King looked like it might continue to prove very difficult.

Atlanta, however, recommended a more direct solution to the FBI's problem: it proposed approaching a young black man who already was working at SCLC headquarters, and whose job was one of the most important in SCLC's low-visibility finance office: accountant James A. Harrison. Headquarters approved the recommendation, and two Atlanta agents arranged to meet with Harrison. Originally from Stockton, California, Harrison was only in his mid twenties and initially had joined SCLC as a bookkeeper in October, 1964. He listened attentively as the two agents made their pitch to him in a conversation that lasted forty-five to sixty minutes. He appeared interested, both by the opportunity to "play detective" and by the weekly stipend that was offered, and promised that he would let the agents know his decision very shortly. Within less than a week Jim Harrison was informing on SCLC and Dr. King to the FBI.[2]

"AT 1387-S," as Harrison was called in Bureau communications, soon eclipsed the wiretaps on the SCLC office as the Bureau's most valuable source of information on Dr. King's organization. Weekly he would meet with Atlanta agent Alan G. Sentinella, who in May of 1965 had taken over primary responsibility for the King, SCLC, and "Communist Influence in Racial Matters" cases from Robert R. Nichols. Generally Harrison would phone Sentinella, arrange a rendezvous time and place, and the agent would come by in his car to pick up the informant. Sentinella then would question Harrison as they drove around the streets of Atlanta, carefully avoiding neighborhoods where someone might recognize Harrison and discern what he was up to. Then, an hour or so later, Sentinella would drop Harrison off within walking distance of his home. The informant would keep in touch by means of occasional phone calls until the following week's meeting took place.

Initially Harrison was paid in cash for his information each time he and Sentinella met. Eventually, though, as Harrison's tenure lengthened and his stipend increased, the payments were made monthly. Also, following an incident in which a white truck driver tried to run the interracial duo off the road, the conversations shifted from the front seat of Sentinella's car to a well-shielded room in an Atlanta motel patronized by few if any blacks. The motel offered a drive-in, underground parking garage, and elevators that lifted you from there to interior corridors. Sentinella would arrive first, wait for

Harrison to slip in, and then record their conversation on a dictabelt device that later could be transcribed by Bureau stenographers. It was a considerable improvement over scribbling notes while driving a car. The interview complete, Sentinella would check the corridor before Harrison stepped out and departed.

The major subjects of the conversations were SCLC finances and demonstration plans, with a heavy smattering of office politics and personnel matters. Although Harrison, after his promotion to comptroller, was a member of SCLC's "Executive Staff," his role was usually peripheral. Rarely did he travel to the sites of SCLC protest campaigns. He did sit in on many important SCLC staff meetings, but only occasionally did he attend the staff retreats where most pivotal discussions of strategy and politics took place. Harrison had very little direct contact with Dr. King. He visited his home once or twice at most. Never was Harrison asked to comment on Dr. King's personal life, though he did volunteer to Sentinella some office gossip.

Harrison's officebound role in SCLC meant that he was of limited help to the Bureau on the subject of SCLC's major activity in 1966, the Chicago Freedom Movement. The Bureau's Chicago office had been notified to keep a close watch on SCLC's initial activities there even before the end of 1965, and when the campaign began in earnest in January, 1966, Chicago kept headquarters posted on developments with almost daily dispatches. The Bureau had a special interest in King's efforts to win the support of Chicago's Catholic archbishop, John P. Cody. After King met with Cody on February 3, Division Five recommended that Chicago SAC Marlin W. Johnson brief Cody on what the Bureau knew about King. Hoover approved that suggestion, and on February 24 SAC Johnson visited Cody at his residence. The Archbishop, headquarters was informed, told Johnson that he had not been impressed with King at their initial meeting. He had thought King "glib" and insincere. Cody had been particularly upset when King described their conversation to reporters after assuring Cody that he would not do so. The Archbishop reportedly "appreciated" hearing the Bureau's information on King, but Cody's subsequent role in the Chicago effort suggests that he supported much of King's campaign despite the FBI's activity.[3]

The spring of 1966 was a quiet time in the King and SCLC cases.

Atlanta twice asked for permission to reinstall a wiretap on King's home, but headquarters said no. King's appearance on the "Today" show on April 18 was summarized for Bureau executives, and Director Hoover reacted strongly to a statement that King had spoken against "loose sex relations." Hoover wrote, "This is positively nauseating coming from a degenerate like King." Meanwhile, Harrison's reports and the information from the SCLC office wiretaps were largely routine. Division Five supervisors had to content themselves with prodding Atlanta to consider COINTEL actions based on the accounts of office rivalries and disagreements within SCLC. There was one office tempest over a story that an ex-SCLC employee had been paid a sum of money to remain silent about certain things she knew. This had led several other staff members to submit resignations. The Atlanta field office wanted to undertake several COINTEL actions against SCLC Voter Registration Director Hosea Williams, who was strongly disliked by a number of Atlanta agents, but Division Five vetoed the proposal on the grounds that Williams had no record of association with subversive organizations. "Any counterintelligence measures instituted," headquarters advised, "should be restricted to exposing and discrediting any communist infiltration within the organization."[4]

Throughout the spring and summer of 1966 the New York wiretaps supplied a continuing flow of information on Stanley Levison's counsel to King about SCLC finances, and whether SCLC's board should approve a formal resolution opposing the Vietnam War. Still afraid that publicizing Levison's supposed Communist ties would also expose "Solo," headquarters instead ordered New York to undertake a thorough search for personal dirt that could be used "to discredit, expose, or otherwise neutralize" Levison. After several months of fruitless inquiry, New York reported that it could come up with no damaging information about Levison's personal life, but that it would attempt to "place Levison in a compromising position" with an unidentified woman. All indications are that the Bureau had no success in this endeavor either.[5]

In May, 1966, King spent several days at Miami's International Airport Hotel and was the subject of intense surveillance by investigators from the Dade County public safety department. The detectives apparently placed a microphone in King's room, and they certainly listened in on his phone calls. They also somehow managed to acquire—either by a break in or by means of a "trash cover"—assorted personal notes and charge-card receipts of King's. The FBI's Miami office was fully aware of the local detectives' activities, and two weeks later Bureau headquarters was sent a list of the material that King and aide Bernard Lee had "left in their rooms" at the hotel. Photocopies of these materials also found their way into the files of the Central Intelligence Agency. The Agency made no effort to explain how it had acquired them when it released them in 1980 in response to a Freedom of Information Act request.[6]

In late April of 1966, in line with the six-month authorization rule for all wiretaps, the Bureau had requested approval from Attorney General Katzenbach to continue the wiretap surveillance of SCLC's Atlanta headquarters. Katzenbach did not act on the request until the middle of June. When he did, he advised the Bureau that the taps should be discontinued. Behind this was a curious circumstance. SCLC's Hosea Williams was one of several people implicated in allegations concerning a stolen-car ring that the Justice Department had been investigating since October, 1965. A continued wiretap on Williams's office would complicate any question of prosecuting him. As it turned out, charges were never filed against Williams in the matter, but on Tuesday, June 21, 1966, Division Five inspector Joseph A. Sizoo called Atlanta SAC Joseph K. Ponder and ordered that the wiretaps be discontinued immediately. At 11:55 A.M. the surveillance was halted, and Atlanta's Peachtree Towers listening post, which had operated round-the-clock for over two and one-half years, was closed down, never to resume operations against SCLC or Dr. King. Jim Harrison would now be the only Atlanta source for information on King and his organization.[7]

The termination of the SCLC headquarters' wiretap greatly reduced the Bureau's flow of information about the organization. The Chicago field office was reprimanded by headquarters for the poor quality of its reports on SCLC activities there, reports that often did little more than summarize stories appearing in the Chicago newspapers. The field office recommended that a wiretap be installed on SCLC's Chicago office, but headquarters said no. Chicago instead was instructed to develop an informant close to the SCLC project to supplement Jim Harrison, who could supply little firsthand information on Chicago developments.[8] Harrison was becoming an extremely productive source on SCLC home-office affairs, and his Bureau stipend was increased accordingly, to a sum that approximated $8,000 to $10,000 annually. He was developing a good rapport with agent Sentinella, and his increasingly responsible role within SCLC's financial operations brought him into some regular contact with Levison and Wachtel, as well as SCLC's Atlanta inner circle. Harrison very much enjoyed the financial benefits of the role, and his life style at times reflected his relative wealth, though even his wife was unaware of his relationship with the Bureau.

Throughout the balance of 1966, however, the Bureau's handling of the King and SCLC cases rarely strayed from the now well developed routine of writing up the information obtained from Harrison and the Levison and Jones wiretaps, and distributing summaries of it within the Bureau and throughout the executive branch intelligence community. The flow of information on King going to the Attorney General and the White House decreased some from what it had been in previous times; in the last six months of 1966 only eight reports on King were sent to President Johnson.[9] The Bureau's assorted COINTEL actions directed against King and SCLC also declined substantially in number; the fall of 1966 witnessed only three notable activities. Division Five prepared a newspaper article criticizing King's indecisive stance on the "Black Power" slogan and detailing the backgrounds of Rustin, Levison, Jones, and Wachtel. Apparently the crime records division was unable to find a reporter willing to print this story. An attempt also was made to block a large Ford Foundation grant reportedly about to be made to SCLC, but foundation president McGeorge Bundy rejected an offer to hear the case against King made by a Bureau intermediary. Division Five also moved, with somewhat greater success, to interfere with a scheduled meeting between King and Teamsters' president Jimmy Hoffa, whom Jones had told King might be a possible source of funds for SCLC. King had indicated that any meeting with the unsavory Hoffa would have to take place without publicity. The Bureau promptly alerted two friendly reporters, Julian Morrison of the *Washington Daily News* and Sid Epstein of the *Washington Star*, plus someone at the *New York Daily News*, to the scheduled meeting. When King was confronted with reporters' questions about his planned meeting with Hoffa, King immediately had the session postponed.[10]

In early 1967 the FBI reported to the White House that its wiretap on Stanley Levison indicated that Levison was advising King to give serious thought to running for president in 1968 as a peace candidate. Several weeks later, when King for the first time since August, 1965, resumed public criticism of American involvement in Vietnam, Division Five recommended that friendly reporters be encouraged to confront King with hostile questions on the subject. Dwight M. Wells, who had replaced Seymor Phillips as headquarters' supervisor of the King and SCLC cases, notified Sullivan that a King antiwar speech of February 25 had included "a statement that might be considered revolutionary. He [King] stated in part, 'we have got to get out and demonstrate and protest until it rocks the very foundations of this Nation.' " Reporters particularly should be encouraged to ask King why he was devoting so much effort to criticizing the war while other civil rights leaders had avoided speaking out on it, Wells said. Shortly thereafter, the FBI again advised the White House that Levison was telling King to run for president in 1968.

King made his strongest attack to date on America's conduct in Vietnam in an April 4 speech at New York's Riverside Church. After that, the hostility towards him in the Bureau and throughout the executive branch emerged more starkly than at any time since late 1964. Johnson adviser John P. Roche, an academic who had once headed Americans for Democratic Action, conveyed a detailed commentary on King's remarks to the President. The Riverside Church speech, Roche said, "indicates that King—in desperate search of a constituency—has thrown in with the commies" and that "the civil rights movement is shot—disorganized and broke. King, who is inordinately ambitious and quite stupid (a bad combination)," Roche went on, "is thus looking back to a promising future. The Communist-oriented 'peace' types have played him (and his driving wife) like trout." King had chosen to oppose the war, Roche suggested, so that he always would have "a crowd to applaud" and "money to keep up his standard of living." He now was "destroying his reputation" and "painting himself into a corner with a bunch of losers" solely to gratify his own ego, Roche implied. King had rejected the advice of people like Bayard Rustin, who had opposed the Riverside speech, and he, Roche, would try to find out for the President exactly who had drafted it for King.[11]

The men around Lyndon Johnson were not alone in reacting

strongly to King's remarks about Vietnam. The *Washington Post* stated that King's criticisms included "sheer inventions of unsupported fantasy" that were "not a sober and responsible comment on the war but a reflection of his disappointment" over the slow pace of progress on civil rights and poverty. By uttering "bitter and damaging allegations and inferences that he did not and could not document," the *Post* added, King "has done a grave injury to those who are his natural allies . . . and . . . an even greater injury to himself. Many who have listened to him with respect will never again accord him the same confidence. He has diminished his usefulness to his cause, to his country and to his people." *Life* magazine attacked King even more strongly, saying that "he goes beyond his personal right to dissent when he connects progress in civil rights here with a proposal that amounts to abject surrender in Vietnam." By making a speech that *Life* termed "a demagogic slander that sounded like a script for Radio Hanoi," King has come "close to betraying the cause for which he has worked so long." King himself sat down and cried, Andrew Young later said, when faced with editorial comments like these on his April 4 speech.[12]

The Johnson White House was extremely pleased at the press reaction to King's speech, and undertook its own Bureau-like initiatives to increase it. On April 8 press secretary George Christian informed the President that he had spoken with black columnist Carl Rowan, former ambassador to Finland and former director of the U.S. Information Agency. Rowan, Christian reported, said that he was "exploring the Martin Luther King matter. He said everyone in the Civil Rights movement has known that King has been getting advice from a communist, and he (Rowan) is trying to firm up in his own mind whether King is still doing this. He wants to take out after King, because he thinks he has hurt the Civil Rights movement with his statements." Rowan wasted little time in making up his mind, writing in an April 14 column that "King is listening most to one man who is clearly more interested in embarrassing the United States than in the plight of either the Negro or the war-weary people of Vietnam."[13]

Rowan was not alone in jumping to that partially incorrect conclusion. The Bureau also quickly assumed that Levison was behind King's Riverside Church speech. On April 10 Division Five requested Bureau approval to distribute a revised version of the King monograph of November, 1964, now retitled "Communist Influence in Racial Matters: A Current Analysis." The new edition was prompted, supervisors Dwight Wells and Robert Shackelford told Sullivan, because "King's strong criticism and condemnation of the Administration's policy on Vietnam . . . shows how much he has been influenced by communist advisers. His speech was a direct parallel of the communist position on Vietnam." Copies of the new report went to the White House, Attorney General Ramsey Clark, Secretary of State Dean Rusk, and Defense Secretary Robert McNamara. In the following weeks a stepped-up flow of "Secret" reports on King, based mainly on the Levison wiretap, went to the White House. One dated April 19, and sent from Hoover's office to President Johnson's personal secretary, Mildred Stegall, stated, "Based on King's recent activities and public utterances, it is clear that he is an instrument in the hands of subversive forces seeking to undermine our nation."[14]

By late April the Bureau was aware that Stanley Levison now was urging King to repudiate publicly the idea that he might run for the presidency in 1968. Many other individuals, however, were trumpeting the idea that King join with Dr. Benjamin Spock on an independent antiwar ticket for 1968. The Bureau kept the White House fully apprised of developments on this score, and in mid-May FBI headquarters asked several field offices to submit ideas for secretly harassing the King-Spock ticket should it actually come to fruition. King himself decided that the candidacy idea should not be pursued.[15]

The FBI undertook few initiatives in the King and SCLC cases during the summer of 1967. In August, however, headquarters established a new "counterintelligence program" directed against what were termed "Black Nationalist Hate Groups" and modeled after the already established COINTEL operations aimed at the Communist party, the Socialist Workers party, Puerto Rican nationalists, and Klan-type "White Hate Groups." SCLC was one of a number of organizations listed for inclusion in this program. Headquarters said it was being set up to "expose, disrupt, misdirect, discredit, or otherwise neutralize the activities of black nationalist, hate-type organizations and groupings, their leadership, spokesmen, membership and supporters, and to counter their propensity for violence and civil disorder.'' Why SCLC was included in the formal program is not explained by Bureau records. In any case the formal designation had no substantive impact on the Bureau's handling of the SCLC or King cases. Both had been the targets of assorted COINTEL tricks over the previous four years without need of any formal program, and establishment of the new rubric brought no increase in that type of activity pertaining to King and his organization.[16]

Another change that affected the form but not the substance of the investigations took place in early October when Division Five was reorganized and a new "racial intelligence section" established with George C. Moore as chief. Both the SCLC and King cases were transferred from the internal security section to this new office, where they continued to be handled by supervisor Dwight M. Wells.

FBI efforts to cause trouble for SCLC did not cease. Division Five sent copies of an editorial critical of King that had appeared in a little-known black newspaper to representatives of a national newspaper chain. Two purposes would be served by this, Wells informed Sullivan. First, attendance at SCLC fund-raising shows featuring King and Harry Belafonte might be reduced. Second, the item would "publicize King as a traitor to his country and race." The effort met with no apparent success. Also a failure was a late-starting effort to block a small contract that the Labor Department was awarding to SCLC. Harrison had reported in mid-October that SCLC had a part in a $60,000 program to provide on-the-job training in grocery stores for a limited number of unemployed Atlanta black people, and Division Five immediately sent Labor Undersecretary James J. Reynolds a copy of the April 10 King monograph. Reynolds told the Bureau's W. J. McDonnell that the agreement could not be nullified, but that he did appreciate the information on King. All of this was duly set forth in a November 8 report to the White House. Division Five also was forced to report that the Ford Foundation had awarded SCLC a $250,000 grant in spite of the Bureau's effort to poison that well.[17]

In early December, 1967, concern began to grow within Division Five over SCLC's plans for a massive Poor People's Campaign in the nation's capital in the spring of 1968. Bureau trepidation was heightened by Jim Harrison's reports on a November retreat to discuss strategy for the protests. As a result, on December 13 the racial intelligence section asked that wiretaps be reestablished on SCLC's Atlanta headquarters. Atlanta was instructed to "survey" SCLC's office. It soon reported back that taps on all of SCLC's ten phone lines would be possible. On December 29 the request to proceed with the taps was forwarded to the Bureau's hierarchy. Division Five's memo read:

> Since SCLC's President, Martin Luther King, Jr., has urged massive civil disobedience throughout the country in an effort to spur Congress into action to help the plight of the Negro, it is felt that we need this installation to obtain racial intelligence information concerning their plans. King has warned that these massive demonstrations may result in riots. Because of this, we should be in a position to obtain intelligence so that appropriate countermeasures can be taken to protect the internal security of the United States.

No mention was made of Levison or any other supposedly subversive influence. Bureau executives endorsed the request, but DeLoach, who handled liaison with the Justice Department, noted that "A. G. will not approve, but believe we should go on record." On January 2 the formal request went to Attorney General Ramsey Clark, asking for the taps "so that we can keep apprised of the strategy and plans of this group. Massive demonstrations could trigger riots which might spread across the Nation." Clark rejected the idea the following day, writing to Hoover, "There has not been an adequate demonstration of a direct threat to the national security. Should further evidence be secured of such a threat, or re-evaluation desired, please resubmit." Thus the Bureau was forced to stay abreast of the quickly developing Poor People's Campaign through Harrison, the New York taps, and newspaper reports alone.[18]

By early February Bureau headquarters was aware that the SCLC staff was falling behind schedule in the preparations for the Washington campaign. Many SCLC field staffers were upset at the Atlanta office's failure to articulate the specific goals of the campaign. The Bureau also was aware that King himself had doubts as to whether SCLC should go forward with the effort, doubts that he had voiced openly at a February 6–7 SCLC board meeting in Washington. Such reports did not ease the fears of the Johnson administration, and planning began on how to cope with King's demonstrators when they arrived in Washington in April.

King himself spent much of February traveling in the Deep South, spurring efforts to recruit demonstrators for the April protests. He took time out on February 23 to deliver a speech praising long-time black scholar and activist W. E. B. DuBois at a fund-raising dinner in New York for *Freedomways* magazine, one of whose editors was Jack O'Dell. The FBI jumped on this but was unsuccessful in drawing press attention to the association.[19] Newspaper commentary on King's Washington plans was extensive, though divided between those who believed his ideas so tame that the campaign would have no effect whatsoever, and others who suggested that the Poor People's descent upon Washington would be a reenactment of the Vandals' occupation of Rome.[20] Both the White House and the Bureau shared the second perspective. One Johnson aide told the President, "We have permitted the Stokely Carmichaels, the Rap Browns, and the Martin Luther Kings to cloak themselves in an aura of respectability to which they are not entitled." King's civil disobedience was really "criminal disobedience," and, "As the time nears for Dr. King's April activities, I hope the President will publicly unmask this type of conduct for what it really is."[21]

The Bureau had exactly that same thought in mind. In late February and early March the flow of reports on King to the White House and other executive branch offices increased once again. A major compendium was distributed to many agencies on February 20. It contained lengthy sections on the Poor People's Campaign plans, SCLC's history, Communist influence on King and SCLC, King's opposition to the Vietnam War, SCLC finances, and King's sexual activities.

The section on the PPC fanned fears that the campaign could lead to violence. This violence might well be the goal, the report claimed, not only of black nationalists waiting to act under cover of King's own demonstrations, but also of King's "shrewd and dedicated Communist" adviser, Stanley Levison. Levison, along with Wachtel and Rustin, also received detailed attention in the section on King's opposition to the war, and the backgrounds of all of them, plus a whole host of others including O'Dell, Mills, Blackwell, and Vivian, were summarized in the section on alleged Communist influence. The final two sections of the monograph dealt solely with King's sexual activities. One part detailed an "all-night sex orgy" at an SCLC workshop in Miami, with no mention of King's presence, and then summarized the four-year-old Willard Hotel happenings, which were termed a "two day, drunken sex orgy." The report added, "Throughout the ensuing years and until this date King has continued to carry on his sexual aberrations secretly while holding himself out to public view as a moral leader of religious conviction." The final portion was entitled "King's Mistress" and described a supposedly long-standing affair that King had been carrying on with the wife of a California dentist. One of the Bureau's major sources on this subject was the woman's own brother, a famous, former professional athlete. He had complained to the Bureau about King, whom he called a "hypocrite." The report went on to allege that Bureau agents had filmed King and the woman emerging from motel rooms and had intercepted phone conversations between them. It also alleged that an unspecified "source," most likely a microphone, had related "an incident which occurred some time ago in a New York City hotel, where King was intoxicated at a small gathering. King threatened to leap from the 13th floor window of the hotel if this woman would not say she loved him." Information like this, the report said, would enable government officials to have "some insight into the nature of the man" scheduled to lead the April demonstrations.[22]

Several days after that report was distributed, a *Washington Post* story on Director Hoover made the first public allusion to the Bureau's efforts to distribute damaging personal information about King. It received little attention, however, and within days the racial intelligence section was recommending a further revision and dissemination of the King monograph so as "again to remind top-level officials in government of the wholly disreputable character of King." That idea was endorsed, and by March 12 a new twenty-one-page report, "Martin Luther King, Jr., A Current Analysis," had been completed. It was sent to the President, Attorney General Clark, and various other officials on March 14. Five days later copies went to the State Department, the Central Intelligence Agency, and a host of military offices.[23]

Headquarters also was moving to direct more energy into the "Black Nationalist Hate Group" COINTELPRO, which had been languishing for six months. On March 4, 1968, Division Five dispatched a lengthy letter to all field offices listing five "long-range goals" for the BNHG COINTELPRO.

1. Prevent the coalition of militant black nationalist groups. . . . An effective coalition of black nationalist groups might be the first step toward a real "Mau Mau" in America, the beginning of a true black revolution.

2. Prevent the rise of a "messiah" who could unify, and electrify, the militant black nationalist movement. Malcolm X might have been such a "messiah"; he is the martyr of the movement today. Martin Luther King, Stokely Carmichael and Elijah Muhammad all aspire to this position. Elijah Muhammad is less of a threat because of his age. King could be a very real contender for this position should he abandon his supposed "obedience" to "white, liberal doctrines" (nonviolence) and embrace black nationalism. Carmichael has the necessary charisma to be a real threat in this way.

3. Prevent violence on the part of black nationalist groups. This is of primary importance.

4. Prevent militant black nationalist groups and leaders from gaining respectability, by discrediting them to. . . . the responsible Negro community. . . . the white community. . . . [and] in the eyes of Negro radicals.

5. A final goal should be to prevent the long-range growth of militant black nationalist organizations, especially among youth.

The "primary targets" of the program, headquarters advised, "should be the most violent and radical groups and their leaders. We should emphasize those leaders and organizations that are nationwide in scope and are most capable of disrupting this country." SNCC, with Stokely Carmichael and H. Rap Brown, SCLC and King, the Revolutionary Action Movement and Maxwell Stanford, and the Nation of Islam and Elijah Muhammad were named as specific targets, and each field office was ordered to move into action within thirty days.

Baltimore, Jackson, Detroit, and Mobile were the four offices that proposed COINTEL actions aimed at King and SCLC between the time of that initial letter of instruction and early April of 1968. Baltimore agents had observed some Black Muslim literature at the newly opened SCLC office there, and wondered if this link could be made embarrassing to one or both groups. Chicago reported that it would not bother the Nation of Islam in the least, though Atlanta advised that it would be nice to tar King with the violent, antiwhite reputation that the Muslims had with many people. The Jackson office suggested a rumor campaign utilizing false information about the timing and place of King's appearances and Poor People's Campaign events, plus stories that King was motivated only by a desire to benefit himself financially, in an effort to reduce participation in the PPC. Detroit recommended that it impede the efforts of that city's Poor People's contingent to get to Washington by having an agent disguised as a supporter promise to supply the necessary buses, and then disappear and fail to do so. Finally, Mobile thought an anonymous letter should be sent to Selma's Reverend F. D. Reese, a leader of the 1965 protests there, in an effort to magnify an existing disagreement between him and SCLC.[24]

While the Bureau weighed these assorted tricks, King was hard at work trying to build popular support for the upcoming Washington demonstrations. In mid-March, however, in response to repeated pleas from long-time friend Reverend James M. Lawson, Jr., King agreed to spend one evening in Memphis, Tennessee, in order to speak in support of a strike that the city's sanitation workers, almost all of whom were black, had been conducting since February 12.

The strike had begun in an effort to win city recognition of the garbage workers' nascent union. Within two weeks, though, the heavy racial overtones of the conflict between the black workers and segregationist Mayor Henry Loeb had come to outweigh the issue of union recognition. The Memphis black community, led by one of the most active NAACP chapters in the nation, had formed an umbrella group, Community on the Move for Equality (COME), to mobilize support for the strikers and organize demonstrations on their behalf. By early March, however, the workers' plight was receiving very little helpful press attention, either locally or nationally. The COME strategy committee, led by reverends Lawson and

H. Ralph Jackson, decided that some nationally recognized person-alities would have to be brought in to draw attention to the sanitation workers' struggle. NAACP official Jesse Turner arranged to have Roy Wilkins visit Memphis on March 14, and both Wilkins and, by chance, Bayard Rustin appeared at that evening's rally.

Lawson had won a promise from King to come in on Monday, March 18. When King arrived, the Memphis movement had over ten thousand people waiting for him at the cavernous Mason Temple church. Extremely impressed by the large and lively crowd, King told them that what the Memphis movement needed was a general work stoppage on some chosen day. While King was speaking, Law-son and other leaders were exchanging comments with King's assis-tants behind the speaker's podium, and they discussed the idea of King returning to Memphis several days later to lead just such a communitywide march. When King finished his address and stepped down, Lawson and others immediately confronted him with the sug-gestion. King, so greatly touched by the crowd, responded affirma-tively and the men quickly settled on Friday as the best date. King walked back to the podium and announced to the crowd that he would return on Friday to lead them.

When the rally concluded, King and his aides, accompanied by Memphis Judge Benjamin Hooks and local Reverend Samuel B. ''Billy'' Kyles, went to the Lorraine Motel, where King had stayed when he was in Memphis from the late-1950s on and which had served as initial headquarters for the 1966 Meredith March into Mis-sissippi. The men sat and talked of the local movement and the Poor People's effort, and King outlined to them his dilemma about whether or not to go forward with it. A girls' choir was spending the night at the Lorraine, and when word circulated that King was there too, the young women assembled and sang for King and his compan-ions in the motel's conference room. The next morning King and his party headed South into Mississippi for a hectic three-day tour of appearances planned to rally support for the Poor People's Cam-paign.[25]

Among the audience at King's March 18 speech at Mason Temple had been Memphis FBI agents William H. Lawrence and Howell S. Lowe. These two men had paid close attention to developments in the sanitation strike since its beginning. They also kept close watch on other events in Memphis's black community, and were well acquainted with a number of its foremost leaders. Throughout the early weeks of the strike, thanks to excellent information provided by three prominent sources in the Memphis chapter of the NAACP— branch president Jesse H. Turner, Dr. Vasco Smith, and his spouse, Maxine Smith—the two agents had been able to furnish FBI head- quarters with extremely acute analyses of the black community's response to the sanitation workers' cause.

One source of concern for both the black political leadership and the local FBI agents was the role that a group of college-age black activists, known as both the "Black Organizing Project" (BOP) and the "Invaders," was playing within the black community. Agents Lowe and Lawrence had targeted the Invaders for Bureau attention under the "Black Nationalist Hate Group" COINTELPRO, and had interviewed the group's two primary leaders in mid-February. Sev- eral weeks later the two agents described the youths' activities in a detailed report to Bureau headquarters. The Memphis agents had a relatively easy time keeping track of the group because an under- cover officer of the Memphis Police Department, Marrell McCollough, had joined the Invaders as a full-fledged member in mid-February. McCollough's superiors had instructed him to attend strike-related meetings, and through his work both local law enforce- ment and the Bureau's field office had remained well informed on developments.[26]

One of the most important developments was a growing split between the young people on one hand and the adult leadership of COME on the other. The Invaders had gotten their start in the sum- mer of 1967 when two local boys, Charles L. Cabbage and Coby Smith, had returned to Memphis from Atlanta's Morehouse College. Both had taken jobs as organizers for Memphis Area Project (MAP) South, a government-funded, antipoverty organization headed by Reverend Lawson. The two young men had been fired from their jobs after repeatedly encouraging poor tenants to engage in rent strikes against their landlords. Subsequently, in conjunction with two other youths, Calvin Taylor and John Smith, they had organized BOP and the Invaders, recruiting several dozen followers, including students from LeMoyne-Owen College and Memphis State Univer- sity. When the strike began, the young men sought a role for their group in the COME effort. From the start relations between the youths and the adults, and particularly between Cabbage and Lawson, were strained. The Invaders had made it clear since the time of the MAP South firings that they considered Lawson insufficiently militant. Lawson, who once had gone to prison as a conscientious objector, deeply resented such criticism from youngsters so new to the movement. When COME's strategy committee, chaired by Lawson, began meeting during the last week of February, the Invaders sought formal representation on it and, over Lawson's objections, were allowed to attend some of the meetings. Lawson, however, generally ignored their presence and gave them no input into COME decision making. "He would knock them down every time they would say anything," one observer noted. Another stated, "Lawson wouldn't recognize them," and a third person concluded that Lawson "was very insecure in the presence of these guys. He felt threatened." By mid-March the Invaders, frustrated both by this treatment and by the very slow escalation in COME's strike support tactics, were no longer sending representatives to the strategy committee's meetings.[27]

The march initially scheduled for Friday, March 22, was cancelled when a freak storm dumped a foot of snow on Memphis Thursday evening and early Friday morning. At 7 A.M. Friday Lawson called King in Atlanta to alert him. They agreed that the event should be rescheduled. After several other phone calls over the weekend, Thursday, March 28 was chosen as the new date. In the interim King continued his travels to recruit people for the April demonstrations in Washington, though the disagreement within SCLC, and within King's own mind, over the wisdom of the campaign continued to simmer. King was particularly disturbed by a memo opposing the demonstrations circulated to the entire SCLC board by one of its officers, Marian Logan. Almost daily he pressed Mrs. Logan to withdraw her objections. She did not, nor did SCLC staff members Jim Bevel and Jesse Jackson, and the uncertainty about what would be done remained. From Monday through Wednesday King made a swing through New York City and northern New Jersey, where two campaign contingents were being organized. On Thursday morning he flew into Memphis for that day's scheduled march.[28]

The week and a half since King's first visit had witnessed no improvement in the relationship between the Invaders and the ministers who predominated in COME. The leaders of the youth group all remained away from the Thursday march. Many of their followers and younger associates, who had heard the accounts of how the adult leadership had treated Cabbage and the others, were present, however, along with large numbers of high-school youths angered by news of a severe injury sustained by a young black girl during a police-student clash earlier that morning at Hamilton High School. King's flight was over an hour late arriving in Memphis. It was not until almost 11 A.M. that he arrived at the march's starting point, Clayborn Temple A.M.E. Church, where a large crowd had been waiting impatiently for the procession to get underway. S. B. "Billy" Kyles had tried to persuade Lawson to calm the atmosphere by beginning the march and having the delayed King join it in progress, but Lawson had chosen to wait. King and Abernathy immediately sensed the impatient, unsettled mood of the crowd when they stepped from their car and set off up Hernando Street at the head of the column. Lawson had assigned a number of the ministers and other adults to serve as marshalls for the march, but the great majority of them crowded to the front of the procession, near Dr. King, leaving the flanks and rear of the column all but unsupervised. The march, aiming for the Memphis City Hall, headed up Hernando and made a left onto Beale, the major thoroughfare of black business in south Memphis. The head of the column had just turned right onto Main, from Beale, when several of the long sticks used to carry placards were thrown from one side of the street into store windows on the opposite side of Beale in the area of the rear half of the column. A pause followed that first fusillade, but within a minute a second barrage of the sticks followed, and some youngsters who had been accompanying or trailing the column began to loot goods from the broken store windows. A number of street persons hanging out on Beale joined in, and the Memphis police waded in to halt the disruption. At the head of the column Lawson and King could hear the commotion to the rear, and the police ordered that they halt. Lawson borrowed a bullhorn and instructed the column to reverse its path. After several moments those in the front did so, turned back onto Beale, and attempted to head back to Clayborn Temple. By then, however, additional police were arriving on the scene and no distinction was being made between active looters and frightened marchers—the police went after them all. Tear gas was released, and the disorganized crowd hurried back toward the church, the police in pursuit.

When the violence first had erupted, Lawson and others immediately had sought to get King away from the scene. King himself, not knowing what was happening, was frightened at first, telling those around him, "I've got to get out of here." Bernard Lee flagged down two black women in a white Pontiac, asked for use of the car for Dr. King, and King and his aides hopped in. The car headed west on McCall, away from Main. Memphis Police Lieutenant M. E. Nichols pulled alongside and asked the driver where King and his party wanted to go. Ralph Abernathy suggested the Sheraton Peabody Hotel, but Nichols said no, that would be back across the path of the disruption. King himself said the Lorraine, but that too was in the wrong direction. Lieutenant Nichols directed them to follow him to the Holiday Inn Rivermont, a short distance south along the bank of the Mississippi River. Nichols's motorcycle led the Pontiac into the Rivermont, and the officer himself went to the desk and requested rooms for King and his aides. After a brief delay the rooms were arranged, and King, Abernathy, and Lee went upstairs. Plans to return to Atlanta that evening were cancelled. King was disturbed by what had happened, and feared how the press would use the incident to raise more doubts about the protests planned for Washington. A call was placed to SCLC headquarters, and all three men spoke with Hosea Williams. Both Lee and Abernathy told Williams that King was extremely dejected and that they, his aides, were certain that the disruption had been deliberately planned by black elements hostile to King. Each man worried that those same elements might try to do personal harm to King.

In Atlanta, Williams shared this information with other staff members at SCLC headquarters, including Jim Harrison. At approximately 4:30 P.M. Harrison called Al Sentinella and relayed what Williams had said. Sentinella immediately called Memphis agent C. O. Halter, and passed on Lee's and Abernathy's reported concern that the violent elements in Memphis might seek to harm King. Halter had another agent convey the report to the Memphis police, and Sentinella himself notified Bureau headquarters.

Back in Memphis, word that King was at the Rivermont circulated quickly. In a short time various members of the movement's local leadership arrived, attempting to explain and apologize for what had happened. King sat on the bed, with his clothes on, under the covers, smoking, as he spoke with the local representatives who came in. Reverend Kyles, who was one of the first to arrive, said later that King "really didn't have any idea of what had happened. . . . he was very disturbed, [but] he wasn't angry . . . just upset." King soon was saying that they would have to hold another march soon to show that one could be conducted without violence. Lee and Abernathy were quite angry that the local leadership had allowed King to be trapped in these developments, and pressed the Memphis figures for an explanation. The adult leadership blamed the disruption on the Invaders, and soon Lawson himself arrived and reinforced that conclusion. Lawson vowed that they would have a march the next day, but the decision was made that Dr. King would not participate in one until more thorough advance planning had taken place.[29]

Once the local people had departed early in the evening, King revealed to Lee and Abernathy just how upset he was because of the afternoon's developments. Abernathy suggested that King call Levison, and King did. Stanley tried hard to cheer him up. King again spoke of cancelling the Poor People's Campaign, and Levison urged him to continue. In New York the Bureau agents manning the wiretap on Levison's phone took down every word of the conversation.

Talking with Levison did not alleviate King's despondency. He wondered to Abernathy whether, "Maybe we just have to admit that the day of violence is here, and maybe we just have to give up and let violence take its course." As Abernathy later described it, "Dr. King was greatly, greatly disturbed. It was the most restless night. It was a terrible and horrible experience for him. I had never seen him in all my life so upset and so troubled." Abernathy added, "I couldn't get him to sleep that night. He was worried, worried. He didn't know what to do, and he didn't know what the press was going to say."

King finally fell asleep at 5 or 6 A.M., and awoke about 10 A.M. The leadership of the Invaders had heard that the disruption of the Thursday march was being attributed to them, and, even though they had not been *directly* or wholly responsible for it, they were aware that they could reap some gains by not denying the accusations with much vehemence. King had told the local leadership Thursday evening that he wanted to meet with these Invaders, and at about 10 A.M. Friday three of the leaders, Charles Cabbage, Calvin Taylor, and Charles Harrington, went to King's room at the Rivermont. King was just arising, and Abernathy gave them a hostile reception when they identified themselves. As Taylor later related it, "We attempted to explain to him that we did not disrupt the march. He insisted that we did, and we insisted that we did not. This went on until Dr. King came out." King emerged from the lavatory in his bathrobe and took a friendlier tack toward the youths. He knew that Cabbage had graduated from his own alma mater, Morehouse, and began the conversation on that note. Cabbage told King that the youths had wanted to speak with him back on March 18, but that Lawson had prevented them from doing so. He also explained to King how Lawson and the other pastors virtually had excluded the youths from any meaningful role in COME's strike-support efforts. King replied that Lawson and the others had told him nothing about the youths, and their unhappiness, prior to the disruption. He asked Cabbage what would have to be done to have a peaceful march a few days hence. Cabbage told King that BOP needed some funds, and transportation, to support their own organizational work in the Memphis black community. King said that he would try to do something about that, but that he certainly would make sure that the young men were accorded a substantive role within COME from now on. With a promise that he would get back in touch with Cabbage, King ended the discussion and prepared to go downstairs for a press conference where he would be confronted with painful charges that he had led a march that had ended in a riot. When that ordeal was over, national union officials Jerry Wurf and William Lucy drove King, Abernathy, and Lee to the airport and their Friday afternoon flight back to Atlanta.[30]

Thursday afternoon, shortly after the first news accounts of the disrupted march reached Washington, Division Five section chief George C. Moore called the second-in-command at the FBI's Memphis field office, C. O. Halter. Moore told Halter that assistant director Sullivan wanted Memphis to submit a lengthy teletype describing King's involvement in the march to headquarters as soon as possible. "The Bureau," Halter wrote in a note to himself, desires the teletype to include: Why was Martin Luther King in Memphis? Why was the march held? Did Martin Luther King do anything to trigger the violence; what part did he play in the march; how much of the violence is attribubable [sic] to King; did he make any statements on joining the march which could have had an effect on the crowd toward violence? What time did the violence start? Was King present at the time the violence started? Did King do anything to control the marchers and to prevent violence? Mr. Sullivan has indicated that although Martin Luther King preaches nonviolence, violence occurs just about everywhere he goes.

Within hours detailed accounts of the day's events were on their way to Washington.

Division Five supervisors at headquarters viewed the news from Memphis as a prediction come true, and as a forerunner of what would be in store for Washington when the Poor People's Campaign arrived in April. Immediately they moved to take the offensive. The supervisor of the BNHG COINTELPRO, T. J. Deakin, recommended to Sullivan that the Bureau alert friendly news reporters to the "hypocrisy" of King's spending Thursday and Friday at the white-owned Rivermont rather than at the Lorraine. Sullivan himself had another idea in mind. Early Friday morning he himself called agent Halter in the Bureau's Memphis office. Sullivan, Halter stated in an account of the conversation,

is most interested in the activities, both official and personal, of King while in Memphis. . . . Sullivan is interested in any improper conduct on the part of King. He had hoped that we would have had coverage which would have made this information available. Mr. Sullivan requested that we get everything possible on King and that we stay on him until he leaves Memphis.

Halter then asked agent Lowe to check with the Memphis Police Department for any indication of whether King had engaged in "improper action" while at the Rivermont.

While Sullivan was making that inquiry, the supervisor of the

King and SCLC cases, Dwight Wells, was drafting a new request for wiretaps on SCLC's Atlanta headquarters because of the violence in Memphis. In the recommendation Wells cited not only the Memphis "riot" but also the New York office's report of the Thursday evening Levison-King phone call, and Levison's urging King to go forward with the Washington demonstrations. On Tuesday, April 2, after being approved by the Bureau's leadership, the wiretap request was forwarded to Attorney General Clark. It requested taps not only on the Atlanta headquarters, but also on SCLC's Washington office. "In view of the recent developments in Memphis, Tennessee, where King led a march that ended in a riot, it is reasonable to assume the same thing could happen later this month when King brings his 'Poor People's March' to Washington,'' the Bureau told Clark. Unlike the previous request that Clark had rejected, this one cited Levison's role as further grounds for the surveillance. Clark did not act on the Bureau's request until more than nine months later, when he rejected it on one of his last days in office.[31]

King and SCLC meanwhile were moving to improve the situation in Memphis. King and the SCLC executive staff held a long and angry meeting Saturday, March 30, at Ebenezer Baptist Church, and once again disagreement erupted over whether the organization should go forward with the Poor People's Campaign. Bevel and Jackson were most vocal about the insufficient planning that had gone into the Washington program. They also were the most forthright in arguing that King and SCLC could not be diverted by Memphis if they intended to have successful demonstrations in Washington. King and others, however, felt that he and SCLC had to return to Memphis and lead a peaceful, successful march in order to counter unfavorable press commentary. King himself was further upset by the disagreements among the staff, and left the meeting for a long period in order to let his assistants argue among themselves. When he returned late in the afternoon, a consensus had been reached that the SCLC staff would commit enough time and energy to Memphis to carry off a successful second march. SCLC staff members James Orange, Jackson, Bevel, and Young were all to be in Memphis by Monday to begin preparations for that march and particularly to work with the Invaders to ensure that there would be no youthful disruption of this second attempt.[32]

On Sunday, March 31, while King preached at Washington's National Cathedral, SCLC's James Orange arrived in Memphis and began discussions with the Invaders. Monday night a number of Invaders met with about half-a-dozen SCLC staff members at the Lorraine Motel, where the SCLC staffers were staying and where several Invaders had taken a room to escape the almost continual harassment of the Memphis police. The Invaders voiced their demands for a more influential role in COME and for financial support of their own organizing efforts by SCLC. If those things could be arranged, they stated, they would work to see that the second march would be peaceful, though they could give no guarantees. On Tuesday SCLC's Orange spoke with Reverend H. Ralph Jackson, vice-chairman of the COME strategy committee, and although the COME adults rejected out of hand an Invader demand that Lawson be replaced as chairman, Jackson himself came to a Tuesday night Invader-SCLC meeting at the Lorraine to offer the youths two formal seats on the strategy committee, which the Invaders filled with Charles Ballard and Edwina Harrell. The Invaders continued to press for financial support from SCLC, and the SCLC staff promised that that would be taken up on Wednesday evening after Dr. King returned to Memphis.

King, Abernathy, and a number of other SCLC staffers, including Jim Harrison, arrived in Memphis from Atlanta at about 10:30 A.M. Wednesday morning. King and Abernathy were driven to the Lorraine Motel, where King held a brief press conference. Jim Harrison meanwhile made a phone call to the ranking agent in the Memphis FBI office, Robert G. Jensen. Harrison explained that he was in town only for the day, did not know precisely what was planned, and would be returning to Atlanta at about 7:30 P.M. If he learned any worthwhile information before then, he would call Jensen again.

At noon King and a number of aides traveled to Lawson's Centenary Methodist Church for a meeting of black ministers who were supporting the strike effort. At about 3 P.M. King returned to the Lorraine, where he was greeted by two U.S. marshals who served him with a temporary restraining order issued just hours earlier by U.S. District Court Judge Bailey Brown, at the request of the city of Memphis. It barred any march unless approved by Judge Brown. In midafternoon King met briefly with Invaders' leaders Cabbage and

John Smith, and he promised them that SCLC would make an effort
to secure some funding and a car for their efforts, if they would serve
as marshals for the second march, now scheduled for the following
Monday.

Just before 4 P.M. King met for about twenty minutes with three
lawyers whom the American Civil Liberties Union had retained to
represent King and SCLC in the federal court hearing that would
determine whether Brown would allow a second march despite the
city's opposition. King stressed to the attorneys his fear that some
incident might occur during the march that would defeat its purpose.
He responded affirmatively when the lawyers explained to him that
their strategy before Judge Brown at the hearing the following day
would be to urge that the judge authorize a Monday march, but that
his order specify in detail the rigorous supervision under which it
would take place, so as to minimize the chance of any disruption. As
one of the attorneys noted, "King was very much afraid that if this
march went on and there was more violence, that he was going to be
irreparably damaged."

After the lawyers left, King and the SCLC staff had another meeting with the Invaders, including police informant McCollough, to
discuss further their demand for SCLC financial support. King continued to be more favorable toward them than were most of his staff,
and he listened as the Invaders detailed their ideas for cultural programs and organizing efforts in the Memphis black community.
King assured them that their ideas had merit, that he would have his
staff give them a hand in drafting a written proposal, and that SCLC
would convey that proposal to people who would be better able to
support them than the financially strained SCLC.[33]

Heavy rain was expected to reduce substantially the attendance at
that evening's rally at Mason Temple. The SCLC staff decided that
Abernathy could suffice as the main speaker, allowing King to have
a bit more rest. Once Abernathy arrived at the church, however, he
sensed that the limited but lively crowd had really been looking forward to hearing King, and was disappointed to see Abernathy arrive
without him. Abernathy called the Lorraine, explained the situation
to King, and King headed for Mason Temple himself. Abernathy
devoted some twenty-five to thirty minutes to introducing King to
the crowd, and when it came King's turn to speak he promised the

crowd that no injunction, not even a federal court injunction, would keep him from leading the second march. He went on to talk about earlier crises in his own life, his own previous brushes with death, and a bomb scare that had delayed his flight into Memphis that very morning. King's emotional remarks about death, and his fatalistic attitude toward it, combined with the sound of the heavy rain and thunder to create an atmosphere that was exceptionally eerie. Rarely before had any of his assistants heard him speak publicly about such subjects. All were deeply moved.

When King finished, however, he was in a buoyant mood. Dinner followed at Ben Hooks's house, and not until the early hours of the morning did King and his aides return to the Lorraine. There they found that King's younger brother A. D. had arrived from Louisville with several other friends, and King sat up talking with them until almost 6:30 A.M., something that had become an almost common practice for him over the previous few years.

King got up just before noon, and the early part of the afternoon was devoted to a meeting of the SCLC staff. They discussed how to handle the Invaders, who had continued to press for a more definite commitment of SCLC support since their Wednesday evening conversation with King. The question of adding Charles Cabbage to the SCLC staff came up, but King emphasized that no one should be put on the payroll who lacked a commitment to at least tactical nonviolence. Hosea Williams chose to quarrel with that, and King lectured him and the others until the meeting broke up without a firm decision on how to handle the Invaders' demands. After the session ended, a number of lesser SCLC staff members who had come to Memphis left to return to Atlanta. Others, including Williams, got into a further heated discussion with the Invaders, who in late afternoon left the Lorraine, angry that the SCLC staff continued to distrust the sincerity of their demands. Andrew Young had spent the entire day in court, along with the movement's lawyers, and returned to the motel at about 5 P.M. to report that it seemed likely that Judge Brown was going to accept the lawyers' suggestion and allow a tightly controlled march on Monday. On that hopeful note King, Abernathy, and the others began preparing to go to dinner at the home of Memphis minister Billy Kyles.[34] When they stepped out onto the balcony of the motel, and the end came, it came on a day no different from so many of those that King had endured over the previous twelve years.

Word of King's fatal shooting reached Bureau headquarters, Attorney General Clark, and President Johnson within thirty minutes of the event. The Bureau immediately turned its energies to the search for King's assassin, and its own six-year-old case on the civil rights leader came to an end.

King's death certainly did not mean the end of the Bureau's surveillance of SCLC and King's associates. Less than a month after King's killing the Bureau renewed its request to Clark for wiretaps on SCLC headquarters, which Clark continued to ignore. Jim Harrison remained a valuable, well paid source, detailing the severe troubles that plagued SCLC's attempt to go forward with the Poor People's Campaign in the wake of King's murder. Though once rebuked by Sentinella for having had his hand in SCLC's till, Harrison remained a paid informant even after he left the SCLC staff in 1969, and he continued to supply information on Atlanta's black community into the early 1970s.[35]

The New York wiretap on Stanley Levison remained in place long after Dr. King's death, and throughout the years 1969–71 the Bureau furnished Nixon White House officials such as Henry Kissinger, Egil Krogh, Jr., and Alexander Butterfield with detailed reports of intercepted phone conversations between Levison and King's widow, Coretta Scott King. Levison himself was still listed in the "Security Index" in 1971, and the Bureau's New York office was still compiling exhaustive reports on his activities as late as 1972.[36]

The Bureau briefly considered requesting authority for an SCLC headquarters wiretap from new Attorney General John N. Mitchell when the Nixon administration took office early in 1969, but the idea was shelved because of continuing public leaks that hinted at the FBI's previous surveillance of King himself. The first public disclosure that King had been wiretapped occurred less than two months after his death, when columnist Drew Pearson reported the story in an effort to damage Robert Kennedy's presidential primary campaign. Bureau executives evidenced an ambivalent attitude towards Pearson's disclosure, reluctant to have so controversial a story surface but eager to see the reports of Kennedy's authorization of the surveillances damage the Senator's presidential effort. In the midst of an election campaign, Kennedy himself chose not to explain his role of five years earlier. After Kennedy's own assassination in June, press discussion of the subject ended too.[37]

King's death had not brought an end to the Bureau's efforts to brief government officials on the material it had collected on him during his lifetime. FBI officials also made a number of attempts to interfere with various King memorial efforts. The May, 1968, Drew Pearson story prompted the White House to request all the information the Bureau had on King, and in early June a six-volume collection, including three volumes of transcripts labeled "obscene," was sent to President Johnson's personal secretary, Mildred Stegall. When the Nixon administration took office seven months later, Attorney General Mitchell and President Nixon were provided with detailed Bureau reports on what its investigation of King had uncovered.[38]

The story of the King wiretaps reemerged in the newspapers in June, 1969, when the government disclosed in court that Muhammad Ali, then known as Cassius Clay, whom the government was prosecuting under the Selective Service Act, had once been overheard in 1964 on the King home wiretap. Agent Robert Nichols, who had overseen the Atlanta office's handling of the King and SCLC cases until 1965, was forced to explain in open court just how the boxing champion had been overheard. This renewed disclosure set off a bitter public controversy between former attorneys general Katzenbach and Clark, and Director Hoover, as to who had approved what sorts of electronic surveillance on King, at what times, and for what reasons. The Bureau undertook a less than subtle campaign to paint the deceased Robert Kennedy as the instigator of the electronic surveillance idea. Kennedy's former associates replied forcefully that the initiative had come from the Bureau, and not the Justice Department. The public arguments spent themselves within several weeks. Not until six years later, when the Senate Select Committee on Intelligence Activities, headed by Idaho Democrat Frank Church, attempted a thorough probe of past misdeeds by American intelligence agencies, did public attention return to the Bureau's activities against Dr. King and SCLC.[39]

Neither the 1975–76 Church Committee investigation, nor the House Assassinations Committee probe two and one-half years later, however, provided a complete and accurate public explanation of the Bureau's conduct in the King and SCLC security investigations. Hardly anyone who had acted in the events of 1962–68 wanted the full story made public. People close to King feared a thoroughgoing account would result only in the public besmirching of his character that the Bureau so long and unsuccessfully had sought. The FBI and many others in government wanted to explain neither the story of "Solo" and the inconclusive case against Stanley Levison nor the perverted motives of Division Five officials, which had made the surveillance of Dr. King's private life the major axis of the King case when the investigation was at its peak. Kennedy administration alumni had no desire to explain further their role in and knowledge of the Bureau's electronic activities against King. Former officials of the Johnson White House did not want to admit how much they had known about the Bureau's conduct in the King case and how they themselves had approved the Bureau's dissemination of information on King throughout the government. Only thus have we come so far and so long without the actual story being told.

6

The Radical Challenge of Martin King

The first two phases of the King investigation have been explained by the FBI's preoccupation first with Stanley Levison's past and then with Martin King's personal life. The third and last phase of the King probe was marked by an emphasis upon information about King's political plans. That focus did not emerge until the late summer or fall of 1965.

Some who support this "political-intelligence" thesis contend that the true purpose of the FBI's pursuit of King and SCLC had *always* been to gather information on political strategy and demonstration plans, information that domestic security police obviously would want to obtain. Any ostensible FBI concern with "subversives" or with King's personal life, this argument says, was either a "cover" for or a concommitant of this larger political purpose. Proponents of this view have based their argument more on this presumption about the natural function of domestic security police than upon specific evidence.

Like the "conservatism" argument, the political-intelligence thesis is true, but only in part. As early as the 1962 wiretapping of Stanley Levison, the Bureau was using what it overheard to report King's and SCLC's political plans to the Attorney General and other officials. In May, 1963, the substance of King-Levison conversations about Birmingham was furnished to the Attorney General and apparently the President. Even in 1964, at the height of the obsession with King's private life, Bureau documents still spoke of how the wiretaps on King's home and office were supplying important "intelligence on the racial movement." Furthermore, what could be a clearer example of the use of FBI surveillance for political-intelligence purposes than the activities of DeLoach's "special squad" at the 1964 Democratic National Convention, and the hourly reports that were furnished to the White House?[1]

All of this, of course, can be cited to support the claim that the Bureau principally used the surveillance of King to gather political information useful to a government worried about racial protests and mass demonstrations.[2] The problem, however, is that indications of such a focus before mid or late 1965 are the exception, rather than the rule, in FBI files on King and SCLC. Nothing presents this contrast more sharply than the Atlantic City events. The communications concerning that operation reflect a clear awareness of the strictly political purpose of the undertaking. Those indications are not mirrored in documents dealing with the Bureau's other electronic activities directed against King and his associates, and it is important to remember that the Atlantic City squad was created not at the Bureau's own initiative, but at the specific behest of Lyndon Johnson. As of the fall of 1964, the FBI had only an incidental interest in using its surveillances of King to gather purely political information for the government's own use.

Why did a greater interest in political intelligence not emerge sooner? First, through late 1963 there was an overpowering focus on the activities of Stanley Levison, and indications of a broader orientation to the King case were rare. Indeed, most of the political information that was collected and reported in 1962–63 was used not to learn King's political plans, but to show how great Stanley Levison's influence was on King. The substance usually received less emphasis than the matter of Levison's involvement. Then, from December,

1963, through mid-1965, the heavy emphasis was on collecting and disseminating material that could be used to "discredit" or "expose" King. Since political information did not suit this purpose, it received low priority. The personal material was paramount.

Throughout 1965 there was a gradual but noticeable decline in the Bureau's animus toward King. File references to the importance of "destroying" him as a public figure decreased sharply. As this occurred, the Bureau essentially had a major investigation that lacked clear purpose. True, an interest remained in identifying supposed "subversives" around SCLC, and in King's personal conduct, but both were greatly reduced from what they once had been. The political emphasis emerged gradually and without any apparent conscious decision to turn the investigation in that direction.[3] It first appeared when King's comments about Vietnam received national press attention in August, 1965. It reemerged in more limited fashion when SCLC began groundwork for its Chicago project in the fall of 1965. Division Five's headquarters supervisors indicated an interest in SCLC's Chicago plans that they had not had for previous SCLC demonstration campaigns in Birmingham, Saint Augustine, and Selma. That interest apparently was grounded not in anything new or unique about the Chicago campaign, but in the fact that there simply was not much else to write reports about. The poor quality of the information from the Chicago field office inhibited the development of even this focus, however.

The lack of substance in the King and SCLC investigations by 1966 led some field agents handling the cases, especially in Atlanta, to believe that the FBI might best turn its attention elsewhere. They kept such views to themselves,[4] however, and even though Division Five made no objection to terminating the SCLC office wiretaps, there was no indication that anyone at headquarters ever considered ending the King and SCLC probes.

To reduce one's own case load voluntarily was a phenomenon rarely witnessed in the statistic-conscious FBI, but a stronger reason for going forward was the presence of Jim Harrison. Harrison was able to supply useful information to the Bureau at a fraction of the cost and effort needed to acquire material from wiretaps. Harrison also was intelligent enough so that his statements about SCLC plans and activities were better informed than the conclusions that could be drawn from dozens of brief summaries of intercepted phone conversations.

Despite even the usefulness of Harrison, the Bureau's investigation of King and SCLC was strikingly quiet from the summer of 1966 through February, 1967. Perhaps it would have remained so had not King decided to speak out strongly against America's involvement in Vietnam. That decision, evidenced first in the late February speech in Los Angeles, and then in the much more widely publicized one of April 4 in Manhattan's Riverside Church, brought about a renewed intensification of FBI and White House interest in King, his advisers, and his political plans.[5] That interest remained acute through the summer of 1967, and it intensified further late that year when the Bureau learned of King's plan to conduct the 1968 Poor People's Campaign.

The FBI's response to both the Vietnam issue and the Poor People's Campaign can be cited to support the argument that after late 1965, and especially after early 1967, the Bureau's interest in King was grounded purely in political-intelligence concerns.

The Bureau was quite aware of how hostile the Johnson White House was toward King. Johnson's particular fear about King's position on the war made him extremely eager for reports on King's political plans, and especially on the possibility that King might run as an independent antiwar presidential candidate in 1968.

Word of the Poor People's Campaign rang another alarm bell at the White House. It also touched a sensitive nerve at FBI headquarters, where supervisors were especially interested in anything that portended urban strife. The late 1967 request for renewed wiretaps on SCLC explicitly stated that the purpose of the surveillance was "to obtain racial intelligence information concerning their plans." Further developments early in 1968 heightened the Bureau's fear of urban disorders, fears most starkly revealed in the early March order warning of a "true black revolution" and intensifying the "Black Nationalist Hate Group" COINTELPRO. FBI headquarter's response to the March 28 "riot" in Memphis was merely one reflection of this broader fear. It was a fear not simply of urban violence per se but of developments in the American black community that the Bureau knew it did not understand.[6]

This evidence of the Bureau's fears and of its responsiveness to the White House's worries is striking. It gives strong and convincing support to the argument that the Bureau's activities against King and SCLC in 1967–68 were based on concern about King's political plans and a desire to know as much as possible about those plans.

In the last twelve months of his life King represented a far greater political threat to the reigning American government than he ever had before. An intensified FBI interest in his political activities was perfectly in keeping with that development. As the fortress mentality of the Johnson White House continued to increase, the FBI's heightened sensitivity to political dissent aimed at the policies of the Johnson administration went hand in hand.

The three successive phases of the FBI's pursuit of King and SCLC thus are accounted for by three seemingly distinct explanations: "communism," "personal conduct," and "political intelligence." However, there is a broader viewpoint that ties all three of these narrower perspectives together and reveals underlying themes they all share.

This broader viewpoint, the "cultural-threat" argument, asserts that certain crucial common themes appear in the Bureau's drastic concern about Stanley Levison, in its obsession with Dr. King's private life, and in the marked fears of King as a pronounced political threat in 1967–68. Each of these three themes from the King case connects with parallel strands of the "cultural-threat" argument that has been suggested by several previous writers. While other arguments about the Bureau's behavior presume that the FBI has been either the instrument of a few particularly influential individuals, or an institution whose functioning largely was the product of certain principles of organizational structure, this perspective focuses on *culture* rather than people or organization, and on how the Bureau actually was more a reflection of American beliefs and society than it was either the product of idiosyncratic individuals or a unique institutional structure.

This cultural-threat thesis has its intellectual roots in Richard Hofstadter's pioneering essay on the importance of the "Paranoid Style in American Politics," and has been applied to the FBI in particular by Frank J. Donner.[7] It argues that the FBI long has been an official representative of just such a "paranoid style," and that the essence of the Bureau's social role has been not to attack critics, Communists, blacks, or leftists per se, but to repress all perceived threats to the dominant, status-quo-oriented political culture. This argument thus appropriates many of the valuable aspects and contributions of previous hypotheses that by themselves are incomplete or overly simplistic. It also makes the powerful and persuasive point that the Bureau was not a deviant institution in American society, but actually a most representative and faithful one.

"Throughout virtually all of Hoover's administration," James Q. Wilson has remarked, "the mission of the FBI was fully consistent with public expectations, beliefs, and values."[8] Though nowadays most reformers would prefer to ignore that point, the cultural perspective argues that the enemies chosen by the FBI were the same targets that much of American society would have selected as its own foes. American popular thought long has had strong themes of nativism, xenophobia, and ethnocentrism. These very same qualities were writ large in the FBI.[9]

Such a conclusion allows for a far more meaningful understanding of the attitudes that the Bureau displayed toward a whole host of groups and individuals. Fear of secret, subversive conspiracies always has played a major role in such paranoid American thought, and the FBI's long-standing obsession with domestic communism was but one reflection of the widespread popular preoccupation with this same xenophobic fear. Anything that appeared foreign or strange to the dominant culture of which the Bureau was so true a reflection thus became the recipient of a hostility that was societal as well as institutional, and this deep-seated fear of those who were distinctly different in any of a number of ways is the common thread that connects the three narrower explanations offered for the distinct phases of the King probe.

Each of the three major themes of the King case connects with a parallel portion of the cultural-threat perspective articulated by Hofstadter and Donner. First, even though the FBI's concern about Levison did have some basis in fact, the Bureau jumped to the conclusion that anyone who had once had close and unrenounced ties to the Communist party must of course be functioning at its behest nearly ten years later. This eagerness to label Levison a Soviet agent even in the early 1960s is but one reflection of the widespread American tendency to see evil conspiracies virtually everywhere. As Hofstadter described this style of thought, its "central preconception

. . . [is] the existence of a vast, insidious, preternaturally effective international conspiratorial network designed to perpetrate acts of the most fiendish character."[10] The conspirators always were thought to be adherents to some foreign, sacrilegious ideology, and to be "strangers" in other ways as well. Communism was far from the first villain in American history to produce this response, and essentially the same dynamics of reaction can be witnessed in the Salem witchcraft trials of the 1690s or the nativist fear of immigration in the nineteenth and early twentieth centuries.[11]

The FBI's exaggerated stance toward communism was a perfect example of exactly this style, as Frank J. Donner in particular has argued. When applied to notable instances of mass domestic dissent, such as the civil rights movement, the paranoid style has been quick to explain the eruption of dissent not by reference to economic or social causes, but by reference to some "outside agitator," identified or unidentified, who is stirring up the happy natives who otherwise would be perfectly satisfied with their lot.[12] This pattern of recourse to the evil, conspiratorial outsider, usually tagged a "Communist," is visible, indeed often pronounced, in local white response to civil rights campaigns from Montgomery in 1956 to Memphis in 1968. It also is reflected in the FBI's eagerness to view Stanley Levison as the malevolent Soviet puppeteer standing secretly behind the entire American civil rights movement.

Another facet of the paranoid style's reaction to the challenge of widespread dissent is a strong tendency to see the challengers not simply as evil foreign puppets but also as immoral, sensually obsessed individuals. As Hofstadter noted, the strange opponent always is perceived as "a perfect model of malice, a kind of amoral superman: sinister, uniquitous, powerful, cruel, sensual, luxury-loving."[13] Again, Hofstadter's observation is a striking description of the Bureau's stance in the King investigation, this time in regard to the second phase, the obsession with King's personal life. Not only was it the case, as in the first phase, that the civil rights movement might be heavily influenced by the goals of a hostile foreign power, but the domestic leaders who were the supposed tools of that international conspiracy were viewed, as the FBI perceived King, as carnally consumed beings. Donner too has noted this, observing how the Bureau "perceived black leaders," and especially King, "as corrupt, criminal, oversexed demagogues who had to be destroyed and replaced by 'respectable' figures who alone could be trusted to lead the ignorant blacks.'' Especially in cases where black people were involved, and visibly so in many COINTELPRO poison-pen letters to black people, themes of sexual misconduct or overindulgence regularly were voiced by the men of Division Five.[14]

The third major strand of the cultural-threat perspective is how the paranoid style fears political change just as much as it is obsessed with foreign agents and notions of the enemy's immoral nature. With reference to the FBI's reaction to the civil rights movement, and especially to King in 1967–68, this third portion of the paranoid-style argument stresses how the Bureau was an institutional opponent of political change and those who embodied it. William Sullivan conceded this point to his interrogators in the mid-1970s, admitting that Director Hoover and most of the Bureau were "opposed to *change* in the social order."[15] This truth was appreciated by some Church Committee staff members, and was utilized with telling effect in the analysis of the FBI's COINTEL efforts of the late 1960s. "The unexpressed major premise of the programs," one report concluded, "was that a law enforcement agency has the duty to do whatever is necessary to combat perceived threats to the existing social and political order."[16] Though the committee did not explicitly note it, this same cast of mind lay behind the Bureau's fear of King in 1967–68 as well as behind the "Black Nationalist" and "New Left" COINTELPROs.

These three strands of the paranoid-style argument, and the three apparently separate themes or phases of the FBI's behavior in the King case, come together to form a wider understanding not only of the conduct of the Bureau itself but of how the Bureau accurately represented many of the major beliefs and fears of American society.[17] Nowhere was this meshing of the strands clearer than in Division Five's 1964 instructions to Bureau field offices that events necessitated a new and more inclusive definition of the Communist threat. Coupled with that new definition was a warning that "we are in the midst of a social revolution with the racial movement as its core." Three years later, when King gave his first 1967 speech attacking America's involvement in Vietnam, Division Five warned its superiors that King's stance was "revolutionary."[18]

What was foreign, unknown, and hence frightening to the FBI was not simply the supposed ties of Stanley Levison, nor the uninhibited nature of King's personal life, nor vocal opposition to the basic policies of the American government. All three of these themes represented a challenge to the established social order that the FBI believed in and faithfully represented. Within the Bureau "Communism" came increasingly to be not a label for any specific organizations or adherence to a certain doctrine, but simply a catchall term of opprobrium to be applied to anyone whose political beliefs and cultural values were at odds with those of mainstream America and the men of the FBI. It was not simply that Stanley Levison excited the paranoid fears of foreign-dominated conspiracies, or that King's opposition to the Vietnam War made him a "traitor,"[19] but that some of his personal conduct represented just as much a challenge to the cultural traditions exemplified by the FBI as did his political stance in the last years of his life. As Frank Donner has written, "the selection of a target embodies a judgment of deviance from the dominant political culture," and that conclusion is borne out not simply by the final phase of the Bureau's activities against Dr. King but by all three of them.[20]

All three strands come together in this question of what Hofstadter termed "ultimate schemes of values."[21] The Bureau's conduct toward King, towards the civil rights movement, and toward a host of people identified with the "Left" in the 1960s is best understood in terms of this conflict of cultural values. This broad analysis is more telling than emphasis on either idiosyncratic individuals such as Hoover and Sullivan or on the organizational behavior of the FBI as an institution. The individuals themselves are best viewed as representatives of that native American culture, and the Bureau itself expressed in its conduct not the self-interested behavior of a rational organization—the activities against King certainly were not "rational" in terms of protecting the FBI—but the underlying attitude of much of American society toward the threat that King and the movement represented. Coretta Scott King later remarked that it seemed in retrospect that "the FBI treated the civil rights movement as if it were an alien enemy attack on the United States." Her comment was right on the mark.[22] The Bureau functioned not simply as a weapon of one disturbed man, not as an institution protecting its own organizational interests, but as the representative, and at times rather irrational representative, of American cultural values that found much about King and the sixties' movements to be frightening and repugnant. The FBI's primary role was to serve as a "relentless guardian" of "acceptable political and cultural values," and to protect and maintain "the existing social order" against those who appeared "to threaten that order." The Bureau was not a renegade institution secretly operating outside the parameters of American values, but a virtually representative bureaucracy that loyally served "to protect the established order against adversary challenges."[23]

Such an analysis of the most important meanings of the Bureau's stance toward Martin Luther King, Jr., does not infer the quite different point that the FBI's hostility toward him was, from its point of view, misdirected or misconceived. Any conclusion that the Bureau's antipathy toward him was thoroughly wrongheaded carries with it the erroneous presumption that King was not so much a threatening challenge to the central values of American society as he was an embodiment of the ideals for which the country always had stood. After his assassination King unfortunately came to be viewed by many people as a thoroughly successful American reformer whose triumph affirmed the myth of American society as both essentially good and increasingly perfectible. In truth Martin King was much more a radical threat than a reassuring reformer. It is ironic that the FBI adopted that view far more readily than did many others.[24]

The FBI's still "Top Secret" quotation of King saying "I am a Marxist" probably would be discounted by most observers as something King could never have said. Actually, however, such a statement would not have been surprising, for King made mention of his distaste for the American economic order to many friends, even in the 1950s.[25] In a divinity school term paper in 1950–51 King spoke of "my present anti-capitalistic feelings,"[26] and he reiterated this theme in several sermons in 1956 and 1957, if not earlier. King's intellectual style was heavily influenced by a rather basic appreciation of the Hegelian dialectic, and as a result he tended to view alternatives as antitheses from which he should create a middle way. That was precisely how he initially handled the thesis of capitalism and the antithesis of communism, and in public remarks he had strong criticisms of both.[27] In private, however, he made it clear to close friends that economically speaking he considered himself what he termed a Marxist, largely because he believed with increasing strength that American society needed a radical redistribution of wealth and economic power to achieve even a rough form of social justice.

As the years passed King increasingly recognized just how extensive and thoroughgoing this change would have to be. In part he was influenced by the realization that purely idealistic and moral appeals to southern white business to support desegregation did not work, while boycotts and protests, which reduced business volume and profits, triggered quick, positive responses.[28] By 1967 King was telling the SCLC staff, "We must recognize that we can't solve our problem now until there is a radical redistribution of economic and political power," and by early 1968 he had taken the final step to the admission that issues of economic class were more crucial and troublesome, and less susceptible to change, than issues of race. "America," he remarked to one interviewer, "is deeply racist and its democracy is flawed both economically and socially." He added that "the black revolution is much more than a struggle for the rights of Negroes. It is forcing America to face all its interrelated flaws—racism, poverty, militarism, and materialism. It is exposing evils that are rooted deeply in the whole structure of our society. It reveals systemic rather than superficial flaws and suggests that radical reconstruction of society itself is the real issue to be faced."

King himself was fully conscious of his journey from reformer to revolutionary. "For the last twelve years," he remarked to the SCLC staff in 1967, "we have been in a reform movement. . . . But after Selma and the voting rights bill [in 1965] we moved into a new era, which must be an era of revolution. I think we must see the great distinction here between a reform movement and a revolutionary movement." The latter would "raise certain basic questions about the whole society. . . . this means a revolution of values and of other things," reaching far beyond the question of race. "The whole structure of American life must be changed," King emphasized, and by early 1968 he publicly was stating, "We are engaged in the class struggle." While his emphasis was not purely materialistic, redistribution of economic power was the central requirement. To one audience King stated, "We're dealing in a sense with class issues, we're dealing with the problem of the gulf between the haves and the have-nots."[29]

This radical and revolutionary vision of King's last years was coupled with a profound change in his view of human nature. Twelve years earlier, at the beginning in Montgomery, King had been a faithful believer in the optimistic notions of human perfectibility propounded by the "social-gospel" theologians whose works he had read during his own religious education.[30] The experiences of the 1960s had taught him that that optimism was unjustified, and that appeals based on persuasion were less effective with reluctant whites that a painful boycott or disruptive street demonstrations. He came increasingly to see the need for political realism and the coercive use of practical power that had been most convincingly set forth as a social philosophy by Reinhold Niebuhr.[31] This shift was reflected in King's changing tactics; it also was revealed by his increasingly radical goals, such as his aspirations for the Poor People's Campaign and his vocal attacks on the American imperialism and militarism manifested by the expanding conflict in Vietnam. At his death King's optimism had been wholly erased. Many who were close to him sensed a profound sadness that had not been present in earlier years. Though even in 1968 King retained a sense of hope that was rooted in his own strong religious faith, his view of man and society was light years different from what it had been a decade or more earlier. As he remarked to an aide less than a week before his death, "Truly America is much, much sicker, Hosea, than I realized when I first began working in 1955."[32]

King's evolution from reformer to revolutionary, from tactics of persuasion to those of coercion, and from optimism to realism was accompanied by an increasingly sophisticated view of himself as a public figure and private man. By 1965 King was aware, as one person articulated it, that "the ability to control his own life had been taken away from him." He told a friend, "I am conscious of two Martin Luther Kings. I am a wonder to myself," and he was greatly troubled by the fame and attention that came to him. Not only was he upset that his position weighed him down with responsibilities and tasks that unrelentingly consumed the great majority of his time, but he was concerned that the Martin Luther King most people knew as a symbol bore little resemblance to his own image of himself. He told one old friend, who recalled it several years later, "I am mystified at my own career. The Martin Luther King that the people talk about seems to be somebody foreign to me." There was, King said, "a kind of dualism in my life," and, the friend recalled, King always said "that that Martin Luther King the famous man was a kind of stranger to him."[33]

King's pronounced ambivalence about his fame and symbolic role led him to agonize over his position much more often than he enjoyed or reveled in it. He frequently thought that he had not done enough to deserve the great acclaim that showered down on him. These doubts made King his own harshest critic. His private questioning of himself, of his motives, and of his political wisdom was never-ending. His penchant for self-criticism often was heartrending for his friends and associates to witness. Stanley Levison saw more of it than most people. "Martin," Stanley explained in 1969,

> could be described as an intensely guilt-ridden man. The most essential element in the feelings of guilt that he had was that he didn't feel he deserved the kind of tribute that he got. [He believed] that he was an actor in history at a particular moment that called for a personality, and he had simply been selected as that personality . . . but he had not done enough to deserve it. He felt keenly that people who had done as much as he had or *more* got no such tribute. This troubled him deeply, and he could find no way of dealing with it because there's no way of sharing that kind of tribute with anyone else—you can't give it away; you have to accept it. But when you don't feel you're worthy of it and you're an honest, principled man, it tortures you. And it could be said that he was tortured by the great appreciation that the public showed for him. If he had been less humble, he could have lived with this kind of acclaim, but because he was genuinely a man of humility, he really couldn't live with it. He always thought of ways in which he could somehow live up to it, and he often talked about

taking a vow of poverty—getting rid of everything he
owned, including his house, so that he could at least feel
that nothing material came to him from his efforts. . . .
The house troubled him greatly. When he moved from a
very small house to one that was large enough to give the
growing family some room, he was troubled by it and
would ask all of his close friends when they came to the
house whether they didn't think it was too big and it wasn't
right for him to have. And though everyone tried to tell
him that this big house wasn't as big as he thought it was—
it was a very modest little house—to him it loomed as a
mansion and he searched in his own mind for ways of making it smaller. . . . Martin found it very difficult to live
comfortably because he had such a sensitive conscience
and such a sense of humility. . . . Martin was always very
aware that he was privileged. . . . and this troubled him.
He felt he didn't deserve this. One of the reasons that he
was so determined to be of service was to justify the privileged position he'd been born into. . . . [He felt] he had
never deserved and earned what he had, and now he didn't
deserve nor had he earned in his own mind the acclaim that
he was receiving. It was a continual series of blows to his
conscience, and this kept him a very restive man all his
life.[34]

That restiveness and self-criticism grew more pronounced in the last
two years of King's life. The evolution of his own political views,
and the increased public criticism of him that followed from it, and
especially from his outspokenness on Vietnam, made both King's
efforts in the public struggle and his private self-examination even
more intense. The frenetic pace of his life increased even further in
the final months as he strove to make the Poor People's Campaign
an effort that would have a dramatic impact even though the sheen
of the civil rights movement was largely gone. His inner tension
increased dramatically. He smoked more, drank more, and slept
less. Sleep, and the sense of aloneness and repose that went with it,
became especially difficult. Almost everyone who knew him well

had vivid experiences where King would sit up talking, arguing, and drinking until nearly dawn, seemingly unable to break away from the companionship of conversation.[35]

The increased anguish manifested itself in many of his public remarks as well. In the last year and one-half of King's life a good number of his sermons ended with a refrain that articulated his deepest sentiments. God, he stated, would not desert one even if everything was going badly, even if criticism was coming from all sides, and even if hope for a better future had grown very dim. One must hold on to some amount of faith, for "He promised never to leave me, never to leave me alone, no, never alone, no, never alone. He promised never to leave me, never to leave me alone."[36]

The endless self-examination that so struck Stanley Levison grew even stronger in King's last months, as he came to as relentlessly frank and realistic an appraisal of himself as he did of American society and the basic tenets of human nature. He became as unremitting in his criticism of himself as he was of the American economic system and America's conduct in Vietnam, and certainly the knowledge that the FBI appeared to be watching his every action increased the intensity of that self-criticism, just as it had in the very painful and anguished days of January, 1965, following receipt of the anonymous tape.[37] On many occasions the belief that the government was sparing no effort to surveil him made King even more determined to pursue his own personal freedom without inhibition. He often would joke with his colleagues about how any chance remark might be immortalized by one of the Bureau's hidden recorders.[38] The determination not to be inhibited or intimidated was only part of King's response, however. The constant reminders that others were standing by to judge him contributed noticeably to the harshness with which King judged himself in his own most reflective moments. The relentless self-analysis came through with striking clarity in many of his sermons, as he returned again and again to the theme that all people are sinners, that everyone's inner self is a mixture of the admirable and the unpleasant. He noted repeatedly that "there is some good in the worst of us and some evil in the best of us," and that there is a "strange mixture in human nature." He told his congregation at Ebenezer Baptist Church that "each of us is two selves. And the great burden of life is to always try to keep that higher self in command. Don't let the lower self take over. . . . every now and then you'll be unfaithful to those that you should be faithful to. It's a mixture in human nature. . . . Because we are two selves, there is a civil war going on within each of us." To admit that one is a sinner is to avoid the far worse fault of being a hypocrite, and Martin King emphasized that to confess that to oneself and one's God was the important challenge. "God's unbroken hold on us is something that will never permit us to feel right when we do wrong, or to feel natural when we do the unnatural," King told his Ebenezer listeners in a sermon he entitled, "Who Are We?" "God has planted within us certain eternal principles, and the more we try to get away from them the more frustrated we will be."[39]

Four weeks before his death King summed up those themes of the last year of his life in a sermon at Ebenezer. Speaking of his life and his disappointments, he said, "We are constantly trying to finish that which is unfinishable. We are commanded to do that, and so we . . . find ourselves in so many instances having to face the facts that our dreams are not fulfilled." Life, he said, "is a continual story of shattered dreams," but one must strive always to hold that dream in one's heart. "There is a schizophrenia . . . within all of us. There are times that all of us know somehow that there is a Mr. Hyde and a Dr. Jekyl in us." Even that truth should not cause one to lose faith, however, for "God does not judge us by the separate incidents or the separate mistakes that we make, but by the total bent of our lives. . . . You don't need to go out this morning saying that Martin Luther King is a saint, oh no; I want you to know this morning that I am a sinner like all of God's children, but I want to be a good man, and I want to hear a voice saying to me one day, 'I take you in and I bless you because you tried. It was well that it was within thy heart.' " The final and essential question, as he had said into that endless phone line that agonizing day three years earlier, "is only between me and my God."[40]

Afterword: "Reforming" the FBI

The last six years have seen a wealth of revelations concerning FBI activities against a myriad of individuals and organizations. They also have seen an extensive effort to reform the FBI, and initial attempts to find some mechanism that will guarantee that never again will the FBI behave as it did in the 1960s and early 1970s. These revelations and reform efforts have drawn unprecedented critical attention to the FBI. This heightened attention, and a visible change in the Bureau's leadership, have reassured many observers that the FBI cannot ever again become a dangerous enemy of the people and principles it was established to protect.

This process of the last half-dozen years, however, has been both incomplete and misleading. The shortcomings and attendant dangers of this reform period fall generally into two categories. First, most discussions of the FBI's past misdeeds have generated more heat than light. Very little effort has been devoted to explaining *why* such offenses occurred; instead most energy has been used to display the "dirty laundry," piece by infinite piece, to rail against each stain

220

and tear. This has been true on all fronts, from press reports of FBI misdeeds and investigations into them, to those government investigating bodies themselves and the academic specialists who have worked for them. Neither the reports produced by these congressional committees of inquiry, nor the subsequent studies authored by academics, have gone beyond description and denunciation of the misdeeds to offer systematic explanations of *why* they occurred. As a reviewer remarked about one such study, it, like all the others, was "long on 'horror stories' and short on analysis."[1]

This "dirty-laundry" school of description and denunciation often has based its accounts on a presumption that such horrors occurred largely because of the idiosyncratic presence and prejudices of one man. As one former official articulated this belief, "the nub of the problems . . . [was] the historical accident of J. Edgar Hoover."[2] This theme has been attractive to many and reassuring to virtually all. Though Hoover's personal influence on FBI conduct was substantial, most accounts of FBI activities have gone too far in seeking to demonstrate that the entire fault for virtually every Bureau misdeed can be placed directly in Hoover's lap.[3] This theme appeals to those who experienced several decades of remarkable propaganda designed to show that J. Edgar Hoover *was* the FBI. Popular belief in this image made for extremely fertile ground when the time for finding fault and attributing responsibility finally came. The belief that all offenses could be assigned to the deceased Hoover also was attractive to FBI officials who survived the Director and were called to account for their own conduct. Many said they had only done what Hoover had ordered them to do. All the important decisions, they asserted, had been made by the "old man" himself. Usually these excuses saved the former subordinates from any further searching inquiries from the investigators.[4]

The focus of all blame upon the person of Hoover had strong appeal in a time eager for reform. Hoover was gone, if not forgotten, and answering the pressing question of how to prevent future FBI misconduct was much easier if "avoiding another Hoover" could serve as a large part of the response. The inclination to see an institution as little more than a large-scale reflection of the image of its leader has always been strong in America, and this "personalization" of both the organization and explanations for its behavior was notably true for the FBI and Director Hoover. The installation of so moderate and mild a figure as former federal appellate judge William H. Webster as FBI director in 1978 thus was immensely reassuring for a society that viewed the Bureau through the image of its director. If the emotional and intolerant Hoover had been the problem, then surely the calm and quiet Webster with his judicial mien and experience was the solution.

The second category of deficiencies in this time of reform shares with the first type an interest in questions of legality. One emphasis of the ''dirty-laundry'' school has been depicting precisely how certain FBI actions violated presidential orders, congressional statutes, Supreme Court decisions, constitutional guarantees, or natural law principles.[5] Such a showing generally has been the bench mark for including FBI misdeeds in the ''dirty-laundry'' exhibitions. This interest in precise questions of law has been shared by a second group of interested observers, whose major preoccupation has been not denunciation but what is best termed ''formal legal'' reform. Though having no more awareness of the need for explanation than the ''dirty-laundry'' school, these erstwhile constitutionalists, unconsciously patterning themselves after an earlier and now much abused generation of American political scholars,[6] have devoted their energies to a struggle to enact into federal law a ''charter'' for the FBI. The charter would specify with some precision just what the Bureau can and cannot do, and who will be assigned to keep watch over the Bureau's activities.

While many of the specialists in denunciation have assumed that a change in the person of the director will prevent any possibility of a repetition of the past, the ''formal legal'' reformers have acted on the belief that passing a new law and implementing the oversight provisions likewise will ensure a safe future. The legalists have become absorbed in an ongoing debate over exactly what the much-heralded charter should contain. Should it allow the Bureau considerable leeway in determining for itself what techniques and procedures are appropriate for different types of intelligence investigations, or should such freedom be heavily restricted by congressional order or Justice Department review?[7] By pursuing the issue in this way, the legalists have largely determined the framework of all present-day discourse about the FBI. They have drawn into the charter debate many of the observers who several years ago were full-fledged members of the "dirty-laundry" school of denunciation. This has resulted in a situation where the left,[8] the center,[9] and the right[10] are all represented in this increasingly ideological debate over how much independence, a little or a lot, the Bureau should be allowed. While the leftist participants argue that the FBI remains a serious threat to Americans' liberties, the conservatives assert that a rising tide of domestic and international terrorism requires that the Bureau be allowed extensive flexibility to meet that challenge.

No position yet has triumphed, since no charter has been enacted into law as of early 1981. The focus of this debate, however, just like the other focus on description and denunciation, has distracted everyone from asking *why* the FBI has behaved as it did in the past. Neither school realizes that intelligent discussion of how to delimit future FBI conduct can take place only after we understand *why* the FBI acted as it did in past times. A presumption that either a new director or a new statute alone will solve the problems is naïve and dangerous.

Public discourse about the FBI has been of poor quality largely because academic and public knowledge of the Bureau is severely limited. One can search almost in vain for serious and well-researched works, even articles, that convey any new or useful information about the internal practices and policies of the FBI. While intelligent studies of other executive agencies such as the Office of Management and Budget appear by the cartload, academic curiosity about the FBI appears almost nil, and this at a time when studies of bureaucratic procedure and organizational behavior are multiplying rapidly in American social science. So little information is publicly available about the Bureau that any effort to examine it from this now well developed academic perspective is almost certainly destined to be unproductive.[11] Two works, however, are valuable. One is a pioneering study of FBI criminal, rather than intelligence, investigations by James Q. Wilson.[12] The second is an insightful but unpublished analysis of the U.S. Army's surveillance of American domestic politics in the 1960s by former army intelligence officer

Christopher H. Pyle.[13] Each supply some insight into how an organizational analysis of so unique a bureaucracy as the FBI should be conducted when the attempt becomes possible.

The two central concepts that should be employed in an examination of the Bureau are "autonomy" and "homogeneity." Autonomy is the degree of independence that an organization has from its formal superiors and from other influential actors in its political environment. Throughout the Hoover era the FBI enjoyed an unparalleled degree of autonomy from both its nominal superiors, the attorney general and president, and from the relevant committees of Congress. This was of paramount importance, for as Wilson has noted, "it is the desire for autonomy, and not for large budgets, new powers, or additional employees, that is the dominant motive of public executives." Director Hoover was a striking example of this principle. Many FBI actions that would appear puzzling from other perspectives, such as the constant *opposition* to proposals that would have expanded the Bureau's powers and jurisdiction, make perfect sense when viewed in this light.[14] Hoover sought with consistent success to maximize the autonomy of the FBI, and it was this pursuit that produced a situation where external controls or checks on the Bureau were virtually nonexistent.

Some participants in the debate of the last six years about the future of the FBI have realized the crucial importance of autonomy, and have sought, as part of the reform efforts, to greatly curtail the independence of the Bureau. Thanks in large part to the initiatives of Attorney General Edward H. Levi in 1975 and 1976, FBI headquarters today possesses only a small fraction of the autonomy from its parent body, the Department of Justice, that it did less than a decade ago. Furthermore, attempts also have been undertaken to *increase* the once almost nonexistent degree of autonomy that FBI field offices have from the detailed commands of headquarters. Arguments can be made for and against this latter development, but most well informed observers of the Bureau have judged the change desirable, largely because it reduces the power of well-insulated supervisors in Washington.

Despite this nascent change, the Bureau remains perhaps the most centrally controlled and rigidly hierarchical organization in the federal government.[15] The difficult challenge that repeatedly will confront anyone seeking to control the Bureau is the rational and inevitable desire of any organization's executives to maximize their institution's autonomy. Hoover demonstrated this in the past and present-day Bureau opposition to a strict charter also reflects it. Controlling the FBI requires that its future autonomy be strictly minimized; the Bureau itself, however, always will seek to raise that level at least incrementally. The innate dynamics of this contraposition will continue unchanged no matter what formal statute if any is enacted to prescribe the processes that FBI domestic intelligence investigations should follow.

If there is no simple fix for the problem of controlling a police agency's autonomy, there also is no simple answer to the other great weakness that helped make the FBI what it became, a weakness that remains a serious problem today—that of homogeneity. If some reformers have recognized the pressing need to reduce drastically the FBI's autonomy, almost none have understood that the FBI has a problem with people as well as with structure. The Bureau was long composed of a strikingly narrow breed of men. This has been noted by a number of observers,[16] but no one has appreciated its importance in discussing FBI reform. Not only did the Bureau recruit mostly white men with small-town backgrounds, parochial educations, and strongly conservative political views, but the socialization new agents underwent in the Bureau strongly inculcated or reinforced just such views and orientations.

Such a procedure comes just as naturally to organization executives as does the urge to maximize autonomy. As Anthony Downs has pointed out, the most effective and cheapest way to create an organization staffed with obedient subordinates is to hire only people whose traits and beliefs mirror those of the superiors. Additionally, "If recruiting is done only at the lowest levels," which is the case with the FBI, "all top officials have to work themselves upward through the hierarchy, presumably by repeatedly pleasing their superiors. Superiors usually approve of continuous development of their policies, rather than sharp breaks with tradition. Therefore, the screening process of upward movement tends to reject radicals and elevate a relatively homogeneous group."[17]

This is precisely what occurred within the FBI. Bureau headquarters was dominated by just such a homogeneous clique, and "that clique,'' as one former assistant director has described it, ''was very selective in trying to keep its own . . . handpicked men in positions of influence in the FBI.''[18] This was particularly true of FBI Division Five, domestic intelligence, which initiated almost all of the Bureau's most harshly criticized activities. Looking back at that headquarters group several years later, William C. Sullivan, former head of the domestic intelligence division, observed, ''We were sealed off from the outside world and the experiences and thinking of others . . . and we remained relatively so and steadily became inbred.''[19]

After the revelations of the mid-1970s came a new rule requiring all FBI agents to leave the Bureau by age fifty-five. The senior men of the Hoover era departed. This turnover was so great that some Bureau executives feared the damage of a ''brain drain.'' Most observers, however, were happy and reassured that the most venerable agents of the old Bureau were gone, like the Director himself. Perhaps it was this perception that accounted for the seemingly total disinterest in Bureau recruitment and personnel policies among the reform advocates of the 1970s. Perhaps the Bureau's public relations emphasis on efforts to recruit women and minority applicants contributed to this quiescence, and no doubt there was some truth to the statements of Bureau executives that the FBI of the 1970s was attracting different and more varied people than the FBI of previous decades.[20]

In any case, this laissez faire attitude toward Bureau personnel practices is both inexcusable and dangerous. We know very little about FBI personnel matters, but what we do know is not reassuring, and gives no grounds for the complacency reformers have exhibited. James Q. Wilson, perhaps the academic observer most knowledgeable about the present-day FBI, wrote in 1978: ''A large part—an estimated 60 percent—of the new agents now come from the military where they have served as officers, often in investigative, security, or counterintelligence work. Three years of appropriate military service will count toward meeting the requirement for postgraduate training or legal/accounting experience. Such recruits have already become familiar with, and even happy with, strict hierarchical controls.''[21]

If a lessening of the Bureau's internal homogeneity is just as crucial to a meaningful reform effort as is a reduction in its external autonomy, present-day practices do not have the FBI headed in the right direction. Pyle's well-informed study of army domestic surveillance in the 1960s contains a particularly important lesson. Army intelligence was then made up heavily of men who were not careerists and who did not share the beliefs and orientations of their superiors. This diversity acted as a major internal brake on how eagerly army intelligence units pursued the desires of their narrow-minded commanders. These "outsiders" also accounted for the public disclosure of the army's misdeeds several years before those of the other, more career-oriented intelligence agencies appeared in the press.[22]

If composition is a serious problem with the present-day FBI, certain practices that heavily influence agents' incentives within the Bureau make matters even worse. Internal dissent remains an extremely risky option in an organization where agents have no civil-service protection and where disciplinary procedures are harsh.[23] Furthermore, the Bureau's extremely remunerative pension plan, which requires a minimum twenty years of service, supplies a powerful disincentive to any action that might propel one out of the organization too early. Many Bureau veterans will testify in private that the prospect of that pension induced them to remain quiet at moments when they might have spoken out.

One hopes that the reform debate will reorient itself and confront these difficult questions of autonomy and homogeneity. The "paranoid style" became so rampant within the FBI largely because the Bureau's autonomy and homogeneity each were so unrestrained. There must be an intensified effort to increase public knowledge of the Bureau's internal practices. These endeavors must be accompanied by a new realization of the pressing need for *explanation* of the Bureau's behavior. Description, denunciation, and prescription all give reform advocates and congressional staffers a warm feeling of relevance. But the important question is still why. Until the "why?" of the Bureau's past abuses is addressed, the reform debate will remain an exercise in legal formalism that is both misleadingly reassuring and, in the long run, downright dangerous. If this book stimulates others to take up these crucial questions, then it will assist in improving our future as well as in better understanding our recent past.

Notes

Preface

1. See particularly U.S., Congress, Senate, Select Committee to Study Governmental Operations with Respect to Intelligence Activities, *Final Report—Book III, Supplementary Detailed Staff Reports on Intelligence Activities and the Rights of Americans,* 94th Cong., 2d sess., 1976; and Senate Select Committee, *Hearings—Federal Bureau of Investigation,* 94th Cong., 1st sess., 1976, vol. 6.

2. See particularly U.S., Congress, House, Select Committee on Assassinations, *Hearings on Investigation of the Assassination of Martin Luther King, Jr.,* 95th Cong., 2d sess., 1978, vols. 1, 6, 7; and *The Final Assassinations Report* (New York: Bantam Books, 1979).

3. Suggestions that the FBI had anything to do with King's assassination are totally baseless, and are convincingly disproven by each and every careful study of the details of the event. People who continue to propound or believe such rumors are, in their own way, prisoners of the "paranoid style" of thought described in chapter 6. While some proponents of the FBI conspiracy notion may well have acted largely out of self-interest, many others who have accepted the idea have reflected only gullibility and ignorance. The wildly irresponsible suggestions of this style of thought appear in Mark Lane and Dick Gregory, *Code Name "Zorro": The Murder of Martin Luther King, Jr.* (Englewood Cliffs, N.J.: Prentice-Hall, 1977); James Lawson, "And the Character Assassination That Followed," *Civil Liberties Review* 5 (July–August 1978): 30–32; "King's Assassins Were FBI Men, Mark Lane Says," *Washington Post,* 28 October 1978, p. A2; Ed Hatcher and Amy Shaw, "Kunstler Blames FBI in King Killing," *Durham* (N.C.) *Morning Herald,* 17 November 1978, p. B5; and David L. Lewis, *King: A*

Biography, 2d ed. (Urbana: University of Illinois Press, 1978), pp. 399–403. For intelligent comments on these notions, see Frank Donner, ''Why Isn't the Truth Bad Enough,'' *Civil Liberties Review* 4 (January–February 1978): 68–72, and ''Hoaxed by a Bogus MP,'' *Civil Liberties Review* 5 (September–October 1978): 50–53; and especially the statements of Delegate Walter E. Fauntroy, House Committee on Assassinations, *Hearings— King,* vol. 6, pp. 1–2, which also are reported in ''Hill Unit Finds No Link between FBI, King Death,'' *Washington Post,* 18 November 1978, pp. A1, A7. Note too the comment in the Justice Department study cited more fully at n. 5 below that ''Logic suggests that the last thing J. Edgar Hoover wanted was to make King a martyr, thereby enhancing his image.'' (Murphy Report, p. 6.) Indeed, as one House investigator concluded, ''Hoover's hatred of King, and the Bureau's extended involvement in security investigations and COINTELPRO activities against the man and his organization, had the ironic effect . . . of increasing the intensity of the investigative effort after the assassination.'' See Peter Beeson, ''An Analysis of the Assassination Investigation of the Department of Justice and the Federal Bureau of Investigation,'' in House Committee on Assassinations, *Hearings—King,* vol. 13, pp. 153–216, at 201.

4. U.S., Department of Justice, *Report of the Department of Justice Task Force to Review the FBI Martin Luther King, Jr., Security and Assassination Investigations,* 11 January 1977.

5. Robert A. Murphy to J. Stanley Pottinger, ''Martin Luther King, Jr.,'' 31 March 1976; and J. Stanley Pottinger to Edward H. Levi, ''Martin Luther King Report,'' 9 April 1976.

6. A number of specialists, such as Professor Athan Theoharis of Marquette University, are making headway on this problem. Although here is not the place for an extended discussion of this subject, three brief points are relevant to the story of the King case. First, most material on King and SCLC was filed by the Bureau under its ''100'' designation, a file series for ''Internal Security'' and ''Subversive Matter'' inquiries. The main headquarters' file on King is ''100–106670,'' and on SCLC, ''100–438794.'' Corresponding but differently numbered ''100'' files on King and SCLC were maintained in most if not all Bureau field offices across the country. Although the Bureau has a ''44'' series entitled ''Civil Rights,'' only criminal investigations involving alleged violations of federal civil rights statutes appear to have been filed under that designation. Most items that generally would be called ''civil rights'' were handled by the Bureau under its ''157'' series, labeled ''Racial Matters.'' Many important Bureau documents about a host of sensitive cases often have been filed in the ''62'' or ''66'' series,

each labeled simply "Administrative Matters." Files on human informants bear either a "134" or "170" designation, the former for "Security" informants and the latter for "Racial" or "Extremist" sources.

Second, it is important to recognize that many important communications on individuals and groups were not reported under, or necessarily filed under, the actual names of that person or organization, but under broader rubrics unknown to most people. For example, many important items concerning King and SCLC are captioned with titles such as "Communist Party USA, Negro Question" (headquarters' file 100–3–116) or "Communist Influence in Racial Matters" (headquarters' file 100–442529).

Third, more needs to be known about the Bureau procedure called *"JUNE* mail," a special filing system for any documents making reference to electronic surveillance activities, and perhaps to physical entries or "black bag jobs" as well. Many items that bear this special *"JUNE"* designation have been released as part of the King and SCLC headquarters' files. How such items were handled in field offices is largely unknown, but apparently depended on the use of multiple "subfiles." For instance, all documents reflecting the Atlanta wiretapping of King, as well as the logs and transcripts from those intercepts, were filed in "subfiles" A through E of Atlanta file 100–6670, "Communist Influence in Racial Matters," or in "subfiles" A through E of Atlanta file 100–6520, "Communist Party USA, Negro Question." In New York, where King was the target of numerous hotel room microphones, the logs and transcripts of those "bugs" were deposited in ten different "subfiles" of the main New York field-office file on King, 100–136585.

The best current sources on FBI filing practices are Ann Mari Buitrago and Leon A. Immerman, *Are You Now or Have You Ever Been in the FBI Files?* (New York: Grove Press, 1981), esp. pp. 1–22; and U.S., Cong., Senate, Committee on the Judiciary, *FBI Statutory Charter—Appendix to Hearings before the Subcommittee on Administrative Practice and Procedure,* 95th Cong., 2d sess., 1979, part 3, pp. 33–73.

7. The Bureau also has shown a strong desire simply to destroy outdated field-office files, thus removing them from the reach of the FOIA. Fortunately a federal court injunction has halted this process. For that, and a good introduction to the entire problem, see Judge Harold H. Greene's opinion and order of 10 January 1980 in *American Friends Service Committee et al.* v. *Webster,* 485 F. Supp. 222. Also see three articles by John Rosenberg: "Catch in the Information Act," *Nation* 226 (4 February 1978): 108–11; "The FBI Would Shred the Past," *Nation* 226 (3 June 1978): 653–55; and "The FBI's Field Files," *Nation* 228 (3 March 1979): 231–32.

8. The FOIA is codified as 5 U.S.C. 552, and (b)(1) and (b)(7)(d) are subsections thereof. Other exemptions, such as (b)(2), "materials related solely to the internal rules and practices of the FBI," also offer potential for Bureau abuse, but have not yet been used extensively for such a purpose. An excellent introduction to the history and use of the FOIA is offered by a series of articles in *Public Administration Review* 39 (July–August 1979): 310–32. The FBI's hostility towards the FOIA can be sampled in William H. Webster, "An FBI Viewpoint Regarding the Freedom of Information Act," *Journal of Legislation* 7 (1980):7–15.

9. See *Lee* v. *Kelley,* Civil Action #76–1185, U.S. District Court for the District of Columbia, Memorandum Opinion and Order, 31 January 1977, Judge John Lewis Smith, Jr.; and Timothy S. Robinson, "FBI Tap Data on King to Go to Archives," *Washington Post,* 1 February 1977, p. A5.

10. Frank J. Donner, *The Age of Surveillance* (New York: Alfred A. Knopf, 1980), pp. 23–24. Also see Victor S. Navasky, *Kennedy Justice* (New York: Atheneum, 1971), p. 88.

11. Clyde Tolson to J. Edgar Hoover, untitled, 17 March 1958, a copy of which is filed but not serialized in 100–438794. Two scholars have described the amusing and disturbing errors they found in their own files after obtaining them under FOIA. See Amitai Etzioni, "What Our FBI Files Tell About the FBI," *Washington Post,* 11 September 1977, pp. B1, B4; and John Kenneth Galbraith, "My Forty Years with the FBI," *Esquire* 88 (October 1977): 122–26, 172–78.

12. This subject is discussed, and the appropriate news stories cited, in n. 41 of chapter 3.

13. See Al Rosen to Alan H. Belmont, "Civil Rights Matters," 22 May 1963, a copy of which is in the series 44 "Civil Rights Policy File," now on deposit at the Kennedy Library, Boston. An excellent preliminary inquiry into the Hobson matter, based on examination of Hobson's main FBI file, 134–12930, is Paul W. Valentine, "FBI Records List Julius Hobson as 'Confidential Source' in '60s," *Washington Post,* 22 May 1981, pp. A1, A18–19.

14. See U.S. Department of Justice, *King Task Force,* pp. 137–39, cited at n. 4 above, which engages in some discussion of this point. I believe there are records reflecting these entries. Whether they are maintained under one of the Bureau's apparent "Do Not File" file procedures, or in the "Official and Confidential" or "Personal and Confidential" files of some long-departed Bureau executive, I do not know. One scholar has reported that field-office documents on such entries regularly were destroyed within one year of the event. See James Q. Wilson, "Buggings, Break-Ins & the FBI," *Commentary* 65 (June 1978): 52–58, at 57.

15. See Joseph Conrad, *The Heart of Darkness* [1899] (New York: W.

W. Norton, 1971), esp. pp. 71–72; and Hannah Arendt, *Eichmann in Jerusalem—A Report on the Banality of Evil* (New York: Viking Press, 1963).

16. The reference is to Niebuhr's *Moral Man and Immoral Society* (New York: Charles Scribner's Sons, 1932), which makes this argument most persuasively.

1. "Solo"—The Mystery of Stanley Levison

1. George H. Scatterday to Alex Rosen, "Martin Luther King, Jr.," 22 May 1961, in U.S., Department of Justice, *Report of the Department of Justice Task Force to Review the FBI Martin Luther King, Jr., Security and Assassination Investigations,* 11 January 1977, pp. 162–64. (Hereinafter *King Task Force.*)

2. Only minimal references to King and the MIA appear in the main headquarters file on the Montgomery "racial situation," 62–101087–5, which has been released under the FOIA. The Mobile office did open a "COMINFIL" investigation of the MIA in 1958, but it lasted less than one year and involved little more than a half-hearted effort to examine the MIA's financial accounts at various banks. The headquarters file on MIA, 100–429326, released under the FOIA, amounts to only a dozen items. The boycott itself had received little attention because the FBI had only a small "resident agency" in Montgomery, and such "RAs" concentrated on criminal matters.

3. Trezz Anderson, "New Rights Group Launched in Dixie," *Pittsburgh Courier,* 17 August 1957, p. 2. The Bureau apparently had missed an earlier item, "Entire South Represented in Leadership Conference," *Pittsburgh Courier,* 2 March 1957, p. 4.

4. Director (by J. G. Kelly) to SAC, Atlanta, "SCLC, Internal Security," 20 September 1957, 100–438794–X1.

5. SAC, Atlanta (by Al F. Miller) to Director, "COMINFIL SCLC, Internal Security—Communist," 5 September 1958, 100–438794–X2. The low level of interest afforded SCLC is indicated by the lag in Atlanta's response: the headquarters' request arrived on July 28, and Miller's answer came five weeks later. The Atlanta "dead file" on SCLC was 100–5718.

6. New York field-office King serial 100–136585–1, 9 September 1958; Birmingham field-office King serial 100–4896–1, 11 September 1958; State Department to Embassy, New Delhi, 28 January 1959, FBI headquarters' serial 100–106670–9; headquarters' serial 100–106670–10, concerning "Meet the Press;" SAC, Chicago to Director, 16 June 1960, filed as Atlanta

serial 100–5586–58; and the seventy–one-page "correlation summary" of 28 September 1960, located in headquarters' file 100–106670.

7. SAC, New Orleans to Director, "SCLC; United Christian Movement," 20 October 1960, 100–438794–X3; and John F. Malone to John P. Mohr, 31 October 1960, 100–106670–unserialized.

8. Martin Luther King, Jr., "Equality Now," *Nation* 192 (4 February 1961): 91–95, at 94; M. A. Jones to Cartha D. DeLoach, "Article in 'The Nation' for February 4, 1961, by Martin Luther King, Jr.," 7 February 1961, 100–106670–12, in U.S., Congress, House, Select Committee on Assassinations, *Hearings on Investigation of the Assassination of Martin Luther King, Jr.,* 95th Cong., 2d sess., 1978, vol. 6, p. 130; and Director to Secretary of State, 4 April 1961, 100–106670–15.

9. Scatterday to Rosen, 22 May 1961. Scatterday could have added, had he known, that King recently had called for clemency for two victims of House Un-American Activities Committee investigations, Carl Braden and Frank Wilkinson, and also had said he favored abolition of HUAC itself. See Douglas Kiker, "King Sees 'McCarthyism' in 2 U.S. Contempt Sentences," *Atlanta Journal,* 2 May 1961. The Progressive party story almost certainly reflected confusion between Martin Luther King, Jr., and his father, Martin Luther King, Sr. King, Jr.'s headquarters' file, 100–1066670, actually had been opened in 1942 in response to an Atlanta report about King, Sr. Only in March, 1962, did the Bureau realize that they had been combining two different Martin Luther Kings. The material on King, Sr., was then shifted to a new file, 100–432863, while King, Jr., inherited what had started out as his father's file.

10. The most complete account of the Labor Day incident is in Frank Adams, *Unearthing Seeds of Fire: The Idea of Highlander* (Winston-Salem: John F. Blair, 1975), pp. 122–27. These photographs later would adorn billboards across the South. Similar characterizations of King as the product of such a training school, which even the Bureau dismissed, are Alan Stang, "The King and His Communists," *American Opinion* 8 (October 1965): 1–14; James D. Bales, *The Martin Luther King Story* (Tulsa: Christian Crusade Publications, 1967); and Ralph de Toledano, *J. Edgar Hoover* (New Rochelle, N.Y.: Arlington House, 1973), p. 332.

11. U.S., Department of Justice, *King Task Force,* p. 113. Also see SAC, Mobile to Director, "Racial Situation, Montgomery, Alabama, RM," 9 February 1960, 100–429326–unserialized, which notified Atlanta of King's move from Montgomery to that city. Mobile reported, "For the information of Atlanta, no investigation has been conducted concerning Rev. King, Jr. From time to time, informants in other matters have furnished information relating to Rev. King, Jr., and a case was opened at one time

captioned 'COMINFIL MIA, IS–C,' when some information appeared indicating the possibility of influence on Rev. King, Jr., on the part of certain subversive suspects.'' On that very limited MIA case, see n. 2 above.

12. SAC, Atlanta (by Robert R. Nichols) to Director, ''Wyatt Tee Walker, Security Matter—Communist,'' 5 July 1961, 100–438794–X5.

13. SAC, Memphis to Director, 'SCLC; Racial Matters,'' 26 September 1961, 100–438794–X6; and SAC, Memphis to Director, ''SCLC; Racial Matters,'' 2 December 1961, 100–438794–X8.

14. SAC, Miami to Director, ''Mass Voting Campaign in Southern States (RM); SCLC (RM),'' 14 November 1961, 100–438794–unserialized; SAC, Miami to Director, ''Mass Voting Campaign in Southern States (RM); SCLC (RM),'' 20 December 1961, 100–438794–unserialized.

15. SAC, Atlanta (by Robert R. Nichols) to Director, ''SCLC, Racial Matters,'' 21 November 1961, 100–438794–X7.

16. J. Edgar Hoover to Robert F. Kennedy, ''Stanley David Levison, SM–C,'' 8 January 1962, 100–392452–131. The Hoover letter was based upon SAC, New York to Director, ''Stanley David Levison, SM–C,'' 4 January 1962, 100–392452–132. Neither document has been released in full by the Bureau. Although Levison's name appeared at least twice in the September, 1960, FBI summary on King (see n. 6 above), and although Assistant Attorney General Burke Marshall had queried Hoover on 9 June 1961 about Levison's relationship to the civil rights movement, not until that New York report of 4 January 1962 did the FBI apparently realize that Levison and King were extremely close friends, rather than just incidental acquaintances, as the September 1960 summary appears to have presumed. Marshall's letter to Hoover, not yet released, is serialized as 100–392452–130. The text of the cited speech, which was written by Levison, can be found in *Proceedings of the Fourth Constitutional Convention of the AFL–CIO* (Washington: AFL–CIO, 1962), vol. 1, pp. 282–89, and *Hotel,* 12 February 1962, pp. 4, 6.

17. See Stanley D. Levison (James Mosby interview, 14 February 1970, New York), Civil Rights Documentation Project Papers, Moorland-Spingarn Research Center, Howard University, pp. 1–6, 10–11; Ella Baker (John Britton interview, 19 June 1968, Washington, D.C.), CRDP Papers, MSRC, Howard University, p. 8; Ella Baker (Sue Thrasher and Casey Hayden interview, 19 April 1977, New York), Southern Historical Collection, University of North Carolina, Chapel Hill, p. 61; Ella Baker (Eugene Walker interview, 4 September 1974, Durham, N.C.), Southern Historical Collection, UNC, part I, pp. 8, 31–32; In Friendship to Cooperating Organizations and Individuals, 27 March 1956, American Civil Liberties Union Papers, Mudd Library, Princeton University; and Coretta Scott King, *My*

Life with Martin Luther King, Jr. (New York: Holt, Rinehart & Winston, 1969), p. 138.

18. See Levison's own characterization in Jacqueline Trescott, ''A Continuing 'King' Controversy,'' *Washington Post,* 14 February 1978, p. B5. As he related it in later years, Levison was drawn to King by the younger man's self-effacing approach to leadership. In one of their first meetings, in Baltimore in 1956, Levison had listened as King talked about his suddenly acquired celebrity status. ''He said, 'If anybody had asked me a year ago to head this movement, I tell you very honestly that I would have run a mile to get away from it. I had no intention of being involved in this way.' He said that, 'As I became involved, and as people began to derive inspiration from their involvement, I realized that the choice leaves your own hands. The people expect you to give them leadership. You see them growing as they move into action, and then you know you no longer have a choice, you can't decide *whether* to stay in it or get out of it, you *must* stay in it.' '' See Levison's 14 February 1970 interview with Mosby, p. 9, cited in n. 17 above.

19. New York: Harper & Brothers, 1958.

20. Letters from Levison to King, 19 October 1957, 29 October 1957, 17 January 1958, 24 January 1958, 28 February 1958, 11 March 1958, and 7 April 1958, all in King Papers, Special Collections Department, Mugar Library, Boston University, Drawers 1, 5 and 16.

21. Two letters from Levison to King, each dated 1 April 1958, King Papers, BU, Drawer 4. Compare, for example, the text of an untitled Levison memo, which begins, ''What are the tasks ahead,'' with a long segment on pp. 214–15 of *Stride Toward Freedom.* The memo is in Drawer 16, King Papers, BU. Also compare another Levison memo, entitled ''A Wind Is Rising,'' given to King in 1957, with pp. 203–4 of *Stride toward Freedom.* This memo is in Drawer 11.

22. Wofford called Levison on August 14. See letters from Levison to King, 28 April 1958, 3 June 1958, 10 June 1958, 14 July 1958, 14 August 1958, and 15 August 1958, all in King Papers, BU.

23. Coretta King, *My Life,* p. 168; letters from Levison to King, 3 November 1958 and 28 November 1958, both in King Papers, BU, Drawer 1.

24. Levison had written to King asking that a coat King had borrowed be returned, and an embarrassed King immediately replied that the coat would be mailed posthaste. He further asked Stanley to bill him for all of his work. This led to Stanley's reply. See letters from Levison to King, 11 December 1958, 16 December 1958, and 8 January 1959, and King to Levison, 15 December 1958, all in King Papers, BU, Drawer 1. Stanley later commented

that King was "very thoughtful, quiet, and shy—very shy. The shyness was accented, I felt, with white people. And even in his relations with me in the early period, there was not always a relaxed attitude, but one of carefully listening to every word that he was saying so that he might not offend me, and that I might not offend him. There was a—a certain politeness, a certain arm's length approach, and you could feel the absence of relaxation. As the years went on this vanished." See Levison's 1970 interview with Mosby, cited in n. 17 above.

25. See letters from Levison to King, 12 January 1959, 26 January 1959, 11 April 1959, 8 May 1959, 24 June 1959, 29 June 1959, 10 July 1959, 1 September 1959, 1 October 1959, 21 December 1959, and 22 December 1959, and King to Levison, 18 May 1959, 19 November 1959, and 25 November 1959, all in King Papers, BU, Drawers 1, 4, and 7. Also see Levison and Rustin telegram to King, 26 February 1960, Drawer 7.

26. Undated letter from Levison to King, King Papers, BU, Drawer 1.

27. See Ella Baker interview, Howard University, p. 18; and Baker interview with Eugene Walker, UNC, part I, pp. 10, 19, and part II, pp. 4, 11, 25, both cited in n. 17 above; and letter from King to Levison, 5 January 1960, King Papers, BU, Drawer 4. The idea of establishing SCLC had originated in a conversation between Levison, Rustin, and Baker, and Levison had interviewed SCLC's first executive director, Rev. John Tilley, before he was hired.

28. See Wyatt T. Walker (John H. Britton interview, 11 October 1967, New York, N.Y.), CRDP Papers, Moorland-Spingarn Research Center, Howard University, p. 77. King, Levison, Walker, and Rustin met in New York to plan matters on May 10–11, 1960. Also see the following letters: Young to King, 24 March 1961, King to Young, 25 April 1961, King to Levison, 25 April 1961, King to Myles Horton, 25 April 1961, all in King Papers, BU, Drawer 7; Young to Robert Spike, 25 April 1961, Young to James Wood, 27 June 1961, both in UCC Race Relations Department Papers, Amistad Research Center, New Orleans, Box 27, Folder 14; and Young to Wyatt Tee Walker, 8 August 1961, and Young to King and Walker, 11 September 1961, both in King Papers, BU, Drawer 7.

29. See letters from O'Dell to King, 21 October 1961 and 11 November 1961, and Levison to King, 1 November 1961, all in King Papers, BU, Drawer 7. O'Dell earlier had assisted Levison in planning a 17 May 1960 benefit in New York for the Committee to Defend Martin Luther King, Jr. More will be said about Jack O'Dell later in this chapter. On Levison's continued writing and financial advice for King, see Levison to King letters of 13 July 1960, 1 August 1960, 13 October 1960, 29 December 1960, 26 May 1961, 20 June 1961, and 24 July 1961, all in King Papers, BU.

30. Author's conversations with Beatrice Levison, Andrew Levison, Janet Kennedy, Jay Kennedy, and Roger W. Loewi.

31. Author's conversations with Beatrice Levison, Andrew Levison, Roy Bennett, Moe Foner, Joseph H. Filner, Nancy Rabson, Eileen Newman, and Paul Cowan. Also see Levison's public comments in Don Oberdorfer, "King Adviser Says FBI 'Used' Him," *Washington Post,* 15 December 1975, p. A4; and Ronald J. Ostrow, "Several Motives Seen for Ordering Dr. King Wiretap," *Los Angeles Times,* 21 December 1975, pp. 1, 6–7.

32. Author's conversations with Roy Bennett, Andrew Levison, Janet Alterman Levison Kennedy, and Jay Kennedy. Also see "Stanley Levison, 67; Adviser to Dr. King," *New York Times,* 14 September 1979, p. B8.

33. Author's conversations with Jay Kennedy, Janet Alterman Levison Kennedy, Beatrice Levison, and Roy Bennett.

34. Author's conversations with Jay Kennedy and Janet Kennedy; and letters from J. Louis Reynolds to Jay Richard Kennedy, 18 October 1944; H. J. Anslinger to George R. Davis, 22 January 1946; Stanley D. Levison to Jay Richard Kennedy, 21 March 1946 and 9 April 1946; H. J. Anslinger to Jay Richard Kennedy, 29 April 1946; Eleanor Roosevelt to Jay Richard Kennedy, 26 April 1947; and Jay Richard Kennedy to Stanley D. Levison, 9 July 1947, 15 August 1947, 18 August 1947, and 25 August 1947, all in author's files. Also see *New York Times,* 15 August 1948, p. X7.

35. Author's conversations with Roy Bennett, Janet Kennedy, and Jay Kennedy. Stanley was to name his only child, Andrew, after the Loewi son who had been Jay's friend and who was killed in the Battle of the Bulge.

36. Letter of agreement from Levison to Kennedy, countersigned by Kennedy, 4 April 1949, in author's files, and author's conversations with Roy Bennett, Jay Kennedy, and Janet Kennedy.

37. Author's conversations with Nancy Rabson, Roy Bennett, Andrew Levison, Eileen Newman, Roger W. Loewi, Joseph H. Filner, and Paul Cowan.

38. Author's conversations with Jay Kennedy, Janet Kennedy, and Roy Bennett.

39. Levison had another acquaintance, Charles Newman, also a Loewi family employee, who too had misgivings about Jay Kennedy. Newman was the first husband of Nancy Loewi, who with her second husband, Mortimer Rabson, became Stanley's partners in the Ecuadorian laundry. Charles's second wife, Eileen, later worked for many years as financial secretary for both Jay and Janet Kennedy. Eileen and Charles subsequently were divorced, as were Nancy and Mortimer. Jay and Janet themselves separated in the mid-1970s.

40. Author's conversations with Clarence B. Jones and Roy Bennett.

41. Kennedy will reappear in our story in 1965 in chapter 3. He went on to publish four successful novels, *Prince Bart* (New York: Farrar, Straus, 1953); *Short Term* (Cleveland: World Publishing Co., 1959); *Favor the Runner* (Cleveland: World Publishing Co., 1965); and *The Chairman* (New York: World Publishing Co., 1969). Kennedy also served as moderator of a television special on 28 August 1963, featuring the leaders of the March on Washington, including Dr. King.

42. See Arthur M. Schlesinger, Jr., *Robert Kennedy and His Times* (Boston: Houghton Mifflin Co., 1978), p. 357.

43. Author's conversations with Roy Bennett and Andrew Levison.

44. On the debate concerning "Fedora," see Edward Jay Epstein, *Legend: The Secret World of Lee Harvey Oswald* (New York: McGraw-Hill, 1978), esp. pp. 20, 36–37, 263–64; Susana Duncan, "The War of the Moles: An Interview with Edward Jay Epstein," *New York* 11 (27 February 1978): 28–38, esp. pp. 31–32, 35–36; and Chapman Pincher, *Their Trade Is Treachery* (London: Sidgwick & Jackson, 1981), pp. 76–77. A useful and necessary counterbalance to the Epstein-Rocca-Angleton view of the world is David C. Martin, *Wilderness of Mirrors* (New York: Harper & Row, 1980). The most beneficial overview of the netherworld of American intelligence is Thomas Powers, *The Man Who Kept the Secrets: Richard Helms and the CIA* (New York: Alfred A. Knopf, 1979). Neither Schlesinger nor Epstein, nor any other name cited here, contributed in any way to this author's identification of Lessiovski. One public reference, not yet declassified, is a four-page letter of 28 June 1965 from J. Edgar Hoover to presidential aide Marvin Watson, on Lessiovski, in WHCF Confidential File ND 19/C0312 at the Lyndon B. Johnson Library, Austin, Texas. On Lessiovski's years in Burma, see the reference to "Victor Lassiovsky," who "ran the entire Burmese effort for Russia," in William J. Lederer and Eugene Burdick, *The Ugly American* (New York: W. W. Norton, 1958), p. 151.

45. John Gates, *The Story of an American Communist* (New York: Thomas Nelson & Sons, 1958), p. 110; Bella V. Dodd, *School of Darkness* (New York: P. J. Kenedy, 1954), pp. 200–203; and Joseph R. Starobin, *American Communism in Crisis, 1943–1957* (Cambridge: Harvard University Press, 1972), pp. 119, 287.

46. See Starobin, *American Communism*, p. 119; *New York Times*, 26 June 1936, p. 4; and U.S., Cong., Senate, Committee on the Judiciary, *Hearings on Scope of Soviet Activity in the United States*, 85th Cong., 1st sess., 1957, appendix I, part 23–A, pp. 107–8.

47. See *New York Times*, 24 August 1980, p. 44. In Bureau documents, Morris Childs was spoken of as "CG–5824–S" and Jack Childs as "NY–

694–S.'' Many Bureau personnel simply referred to the two men as "five eight" and "six nine," respectively. Oftentimes in written references an effort was made to imply that these sources were electronic intercepts rather than human informants.

48. Only the most incomplete information about the actual content of the FBI's earliest documents on Levison is available. The initial item apparently is SAC, New York to Director, 9 June 1952, which is followed by Director to SAC, New York, 24 June 1952, 100–392452–1. The first large report on Levison, prepared by the New York office on 19 June 1953, is serialized as headquarters' document 100–392452–2 and as New York 100–111180–26. On 29 July 1953 Attorney General Herbert Brownell asked the Treasury Department to furnish copies of Levison's recent income tax returns (100–392452–5). Another major New York report on Levison, 41 pages long and dated 21 September 1953, is serialized as 100–392452–12. The IRS furnished Levison's 1950 and 1951 tax returns to FBI headquarters in late September, and they promptly were forwarded to the Bureau's New York office (100–392452–15). SAC, Newark to Director, 29 October 1953, 100–392452–16, and SAC, Chicago to Director, 30 October 1953, 100–392452–17, both detail efforts to trace Levison's long-distance phone calls.

49. Author's conversations with Beatrice Levison and Roy Bennett. Obituaries on Needleman appear in the *New York Times,* 25 September 1975, p. 46; and the *Daily World,* 26 September 1975, p. 9.

50. Major Bureau documents on Levison in 1954, none of which is available in complete form, include SAC, New York to Director, 14 January 1954, 100–392452–26; SAC, Newark to Director, 12 February 1954, 100–392452–27; SAC, New York to Director, 15 March 1954, 100–392452–34; an 83 page SAC, New York to Director report dated 29 April 1954, 100–392452–50; Alan H. Belmont to J. Edgar Hoover, 28 April 1954, 100–392452–51, informing Hoover that Belmont had approved the Chicago bug; SAC, Chicago to Director, 1 May 1954, 100–392452–58X, transmitting a seven-page summary transcript of the surveillance; SAC, New York to Director, 6 July 1954, 100–392452–66, which placed Levison on the select list of "key figure" Communists; and SAC, New York to Director, 8 December 1954, 100–392452–85. Levison was the target of physical surveillance in Washington, D.C., on 20 and 21 June 1955, but summaries of Bureau documents from fall 1955 appear to suggest that by that time Levison no longer was playing his previous role. These include SAC, New York to Director, 1 September 1955, 100–392452–101, and an internal New York office memo of 9 November 1955, serialized as 100–111180–657.

51. Levison's lack of CP activity is noted in an internal New York office memo of 25 July 1956, serialized as 100–111180–679; his fund–raising

work with In Friendship is detailed in an internal New York memo of 22 October 1956, 100–111180–697; SAC, New York to Director, 28 November 1956; and SAC, New York to Director, 24 January 1957. Levison was removed from the "key figure" list on 22 March 1957 (New York serial 100–111180–805); subsequent reports on him were sent by New York to headquarters on 29 April 1957 and 1 August 1957 and are serialized as 100–392452–114 and 116, respectively. The Bureau maintained an interest in Levison's travel to Ecuador, as Miami field-office serials 100–14165–1 and 2, dated 27 November 1957 and 20 February 1958, indicate.

52. Bureau documents detailing the effort to recruit Levison as an informant include SAC, New York to Director, 27 November 1959; Fred J. Baumgardner to Alan H. Belmont, 8 December 1959; Director to SAC, New York, 9 December 1959; SAC, New York to Director, 9 February 1960; SAC, New York to Director, 4 March 1960; and Director to SAC, New York, 9 March 1960, all of which are in file 100–392452 but none of which has been released in full. Speculation by some Justice Department officials in the mid–1970s, such as Jack Fuller, special assistant to Attorney General Edward H. Levi, that Levison did become a Bureau informant is inaccurate. See Jack Fuller to File, "King Investigation," 11 December 1975, copy in author's files.

53. Author's conversations with Roy Bennett, Beatrice Levison, Andrew Levison, Roger W. Loewi, and Lem Harris, among others.

54. Author's conversations with John Seigenthaler.

55. Author's conversations with Harris Wofford and Burke Marshall; Wofford, *Of Kennedys and Kings* (New York: Farrar, Straus & Giroux, 1980), p. 216; Robert F. Kennedy and Burke Marshall (Anthony Lewis interview, 4 December 1964, New York, N.Y.), John F. Kennedy Library, Boston, Mass., pp. 31–33; Harris Wofford (Berl Bernhard interview, 29 November 1965, Washington, D.C.), John F. Kennedy Library, Boston, Mass., pp. 143–44.

56. Author's conversations with Harris Wofford and John Seigenthaler; Stanley D. Levison (Arthur Schlesinger, Jr., interview, 3 August 1976, New York, N.Y.); Wofford, *Of Kennedys and Kings,* p. 216; John Seigenthaler (Robert F. Campbell interview, 10 July 1968, Nashville, Tenn.), Civil Rights Documentation Project, Moorland-Spingarn Research Center, Howard University, pp. 17–18. Unfortunately the precise date of this meeting has not yet been established. Accounts that suggest it occurred in early 1961 are quite wide of the mark; Andrew Young, whom everyone recalls was present, did not join the SCLC staff until early in the fall of 1961. A number of Kennedy administration personnel mistakenly place these events of early 1962 in early or mid-1961.

57. White's initial conversation with Evans took place on 2 February, and a second on 6 February. See Courtney A. Evans to Alan H. Belmont, "Stanley David Levison, SM–C," 2 February 1962, 100–392452–134; James F. Bland to William C. Sullivan, "Stanley David Levison, SM–C," 3 February 1962, 100–392452–135; and Courtney A. Evans to Alan H. Belmont, "Stanley David Levison, SM–C," 6 February 1962, 100–392452–136. Hoover's annotation appears on the Bland memo.

58. Bureau headquarters had prepared a 32-page summary report on King, 100–106670–23, on 5 February. Director to SAC, New York, 2 March 1962, 100–392452–139, granted authority to "survey" Levison's office. Director to SACs, Atlanta and New York, "Martin Luther King, Jr., SM–C," 27 February 1962, 100–106670–26, ordered the file review. New York responded on 13 April with a 25-page report (100–106670–40) and Atlanta on 25 April with a 37-page document (100–106670–49), neither of which contained any new information. Also see Hoover to Robert Kennedy, and Hoover to O'Donnell, 14 February 1962, 100–106670–24 and 25; J. F. Bland to William C. Sullivan, 2 March 1962; and Hoover to Robert F. Kennedy, 6 March 1962. Accounts that imply that Levison himself was not tapped are of course incorrect; see Victor S. Navasky, "The Government and Martin Luther King," *Atlantic* 226 (November 1970): 43–52, at 50; and *Kennedy Justice* (New York: Atheneum, 1971), p. 150; and Ovid Demaris, *The Director: An Oral Biography of J. Edgar Hoover* (New York: Harper & Row, 1975), p. 197.

59. Hoover (by T. W. Kitchens) to Robert Kennedy, "Martin Luther King, Jr., SM–C," 20 April 1962, 100–106670–48. Also see Schlesinger, *Robert Kennedy,* pp. 353–54. An almost identical memo of the same date to O'Donnell is serial 45. A Hoover memo of 16 March 1962 (100–106670–31) had told Robert Kennedy that Jack O'Dell was writing an article under King's name, and ones of 2 April (100–106670–32) and 13 April (100–106670–39) had further detailed Levison's influence. A very similar version of the 13 April one had reported the Levison-King relationship to Vice-President Lyndon B. Johnson (100–106670–41). The Gandhi Society for Human Rights—which was announced at the 17 May luncheon—was the idea of New York lawyer Harry Wachtel, who had met King through Clarence Jones. Wachtel had learned from King that SCLC, which did not have tax-exempt status, was losing some potential contributions because it lacked an arm to which tax–deductible contributions could be made. Wachtel volunteered to remedy this problem, and the Gandhi Society, begun initially with Kheel as president, but actually run by Jones and Wachtel, was the result. Author's conversations with Harry Wachtel and Clarence B. Jones.

60. A transcript of the 30 April hearing, still classified, is in the Robert

F. Kennedy Papers, John F. Kennedy Library, Boston. Bureau documents concerning Levison's appearance include SAC, New York to Director, 26 April 1962, 100–392452–152; SAC, New York to Director, 3 May 1962, 100–392452–153; and James F. Bland to William C. Sullivan, 7 May 1962, 100–392452–154. Memos went to Robert Kennedy on 4 May (100–106670–63) and 8 May (100–392452–unserialized) and to O'Donnell on 4 May (100–106670–58). Also, author's conversations with Roy Bennett and Andrew Levison; Navasky, *Kennedy Justice,* p. 148; and Schlesinger, *Robert Kennedy,* p. 354.

61. SAC, Atlanta to Director, "Martin Luther King, Jr., SM–C," 25 April 1962, 100–106670–49; Director to SAC, Atlanta, "Martin Luther King, Jr., SM–C," 10 May 1962, 100–106670–60; Director to SAC, New York, "Martin Luther King, Jr., SM–C," 100–106670–57; Hoover (by T. W. Kitchens) to Kenneth O'Donnell, 4 May 1962, 100–106670–58; and Director to SAC, Atlanta, "Martin Luther King, Jr., SM–C," 11 May 1962, 100–106670–65. On the details of the Security and Reserve Indices, see U.S., Congress, Senate, Select Committee to Study Governmental Operations with Respect to Intelligence Activities, *Final Report—Book III, Supplementary Detailed Staff Reports on Intelligence Activities and the Rights of Americans,* 94th Cong., 2d sess., 1976, pp. 436–47; and Athan Theoharis, *Spying on Americans: Political Surveillance from Hoover to the Huston Plan* (Philadelphia: Temple University Press, 1978), pp. 43–62. Also see two articles by Robert J. Goldstein: "The FBI's Forty-Year Plot," *Nation* 227 (1 July 1978): 10–15; and "An American Gulag?—Summary Arrest and Emergency Detention of Political Dissidents in the United States," *Columbia Human Rights Law Review* 10 (1978): 541–73.

62. SAC, Atlanta (by Robert R. Nichols) to Director, "SCLC; Racial Matters," 17 May 1962, 100–438794–X10; and SAC, Atlanta (by Robert R. Nichols) to Director, "SCLC; Racial Matters," 26 June 1962, 100–438794–X21.

63. See SAC, Atlanta to Director, "SCLC; RM," 5 June 1962, 100–438794–X11; Director (by R. B. Long) to Attorney General, "SCLC; RM," 6 June 1962, 100–438794–X12; SAC, Atlanta to Director, "SCLC; RM," 6 June 1962, 100–438794–X13; and three memos from Al Rosen to Alan H. Belmont, all captioned "SCLC; RM," and all dated 6 June, and serialized as 100–438794–X15 through X17.

64. SAC, New York to Director, "Martin Luther King, Jr., SM–C," 21 June 1962, 100–106670–80; Hoover (by I. D. Haack) to Robert Kennedy, "Martin Luther King, Jr., SM–C," 25 June 1962, 100–106670–79; and SAC, New York to Director, "COMINFIL SCLC, IS–C," 21 August 1962, 100–438794–4. The Bureau also was seeking public source information

showing Levison's and O'Dell's ties to King. See SAC, New York to Director, 4 June 1962, 100–392452–158, and Director to SAC, New York, 12 June 1962, both unreleased. No one has ever questioned O'Dell's ability or intelligence. Former SCLC Executive Director Wyatt T. Walker has stated several times that O'Dell was the most capable staff member the organization ever had. See Wyatt T. Walker interview, Howard University, p. 79; author's conversations with Wyatt T. Walker.

65. See U.S., Congress, Senate, Committee on the Judiciary, Subcommittee to Investigate the Administration of the Internal Security Act and Other Internal Security Laws, *Hearings on the Scope of Soviety Activity in the United States,* part 13, 84th Congress, 2d sess., 1956, pp. 755–76; U.S., Congress, House, Committee on Un–American Activities, *Hearings on Communist Infiltration and Activities in the South,* 85th Cong., 2nd sess., 1958, pp. 2714–17; and letters from O'Dell to King, 22 August 1959, 18 January 1960, and 8 September 1960; and King to O'Dell, 14 September 1959; and Maude L. Ballou to O'Dell, 1 February 1960, all in King Papers, Boston University, Drawers 4 and 7.

66. See SAC, New York to Director, "Martin Luther King, Jr., SM–C," 13 April 1962, 100–106670–40, pp. 16–17; SAC, New York to Director, "COMINFIL SCLC, IS–C," 21 August 1962, 100–438794–4; SAC, Atlanta (by Robert R. Nichols) to Director, "COMINFIL SCLC, IS–C," 11 October 1962, 100–438794–9; and SAC, New York (by Patrick J. Stokes) to Director, "COMINFIL SCLC, IS–C," 14 December 1962, 100–438794–15. Stokes's report states that a pretext call had been made to the In Friendship office on 14 July 1958.

67. King's message books at Boston University reflect calls from or to O'Dell, or in-person contact, on 12 and 13 June, 5 and 6 July, 24 August, and 10 and 11 October, 1962.

68. Director (by R. J. Rampton) to SAC, Atlanta, "COMINFIL SCLC, IS–C," 20 July 1962, 100–438794–1; and Director (by R. J. Rampton) to SAC, Mobile, "COMINFIL SCLC, IS–C," 20 July 1962, 100–438794–1X.

69. See SAC, New York to Director, "COMINFIL SCLC, IS–C," 3 August 1962, 100–438794–2; SAC, New York to Director, "COMINFIL SCLC, IS–C," 3 August 1962, 100–438794–3; Director (by R. J. Rampton) to SAC, New York, "COMINFIL SCLC, IS–C," 7 August 1962, 100–438794–3; SAC, New York to Director, "COMINFIL SCLC, IS–C," 21 August 1962, 100–438794–4; and Director to SAC, New York, "COMINFIL SCLC, IS–C," 29 August 1962, 100–438794–4. An 8 August memo from Hoover to Robert Kennedy (100–106670–87), not yet released, apparently reported on a phone conversation that Kennedy himself had had with

King. The "bug" or microphone surveillance on Levison's office was ended on 16 August, as an unreleased communication of that date from SAC, New York to Director reports. Why it was discontinued at that time remains unknown.

70. See SAC, Savannah to Director, "SCLC, IS–C," 29 August 1962, 100–438794–5; Director (by R. J. Rampton) to SAC, Savannah, "COM-INFIL SCLC, IS–C," 17 September 1962, 100–438794–5; SAC, Atlanta (by Robert R. Nichols) to Director, "COMINFIL SCLC, IS–C," 20 September 1962, 100–438794–6; and SAC, Savannah to Director, "COMIN-FIL SCLC, IS–C," 25 September 1962, 100–438794–7.

71. Director (by R. J. Rampton) to SAC, Atlanta, "COMINFIL SCLC, IS–C," 1 October 1962, 100–438794–6.

72. SAC, Atlanta (by Robert R. Nichols) to Director, "COMINFIL SCLC, IS–C," 11 October 1962, 100–438794–9.

73. Fred J. Baumgardner (by R. J. Rampton) to William C. Sullivan, "COMINFIL SCLC, IS–C," 22 October 1962, 100–438794–10; Director (by R. J. Rampton) to SAC, Atlanta, "COMINFIL SCLC, IS–C," 23 October 1962, 100–438794–9; and James F. Bland (by I. D. Haack) to William C. Sullivan, "Martin Luther King, Jr., SM–C," 27 September 1962, 100–106670–94.

74. See "Red Aids King's Efforts," *Augusta Chronicle,* 25 October 1962, p. A4; "Communist Revealed As Rev. King's Aid [*sic*]," *St. Louis Globe-Democrat,* 26 October 1962, p. A1; "Communist in High Post with King's Mixing Group," *Birmingham News,* 26 October 1962, p. 1; and "A Communist Has Infiltrated Martin Luther King's Top Ranks," *Long Island Star-Journal,* 26 October 1962, pp. 1–2. The Bureau's New York office made a pretext call to the SCLC office there on 24 October, presumably to make certain that O'Dell was still with SCLC. The entire operation first had been recommended in SAC, New York to Director, "CPUSA, COINTEL-PRO, IS–C," 28 September 1962, 100–3–104–34–295; and then in an 8 October memo from Baumgardner to Sullivan (unreleased), who had approved it and forwarded the matter to DeLoach, who, a notation indicates, made the necessary contacts.

75. See "King Reports Alleged Red Has Quit Post," *Birmingham News,* 2 November 1962, p. 1; and "Communist Resigns from Rev. King's Group," *Long Island Star-Journal,* 2 November 1962, pp. 1–2.

76. The message books at Boston University reflect calls from O'Dell on 21 and 23 November and 18 December, 1962, and 28 January, 12 March, and 6, 7, and 10 June, 1963. Also see O'Dell to King, 14 May 1963, King Papers, Drawer 5, BU. The Bureau knew as early as 7 December, 1962, from the Levison wiretap, that O'Dell would be remaining with SCLC. See

SAC, New York to Director, "Hunter Pitts O'Dell, IS–C," 12 December 1962, 100–438794–unserialized.

77. See Howard Zinn, *Albany: A Study in National Responsibility* (Atlanta: Southern Regional Council, 14 November 1962), p. 31. Zinn had done an earlier report on Albany for the SRC as well, dated 8 January 1962. Also see James Wechsler, "The FBI's Failure in the South," *Progressive* 27 (December 1963): 20–23.

78. "Dr. King Says F.B.I. in Albany, Ga., Favors Segregationists," *New York Times*, 19 November 1962, p. 21; and *Atlanta Constitution*, 19 November 1962, p. 18.

79. SAC, Atlanta to Director, "Racial Situation, Albany, Georgia, RM," 19 November 1962, in House Committee on Assassinations, *Hearings— King*, vol. 6, p. 95; Alex Rosen to Alan H. Belmont, 20 November 1962 (unreleased); Belmont to Clyde Tolson, 26 November 1962 (unreleased); and Rosen to Belmont, "Racial Situation, Albany, Georgia, RM," 3 December 1962, 157–6–2–932.

80. King message books, Boston University; C. D. DeLoach to John P. Mohr, 3 December 1962, 100–106670–104; and ASAC Hitt to SAC, 4 December 1962, Atlanta serial 100–5586–441 (unreleased).

81. See Murtagh's testimony in House Committee on Assassinations, *Hearings—King*, vol. 6, pp. 91–94.

82. See DeLoach's testimony in House Committee on Assassinations, *Hearings—King*, vol. 7, pp. 41–43. Also see Don Whitehead, *Attack on Terror: The FBI Against the Ku Klux Klan in Mississippi* (New York: Funk & Wagnalls, 1970), pp. 193–95.

83. Hoover to Kennedy, "Martin Luther King, Jr., SM–C," 8 August 1962, 100–106670–88; Hoover to Kennedy, "Racial Situation, Albany, Georgia, RM," 11 August 1962, 157–6–2–617; Hoover to Kennedy, "Racial Situation, Albany, Georgia, RM," 11 September 1962, 100–106670–92; Hoover to Kennedy, "Martin Luther King, Jr., SM–C," 16 October 1962, 100–106670–95; Hoover to Kennedy, 20 November 1962 (unreleased); Director to SAC, New York, 23 November 1962 (unreleased); Hoover to Kennedy, "Hunter Pitts O'Dell, IS–C," 6 December 1962, 100–358916–223; and Hoover to Kennedy, "Martin Luther King, Jr., SM–C," 7 December 1962, 100–106670–102. A similar 7 December memo (100–106670–100) went to White House aide Kenneth O'Donnell. A 27 December 1962 report to both the Attorney General and O'Donnell (100–106670–105 and 106) related that Clarence Jones had told Levison that King, in a recent meeting with President Kennedy, had been extremely impressed at Kennedy's familiarity with King's published writings.

84. See SAC, Atlanta (by Robert R. Nichols) to Director, "COMINFIL

SCLC, IS–C,'' 7 December 1962, 100–438794–13; SAC, New York (by Stokes) to Director, ''COMINFIL SCLC, IS–C,'' 14 December 1962, 100–438794–15; Director (by R. J. Rampton) to SAC, New York, ''COMINFIL SCLC, IS–C,'' 27 December 1962, 100–438794–16; and SAC, Atlanta (by Nichols) to Director, ''COMINFIL SCLC, IS–C,'' 10 January 1963, 100–438794–unserialized.

85. Hoover to Kennedy, ''Martin Luther King, Jr., SM–C,'' 10 January 1963, 100–106670–107; SAC, New York to Director, ''Martin Luther King, Jr., SM–C,'' 7 January 1963, 100–106670–109; James F. Bland (by William T. Forsyth) to William C. Sullivan, ''Martin Luther King, Jr., SM–C,'' 11 January 1963, 100–106670–108; SAC, Atlanta (by Nichols) to Director and SACs, New York and Savannah, ''Hunter Pitts O'Dell,'' 15 January 1963, 100–438794–unserialized; SAC, Savannah to Director, ''Hunter Pitts O'Dell, IS–C,'' 16 January 1963, 100–358916–228; SAC, New York to Director, ''Stanley D. Levison, IS–C,'' 28 January 1963, 100–438794–unserialized; Hoover to Burke Marshall, ''Martin Luther King, Jr., SM–C,'' 31 January 1963, 100–106670–111; and SAC, Atlanta (by Nichols) to Director, ''COMINFIL SCLC, IS–C; Dorothy F. Cotton,'' 23 September 1964, 100–438794–157, p. 4. Also, SAC, New York to Director, ''Hunter Pitts O'Dell, IS–C,'' 12 December 1962, 100–358916–223; and Hoover to Kennedy, ''Martin Luther King, Jr., SM–C,'' 30 January 1963, 100–106670–113.

86. Levison described the meeting in a 21 November 1969 interview in New York with Jean Stein vanden Heuvel, who graciously supplied a copy of the transcript to this author, and also in a November 1968 interview with David L. Lewis.

87. Kennedy's annotation was on the Hoover memo of 10 January, cited in n. 85 above. Also see Hoover to Marshall, 31 January, cited in n. 85 above, C. D. DeLoach to John Mohr, ''Racial Situation, Albany, Georgia, RM,'' 15 January 1963, 157–6–2–965; and Hoover to Kennedy, 18 January 1963 (unreleased).

88. Alex Rosen to Alan H. Belmont, 4 February 1963 (unreleased); Burke Marshall to J. Edgar Hoover, ''Hunter Pitts O'Dell,'' 20 September 1963, Marshall Papers, Kennedy Library, Boston; Director to SAC, New York, ''Stanley David Levison, SM–C,'' 25 January 1963, NY serial 100–111180–1129; J. Walter Yeagley to Hoover, 8 February 1963, and Hoover to Yeagley, 13 February 1963, 100–392452–187 and 188; SAC, New York to Director, ''Stanley David Levison, SM–C,'' 21 February 1963, 100–392452–190; and ASAC Donald E. Roney to SAC, 12 February 1963, New York serial 100–111180–1143.

89. Hoover to Kennedy, and Hoover to O'Donnell, ''Martin Luther King,

Jr., SM–C,'' 12 March 1963, 100–106670–118X and 117; Hoover to Kennedy, and Hoover to O'Donnell, ''Martin Luther King, Jr., RM,'' 26 March 1963, 100–106670–119 and 120; Director to SAC, New York, ''Stanley D. Levison, IS–C,'' 26 March 1963 (unreleased); SAC, New York to Director, ''Sit Ins, Birmingham, Ala., RM,'' 21 May 1963, 157–6–4–1067; Alex Rosen to Alan Belmont, ''Martin Luther King, Jr., RM,'' 31 May 1963, 100–106670–132; Hoover to Kennedy, and Hoover to O'Donnell, ''Martin Luther King, Jr., RM,'' 31 May 1963, 100–106670–127 and 129; Hoover to Kennedy, ''Rev. Martin Luther King, Jr., SM–C; RM,'' 3 June 1963, 100–106670–128; Hoover to Kennedy, ''Rev. Martin Luther King, Jr., RM,'' 7 June 1963, 100–106670–134; Hoover to Kennedy, ''Rev. Martin Luther King, Jr., RM,'' 11 June 1963, 100–106670–145; Hoover to Kennedy, ''Rev. Martin Luther King, Jr., SM–C, RM,'' 12 June 1963, 100–106670–133; Hoover to O'Donnell, 14 June 1963, 100–106670–149; and SAC, New York (by P. J. Stokes) to Director, ''COMINFIL SCLC, IS–C,'' 12 July 1963, 100–438794–21, pp. 9–10. Levison's and O'Dell's phone calls to King about the magazine article are reflected in King's message book for 12 and 13 March; the article itself appeared as ''Bold Design for a New South,'' *Nation* 196 (30 March 1963): 259–62. President Kennedy's televised speech took place on 11 June.

90. See Hoover to Clyde Tolson, 17 June 1963, 100–106670–150; Burke Marshall to Hoover, 12 September 1963 (unreleased); and Marshall to Hoover, ''Hunter Pitts O'Dell,'' 20 September 1963, cited in n. 88 above. Kennedy on June 19 received a Hoover memo detailing a Levison-Clarence Jones conversation (100–106670–151); it was based on SAC, New York to Director, 19 June 1963, 100–106670–152.

91. The most detailed description of King's account of the conversation was given by Levison to Arthur Schlesinger, Jr., in 1976, and Schlesinger graciously made it available. Also see Schlesinger, *Robert Kennedy*, p. 357; Leon Howell, ''An Interview with Andrew Young,'' *Christianity & Crisis* 36 (16 February 1976): 14–20, at 17; ''Andrew Young Remembers Martin Luther King,'' *Bill Moyers' Journal*, Program 409, 2 April 1979, p. 4; Young's comments in Howell Raines, *My Soul Is Rested* (New York: G. P. Putnam's Sons, 1977), pp. 430–31; and Andrew Young, ''But His Truth Is Marching On,'' *New York Times*, 15 January 1974, p. 37.

92. James Free, ''King's SCLC Pays O'Dell Despite Denial,'' *Birmingham News*, 30 June 1963, p. 1.

93. Martin Luther King, Jr., to Jack H. O'Dell, 3 July 1963, Marshall Papers, Kennedy Library, Boston.

94. Levison's 1976 interview with Schlesinger, noted in n. 91 above; Ronald J. Ostrow, ''Why King Wiretap?,'' *Atlanta Constitution*, 21 Decem-

ber 1975, pp. A1, A14; author's conversations with Harry Wachtel and Burke Marshall. Marshall does not recall using the reference to Abel, but does not quarrel with accounts that he did.

95. Author's conversations with Clarence B. Jones; King, *Why We Can't Wait* (New York: Harper & Row, 1964) Mentor edition, p. 75. The FBI had first taken detailed note of Jones's presence in the King entourage in SAC, New York to Director, "Martin Luther King, Jr., SM–C," 12 September 1962, 100–106670–93.

96. Courtney A. Evans to Alan H. Belmont, "Communist Influence in Racial Matters (*JUNE*)," 16 July 1963, 100–3–116–41; Richard L. Lyons, "Red 'Rights Plot' Seen By Barnett," *Washington Post*, 13 July 1963, pp. A1, A4; Warren G. Magnuson to Hoover, 16 July 1963, 105–72120–3; Evans to Belmont, "Martin Luther King, Jr., SM–C, RM," 16 July 1963, 100–106670–166. The Bureau again privately dismissed the Highlander story, with a 13 July memo from Bland to Sullivan (100–106670–160) noting that Highlander was not and never had been a communist facility.

97. Hoover to Kennedy, 17 July 1963 (unreleased); Hoover to Magnuson, 18 July 1963, 105–72120–3; Hoover to Kennedy, 18 July 1963, 100–106670–157; Carl M. Brauer, *John F. Kennedy and the Second Reconstruction* (New York: Columbia University Press, 1977), p. 286; Hoover to Kennedy, 22 July 1963 (unreleased); Fred J. Baumgardner (by W. G. Shaw) to William C. Sullivan, "Martin Luther King, Jr., SM–C (*JUNE*)," 22 July 1963, 100–106670–168; Hoover to Kennedy, "Martin Luther King, Jr., SM–C (*JUNE*)," 23 July 1963, 100–106670–165; SAC, Atlanta to Director, "Communist Influence in Racial Matters (*JUNE*)," 24 July 1963, 100–3–116–48; Courtney A. Evans to Alan H. Belmont, "Martin Luther King, Jr. (*JUNE*)," 25 July 1963, 100–106670–171; and Hoover to Robert Kennedy, "Martin Luther King, Jr., SM–C, RM," 2 August 1963, 100–106670–174. The source of the Bureau's allegation that Jones had been a member, and perhaps a leader of the LYL was Albert Brown, Columbia University LYL chairman in 1954, and apparently an FBI informant. The allegation may have rested on nothing more than an identification of a photograph of Jones. See Hoover to Burke Marshall, "Clarence Benjamin Jones, SM–C," 13 September 1962, 100–407018–12; and SAC, New York to Director, "COMINFIL SCLC, IS–C," 8 November 1965, 100–438794–886. The tap on Jones was begun on 29 July 1963, and was not disconnected until 29 November 1966.

98. See E. W. Kenworthy, "U.S. Denies Reds Lead Integrationists," *New York Times*, 26 July 1963, p. 1; Robert Kennedy's and Burke Marshall's comments in their 1964 oral history interview with Anthony Lewis, Tape 6, pp. 2–4, cited at n. 51 above; Burke Marshall (Larry J. Hackman

interview, 19–20 January 1970, Bedford, N.Y.), John F. Kennedy Library, Boston, pp. 45–46; author's conversations with Burke Marshall and Nicholas deB. Katzenbach. President Kennedy himself had made a similar declaration at a 17 July news conference.

99. See Bill Shipp, "Onetime Communist Organizer Heads Rev. King's Office in N.Y.," *Atlanta Constitution,* 25 July 1963, pp. 1, 17; and Ted Simmons, "Rev. King Denies O'Dell Link but His Office in N.Y. Differs," *Atlanta Constitution,* 26 July 1963, p. 1. Also see William A. Fowlkes, "Dr. King Says O'Dell Left SCLC June 26," *Atlanta Daily World,* 26 July 1963, p. 1; "Dr. King Tells Role of His Accused Aide," *New York Times,* 27 July 1963, p. 8; Eugene Patterson, "Reds and Racists vs. Dr. King," *Atlanta Constitution,* 27 July 1963, p. 4; Al Kuettner (UPI), "King Suffers Red Troubles," *Jackson* (Miss.) *Daily News,* 29 July 1963, p. 9; "Dr. King's Affidavit on Ex-Aide Sought," *New York Times,* 30 July 1963, p. 13; Bill Shipp, "Dr. King to Give Cook a Statement on O'Dell," *Atlanta Constitution,* 30 July 1963, p. 5; and Bill Shipp, "King Withheld No Data, Aide Replies to Cook," *Atlanta Constitution,* 17 August 1963, p. 3.

100. SAC, New York to Director, "Martin Luther King, Jr., SM–C," 22 July 1963, 100–106670–162; Evans to Belmont, 29 July 1963 (unreleased); Evans to Belmont, "Martin Luther King, Jr., SM–C," 1 August 1963, 100–106670–202; and Hoover (by Theron D. Rushing) to Kennedy, 2 August 1963, 100–106670–203.

101. Hoover to Kennedy, "Martin Luther King, Jr., SM–C, RM," 7 August 1963, 100–106670–212; Hoover to Kennedy, "Martin Luther King, Jr., SM–C, RM," 12 August 1963, 100–106670–178; Hoover to Katzenbach, 13 August 1963, 100–106670–180, Marshall Papers, Box 8, and President's Office Files, Box 97, Kennedy Library, Boston; Evans to Belmont, 20 August 1963 (unreleased); and Hoover to Kennedy, "Martin Luther King, Jr., SM–C," 26 August 1963, 100–106670–191. The August 12 memo enclosed a four-page account of derogatory information on Bayard Rustin. On August 5 Katzenbach had been sent fifteen different reports on Rustin dating from 1942 to 1963.

102. See Fred J. Baumgardner to William C. Sullivan, "March on Washington, August 28, 1963, Possible Subversive Influence," 22 August 1963, 100–3–116–230; Baumgardner to Sullivan, "Communist Party, USA, Negro Question; IS–C," 23 August 1963, 100–3–116–253X; the report itself, entitled simply "Communist Party, USA—Negro Question," dated 23 August 1963 and filed as an attachment to 100–3–116–253X; and Baumgardner to Sullivan, "March on Washington, August 28, 1963, Possible Subversive Influence," 27 August 1963, 157–970–992. The second of these memos, like other Bureau documents, speaks of Stanley "Levinson" [*sic*],

as do a number of the few published accounts of the movement that even mention Levison. See, for instance, Howard Zinn, *SNCC: The New Abolitionists,* 2d ed. (Boston: Beacon Press, 1965), p. 32; and a very poor unpublished study, Eugene P. Walker, "A History of the Southern Christian Leadership Conference, 1955–1965: The Evolution of a Southern Strategy for Social Change," Ph.D. diss., Duke University, 1978, pp. 39–40, 45, 58, 82.

103. Sullivan to Alan H. Belmont, "Communist Party, USA, Negro Question; IS–C," 30 August 1963, 100–3–116–253X. This memo is easily accessible in both House Committee on Assassinations, *Hearings—King,* vol. 6, pp. 143–44; and in U.S., Department of Justice, *King Task Force,* pp. 165–66.

104. Hoover (by William T. Forsyth) to Kennedy, "Martin Luther King, Jr., SM–C," 4 September 1963, 100–106670–206; Hoover to Kennedy, 5 September 1963 (unreleased); ASAC to SAC, 3 September 1963, New York serial 100–111180–1229; James F. Bland to William C. Sullivan, "Martin Luther King, Jr., SM–C (*JUNE*)," 6 September 1963, 100–106670–207; Director to SACs, Atlanta and New York, "Martin Luther King, Jr., SM–C, (*JUNE*)," 6 September 1963, 100–106670–illegible; and Marshall to Hoover, "Hunter Pitts O'Dell," 20 September 1963, Marshall Papers, Kennedy Library, Boston. The Bland memo, though released, has 95 percent of its substance deleted, thus clouding the story.

105. SAC, New York to Director, "Martin Luther King, SM–C, RM," 11 September 1963, 100–106670–225. Hoover to Robert Kennedy, "Martin Luther King, Jr., SM–C, RM," 13 September 1963, 100–106670–208, enclosed a copy of the New York report for the Attorney General. At a 7 September news conference in Richmond, where the SCLC was holding its annual convention—under the very watchful eye of the local Bureau field office—King had remarked that "there are about as many Communists in the movement as there are Eskimoes in Florida." See "Dr. King Calls Wallace Move Irresponsible," *Richmond News Leader,* 8 September 1963, p. A2. On the Bureau's interest in the convention, see SAC, Richmond to Director (Attn.: Civil Rights Section, General Investigative Division), "National Convention, SCLC, Richmond, Va., 9/23–27/63, RM," 20 September 1963, 100–438794–24X3; and similar captioned reports of September 25 (24X9); September 26 (two, 24X4 and 24X5); September 27 (24X8); September 28 (two; 24X6 and 24X7); and October 4 (24X10). Six months later Levison advised Jones that he and King had decided that Rustin should be hired to oversee the New York office, but that no announcement would be made until the Senate filibuster on the civil rights bill had ended. See the account of a 11 March 1964 conversation in SAC, Atlanta (by Robert R.

Nichols) to Director, "COMINFIL SCLC, IS–C," 23 June 1964, 100–438794–94, p. 15.

106. Hoover to Kennedy, "Clarence Benjamin Jones, SM–C, RM," 11 September 1963, 100–407018–30; Hoover to Kennedy, "Martin Luther King, Jr., SM–C, RM," 17 September 1963, 100–106670–213; Evans to Belmont, 20 September 1963 (unreleased); Hoover to Kennedy, 24 September 1963, 100–392452–217; Hoover to Kennedy, "CPUSA, NQ; CIRM, IS–C," 26 September 1963, 100–3–116–388; and Bland to Sullivan, 18 September 1963, 100–392452–220. On the latter memo Hoover once again made light of Division Five's analysis of CP influence.

107. Fred J. Baumgardner (by Seymor F. Phillips) to Sullivan, "CPUSA, NQ; CIRM, IS–C," 16 September 1963, 100–3–116–367, which appears in both U.S., Department of Justice, *King Task Force,* pp. 167–68, and in House Assassinations Committee, *Hearings—King,* vol. 6, pp. 147–48; and Clyde Tolson to Hoover, "Memorandum for the Director," 18 September 1963, 100–3–116–253X, which appears in *King Task Force,* p. 169.

108. William C. Sullivan to Alan H. Belmont, "Communist Party, USA, Negro Question; Communist Influence in Racial Matters, IS–C," 25 September 1963, which appears in both *King Task Force,* pp. 170–74, and House Assassinations Committee, *Hearings—King,* vol. 6, pp. 149–53; and J. Edgar Hoover (by Seymor F. Phillips) to All SACs, "Communist Party, USA, Negro Question; Communist Influence in Racial Matters," 24 September 1963, 100–3–116–illegible.

109. James F. Bland (by William T. Forsyth) to William C. Sullivan, "Martin Luther King, Jr., Security Matter—Communist; Communist Influence in Racial Matters," 4 October 1963, 100–106670–251; and Hoover to Kennedy, "Martin Luther King, Jr., SM–C; Communist Influence in Racial Matters," 7 October 1963, 100–106670–250. Also, Hoover to Kennedy, "Rev. Martin Luther King, Jr., RM," 3 October 1963, 100–106670–227.

110. Kennedy to Evans, "Courtney, Speak to Me, RFK," 10 October 1963, 100–106670–171; Evans to Alan H. Belmont, "Martin Luther King, Jr., Security Matter—Communist," 10 October 1963, 100–106670–254.

111. Charles D. Brennan, "Communism and the Negro Movement—A Current Analysis," 16 October 1963, 100–3–116–416; Sullivan (by Brennan) to Belmont, 15 October 1963 (unreleased); Belmont to Tolson, 17 October 1963, in U.S., Department of Justice, *King Task Force,* p. 176; and Hoover to Kennedy, 18 October 1963 (unreleased).

112. James F. Bland to William C. Sullivan, "Martin Luther King, Jr., SM–C; Communist Influence in Racial Matters," 18 October 1963, 100–106670–illegible; Hoover to Kennedy, "Martin Luther King, Jr., SM–C; Communist Influence in Racial Matters," 18 October 1963, 100–106670–

illegible; Evans to Belmont, "Martin Luther King, Jr., SM–C; Communist Influence in Racial Matters," 21 October 1963, 100–106670–259.

113. Evans to Belmont, 25 October 1963, 100–3–116–483; Robert Kennedy, in 1964 oral history interview with Anthony Lewis, tape 6, pp. 9–10, cited at n. 55 above; Hoover to Kennedy, "Communism and the Negro Movement—A Current Analysis," 25 October 1963, unserialized; Hoover to Clyde Tolson, et al., 25 October 1963, unserialized; Helen W. Gandy to Hoover, n.d. [26 October 1963], unserialized; and Hoover to Clyde Tolson, et al., 7 November 1963, 100–3–116–483.

114. Courtney A. Evans to Alan H. Belmont, "Communist Influence in the Negro Movement," 1 November 1963, 100–3–116–518; Belmont to Clyde Tolson, "Communist Influence in the Negro Movement," 1 November 1963, 100–3–116–517; Evans to Belmont, "Dr. Martin Luther King, Jr., Information Concerning," 6 February 1964, 100–106670–307; and author's conversations with Nicholas deB. Katzenbach.

115. SAC, New York to Director, "Martin Luther King, Jr., SM–C; CIRM (*JUNE*)," 25 October 1963, 100–106670–246; SAC, New York to Director, "CPUSA, NQ," 31 October 1963, 100–3–116–485; SAC, New York to Director, "Martin Luther King, Jr., SM–C; CIRM (*JUNE*)," 1 November 1963, 100–106670–249; and SAC, Atlanta to Director, "COMINFIL, RM; Dr. Martin Luther King, Jr., SM–C (*JUNE*)," 27 November 1963, 100–438794–43. New York also continued to report on conversations overheard on the Jones and Levison wiretaps. See SAC, New York to Director, "COMINFIL SCLC, IS–C," 4 November 1963, 100–438794–42; and Hoover to Robert Kennedy, "Martin Luther King, Jr., SM–C," 8 November 1963, 100–106670–257. In early 1964 a wiretap was added on Rustin, though apparently not on Bennett.

2. Criticism, Communism, and Robert Kennedy

1. Possible examples of these words, even just in the King and SCLC case files, number in the hundreds. See, for example, Director (by Seymor F. Phillips) to SACs, Birmingham and New York, "COMINFIL SCLC, IS–C," 4 August 1965, 100–438794–472; and Director (by Phillips) to SAC, Indianapolis, "COMINFIL SCLC, IS–C," 28 July 1965, 100–438794–441.

2. Author's conversations with Nicholas deB. Katzenbach, and Katzenbach's testimony in U.S., Congress, Senate, Select Committee to Study Governmental Operations with Respect to Intelligence Activities, *Hear-*

ings—Federal Bureau of Investigation, 94th Cong., 1st sess., 1976, vol. 6, pp. 198, 209.

3. Senate Select Committee, *Hearings—FBI,* vol. 6, p. 173; and U.S., Congress, House, Select Committee on Assassinations, *Hearings on Investigation of the Assassination of Martin Luther King, Jr.,* 95th Cong., 2d sess., 1978, vol. 7, pp. 41–44, 55.

4. William C. Sullivan, *The Bureau: My Thirty Years in Hoover's FBI* (New York: W. W. Norton, 1979), pp. 135, 139, 142. Also see Mark Felt, *The FBI Pyramid* (New York: G. P. Putnam's Sons, 1979), p. 121.

5. See Wallace Turner, "FBI Taps Called Plan to Discredit Dr. King," *New York Times,* 21 May 1973, p. 25; Arthur L. Murtagh, "An Agent's View of Hoover," *Nation* 220 (19 April 1975): 467–68; and Murtagh's statements in Mark Lane and Dick Gregory, *Code Name "Zorro" The Murder of Martin Luther King, Jr.* (Englewood Cliffs, N.J.: Prentice-Hall, 1977), pp. 90–91.

6. See Laurence Stern and Richard Harwood, " 'King Tape' Emerges From Legend to Underline a Danger to Liberties," *Washington Post,* 11 June 1969, p. A27; " 'A Dirty Business,' " *Nation* 208 (23 June 1969): 780–81; and also Arlie Schardt, "Civil Rights: Too Much, Too Late," in *Investigating the FBI,* ed. Pat Watters and Stephen Gillers (Garden City, N.Y.: Doubleday, 1973), pp. 167–205, at 188.

7. Senate Select Committee, *Hearings—FBI,* vol. 6, p. 30. Also see the remarks of John T. Elliff, *Hearings—FBI,* vol. 6, p. 159; and Eugene Lewis, *Public Entrepreneurship: Toward A Theory of Bureaucratic Political Power* (Bloomington: Indiana University Press, 1980), p. 152.

8. See Nicholas M. Horrock, "Senate Intelligence Panel Told of FBI Attempt to Discredit Dr. King in 1964," *New York Times,* 19 November 1975, p. 16; Horrock, "FBI Aide Terms Effort to Vilify Dr. King Illegal," *New York Times,* 20 November 1975, pp. 1, 30; "The Crusade to Topple King," *Time,* 1 December 1975, pp. 11–12; and Sandra Salmans, "Tales of the FBI," *Newsweek,* 1 December 1975, pp. 35–36. Also see Jerry J. Berman, "The FBI's Vendetta against Martin Luther King, Jr.," in Morton Halperin et al., *The Lawless State: The Crimes of the U.S. Intelligence Agencies* (New York: Penguin Books, 1976), pp. 66, 68, which is generally a rehash of material disclosed in Church Committee publications.

9. See Peter Beeson, "An Analysis of the Assassination Investigation of the Department of Justice and the Federal Bureau of Investigation," in House Committee on Assassinations, *Hearings—King,* vol. 13, pp. 153–216, at 178–79; and House Committee on Assassinations, *The Final Assassinations Report* (New York: Bantam Books, 1979), pp. 569–70.

10. One rather egregious example is Iris L. Washington, "The FBI Plot

against Black Leaders,'' *Essence* 9 (October 1978): 70–73, 97–105, 146, at 72.

11. Frank J. Donner, *The Age of Surveillance* (New York: Alfred A. Knopf, 1980), p. 122.

12. J. Edgar Hoover to Robert F. Kennedy, 30 September 1963, FBI "Civil Rights Policy File," Series "44," Kennedy Library, Boston.

13. See nn. 8, 78–80, 87, chapter 1.

14. Senate Select Committee, *Final Report—Book III,* p. 85. Also see House Committee on Assassinations, *The Final Assassinations Report,* p. 570.

15. See n. 108, chapter 1.

16. See n. 109, chapter 1.

17. See Anthony Downs, *Inside Bureaucracy* (Boston: Little Brown, 1967), pp. 1–7, 118. Also see William A. Niskanen, *Bureaucracy and Representative Government* (Chicago: Aldine-Atherton, 1971), chapter 4; Niskanen, "Bureaucrats and Politicians," *Journal of Law and Economics* 18 (December 1975): 617–43; and Niskanen, "Competition among Government Bureaus," *American Behavioral Scientist* 22 (May–June 1979): 517–24.

18. Senate Select Committee, *Final Report—Book III,* pp. 15, 106–11; and *Final Report—Book II,* p. 250.

19. See Sullivan, *The Bureau,* p. 139; and C. D. Brennan's remarks in House Committee on Assassinations, *Hearings—King,* vol. 6, p. 154. Also see Adam Przeworski and Henry Teune, *The Logic of Comparative Social Inquiry* (New York: Wiley-Interscience, 1970), pp. 17, 20–21.

20. See n. 100, chapter 1.

21. Victor S. Navasky, *Kennedy Justice* (New York: Atheneum, 1971), pp. 147, 151; Courtney Evans's comments in Ronald J. Ostrow, "Why King Wiretap?" *Atlanta Constitution,* 21 December 1975, pp. A1, A14; and author's conversations with Ed Guthman. Arthur Schlesinger too has indicated a sympathy for this view: "The Kennedys authorized the taps on King for defensive purposes—in order to protect King, to protect the civil rights bill, to protect themselves." *Robert Kennedy and His Times* (Boston: Houghton Mifflin, 1978), p. 360.

22. See nn. 110–13, chapter 1.

23. Do note, however, Navasky's statement, "If they really believed . . . that Dr. King himself was above suspicion, then a tap on *him* was redundant." *Kennedy Justice,* p. 150.

24. Robert F. Kennedy and Burke Marshall (Anthony Lewis interview, 4 December 1964, New York, N.Y.), Kennedy Library, Boston, tape V, pp. 22–25, 28–39, and tape VI, pp. 1–8.

25. Burke Marshall (Larry J. Hackman interview, 19–20 January 1970, Bedford, N.Y.), Kennedy Library, Boston, pp. 44–45; and Senate Select Committee, *Final Report—Book III,* p. 117. Also see Navasky, *Kennedy Justice,* p. 147, and Nicholas Katzenbach's comments in William Safire, "Of Kennedys and Kings," *New York Times,* 20 June 1975, p. 35.

26. Both Burke Marshall and Nicholas Katzenbach, along with Guthman and Seigenthaler, explain today that Kennedy's attitude was a complicated one and difficult to grasp in retrospect. On one hand he had no doubt that Levison was both a Communist agent and King's most influential adviser. On the other, he reacted as much with bemusement as with anger at King's seeming inability to take the allegations and warnings seriously. The statements of Marshall and others that Kennedy never articulated any concrete doubts about King's conscious loyalty are no doubt quite accurate, but Kennedy's puzzlement and disappointment over King's maintaining contact with Levison deserves to receive equal emphasis. Author's conversations with Marshall, Katzenbach, Guthman, and Seigenthaler. These mixed sentiments come through clearly at pp. 8–9 of tape VI of the Kennedy-Marshall conversation with Lewis cited in n. 24 above. Also see Navasky, *Kennedy Justice,* pp. 140, 143.

27. See Harris Wofford, *Of Kennedys and Kings* (New York: Farrar, Straus & Giroux, 1980), pp. 32–33; Schlesinger, *Robert Kennedy,* pp. 121–26; and Navasky, *Kennedy Justice,* p. 139. All indications are that Robert Kennedy never was told the "Solo" story by anyone from the Bureau.

28. Senate Select Committee, *Final Report—Book III,* p. 84; Schlesinger, *Robert Kennedy,* p. 355; author's conversations with Burke Marshall, Ed Guthman, John Seigenthaler, and Nicholas deB. Katzenbach.

29. See especially Burke Marshall, *Federalism and Civil Rights* (New York: Columbia University Press, 1964), as well as Simon Lazarus III, "Theories of Federalism and Civil Rights," *Yale Law Journal* 75 (May 1966): 1007–52. Critical comments appear in Navasky, *Kennedy Justice,* pp. 132, 176, 185, 207; and Richard A. Wasserstrom, "Federalism and Civil Rights," *University of Chicago Law Review* 33 (Winter 1966): 406–13. Interestingly, Marshall's book contains not one reference to the FBI. The Bureau's position can be sampled in J. Edgar Hoover, "The Role of the FBI in Civil Rights Disputes," *Yale Political* 2 (August 1963): 12, 31–32; and a lengthier but quite similar Bureau monograph entitled "The Role of the FBI in Protecting Civil Rights," 24 October 1962, Berl I. Bernhard Papers, Kennedy Library, Boston.

30. As an outstanding study by John T. Elliff concludes, both Marshall and Hoover "shared (perhaps for different reasons) a reluctance to assert maximum federal power in the South." Up through 1964, "there was sel-

dom a direct adversary relationship between the Bureau and executives of the Civil Rights Division." "Aspects of Federal Civil Rights Enforcement: The Justice Department and the FBI, 1939–1964," *Perspectives in American History* 5 (1971): 605–73, at 670. Also see Navasky, *Kennedy Justice,* pp. 9, 100. This conclusion receives implicit endorsement in John Doar and Dorothy Landsberg, "The Performance of the FBI in Investigating Violations of Federal Laws Protecting the Right to Vote—1960–1967," in Senate Select Committee, *Hearings—FBI,* vol. 6, pp. 888–991. Furthermore, as Robert Kennedy himself stressed privately in 1964, up through the time of his brother's assassination relations between him and Director Hoover were "reasonably cordial." Robert F. Kennedy (John B. Martin interview, 13 April 1964, New York, N.Y.), Kennedy Library, Boston, p. 32. Also see Edwin Guthman, *We Band of Brothers* (New York: Harper & Row, 1971), p. 261; and Courtney Evans's remark in Scott J. Rafferty, "Building the Consensus: Civil Rights and the Department of Justice, 1961–1963," Unpublished B.A. thesis, Princeton University, 1976, p. 24. Some well-informed critics, such as the Civil Rights Commission's Erwin Griswold, are as harsh on the Kennedy Justice Department as most observers are on the Bureau. "Marshall was a distinctly negative influence . . . he was so conservative, so cautious, and had no broad vision of the whole thing at all. . . . he would only deal with the specific crisis at hand." Erwin Griswold (Scott J. Rafferty interview, 29 October 1975, Washington, D.C.), Kennedy Library, Boston. Suggestions that the Bureau used the information it possessed on President Kennedy's relationship with Mafia moll Judith Campbell to blackmail the Kennedy brothers into approving the King wiretaps lack supporting evidence. See William Safire, "The President's Friend," *New York Times,* 15 December 1975, p. 31.

31. The various congressional and Justice Department probes of the Bureau have all concluded that no dependable judgment on the Levison issue is possible. See Senate Select Committee, *Final Report—Book III,* p. 84; Murphy Report, 31 March 1976, p. 11; U.S., Department of Justice, *King Task Force,* pp. 123, 125, 141; and House Committee on Assassinations, *The Final Assassinations Report,* p. 535. Of course, none of these investigators knew the full story of the "Solo" operation. Suggestions by a number of the investigators that secondhand information received in early 1963 (presumably from Jack Childs) that Levison reportedly had expressed great unhappiness with the Communist party's stance on civil rights questions should have caused the Bureau to close down the entire investigation are well taken, but that report, like all the others on Levison, was inconclusive on the larger question that preoccupied the Bureau. See especially *King Task Force,* pp. 125, 141.

32. The possibility that Levison did perjure himself on that question is extremely remote. Levison repeatedly denied that he ever was a member of the party, and that statement, interpreted literally, is in all likelihood both accurate and misleading. Interviewers who questioned Levison on his past associations apparently always took that denial as a statement that he had had no meaningful involvement with the CP whatsoever—which, as any careful observer immediately will realize, is a much different matter from the simple question of formal membership—and pressed him no further on the issue. See Don Oberdorfer, "King Adviser Says FBI 'Used' Him," *Washington Post,* 15 December 1975, p. A4; Carl T. Rowan, "King's 'Communist Adviser,' " *New York Post,* 19 December 1975, p. 35; Laurence Stern, "King 'Influencer' Named," *Washington Post,* 8 December 1975, pp. A1, A8; Navasky, *Kennedy Justice,* p. 148; and Arthur M. Schlesinger, Jr.'s notes of a 3 August 1976 conversation with Levison, and Levison to Schlesinger, 27 September 1977, both kindly supplied to the author by Schlesinger. To his closest relatives, Levison made it clear that he saw an immense difference between the allegation that he had been a close friend of the CP, and the accusation that he was or had been the agent of a foreign power. While he would not disclaim the former, he angrily denied the latter. To the FBI, however, which viewed everything through the prism of "Solo," that distinction was largely formal and rather minor.

33. Author's conversations with Andrew Levison, Beatrice Levison, Roy Bennett, Joseph H. Filner, Harry Wachtel, and Clarence B. Jones.

34. See n. 60, chapter 1.

35. For the standard comment, see Oberdorfer, "King Adviser Says FBI 'Used' Him," cited in n. 32 above.

36. Young's characterization of Levison as a "conservative force" or "conservative influence" who was "very cautious about becoming involved with the war in Vietnam" appears in both Leon Howell, "An Interview with Andrew Young," *Christianity & Crisis* 36 (16 February 1976): 14–20, at 18; and Oberdorfer, "King Adviser Says FBI 'Used' Him," cited in n. 32 above.

37. Levison always remained self-effacing and reluctant to talk about his close friendship with King. Only the 1978 controversy over Abby Mann's "King" docudrama persuaded Levison to speak out concerning his role. See Jay Lawrence, " 'King' Movie Distorts Man, Movement, Followers Assert," *Atlanta Constitution,* 10 August 1977, pp. A1, A7; and Jacqueline Trescott, "A Continuing 'King' Controversy," *Washington Post,* 14 February 1978, p. B5.

3. "They Are Out to Break Me"—The Surveillance of Martin King

1. James F. Bland (by William T. Forsyth) to William C. Sullivan, "Communist Influence in Racial Matters; SCLC; Martin Luther King, Jr., SM–C, (*JUNE*)," 20 December 1963, 100–438794–unserialized; SAC, New York to Director, "Martin Luther King, Jr., SM–C, (*JUNE*)," 12 December 1963, 100–106670–285; and SAC, New York to Director, "Justification for Continuation of Technical or Microphone Surveillance, Martin Luther King, Jr., SM–C, (*JUNE*)," 22 November 1963, 100–438794–unserialized.

2. See SAC, New York to Director, "CPUSA, NQ; CIRM, IS–C," 21 November 1963, 100–3–116–562; Hoover (by Seymor F. Phillips) to Kennedy, "CPUSA, NQ; CIRM, IS–C," 22 November 1963, 100–3–116–530; Hoover (by William T. Forsyth) to Kennedy, "Martin Luther King, Jr., SM–C," 22 November 1963, 100–106670–271; Hoover (by R. C. Denz) to Kennedy, "CPUSA, NQ; CIRM, IS–C," 26 November 1963, 100–3–116–536; Hoover (by Denz) to Kennedy and Kenneth O'Donnell, "CPUSA, NQ; CIRM, IS–C," 27 November 1963, 100–3–116–539; SAC, New York to Director, "CPUSA, NQ," 2 December 1963, 100–3–116–577; SAC, New York to Director, "CPUSA, NQ; CIRM, IS–C," 10 December 1963, 100–3–116–631; SAC, New York to Director, "CPUSA, NQ; CIRM, IS–C," 12 December and 17 December 1963, both unserialized in 100–438794; SAC, New York to Director, "CPUSA, NQ; CIRM, IS–C," 18 December and 20 December 1963, 100–3–116–666 and 627; Bland to Sullivan, 20 December 1963, cited in n. 1 above, and Hoover (by Denz) to Kennedy, "CPUSA, NQ; CIRM, IS–C," 30 December 1963, 100–3–116–illegible. One memo, Baumgardner (by Phillips) to Sullivan, "CPUSA, NQ; CIRM, IS–C," 21 November 1963, 100–3–116–549, speaks of a "highly sensitive and anonymous–type investigative technique concerning Levison [that] was used by our New York office on 10/19/63 and 10/21/63 but proved negative." This may well indicate a break-in.

3. Baumgardner (by Gurley) to Sullivan, "CPUSA, NQ; CIRM, IS–C," 19 December 1963, 100–3–116–illegible; Sullivan (by Baumgardner) to Belmont, "CPUSA, NQ; CIRM, IS–C," 24 December 1963, 100–3–116–684. The second memo is reprinted in House Committee on Assassinations, *Hearings—King,* vol. 6, pp. 156–58.

4. "Questions to be Explored at Conference 12/23/63 re Communist Influence in Racial Matters," 100–3–116–684, and most easily available in House Committee on Assassinations, *Hearings—King,* vol. 6, pp. 159–61.

5. See *Time,* 3 January 1964; SAC, New York to Director, "Communist Party USA, Negro Question; Communist Influence in Racial Matters, IS–C," 6 January 1964, 100–438794–unserialized; and SAC, New York to Director, 18 December 1963, cited in n. 2 above.

6. William C. Sullivan to Alan H. Belmont, "CPUSA, Negro Question; CIRM, IS–C," 6 January 1964, 100–3–116–714, and most easily available in House Committee on Assassinations, *Hearings—King,* vol. 6, p. 192. Two unreleased New York field-office serials of 3 December 1963, 100–151548–752 and 754 indicate that Sullivan's immediate assistant, Joseph A. Sizoo, had called ASAC Donald E. Roney on that date to ask if it would be possible to bug King's room at the Park Sheraton, where headquarters believed he soon would be staying. Roney did not pursue the idea after learning from the hotel that King did not have a reservation there.

7. Fred J. Baumgardner (by Phillips) to Sullivan, "CPUSA, NQ; CIRM, IS–C," 8 January 1964, 100–3–116–724; and Director (by Phillips) to SAC, New York, "CPUSA, NQ; CIRM, IS–C," 9 January 1964, 100–3–116–701. Phillips explained his role in the administrative handling of the King and SCLC cases to two Justice Department lawyers, James R. Kieckhefer and Joseph F. Gross, Jr., in a 21 December 1976 interview, a summary of which is filed in appendix B of U.S., Department of Justice, *Report of the Department of Justice Task Force to Review the FBI Martin Luther King, Jr., Security and Assassination Investigations,* 11 January 1977.

8. William C. Sullivan to Alan H. Belmont, "Samuel Riley Pierce, Jr.," 8 January 1964, 77–56944–19. Also see Anthony Marro, "Lawyer Is Identified as FBI's Candidate," *New York Times,* 10 June 1978, p. 8; and Victor S. Navasky, "The FBI's Wildest Dream," *Nation* 226 (17 June 1978): 716–18. As both these accounts note, Pierce was both totally unaware of Sullivan's interest in him, and scarcely suited to any public leadership role in the black freedom movement. In 1981 Pierce became secretary of housing and urban development in the Reagan cabinet.

9. Sullivan to Alan H. Belmont, "Communist Party USA, Negro Question; Communist Influence in Racial Matters, IS–C," 13 January 1964, 100–3–116–761, most easily accessible in House Committee on Assassinations, *Hearings—King,* vol. 6, pp. 193–94; and DeLoach to Hoover, 14 January 1964 (unreleased). The eight-page account, still classified "Top Secret" and never released, is in the extensive "Stegall File" (after Johnson's private secretary) on Dr. King at the Johnson Library, Austin, Texas. Also in that file is the one earlier Bureau communication sent to the Johnson White House, a two-page Hoover to Jenkins letter of 3 December 1963, the date of King's first meeting with the new president. No Stegall Files have yet been opened by the Johnson Library. A much later memo, George C.

Moore to William C. Sullivan, "Martin Luther King, Jr., SM–C," 2 July 1969, 100–106670–3638, reports that DeLoach sometime in December gave President Johnson a copy of the recalled Brennan monograph, which Johnson returned to DeLoach the next day.

10. See four different communications from SAC, New York to Director, all dated 10 January 1964 and all located in 100–438794. Three—two captioned "Communist Party USA, Negro Question; Communist Influence in Racial Matters, IS–C;" and one headed "Justification for Continuation of Technical or Microphone Surveillance, Martin Luther King, Jr., SM–C,"— are unserialized. The fourth, captioned "COMINFIL SCLC, IS–C," is serial 61. Also see Hoover to Robert Kennedy, "CPUSA, NQ; CIRM, IS–C," 17 January 1964, 100–3–116–illegible; Director (by William T. Forsyth) to SAC, New York, "Martin Luther King, Jr., SM–C," 17 January 1964, 100–438794–unserialized, which states that "no information of any value has been received to date from this source;" SAC, New York to Director, "Martin Luther King, Jr., SM–C (*JUNE*)," 27 January 1964, 100–106670–294; and the notations on SAC, New York to Director, "Martin Luther King, Jr., SM–C (*JUNE*)," 12 December 1963, 100–106670–285. The burglary is reflected in subfile 1 of New York file 100–136585.

11. See three communications, all from Director (by Seymor F. Phillips), all captioned "Communist Party USA, Negro Question; Communist Influence in Racial Matters, IS–C," dated 10, 16, 17 January 1964, and all unserialized in 100–438794. The first and last are to SACs, Charlotte, Atlanta, and New York; the 16 January one is to SAC, Atlanta.

12. See Sullivan to Alan H. Belmont, 17 January 1964, 100–106670 (*JUNE*), unreleased; Fred J. Baumgardner to Sullivan, "Communist Party USA, Negro Question; Communist Influence in Racial Matters, IS–C, (*JUNE*)," 23 January 1964, 100–3–116–illegible; and two Sullivan to Belmont memos of 27 and 28 January, each with that same double caption and serialized as 100–3–116–792 and 801.

13. Baumgardner (apparently by Phillips) to Sullivan, 28 January 1964 (unreleased); Baumgardner (apparently by Phillips) to Sullivan, "Communist Party USA, Negro Question; Communist Influence in Racial Matters, (*JUNE*)," 4 February 1964, 100–3–116–900; SAC, San Francisco (by Harry F. Clifford, Jr.) to Director, attn. William C. Sullivan, "Communist Party USA, Negro Question; Communist Influence in Racial Matters, IS–C," 25 February 1964, 100–3–116–illegible, and most easily accessible in House Committee on Assassinations, *Hearings—King,* vol. 6, pp. 195–204; Joseph A. Sizoo to William C. Sullivan, 20 February 1964 (unreleased); Sullivan to Alan H. Belmont, "CPUSA, NQ; CIRM, IS–C (*JUNE*)," 20 February 1964, 100–3–116–975; SAC, San Francisco to

Director, 27 February 1964 (unreleased), which transmitted a 31-page summary transcript; SAC, San Francisco to Director, 25 March 1964 (unreleased); SAC, Los Angeles to Director, attn. William C. Sullivan, "CPUSA, NQ; CIRM, IS–C (*JUNE*)," 24 February 1964, 100–3–116–975; and three other similarly addressed and captioned communications of 24 February, 26 February, and 5 March 1964, serialized as 100–3–116–976, 977, and 1022, respectively.

14. See particularly Fred J. Baumgardner (by Phillips) to Sullivan, "CPUSA, NQ; CIRM, IS–C (*JUNE*)," 4 March 1964, 100–3–116–illegible, and most easily accessible in House Committee on Assassinations, *Hearings—King,* vol. 6, pp. 205–6; the other phrase is from a blind memorandum of 9 April 1968 entitled "Martin Luther King, Jr.," and serialized as 100–106670–3413. In another memo sent to Sullivan under Baumgardner's name on 3 March 1964 (100–3–116–986), the writer remarked, "It is shocking indeed that King continues to increase his influence and status in government circles notwithstanding the information which the White House has concerning his communist connections" and personal conduct. Why officials continued to treat with respect "an individual so fraught with evil as King" was unfathomable to the Bureau.

15. Eleven letters about King went from Hoover to Walter Jenkins between early February and late April, 1964. Ones dated 5, 10, and 13 February, 9 March, and 27 April have been released; ones dated 11 and 28 February, 5 March, and 14, 17, and 24 April have not. Copies of most of them also went to Robert Kennedy. Also see Baumgardner to Sullivan, 4 March 1964, cited in n. 14 above. The hunger strike news was conveyed in the 14 April letter, with a copy going to Burke Marshall (100–106670–340 and 338). It also is discussed in the "Murphy Report," 31 March 1976, p. 31. Hoover's January testimony, Kennedy's complaint, and Smith's request are the subjects of Evans to Belmont, "Testimony Concerning Martin Luther King Before the House Appropriations Committee," 31 January 1964, 100–106670–299; Nicholas P. Callahan to John P. Mohr, "USIA Film—'March for Freedom,' " 31 January 1964, 100–106670–302; Hoover to Tolson, et al., 5 February 1964, 100–106670–297; and DeLoach to Mohr, "Martin Luther King, Information Concerning," 16 March 1964, 100–106670–320.

16. Baumgardner to Sullivan, "CPUSA, NQ; CIRM, IS–C," 4 February and 5 February 1964, 100–3–116–illegible and 861; Evans to Belmont, "CPUSA, NQ; CIRM, IS–C," 5 February 1964, 100–3–116–866; Edwin Guthman memorandum, 5 February 1964, in U.S., Congress, Senate, Select Committee to Study Governmental Operations with Respect to Intelligence Activities, *Final Report, Book III, Supplementary Detailed Staff Reports on*

Intelligence Activities and the Rights of Americans, 94th Cong., 2d sess., 1976, pp. 149–50; DeLoach to John Mohr, "Martin Luther King," 5 February and 12 February 1964, 100–106670–unserialized and 303; Marshall to Moyers, 13 February 1964, 100–106670–315; Moyers to Marshall, 18 February 1964 (unreleased); DeLoach to Hoover, 18 February and 19 February 1964, 100–106670–315 and 316; and three memos from Al Rosen to Belmont, one dated 25 February 1964 and two 26 February 1964, 100–106670–317, 318 and 319. The Bureau strongly suspected that Cleghorn's original source was a supervisor in the Atlanta FBI office.

17. Joseph Alsop, "Matter of Fact," *Washington Post,* 15 April 1964, and *New York Herald Tribune,* 15 April 1964; SAC, New York to Director, "CPUSA, NQ; CIRM, IS–C," 4 March 1964, 100–438794–unserialized; SAC, Atlanta to Director and SAC, New York, "CPUSA, NQ; CIRM, IS–C; COMINFIL SCLC, IS–C," 10 March 1964, 100–438794–unserialized; Hoover to Walter Jenkins, 17 March 1964, 100–3–116–1054, Johnson Library; SAC, New York to Director, "CPUSA, NQ; CIRM, IS–C," 2 April 1964, 100–438794–unserialized; SAC, New York to Director, "CPUSA, NQ; CIRM, IS–C," 21 April 1964, 100–438794–unserialized; Fred J. Baumgardner to William C. Sullivan, 21 April 1964 (unreleased); SAC, Atlanta to Director, "CPUSA, NQ; CIRM, IS–C; COMINFIL SCLC, IS–C," 22 April 1964, 100–3–116–1322; SAC, New York to Director, "CPUSA, NQ; CIRM, IS–C," 22 April 1964, 100–438794–unserialized; SAC, New York to Director, "COMINFIL SCLC, IS–C," 5 June 1964, 100–438794–90, pp. 14–16; and SAC, Atlanta (by Robert R. Nichols) to Director, "COMINFIL SCLC, IS–C; Ralph David Abernathy," 24 September 1964, 100–438794–158.

18. "Hoover Says Reds Exploit Negroes," *New York Times,* 22 April 1964, p. 30; "King Admits 'Reds Here and There,' " *Nashville Banner,* 24 April 1964, p. 1; and "King Says FBI Abets Racists," *Newark Star-Ledger,* 24 April 1964, p. 9. King's statement was drafted by Clarence Jones. See SAC, New York to Director, "CPUSA, NQ; CIRM, IS–C," 27 April 1964, 100–438794 and 100–106670, unserialized; and New York's report of 5 June 1964, p. 16, cited in n. 17 above.

19. King interview, 10 May 1964, *Face the Nation,* CBS, vol. 7 (1964), pp. 210–11; and Baumgardner to Sullivan, "CPUSA, NQ; CIRM, IS–C," 11 May 1964, 100–3–116–1310.

20. Baumgardner (by Phillips) to Sullivan, "Martin Luther King, Jr., SM–C," 4 March 1964, 100–106670–312, and an identically addressed and captioned memo of 2 April, 100–106670–348. The Springfield attempt, which proved unsuccessful, was handled by having DeLoach provide the King material to Massachusetts Senator Leverett Saltonstall. See DeLoach

to John Mohr, "Martin Luther King, Jr., SM–C," 8 April 1964, 100–106670–349. All three items appear in House Committee on Assassinations, *Hearings—King,* vol. 6, pp. 268–74. The Detroit bug is the subject of Sullivan to Belmont, "CPUSA, NQ; CIRM, IS–C (*JUNE*)," 19 March 1964, 100–3–116–1153. The Bureau also disseminated information on King to Thomas Hughes, Director of the State Department's Bureau of Intelligence and Research, and U.S. Information Agency security director Paul J. McNichol. See Daniel J. Brennan, Jr. (by O. H. Bartlett) to Sullivan, "CPUSA, NQ; CIRM, IS–C," 3 April 1964, 100–106670–337; and Hoover to McNichol, 5 March 1964, 100–106670–311.

21. Director to SAC, Atlanta, "CPUSA, NQ; CIRM, IS–C," 19 March 1964, 100–438794–unserialized; Daniel Brennan to Sullivan, 27 March 1964, Baumgardner to Sullivan, 27 March 1964, headquarters' serials 100–3–116–1200 and 1201, New York serials 100–111180–1391 and 1414, dated 9 March 1964 and 17 April 1964, respectively, Director to SAC, New York, "CPUSA, NQ," 19 March 1964, Director to SACs, Atlanta and New York, 1 April 1964, SAC, New York to Director, 2 April 1964, SAC, New York to Director, 14 April 1964, 100–392452–229, SAC, Atlanta to Director, 14 April 1964, and headquarters' serial 100–3–116–1243, all unreleased; Director (by David Ryan) to SACs, New York and Atlanta, "CPUSA, COINTELPRO, IS–C (NQ)," 13 April 1964, 100–438794–unserialized and 100–3–104–34–illegible; Director (by David Ryan) to SAC, New York, "CPUSA, COINTELPRO, IS–C (NQ)," 20 April 1964, 100–438794–unserialized; SAC, Atlanta (by Al F. Miller) to Director, "CPUSA, NQ; CIRM, IS–C," 23 April 1964, 100–438794–unserialized; Director to SAC, Atlanta, 24 April 1964, unreleased; and Director (by T. P. Rosack) to SAC, Atlanta, "COMINFIL SCLC, IS–C," 7 May 1964, 100–438794–85. Also, Director to SAC, New York, "CPUSA, NQ; CIRM, IS–C," 24 April 1964, in U.S., Congress, Senate, Select Committee to Study Governmental Operations with Respect to Intelligence Activities, *Hearings—Federal Bureau of Investigation,* 94th Cong., 1st sess., 1976, vol. 6, pp. 695–96; and two unreleased headquarters' documents, a large report dated 27 April 1964 (100–3–116–1309) and a Baumgardner to Sullivan memo of 29 April 1964, each of which terms King a "communist tool." The Atlanta office's recommendations are discussed in Beau Cutts, "FBI Asked Tax Scare for SCLC," *Atlanta Constitution,* 3 October 1975, pp. A1, A19; and Claudia Townsend, "IRS Gave FBI Names of Secret SCLC Contributors," *Atlanta Constitution,* 12 May 1976, p. C1.

22. See SAC, New York to Director, "CPUSA, NQ; CIRM, IS–C (*JUNE*)," 15 April 1964, 100–438794–unserialized; Director to SAC, New York, "CPUSA, NQ; CIRM, IS–C (*JUNE*)," 22 April 1964, 100–

438794–unserialized; SAC, New York to Director, "CPUSA, NQ; CIRM, IS–C (*JUNE*)," 28 April 1964, 100–438794–unserialized; SAC, New York to Director, "Recommendation for Installation of Technical or Microphone Surveillance (*JUNE*)," 29 April 1964, 100–438794–unserialized; Baumgardner (by R. C. Denz) to Sullivan, "CPUSA, NQ; CIRM, IS–C (*JUNE*)," 6 May 1964, 100–3–116–1341; and Director (by R. C. Denz) to SAC, New York, "CPUSA, NQ; CIRM, IS–C (*JUNE*)," 7 May 1964, 100–3–116–1328.

23. See Sullivan to Belmont, "CPUSA, NQ; CIRM, IS–C," 22 April 1964, 100–3–116–1382; Sullivan to Belmont, "Martin Luther King, Jr.; CPUSA, NQ; CIRM, IS–C," 23 April 1964, 100–106670–360; SAC, Los Angeles to Director, "CPUSA, NQ; CIRM, IS–C," 24 April 1964, 100–3–116–1373; SAC, Los Angeles to Director, "CPUSA, NQ; CIRM, IS–C," 26 April 1964, 100–3–116–1389; and SAC, San Francisco to Director, 6 May 1964, which enclosed a 23-page summary transcript from the Sacramento bug. A phone wiretap as well as a microphone was employed during the Hyatt House stay. See George C. Moore (by C. E. Glass) to Sullivan, "Martin Luther King, Jr., SM–C (*JUNE*)," 9 June 1969, 100–106670–unserialized.

24. SAC, Las Vegas to Director, "CPUSA, NQ; CIRM, IS–C," 15 May 1964, 100–438794–unserialized; [SAC Elson, Las Vegas] to J. Edgar Hoover, 20 May 1964, "O & C" File 24; and SAC, Las Vegas to Director, "Martin Luther King, Jr.," 12 December 1975, 100–106670–4024. Although no bug had been deployed, Sullivan had called the Las Vegas office to ask that King be photographed gambling if at all possible. This did not develop. The four-page report to the White House, dated 1 June 1964, is in the Stegall Files, Johnson Library.

25. See SAC, Atlanta (by Robert R. Nichols) to Director, "CPUSA, NQ; CIRM, IS–C; Cordy Tindell Vivian, SM–C," 31 March 1964, 100–438794–unserialized; Director (by T. P. Rosack) to SAC, Atlanta, "COMINFIL SCLC, IS–C," 5 May 1964, 100–438794–84; SAC, Atlanta (by Robert R. Nichols) to Director, "CPUSA, NQ; CIRM, IS–C," 26 May 1964, and a similarly addressed and captioned item of 2 June, both 100–438794–unserialized; and SAC, Baltimore to Director, "Lawrence Dunbar Reddick," 15 June 1964, 100–438794–unserialized. SAC, Atlanta (by Robert R. Nichols) to Director, "COMINFIL SCLC, IS–C," 23 June 1964, 100–438794–95, p. 7, indicates that the allegation against Reddick by Budenz was made on three different occasions. Reddick, the Baltimore report indicates, denied that he had been either a CP member or sympathizer. On Mills, see SAC, Atlanta to Director, "Martin Luther King, Jr., SM–C," 26 May 1964, 100–106670–388, p. 28; and SAC, New York to Director,

"COMINFIL SCLC, IS–C," 17 November 1965, 100–438794–908, which details another informant's claim that Mills "had been one of the most important persons in the CP" in the early 1940s.

26. See six communications, all addressed SAC, New York to Director, "CPUSA, NQ; CIRM, IS–C," dated 21 May, 4, 9, 11, 16, and 17 June 1964, and all unserialized in file 100–438794; and SAC, New York to Director, "COMINFIL SCLC, IS–C," 5 June 1964, 100–438794–90; and Director (by Seymor F. Phillips) to SAC, New York, "CPUSA, NQ; CIRM, IS–C, (*JUNE*)," 23 June 1964, 100–3–116–1626.

27. See two communications of 25 and 26 June, each addressed and captioned SAC, New York to Director, "CPUSA, NQ; CIRM, IS–C," and unserialized in 100–438794; and SAC, Miami to Director, "Racial Situation, St. Johns County, Florida," 1 July 1964, unserialized but located in Justice Department file 144–17M–181. Hoover to Jenkins letters of 3 June and 10 June (100–106670–377) passed the wiretap information along to the White House.

28. See eight items, all captioned "CPUSA, NQ; CIRM, IS–C; (*JUNE*)," : SAC, Atlanta (by Al F. Miller) to Director, 27 May 1964, 100–438794–unserialized; Director (by Seymor F. Phillips) to SAC, Atlanta, 2 June 1964, 100–438794–unserialized; Baumgardner (by T. P. Rosack) to Sullivan, 7 July 1964, 100–3–116–1789; Director (by T. P. Rosack) to SAC, Atlanta 8 July 1964, 100–3–116–1787; SAC, Atlanta (by Al F. Miller) to Director, attn. William C. Sullivan, 11 July 1964, 100–3–116–1796; SAC, New York to Director, 13 July 1964, 100–3–116–1764; SAC, New York to Director, 1 August 1964, 100–442529–17; and Director (by T. P. Rosack) to SAC, New York, 7 August 1964, 100–438794–unserialized; and SAC, New York to Director, "CIRM," 25 August 1964, 100–3–116–2226.

29. Baumgardner (by Phillips) to Sullivan, "CPUSA, NQ; CIRM, IS–C, (*JUNE*)," 2 July 1964, 100–3–116–1664; Joseph A. Sizoo to Sullivan, "CPUSA, NQ; CIRM, IS–C, (*JUNE*)," 7 July 1964, 100–3–116–1723; Baumgardner to Sullivan, 15 July 1964, unreleased; and Hoover to Jenkins, 17 July 1964, Stegall Files, Johnson Library. Reports on the overheard phone conversations for the month went to the White House on 10 and 23 July.

30. Hoover to Jenkins, "CPUSA, NQ; CIRM, IS–C," 12 July 1964, 100–3–116–1649; Hoover to Jenkins, "CPUSA, NQ; CIRM, IS–C," 29 July 1964, 100–3–116–2051; Hoover to Jenkins, "CPUSA, NQ; CIRM, IS–C," 30 July 1964, 100–3–116–2070; Hoover to Jenkins, "CPUSA, NQ; CIRM, IS–C," 8 August 1964, 100–3–116–2108; Director (by Seymor F. Phillips) to SAC, New York, "CIRM (*JUNE*)," 11 August 1964,

100–3–116–2048; SAC, New York to Director, "CIRM (*JUNE*)," 17 August 1964, 100–3–116–2155; Hoover to Jenkins, "CPUSA, NQ; CIRM, IS–C," 19 August 1964, 100–3–116–2224; Sullivan to Alan H. Belmont, 21 August 1964 (unreleased), and Joseph A. Sizoo to Sullivan, "Martin Luther King, Jr., SM–C (*JUNE*)," 24 August 1964, 100–106670–illegible. Also, Coretta Scott King, *My Life with Martin Luther King, Jr.* (New York: Holt, Rinehart & Winston, 1969), p. 247.

31. Director to SAC, New York, 11 August, cited in n. 30 above; Baumgardner to Sullivan, "Martin Luther King, Jr., SM–C," 13 August 1964, 100–106670–438; "Note," 19 August 1964, DeLoach Name File, Johnson Library, Austin; DeLoach to Walter Jenkins, 24 August 1964 (unreleased); DeLoach to John Mohr, "Racial Matters, 1964 Democratic National Convention, Atlantic City, N.J.," 25 August 1964, 100–106670–unserialized; DeLoach to Jenkins, "Morning Summary of Activities, Democratic National Convention," 25 August 1964, in Senate Select Committee, *Hearings—FBI*, vol. 6, pp. 714–17; DeLoach to Mohr, "Special Squad, Atlantic City, New Jersey, Democratic National Convention, August 22–28, 1964," 29 August 1964, in U.S., Congress, House of Representatives, Committee on Government Operations, *Inquiry into the Destruction of Former FBI Director J. Edgar Hoover's Files and FBI Recordkeeping*, 94th Cong., 1st sess., 1975, pp. 75–82, and in Senate Select Committee, *Hearings—FBI*, vol. 6, pp. 495–502; H. N. Bassett to Nicholas P. Callahan, "Special Squad at Democratic National Convention, Atlantic City, New Jersey, 8/22–28/64," 29 January 1975, in Senate Select Committee, *Hearings—FBI*, vol. 6, pp. 503–9; DeLoach's own 1975 testimony in Senate Select Committee, *Hearings—FBI*, vol. 6, pp. 175–77; and DeLoach to Moyers, 10 September 1964, DeLoach Name File, Johnson Library. Detailed accounts of the Bureau's activities at the convention include Ronald Kessler, "FBI Tapped King at 1964 Convention," *Washington Post*, 26 January 1975, pp. A1, A6; and David Wise, *The American Police State* (New York: Random House, 1976), pp. 289–91. Bureau reports on King from that period that went to the White House include Hoover to Jenkins letters of 7, 8, 10, 11, 14, 18, and 19 August 1964, all in the Stegall Files.

32. Director to SAC, Atlanta, 28 August 1964, unreleased; Director (by T. P. Rosack) to SAC, Savannah, "SCLC, IS–C," 9 September 1964, 100–438794–138; SAC, Savannah to Director, "SCLC, IS–C,," 15 September 1964, 100–438794–149; SAC, Savannah to Director, "CIRM; COMINFIL SCLC, IS–C, (*JUNE*)," 18 September 1964, 100–438794–unserialized; Director (by T. P. Rosack) to SAC, Savannah, "CIRM, (*JUNE*)," 22 September 1964, 100–438794–unserialized; SAC, Savannah to Director, "CIRM; COMINFIL SCLC, IS–C, (*JUNE*)," 26 September 1964, 100–

438794–unserialized; Baumgardner to Sullivan, 28 September 1964, unreleased; Director (by T. P. Rosack) to SAC, Savannah, "CIRM; COMINFIL SCLC, IS–C," 28 September 1964, 100–438794–unserialized; Joseph A. Sizoo to Sullivan, "SCLC, IS–C, (*JUNE*)," 30 September 1964, 100–438794–174; SAC, Savannah to Director, "COMINFIL SCLC, IS–C," 1 October 1964, 100–438794–171; SAC, Savannah to Director, "CIRM; COMINFIL SCLC, IS–C," 5 October 1964, 100–442529–167; SAC, Savannah to Director, "CIRM, IS–C; COMINFIL SCLC, IS–C (*JUNE*)," 12 October 1964, 100–442529–186; and SAC, New York to Director, "CIRM, IS–C," 17 February 1965, 100–442529–778.

33. On Blackwell, see SAC, Atlanta to Director, "COMINFIL SCLC," 15 September 1964, 100–438794–143; SAC, Atlanta (by Robert R. Nichols) to Director, "COMINFIL SCLC, IS–C," 21 September 1964, 100–438794–147; SAC, Atlanta (by Robert R. Nichols) to Director, "CIRM; Randolph Talmadge Blackwell, SM–C," 8 October 1964, 100–438794–unserialized; and SAC, Atlanta to Director, "COMINFIL SCLC, IS–C," 15 February 1965, 100–438794–253. On Daddy King, see SAC, Atlanta (by Robert R. Nichols) to Director, "COMINFIL SCLC, IS–C; Martin Luther King, Sr.," 28 September 1964, 100–438794–164; and Director (by Seymor F. Phillips) to SAC, Atlanta, "COMINFIL SCLC, IS–C," 20 October 1964, 100–438794–190.

34. Concerning the Pope and Spellman, see Baumgardner (by Phillips) to Sullivan, "Martin Luther King, Jr., SM–C," 31 August 1964, 100–106670–450; Baumgardner to Sullivan, "Martin Luther King, Jr., SM–C," 8 September 1964, 100–106670–452; two *Washington Post* clippings of 17 and 19 September 1964, serialized as 100–106670–456 and 461; Baumgardner (by C. D. Brennan) to Sullivan, "Martin Luther King, Jr., SM–C," 17 September 1964, 100–106670–479, which appears in House Committee on Assassinations, *Hearings—King,* vol. 6, pp. 256–58; and Joseph A. Sizoo to Sullivan, "SCLC, IS–C," 6 October 1964, 100–438794–185. The review memos are James F. Bland (by William T. Forsyth) to Sullivan, "Martin Luther King, Jr., SM–C, (*JUNE*)," 6 October 1964, 100–106670–483; and Fred J. Baumgardner (by T. P. Rosack) to Sullivan, "CIRM, IS–C, (*JUNE*)," 6 October 1964, 100–438794–unserialized.

35. News reports of 7 and 14 October 1964, serialized as 100–106670–480 and 484; Hoover to Bill Moyers, 20 October 1964, 100–442529–223; Hoover to Moyers, 21 October 1964, 100–442529–239 (terming Levison a "long–time Communist"); SAC, New York to Director, "CIRM, IS–C," 13 October 1964, 100–442529–190; Hoover to Moyers, 27 October 1964, 100–442529–unserialized; Hoover to Moyers, 2 November 1964, 100–442529–309; Hoover to Moyers, 2 November 1964, 100–442529–297;

Hoover to Moyers, 3 November 1964, 100–442529–333; Hoover to Moyers 6 November 1964, 100–106670–unserialized; SAC, Atlanta to Director, "CIRM, IS–C," 6 November 1964, 100–442529–392; Hoover to Moyers, "CIRM, IS–C," 6 November 1964, 100–442529–405; Baumgardner (by Phillips) to Sullivan, "Martin Luther King, Jr., SM–C," 10 November 1964, 100–106670–528, in House Committee on Assassinations, *Hearings—King,* vol. 6, pp. 227–28; Baumgardner to Sullivan, 12 November 1964, unreleased; and Hoover to Moyers, "Martin Luther King, Jr., SM–C," 12 November 1964, 100–106670–527 (detailing King's Nobel trip plans). Also see George C. Moore (by J. J. Dunn) to Sullivan, "Martin Luther King, Jr., SM–C," 19 June 1969, 100–106670–unserialized. Other letters from Hoover to Moyers went to the White House on 20, 22, 26, and 28 October and 3 November 1964, and all are in the Stegall Files, Johnson Library. Reports went to Katzenbach on 20 and 22 October and 3, 6, 12, and 23 November.

36. C. D. DeLoach to John Mohr, 18 November 1964, 62–109811–3513; Elizabeth Shelton, "Hoover in Blast at Police Corruption Opens Fire on Some Other Targets," *Washington Post,* 19 November 1964, pp. A1, A3; Ben A. Franklin, "Hoover Assails Warren Findings," *New York Times,* 19 November 1964, pp. 1, 28; "Off Hoover's Chest," *Newsweek,* 30 November 1964, pp. 29–30; "The FBI and Civil Rights—J. Edgar Hoover Speaks Out," *U.S. News & World Report,* 30 November 1964, pp. 56–58; Ralph de Toledano, *J. Edgar Hoover* (New Rochelle, N.Y.: Arlington House, 1973), p. 333; Sanford J. Ungar, *FBI* (Boston: Little, Brown, 1975), p. 294; and Robert E. Wick's comments in Ovid Demaris, *The Director: An Oral Biography of J. Edgar Hoover* (New York: Harper & Row, 1975), pp. 194–95. The Bureau's attempt to document the charge that King refused proffered meetings appears in Alex Rosen to Belmont, "Difficulties Encountered in Attempting to Contact Martin Luther King, Jr.," 1 December 1964, 100–106670–592; and "Next: A National Police Force?" *U.S. News & World Report,* 7 December 1964, pp. 44–48.

37. King to Hoover, 19 November 1964, 100–106670–584; John Herbers, "Dr. King Rebuts Hoover Charges," *New York Times,* 20 November 1964, pp. 1, 18; " 'Nothing But Sympathy' For Hoover, Dr. King Replies to 'Liar' Charge," *SCLC Newsletter* 2 (October-November 1964): 9; Anthony Lewis, "Negro Leaders Support Dr. King," *New York Times,* 20 November 1964, p. 18; "Leaders Defend Dr. M. L. King," *New York Amsterdam News,* 28 November 1964, pp. 1–2.

38. "Murphy Report," 31 March 1976, pp. 36–37, 44; Baumgardner to Sullivan, "Martin Luther King, Jr., SM–C," 19 and 20 November 1964, 100–106670–537 and 543; Rosen to Belmont, "Telegram from Martin

Luther King, Jr.,'' 20 November 1964, 100–106670–581; SAC, Atlanta to Director, ''CIRM, IS–C,'' 20 November 1964, 100–442529–445; and Jones to DeLoach, ''Martin Luther King, Jr.,'' 1 December 1964, 100–106670–647, pp. 10–11. Whitsun did not apparently know what was in the package he mailed. Other King advisers who recommended a more combative response were Jones and Kenneth Clark. See Arthur M. Schlesinger, Jr., *Robert Kennedy and His Times* (Boston: Houghton Mifflin, 1978), pp. 364–65. Later stories on these events, some of which incorrectly say that the thirty-four-day ''deadline'' was the Nobel ceremony, include Nicholas M. Horrock, ''Ex-Officials Say FBI Harassed Dr. King to Stop His Criticism,'' *New York Times,* 9 March 1975, p. 40; Horrock, ''Senate Intelligence Panel Told of FBI Attempt to Discredit Dr. King in 1964,'' *New York Times,* 19 November 1975, p. 16; George Lardner, Jr., ''FBI Bugging and Blackmail of King Bared,'' *Washington Post,* 19 November 1975, pp. A1, A7; and William M. Kunstler, ''Writers of the Purple Page,'' *Nation* 227 (30 December 1978): 721, 735–40.

39. SAC, Atlanta to Director, ''Martin Luther King, Jr., SM–C,'' 23 November 1964, 100–106670–540; Hoover to Moyers, ''Martin Luther King, Jr., SM–C,'' 23 November 1964, 100–106670–542; Hoover to Moyers, 23 November 1964 (unreleased), Stegall Files, Johnson Library; Robert E. Baker, ''FBI Hits Back at Rights Groups, Lists Accomplishments in South,'' *Washington Post,* 26 November 1964, p. A2; Victor Riesel, ''Hoover Bided Time to Answer King,'' *Memphis Commercial Appeal,* 26 November 1964, p. 7. Hoover sent Moyers another letter on 25 November. A State Department request that the Bureau ask the Central Intelligence Agency to surveil King closely while he was in Europe was turned down on Tuesday. See Fred J. Baumgardner to Sullivan, ''COMINFIL SCLC, IS–C,'' 24 November 1964, 100–438794–209. Contrary to Riesel, some former Bureau executives believe that the timing of Hoover's outburst is explained by the announcement of King's Nobel Prize.

40. Wise, *The American Police State,* pp. 303–6; Howard Bray, *The Pillars of the Post* (New York: W. W. Norton, 1980), pp. 109–11; Demaris, *The Director,* p. 198; DeLoach to John Mohr, 1 December 1964, unreleased; Burke Marshall (Larry J. Hackman interview, 19–20 January 1970, Bedford, N.Y.), Kennedy Library, Boston, pp. 43–44; and author's conversations with Burke Marshall and Nicholas deB. Katzenbach. Katzenbach subsequently was contacted by another reporter with a similar story, and then confronted DeLoach about the matter. DeLoach denied making any such offers. DeLoach has denied both the substance of the Bradlee encounter, and any such conversation with Katzenbach. Senate Select Committee, *Hearings—FBI,* vol. 6, p. 210, and Wise, *The American Police State,* p. 306.

41. DeLoach to John Mohr, 27 November 1964, and Hoover to Johnson, 30 November 1964, unreleased; and Joseph A. Sizoo to Sullivan, 1 December 1964, unserialized, in Hoover's "Official & Confidential" File 24. Wilkins' column in the 28 November *New York Amsterdam News,* "Dr. King Needs No Defense," was devoted not to an endorsement of King, but only to comments about the desirability of federal officers enforcing laws to protect black citizens. Although Wilkins's long-standing personal dislike for King should not be minimized, his 1978 denials of the statements DeLoach attributed to him are almost certainly correct. Several former Bureau and Justice Department officials voice a low opinion of the accuracy of many such DeLoach memos. For Wilkins's denials, see two *Washington Post* stories by George Lardner, Jr.: "Black Reportedly Worked With FBI to Discredit King," 29 May 1978, p. 1, and "Wilkins Denied Any Link to FBI Plot to Discredit Dr. King," 31 May 1978, p. A6, as well as a smaller item in the 2 June 1978 *Post,* p. A2.

42. James Farmer (Paige Mulhollan interview, 20 July 1971, Washington, D.C.), Johnson Library, Austin, pp. 29–31; author's conversations with James Farmer; and SAC, New York to Director, "CIRM," 1 December 1964, 100–442529–475, which indicates that agents watched King arrive for his airport meeting with Farmer.

43. DeLoach to Mohr, "Martin Luther King," 1 December 1964, 100–106670–570; DeLoach to Mohr, "Martin Luther King, Appointment with Director," 2 December 1964, 100–106670–634, available in House Committee on Assassinations, *Hearings—King,* vol. 6, pp. 167–77; Richard L. Lyons, "Hoover, Dr. King Meet, See New Understanding," *Washington Post,* 2 December 1964, p. A1; Anthony Lewis, "Hoover and King Discuss Dispute," *New York Times,* 2 December 1964, pp. 1, 32; "The Hoover-King Meeting," *Newsweek,* 14 December 1964, pp. 22–24; Drew Pearson, "Meeting With Hoover Amazes King," *Washington Post,* 5 December 1964, p. E15; and James Phelan, "Hoover of the FBI," *Saturday Evening Post* 238 (25 September 1965): 23–33, at 32. As Phelan observed in an identically titled article ten years later, Hoover, "When he was not sure of his visitor, . . . launched into a monologue that ended only when the allotted time was up." King was one of many people who produced this reaction. (*Saturday Evening Post* 247 [December 1975] 30–35, 104–7, at 31.) Hoover himself later circulated grossly inaccurate accounts of the meeting. See "J. Edgar Hoover Speaks Out with Vigor," *Time,* 14 December 1970, pp. 16–17; as well as "Posthumous Pillory," *Time,* 17 August 1970, pp. 12–13, and "Mrs. King Denies Time's Account of Husband's Meeting with Hoover," *Washington Post,* 11 August 1970, p. A4.

44. Young has described his recollections of and feelings about the meeting and its aftermath in a number of interviews. See Valerie Price, "King-

Hoover Talk Recalled,'' *Atlanta Constitution,* 6 December 1975, p. A2;
Leon Howell, ''An Interview with Andrew Young,'' *Christianity & Crisis*
36 (16 February 1976): 14–20, at 16–17; ''Andrew Young Remembers
Martin Luther King,'' *Bill Moyers' Journal,* Program 409, 2 April 1979,
p. 3; Peter R. Range, ''Interview with Andrew Young,'' *Playboy* 24 (July
1977): 61–83, at 75; Andrew J. Young (T. H. Baker interview, 18 June
1970, Atlanta, Ga.), Lyndon B. Johnson Library, Austin, pp. 24–25; and
Howell Raines, *My Soul Is Rested* (New York: G. P. Putnam's Sons, 1977),
pp. 428–30. McCartney's story is detailed in Paul Clancy, ''The Bureau
and the bureaus,'' *Quill,* February 1976, pp. 12–18, at 14–15. The Farmer-
DeLoach meeting is described in DeLoach to Mohr, 1 December 1964, 100–
106670–unserialized, and in Farmer's Johnson Library interview, cited in
n. 42 above. Farmer also states (pp. 30–31) that he understood that Whitney
Young of the Urban League subsequently heard the tapes and viewed pictures of King after personally asking President Johnson about the matter.
This has not been confirmed.

45. Baumgardner to Sullivan, 30 November 1964 (unreleased); Hoover
to Moyers, 1 December 1964 (unreleased); Hoover to Moyers, ''Martin
Luther King, Jr., SM–C,'' 2 December 1964, 100–106670–562; Hoover to
Johnson, ''Martin Luther King, Jr.,'' 2 December 1964, 100–106670–607
(a four-page account of the Hoover-King meeting); DeLoach to Mohr,
''Martin Luther King, Dissemination of Monograph,'' 7 December 1964,
100–106670–618; Hoover to Moyers, Rusk, McNamara, Helms, Katzenbach, Rowan, and the chiefs of naval intelligence, air force intelligence, and
the Defense Intelligence Agency, all dated 7 December 1964 and serialized
as 100–442529–486 through 490, 492–493, 502–503, and 505; Hoover to
Director, National Science Foundation, 8 December 1964, 100–442529–
538; Hoover to Moyers, 9 December 1964 (unreleased); and Legal Attaché,
London to Director, ''Martin Luther King, Jr., SM–C,'' 10 December 1964,
100–106670–638. Press commentary on the issue of Hoover's retirement
includes ''Retirement Time,'' *New York Amsterdam News,* 28 November
1964, p. 8; Gardner L. Bridge, ''Talk of Replacing Hoover Disclaimed by
the White House,'' and Paul Good, ''Negro Criticism of Hoover Grows
Louder,'' both on p. A3 of the 1 December 1964 *Washington Post;* Jackie
Robinson, ''Strange Case of Mr. Hoover,'' *New York Amsterdam News,*
5 December 1964, p. 11; and ''Hoover, 69, Feels Fit to Continue in FBI
Post,'' *New York Times,* 5 December 1964, p. 18, and written by Hoover's
long-time friend, AP correspondent Don Whitehead. The most unique perspective is that of Daniel H. Watts, ''King vs. Hoover: The Cry Baby and
the Great White Father,'' *Liberator* 4 (December 1964): 3, who endorses
the characterization of King as a ''notorious liar'' but ''for completely oppo-

site reasons'' than those held by Hoover. Watts cited alleged misuse of movement funds as one specific complaint.

46. The Rockefeller item is the subject of Baumgardner (by Phillips) to Sullivan, ''Martin Luther King, Jr., SM–C,'' 8 December 1964, 100–106670–643. The BWA contacts are described in Milton A. Jones to DeLoach, ''Martin Luther King, Jr., Possible Appearance before Baptist World Alliance Congress,'' 8 December 1964, 100–106670–624; Jones to Thomas Bishop, 8 December 1964, unreleased; and Hays to Moyers, 14 December 1964, WHCF Confidential File FG 135–6, Johnson Library. Sullivan's accounts of his contacts with Espy are the subject of three memos from him to Alan Belmont, all titled ''Martin Luther King, Jr., SM–C''— 12 June 1964, 100–106670–383; 15 December 1964, 100–106670–628; and 16 December 1964, 100–106670–636. Sullivan's story about Espy, however, may be no more dependable than DeLoach's about Wilkins. Despite the circulation of so many reports, Sullivan still told Belmont in mid-December that ''this Bureau has not yet emerged victorious in its conflict with Martin Luther King . . . realism makes it mandatory that we take every prudent step that we can take to emerge completely victorious in this conflict.'' See Sullivan to Belmont, ''Martin Luther King, Jr., SM–C,'' 14 December 1964, 100–106670–627; and Baumgardner to Sullivan, 17 December 1964 (unreleased).

47. Headquarters' serial 100–106670–630 (unreleased); Hoover to Moyers, ''Martin Luther King, Jr., SM–C,'' 17 December 1964, 100–106670–622; two other Hoover letters of 17 December, to Moyers and Katzenbach, both unreleased; Hoover to Rusk, McNamara, Helms, Rowan, the National Science Foundation, the chiefs of army intelligence, naval intelligence, air force intelligence, and the Defense Intelligence Agency, and Vice–President-elect Humphrey, all dated 21 December 1964 and serialized as 100–442529–539 through 542, 549–52, 554–55, and 562; Hoover to Katzenbach, ''Martin Luther King, Jr., SM–C,'' 21 December 1964, 100–106670–629; Hoover to Moyers, 21 December 1964, 100–106670–650; and Hoover to Moyers, ''COMINFIL SCLC, IS–C,'' 22 December 1964, 100–438794–221. Also see two George C. Moore to Sullivan memos of 25 and 27 June 1969, captioned ''Martin Luther King, Jr., SM–C,'' and serialized as 100–106670–3639 and 3660.

48. ''Dr. King Says He Needs 'A Long Period of Rest,' '' *New York Times,* 5 December 1964, p. 19; SAC, Atlanta to Director, ''Martin Luther King, Jr., SM–C,'' 29 and 30 December 1964, 100–106670–701 and 702; Hoover to Moyers, 30 December 1964, 100–442529–569; Hoover to Moyers, and Hoover to Katzenbach, both dated 31 December 1964 and both unreleased; ''Murphy Report,'' 31 March 1976, pp. 43–47; SAC, Atlanta

to Director, "Martin Luther King, Jr., SM–C," 5 and 6 January 1965, 100–106670–715 and 716; Baumgardner to Sullivan, "Martin Luther King, Jr., SM–C," 6 January 1965, 100–106670–712; Joseph A. Sizoo to Sullivan, "Martin Luther King, Jr., SM–C (*JUNE*)," 8 January 1965, 100–106670–698; Hoover to Katzenbach, "Martin Luther King, Jr., SM–C," 8 January 1965, 100–106670–673; Hoover to Moyers, 8 January 1965 (unreleased); SAC, New York to Director, "Martin Luther King, Jr., SM–C (*JUNE*)," 9, 10, and 11 January 1965, 100–106670–719, 721, and 697; and DeLoach to Mohr, "Martin Luther King, Jr., SM–C," 8 and 11 January 1965, 100–106670–713 and 730. Also, Nicholas M. Horrock, "Ex-Officials Say FBI Harassed Dr. King to Stop His Criticism," *New York Times,* 9 March 1975, p. 40; Jack Anderson and Les Whitten, "Hoover's Campaign against King," *Washington Post,* 26 November 1975, p. C10; Joyce Leviton, "Once the Woman behind the Martyr, Coretta King at 50 Becomes a Power on Her Own," *People* 9 (20 February 1978): 72–74, 79–83, at 79; Andrew Young (Baker interview), Johnson Library, pp. 24–26; Howell, "An Interview with Andrew Young," pp. 17–18; Raines, *My Soul Is Rested,* pp. 428–30; Range, "Interview with Andrew Young," p. 75; and Senate Select Committee, *Final Report—Book III,* p. 159.

49. Raines, *My Soul Is Rested,* pp. 368–70; Clancy, "The Bureau and the bureaus," pp. 15–16; Claudia Townsend, "LBJ Knew of Anti-King Drive?" *Atlanta Constitution,* 29 April 1976, p. A16; Eugene C. Patterson, "More FBI Double Dealing," *Washington Post,* 18 May 1976, p. A19, and "Secret Lies Soothe Hoover," *Atlanta Constitution,* 31 May 1976, p. A5; Claudia Townsend and Beau Cutts, "Johnson Put FBI on King," *Atlanta Constitution,* 6 May 1976, pp. A1, A14; Sullivan to Belmont, 21 December 1964 (unreleased); Sullivan to Belmont, "Martin Luther King Jr., SM–C," 21 January 1965, 100–106670–781; Hoover to Moyers, 22 January 1965, 100–106670–756; and author's conversations with John Doar. McGill subsequently wrote to Johnson aide Bill Moyers, warning the administration to be alert to the danger of a right-wing smear of the civil rights movement with allegations of Communist influence, and recommending that William Sullivan of the FBI be asked for counsel on this. The letter reflects no animus toward King, though also this positive regard for Sullivan, and hence lends clear support to neither the Bureau nor Patterson versions of the story. McGill to Moyers, 1 April 1965, WHCF Gen HU 2, Johnson Library, Austin. Sullivan unsuccesssfully attempted to speak with the Catholic archbishop of Atlanta, Paul Hallinan, for the same purpose as well.

50. U.S., Department of Justice, *Report of the Department of Justice Task Force to Review the FBI Martin Luther King, Jr., Security and Assassination Investigations,* 11 January 1977, p. 134; Sullivan to Belmont,

"Martin Luther King, Jr., SM–C," 22 January 1965, 100–106670–786; Baumgardner to Sullivan, "Martin Luther King, Jr., SM–C," 28 January 1965, 100–106670–780, Raines, *My Soul Is Rested,* p. 354; Jack Anderson and Les Whitten, "Associates Ask Probe to Clear King's Name," *Washington Post,* 9 October 1975, p. A24; Herbert T. Jenkins (T. H. Baker interview, 14 May 1969, Atlanta, Ga.), Johnson Library, Austin, pp. 14–18; and author's conversations with Chief Jenkins and Major Howard Baugh. A childhood acquaintance of King's and the highest ranking black officer on the Atlanta force, Baugh often was the target of Bureau agents' promptings. His one visit to the Waluhaje, where he discovered the meeting, occurred at about the same time as the false fire alarm.

51. Joseph A. Sizoo to Sullivan, "Martin Luther King, Jr., SM–C (*JUNE*)," 29 January 1965, 100–106670–800; SAC, New York to Director, "'Martin Luther King, Jr., SM–C (*JUNE*)," 29 January 1965, 100–106670–779; SAC, New York to Director, "Martin Luther King, Jr., SM–C (*JUNE*)," 31 January 1965, 100–106670–778; SAC, Atlanta to Director, "CIRM, IS–C," 2 February 1965, 100–442529–unserialized; Baumgardner to Sullivan, "Martin Luther King, Jr., SM–C," 27 February 1965, 100–106670–937; SAC, New York to Director, COMINFIL SCLC, IS–C," 23 April 1965, 100–438794–306, pp. 23–28; Levison to Lyndon Johnson, 14 February 1965, Levison Name File, Johnson Library; and Clarence B. Jones to Johnson, 4 March 1965, Jones Name File, Johnson Library. Letters from Hoover went to Bill Moyers on 3 and 4 February 1965 (100–106670–804), and to Johnson aide Marvin Watson on 8 and 17 February (100–106670–808 and 912) and 5 and 9 March 1965 (100–106670–931 and 971). Copies of most of these went to Katzenbach as well.

52. A surveillance at New York's Park Sheraton Hotel in late March is the subject of Director (by Seymor F. Phillips) to SACs, Atlanta, Baltimore, and New York, "CIRM; COMINFIL SCLC, IS–C," 30 March 1965, 100–438794–unserialized; and SAC, New York to Director, "Martin Luther King, Jr., SM-C, (*JUNE*)," 31 March 1965, 100–106670–1153. Various dissemination ideas developed in Division Five are detailed in three memos from Baumgardner (by Phillips) to Sullivan of 1 February, 2 and 23 March 1965, all available in House Committee on Assassinations, *Hearings—King,* vol. 6, pp. 232–34, 254–55. Also see Hoover to LeRoy Collins, 24 March 1965, 100–442529–931; Baumgardner to Sullivan, 31 March 1965 (unreleased); Hoover to Fred Robinette, Internal Revenue Service, 2 April 1965, 100–106670–1101; and Director (by Seymor F. Phillips) to SAC, Boston, "COMINFIL SCLC, IS-C," 10 May 1965, 100–438794–323. In May Crime Records did approve on Atlanta request that UPI reporter Al Kuettner, a friend of Atlanta SAC Joseph K. Ponder, be given some infor-

mation on King. Kuettner's resulting story stated that "King has many critics. They privately, and sometimes publicly, question his sources of income, his private life and his political leanings." When shown a copy, Hoover scribbled, "a 'whitewash' if there ever was one." See Joseph A. Sizoo to Sullivan, "Martin Luther King, Jr., SM-C," 24 May 1965, 100–106670–1403: and an unserialized teletype copy of Kuettner's 15 June text in file 100–438794. The unactivated April bug at the Americana is detailed in SAC, New York to Director, "Martin Luther King, Jr., SM–C (*JUNE*)," 5 April 1965, 100–106670–1195. Another Bureau report on King went to White House aide Marvin Watson on 30 March 1965.

53. Director (by Phillips) to SAC, Atlanta, "CIRM (*JUNE*)," 19 April 1965, 100–442529–933; SAC, Atlanta to Director, "CIRM (*JUNE*)," 19 May 1965, 100–442529–illegible; Joseph A. Sizoo to Sullivan, and SAC, New York to Director, both captioned "Martin Luther King, Jr., SM–C (*JUNE*)," and both dated 13 May 1965, 100–106670–1346 and 1347; Hoover to Watson, 15 May 1965, 100–442529–1073; Hoover to Katzenbach, "Martin Luther King, Jr.," 17 May 1965, 100–106670–1373; and SAC, New York to Director, "Martin Luther King, Jr., SM–C (*JUNE*)," 7 June 1965, 100–106670–1444. Two similarly captioned items dated 21 and 28 May 1965, the first from Hoover to New York and the second from New York to headquarters (100–106670–1382 and 1407) indicate that King and his aides now searched their hotel rooms for listening devices. An Atlanta report of 16 July ("CIRM, IS–C," 100–442529–1218) indicated that King had suggested to Young putting scramblers on SCLC's phones.

54. Author's conversations with Jay Richard Kennedy.

55. "Memorandum for the Record," 11 May 1965, Office of Security, Central Intelligence Agency. King's CIA "security file" was numbered 353–062. An earlier memo in the same file, entitled "Notes Made During Conversations with [deletion] in New York City, 26 February 1965," may well relate to Kennedy also, as may a "Memorandum for the Record" dated 10 March 1965.

56. Director to SAC, New York, "CIRM, IS–C," 13 May 1965, New York serial 100–153735–1449; SAC, New York to Director, "CIRM, IS–C," 25 May 1965, New York serial 100–153735–1484; SAC, New York to Director, "CIRM, IS–C," 1 June 1965, New York serial 100–153735–1546; and SAC, New York to Director, "CIRM, IS–C," 1 June 1965, New York serial 100–153735–1547. An internal New York memo of 21 June 1965, serialized as 100–153735–1560, may also relate to a conversation with Kennedy.

57. "Memorandum for Chief, Security Research Staff," 9 June 1965, CIA King security file 353–062. The July conversations are the subject of

Chief, Liaison & External Operations Branch, SRS, to Chief, Security Research Staff, 7 July 1965, and an untitled memo of 21 July 1965. Three memos dated 8 February 1968, 5 April 1968, and 8 April 1968, and all directed to the Chief, Security Research Staff, also in all likelihood concern information that was provided by Jay Kennedy. Both the first and the last contain references to "Chicoms" or "Peking communists." CIA memos written in 1975 contain Agency denials of ever engaging in any electronic surveillance or "mail covers" against King, plus a statement that no Agency representatives reported on King's activities when King was overseas. Office of Security, CIA, "Memorandum for Chief, Security Analysis Group," 28 November 1975.

58. Author's conversations with Harry Wachtel; Victor Navasky, *Kennedy Justice* (New York: Atheneum, 1971), p. 146; SAC, New York to Director, "CIRM, IS–C," 5 March 1965, 100–438794–unserialized; SAC, New York to Director, "COMINFIL SCLC, IS–C; Stanley Levison, IS–C," 15 April 1965, 100–438794–296; SAC, New York to Director, "CIRM, IS–C; SCLC, IS–C," 11 June 1965, 100–438794–unserialized; and SAC, Richmond to Director, "CIRM; COMINFIL SCLC, IS–C," 11 June 1965, 100–438794–unserialized. Levison had opposed the general economic boycott of Alabama that King announced in late March, and also feared that SCLC was moving into the summer months without a well-planned program. No fan of Hosea Williams, Levison believed that spreading SCOPE workers across seventy counties was extremely inadvisable. Bureau intercepts also indicated that Bayard Rustin strenuously opposed the Alabama boycott plan. See SAC, New York to Director, 23 April 1965, pp. 27–28, cited at n. 51 above; SAC, Atlanta (by Al F. Miller) to Director, "COMINFIL SCLC, IS–C," 8 July 1965, 100–438794–393, pp. 29–30; SAC, New York to Director and SAC, Baltimore, "CIRM, IS–C; COMINFIL SCLC, IS–C," 1 April 1965, 100–438794–unserialized; SAC, New York to Director, "CIRM, IS–C; COMINFIL SCLC, IS–C," 2 April 1965, 100–438794–unserialized; and Hoover to Katzenbach, "Boycott of Alabama by the SCLC to Protest Voting Discrimination, RM," 2 April 1965, 100–438794–279. Additional reports on King went to the White House on 2 and 15 (100–106670–1238) April and 8 and 17 (100–106670–1489) June 1965. At Warrenton, headquarters learned, "the discussions centered around the moving of SCLC operations North, specifically New York and Chicago. The purpose for moving North . . . would be to make gains in housing, schools, and other basic needs." SAC, New York to Director, "CIRM, IS–C; SCLC, IS–C," 15 June 1965, 100–438794–unserialized.

59. Director (by Phillips) to SAC, New York, "COMINFIL SCLC, IS–

C,'' 13 May 1965, 100–438794–328; Director (by Phillips) to SAC, Atlanta, "COMINFIL SCLC, IS–C,'' 10 June 1965, 100–438794–346. On the efforts to find subversives among the SCOPE workers, see Director (by J. F. Martin) to SAC, Springfield, "COMINFIL SCLC, IS–C,'' 4 February 1965, 100–438794–245; Director (by J. F. Martin) to SAC, Albany, "SCOPE Program,'' 8 April 1965, 100–438794–unserialized; Baumgardner (by Martin) to Sullivan, "SCOPE Program,'' 8 April 1965, 100–438794–unserialized; and Director (by Martin) to SAC, Springfield, "COMINFIL SCLC, IS–C,'' 14 April 1965, 100–438794–280.

60. On the search for the foreign account—the Bureau checked the Bahamas as well as Switzerland—see Baumgardner to Sullivan, 29 June 1965, 15 July 1965, and 10 December 1965, and Director to SAC, New Orleans, 3 December 1965, all unreleased. The search for Ms. Farnsworth begins with Director (by Phillips) to SACs, New York and Atlanta, "COMINFIL SCLC, IS–C,'' 23 July 1965, 100–438794–435. The Ebenezer connection is detailed in SAC, New York to Director, "COMINFIL SCLC,'' 17 June 1965, 100–438794–360. Phillips had assumed responsibility for the King case, in addition to the SCLC one, in early 1965.

61. Atlanta's strenuous efforts to answer Abernathy's statement—and to assure headquarters that there was no truth to it—are chronicled in two Baumgardner to Sullivan memos of 1 July, each captioned "SCLC, IS–C,'' 100–438794–392 and 408; a UPI teletype story of 1 July, serialized as 100–438794–465; DeLoach (by Robert E. Wick) to John Mohr, "SCLC, IS–C, Statement re FBI by Ralph Abernathy,'' 1 July 1965, 100–438794–391; and SAC, Atlanta (by Alan G. Sentinella) to Director, "COMINFIL SCLC, IS–C,'' 2 July 1965, 100–438794–396.

62. See SAC, Atlanta (by Al F. Miller) to Director, "COMINFIL SCLC, IS–C,'' 8 July 1965, 100–438794–393; and three communications addressed Director (by Phillips) to SAC, Atlanta, "COMINFIL SCLC, IS–C,'' dated 27 July 1965, 4 August 1965, and 27 September 1965, and serialized as 100–438794–443, 463, and 657.

63. Bureau activity regarding the Birmingham convention and the Vietnam question is reflected in Director (by Phillips) to SAC, Birmingham, "COMINFIL SCLC, IS–C,'' 15 July 1965, 100–438794–410; SAC, New York to Director, "COMINFIL SCLC, IS–C,'' 4 August 1965, 100–438794–477; SAC, Birmingham to Director, "COMINFIL SCLC, IS–C,'' 10 August 1965, 100–438794–497; SAC, New York to Director, "COMINFIL SCLC, IS–C,'' 10 August 1965, 100–438794–505; Director (by Phillips) to SAC, Birmingham, "COMINFIL SCLC, IS–C,'' 13 August 1965, 100–438794–504; SAC, New York to Director and SAC, Atlanta, "COMINFIL SCLC, IS–C; Martin Luther King, Jr., SM–C,'' 14 August

1965, 100–438794–unserialized; SAC, New York to Director, "COMIN-FIL SCLC, IS–C," 15 August 1965, 100–438794–536; SAC, New York to Director, "COMINFIL SCLC, IS–C; Martin Luther King, Jr., SM–C," 17 August 1965, 100–438794–530; and "SCLC" (by Phillips), 4 October 1965, 100–438794–687. The odd format of the last item is explained by a note indicating "Original delivered to White House." Various letters and reports on King went to the President on 7, 16, 19, 20, and 23 July; 5, 12, 16 (the Levison answers), 23, and 26 August; and 3, 7, 9 (two), 10, 15, 16, and 30 (two) September 1965. For a sampling of their content, see Baumgardner (by R. F. Bates) to Sullivan, "COMINFIL SCLC, IS–C (*JUNE*)," 14 January 1966, 100–438794–1064. Also see SAC, New York to Director, "COMINFIL SCLC, IS–C; Martin Luther King, Jr., SM–C," 4 October 1965, 100–438794–717; SAC, New York to Director, "COMINFIL SCLC, IS–C," 8 November 1965, 100–438794–886; Baumgardner (by Phillips) to Sullivan, "COMINFIL SCLC, IS–C," 10 November 1965, 100–438794–880; and SAC, New York to Director, "COMINFIL SCLC, IS–C," 15 November 1965, 100–438794–888. Assistant Director DeLoach also briefed House Speaker John McCormack on "the background and activities" of King, as a 14 August 1965 memo from DeLoach to John Mohr, 100–106670–1782, details. King's position on Vietnam at this time—he first had spoken publicly on the subject in Petersburg, Virginia, on July 2—is best seen in a *Face the Nation* interview of 29 August (vol. 7, pp. 206–11). Also see "Dr. King Calls for End to War in Viet Nam," *Richmond Times Dispatch,* 3 July 1965.

64. Sullivan (by Phillips) to Alan H. Belmont, "Martin Luther King, Jr., SM–C (*JUNE*)," 14 October 1965, 100–106670–1981; SAC, New York to Director, "Martin Luther King, Jr., SM–C (*JUNE*)," 15 October 1965, 100–106670–1988; SAC, New York to Director, "COMINFIL SCLC, IS–C," 18 October 1965, 100–438794–773; Hoover to Katzenbach, "Martin Luther King, Jr.," 19 October 1965, 100–106670–1990; Baumgardner to Sullivan, "Martin Luther King, Jr., SM–C (*JUNE*)," 29 October 1965, 100–106670–illegible; and SAC, New York to Director, "Martin Luther King, Jr., SM–C (*JUNE*)," 8 November 1965, 100–106670–2034.

65. Hoover to Katzenbach, "Communist Influence in Racial Matters," 27 October 1965, 100–442529–illegible.

66. See two memos from Baumgardner (by Phillips) to Sullivan, "CIRM, IS–C," 8 November 1965 and 18 November 1965, both unserialized in 100–438794; Hoover to Marvin Watson, "CIRM, IS–C," 9 November 1965, 100–442529–1576; Baumgardner (by Phillips) to Sullivan, "Martin Luther King, Jr., SM–C (*JUNE*)," 29 November 1965, 100–106670–2182; SAC, New York to Director, "Martin Luther King, Jr., SM–C (*JUNE*),"

1 December 1965, 100–106670–2103; Hoover to Katzenbach, "Martin Luther King, Jr.," 1 December 1965, 100–106670–2183; and Katzenbach to Hoover, 10 December 1965, 100–106670–2184. Katzenbach acknowledges that he wrote this note, and initialed several memos reporting on the King microphone surveillances, but denies any recollection that he authorized the Bureau's bugging efforts. Reports specifically on King went to the White House on 12 October, 5 and 12 November, and 22 December 1965.

67. See Sullivan (by R. F. Bates) to DeLoach, "Martin Luther King, Jr., SM–C (*JUNE*)," 21 January 1966, 100–106670–illegible; Hoover (by R. F. Bates) to Katzenbach, "Martin Luther King, Jr.," 21 January 1966, 100–106670–illegible; and U.S. Department of Justice, *King Task Force,* pp. 127–29. Ironically, King personally sent DeLoach a congratulatory telegram on 6 December 1965 when a Bureau promotion for him was announced publicly. The ongoing SCLC headquarters wiretap also was reviewed at the same time, but was continued without hesitation, apparently because of the political information that it allowed the Bureau to furnish the White House. See Baumgardner (by Bates) to Sullivan, "COMINFIL SCLC, IS–C (*JUNE*)," 14 January 1966, 100–438794–1064. The Long subcommittee investigation is described in Senate Select Committee, *Final Report—Book III,* pp. 307–10. During the one month, FBI reports on King went to the White House on 5, 14, 18, 20, and 26 (two) January 1966.

4. Puritans and Voyeurs—Sullivan, Hoover, and Johnson

1. See n. 3, chapter 3.

2. David Wise, *The American Police State* (New York: Random House, 1976), p. 298. Also see David Wise, "The Campaign to Destroy Martin Luther King," *New York Review of Books* 23 (11 November 1976): 38–42.

3. See Senate Select Committee, *Final Report—Book III,* p. 91; William C. Sullivan, *The Bureau: My Thirty Years in Hoover's FBI* (New York:W. W. Norton, 1979), p. 138; William C. Sullivan to Senator Walter F. Mondale, 17 April 1976; and Sullivan's comments in Ovid Demaris, *The Director: An Oral Biography of J. Edgar Hoover* (New York: Harper & Row, 1975), p. 220.

4. See Jack Levine, "Racism in the FBI," *Liberator* 2 (November–December 1962): 10; Robert Wall, "Special Agent for the FBI," *New York Review of Books* 17 (27 January 1972): 12–18, at 17; and Murtagh's testimony in House Committee on Assassinations, *Hearings—King,* vol. 6, pp. 92–94, 96–97, 110–14.

5. See John A. Williams, *The King God Didn't Save* (New York: Coward, McCann, 1970), p. 189, and especially "The King Wiretap," *Atlantic* 227 (January 1971): 35–36. Also see "Posthumous Pillory," *Time*, 17 August 1970, pp. 12–13, and an excellent commentary by Richard Neuhaus, "Slur of the Year," *Christian Century* 87 (16 September 1970): 1079–80.

6. See Jesse Jackson, "On the Case," *Chicago Defender*, 15 August 1970, p. 1; and L. F. Palmer, Jr., "King 'File' Has Ominous Overtones," *Seattle Times*, 16 August 1970, p. D10.

7. See Sanford J. Ungar, *FBI* (Boston: Little, Brown, 1975), pp. 255–56, 328, 408; Hank Messick, *John Edgar Hoover* (New York: David McKay, 1972), p. 207; Arthur M. Schlesinger, Jr., *Robert Kennedy and His Times* (Boston: Houghton Mifflin, 1978), p. 291; Senate Select Committee, *Hearings—FBI*, vol. 6, p. 33; and "Beyond the Call of Duty," *Economist* 257 (29 November 1975): 72.

8. See Ungar, *FBI*, pp. 327–29; and Sullivan, *The Bureau*, pp. 268–69. Also see Simeon Booker, "The Negro in the FBI," *Ebony* 17 (September 1962): 29–32, which is one of the most hilarious public-relations snowjobs in recent American history. Booker's comment that Hoover's relationship with his office assistant, Sam Noisette, "virtually sets the race relations pattern for the huge agency," was right on the mark, though not in the way Booker intended. On Booker's treatment, see Jack Levine, "Racism in the FBI," *Liberator* 2 (November–December 1962): 10, and a transcript of "The FBI—A Panel Discussion," WBAI radio, New York, 29–30 November 1962, p. 3, in ACLU Papers, 1962, vol. 50, Princeton University.

9. On Bureau surveillance of Elijah Muhammad and the NOI, see Hoover to Herbert Brownell, "Elijah Mohammed [sic], Internal Security—Muslim Cult of Islam," 31 December 1956; Fred J. Baumgardner to William C. Sullivan, "Nation of Islam, IS–NOI," 8 September 1961, 25–330971–5331; SAC, Phoenix to Director, "Nation of Islam, IS–NOI," 30 June 1965, 25–330971–illegible; Hoover to Katzenbach, "Nation of Islam, IS–NOI," 1 July 1966, 25–330971–unserialized; blind memo, "Elijah Muhammad–Reasons for Request of Electronic Surveillance Authorization," 13 May 1969, 25–330971–unserialized; and George C. Moore (by C. E. Glass) to William C. Sullivan, "Martin Luther King, Jr., SM–C; Elijah Muhammad, IS–NOI (*JUNE*)," 10 June 1969, 100–106670–unserialized. There is also a "105" series headquarters file on the Muslims, as well as a twenty-three-hundred-page surveillance file on Malcolm X, which has been released under the FOIA.

10. On SNCC, see the brief description in Clayborne Carson, *In Struggle: SNCC and the Black Awakening of the 1960s* (Cambridge: Harvard Univer-

sity Press, 1981), pp. 261–64, 298; on the Panthers, see "The FBI's Covert Action Program to Destroy the Black Panther Party," in Senate Select Committee, *Final Report—Book III,* pp. 187–223; and C. Gerald Fraser, "FBI Files Reveal Moves against Black Panthers," *New York Times,* 19 October 1980, pp. 1, 16.

11. See particularly the three memos cited in n. 41, chapter 3, especially Sizoo to Sullivan, 1 December 1964.

12. See n. 8, chapter 3.

13. An additional example is the previously mentioned Reverend Archibald Carey of Chicago's Quinn Chapel AME Church, a long-time friend of Director Hoover and the intermediary used by King for setting up the December 1 meeting. See "FBI Chief Blasts KKK," *Pittsburgh Courier,* 30 April 1960, p. 9, which is an account of a Hoover appearance at Reverend Carey's church, plus the accompanying photograph.

14. "The failure," Clark told the Church Committee, "was that the Bureau became ideological." Senate Select Committee, *Hearings—FBI,* vol. 6, p. 238. Also see Schlesinger, *Robert Kennedy,* pp. 247, 266.

15. Charles Morgan, Jr., *One Man, One Voice* (New York: Holt, Rinehart & Winston, 1979), p. 37. Morgan was the lawyer representing Muhammad Ali when the wiretapping of King was first publicly confirmed in June, 1969 by a Bureau disclosure that Ali, then Cassius Clay, had been overheard once on the tap in September, 1964. Ali also had been overheard several times on the aforementioned taps of Elijah Muhammad.

16. Athan Theoharis, *Spying on Americans: Political Surveillance from Hoover to the Huston Plan* (Philadelphia: Temple University Press, 1978), pp. 12, 172, 175, 194, 285. Also see James Jacobs, "An Overview of National Political Intelligence," *University of Detroit Journal of Urban Law* 55 (1978): 853–75, at 854–56. On balance Theoharis believes that the Bureau's endemic, organizationwide political conservatism was key, rather than the personal conservatism of Hoover himself. On "conservatism" too, like criticism and racism, both variations can be asserted, and comments such as Morgan's (see n. 15 above) reflect a preference for the other, Hoover-centered version. The strong and widespread conservatism of the Bureau is noted in Ungar, *FBI,* pp. 325–27, 329–31; and James Q. Wilson, *The Investigators* (New York: Basic Books, 1978), pp. 176–77.

17. See nn. 3–4, chapter 3.

18. See n. 101, chapter 1.

19. See n. 6, chapter 3.

20. See n. 5, chapter 3.

21. See nn. 9 and 12, chapter 3.

22. See nn. 8–14, chapter 3.

23. See nn. 20, 23–26, 29, 32–33, chapter 3.

24. See House Committee on Assassinations, *The Final Assassinations Report*, p. 573, and *Hearings—King*, vol. 6, p. 70; Senate Select Committee, *Final Report—Book III*, pp. 199, 318; and J. Stanley Pottinger to Edward H. Levi, "Martin Luther King Report," 9 April 1976, p. 3.

25. Senate Select Committee, *Final Report—Book III*, p. 85.

26. See n. 38, chapter 3.

27. Sullivan, *The Bureau*, p. 135.

28. See Sullivan, *The Bureau*, p. 137. Sullivan believed that there was no real meaning in King's use of "Marxist." He also believed that King was not a Communist, and had no coherent ideology whatsoever. Sullivan stated these views in a 17 April 1976 letter to Senator Walter F. Mondale, a Church Committee member.

29. See Sullivan, *The Bureau*, pp. 135–39, esp. 138.

30. See Sullivan, *The Bureau*, p. 142; Wise, *The American Police State*, pp. 306–8; and Senate Select Committee, *Final Report—Book II*, p. 221, and *Final Report—Book III*, pp. 158–60.

31. See Sullivan, *The Bureau*, p. 144.

32. Sullivan expressed these views in a 4 February 1976 letter to his attorney, Joseph E. Casey.

33. Sullivan detailed these sentiments in two letters to Casey, one dated 22 December 1975 and the other 4 February 1976.

34. Sullivan made these statements in his 22 December 1975 letter to Casey and in his 17 April 1976 one to Senator Mondale.

35. On Sullivan himself, see Ungar, *FBI*, pp. 295–314, and Ungar's review of Sullivan's posthumous book in the *New Republic*, 13 October 1979, pp. 35–36, where Ungar prints the much-whispered story that Sullivan was hospitalized on a number of occasions for severe psychiatric problems. Also see J. Y. Smith, "William C. Sullivan, Once High FBI Aide, Killed by Hunter," *Washington Post*, 10 November 1977, p. C8.

36. See n. 8, chapter 3.

37. See Winthrop D. Jordan, *White over Black: American Attitudes toward the Negro, 1550–1812* (Baltimore: Penguin Books, 1969), pp. 28–40, 150–63, esp. at 38. Also see Charles H. Stember's important but little-cited *Sexual Racism* (New York: Elsevier, 1976), esp. pp. 44–46, 60–62, 159–64; as well as Calvin C. Hernton's two useful books, *Sex and Racism in America* (Garden City, N.Y.: Doubleday, 1965), and *Coming Together: Black Power, White Hatred and Sexual Hang-ups* (New York: Random House, 1971); and James P. Comer, "White Racism: Its Root, Form, and Function," *American Journal of Psychiatry* 126 (December 1969): 802–6.

38. See Ungar, *FBI*, pp. 269–70; Sullivan, *The Bureau*, pp. 140–41; and Demaris, *The Director*, p. 94.

39. W. Mark Felt, *The FBI Pyramid* (New York: G. P. Putnam's Sons,

1979), pp. 125–26, 197; and Ralph de Toledano, *J. Edgar Hoover* (New Rochelle, N.Y.: Arlington House, 1973), p. 333.

40. John M. Goshko, "Hoover's Files Focus on Sex Scandals," *Washington Post,* 24 November 1976, pp. Al, A8, notes that "a preoccupation with homosexuality runs through the files like a connecting thread. Reference after reference is made to allegations that various politicians, government officials and other well-known people were homosexuals." One close aide to Robert Kennedy can recall his own initial meeting with Director Hoover, at which Hoover launched into a long monologue about how a well-known national politician, "Governor Smith," supposedly was the country's most notorious homosexual. The aide found the rendition "disconcerting," and happened to encounter the Attorney General when he returned to his own office. Kennedy asked him where he had been, and when the aide replied, "Being introduced to Director Hoover," Kennedy responded, "Did he tell you that 'Governor Smith' was the country's most notorious homosexual?" The aide was startled, but realized that he was not the only person Hoover had volunteered the information to. The aide believed that Robert Kennedy did not know whether to take Hoover seriously on this or many other subjects.

41. See Ramsey Clark (T. H. Baker interview, 21 March, 16 April, and 3 June 1969, Falls Church, Va.), Johnson Library, Austin, part II, pp. 20–21; and Clark's comments in Demaris, *The Director,* p. 233; and House Committee on Assassinations, *Hearings—King,* vol. 7, pp. 141, 150; and Nina Totenberg, "Hoover: Life and Times of a 76-Year-Old Cop," *National Observer,* 12 April 1971, pp. 1, 13.

42. Frank Donner, *The Age of Surveillance* (New York: Alfred A. Knopf, 1980), p. 113, also endorses this evaluation of Hoover. It also can be asserted that if Hoover himself had been as totally committed to destroying King as Sullivan was, that the simple refusal of numerous journalists to print the FBI's material would not have kept the Bureau from "getting its man."

43. Burke Marshall (Larry J. Hackman interview, 19–20 January 1970, Bedford, N.Y.), Kennedy Library, Boston, p. 43.

44. See Marshall interview, cited in n. 43 above, pp. 36–37, 46; Anthony Lewis (Larry J. Hackman interview, 23 July 1970, New York, N.Y.) Kennedy Library, Boston, p. 19; and Schlesinger, *Robert Kennedy,* p. 362.

45. See Hugh Sidey, "LBJ, Hoover and Domestic Spying," *Time,* 10 February 1975, p. 16; Bill Moyers, "LBJ and the FBI," *Newsweek,* 10 March 1975, p. 84; George E. Reedy (Joe B. Frantz interview, 14 February 1972, Washington, D.C.), Johnson Library, Austin, part V, p. 39; and George E. Reedy (Michael L. Gillette interview, 7 June 1975, Washington, D.C.), Johnson Library, Austin, p. 54. Reedy's comment that Johnson

"enjoyed gossip for the sake of gossip" was echoed by Moyers, who observed that Johnson "sometimes found gossip about other men's weaknesses a delicious hiatus from work."

46. Harry C. McPherson (T. H. Baker interview, 9 April 1969, Washington, D.C.), Johnson Library, Austin, part VII, pp. 13–14.

47. See Sidey, "LBJ, Hoover and Domestic Spying," cited in n. 45 above.

48. Ramsey Clark, *Crime in America* (New York: Simon & Schuster, 1970), p. 293. Many of the standard books on the Johnson presidency, including Johnson's own, contain scant mention of Hoover, DeLoach, or even King. See Lyndon B. Johnson, *The Vantage Point* (New York: Holt, Rinehart & Winston, 1971); Eric F. Goldman, *The Tragedy of Lyndon Johnson* (New York: Alfred A. Knopf, 1968), who does note that LBJ was "no great admirer" of King (Dell edition, p. 369); and Doris Kearns, *Lyndon Johnson and the American Dream* (New York: Harper & Row, 1976). Also see Gary Wills, "Singing 'Mammy' to Doris," *New York Review of Books* 23 (24 June 1976): 8, 10–11, who observes that "vast areas of the Johnson psyche are missing" from Kearns's book and that "she has nothing useful to say about the Johnson presidency." Merle Miller's recent account of Johnson's life (*Lyndon: An Oral Biography* [New York: G. P. Putnam's Sons, 1980]) partially corrects a few of the broader omissions.

49. See Moyers, "LBJ and the FBI," cited in n. 45 above; Senate Select Committee, *Final Report—Book III,* pp. 92–93, 122, 146, and *Hearings—FBI,* vol. 6, p. 159; Claudia Townsend and Beau Cutts, "Johnson Put FBI on King," *Atlanta Constitution,* 6 May 1976, pp. A1, A14; and Harris Wofford, *Of Kennedys and Kings* (New York: Farrar, Straus & Giroux, 1980), p. 219.

50. See Harry C. McPherson (T. H. Baker interview, 5 December 1968 and 9 April 1969, Washington D.C.), Johnson Library, Austin, part I, p. 16, part VII, p. 18, and part VIII, p. 12.

51. Author's conversations with Ralph D. Abernathy.

52. See nn. 34, 46, chapter 3.

53. See n. 49, chapter 3.

54. See nn. 52–53, chapter 3.

55. This decline also has been noted by others. See Senate Select Committee, *Final Report—Book III,* pp. 121, 180.

56. See nn. 64, 66–67, chapter 3.

57. This implication is heavy in Felt, *The FBI Pyramid,* pp. 125–26, who states that "it was his personal private conduct, more than the attacks on the Bureau and his association with Communists, which inflamed Hoover and led him to embark on a campaign to discredit Martin Luther King." Making

the same point, though less pregnant with meaning, is the argument of former agent Joseph L. Schott, who wrote that "Hoover's unhappiness with Dr. Martin Luther King, Jr., had more to do with sex than anything else," and particularly with activities that were interracial. See "Hoover's Ghost Still Hangs over FBI," *Trenton* (N.J.) *Times,* 16 March 1980, p. H5.

58. Jackson's angry remarks were more accurate than many people would care to admit. Jackson attacked Hoover's "sick and Peeping Tomism interest of the white male in black sexuality, especially as it concerns the intimate, bedroom activities of the black male." He went on to demand a psychiatric examination of Hoover, who at that time was still FBI Director. See Sheryl M. Butler, "Hits Hoover on Smear," *Chicago Defender,* 11 August 1970, p. 3; and Jesse Jackson, "On the Case," *Chicago Defender,* 15 August 1970, p. 1.

5. *Informant: Jim Harrison and the Road to Memphis*

1. No documents concerning the Young idea have been released. SAC, Atlanta to SAC, Philadelphia, 2 July 1962, Atlanta serial 100–5586–387, suggests someone as a possible informant on King. The fall, 1964, developments, which remain somewhat unclear, are the subject of Atlanta serial 100–5586–1284; SAC, Atlanta to Director, "CIRM, IS–C," 2 November 1964, 100–442529–352; Director to SAC, Atlanta, 6 November 1964; SAC, Atlanta to Director, 27 November 1964; and Director to SAC, Atlanta, date unknown, 100–106670–569; all unreleased. It is quite possible that these fall 1964 developments concern James A. Harrison, and that he had this brief earlier relationship with the Bureau prior to beginning his more extensive role in October, 1965. The Hunter idea is the subject of Director (by Phillips) to SAC, Atlanta, "COMINFIL SCLC, IS–C," 18 August 1965, 100–438794–526.

2. See Director (by Seymor F. Phillips) to SAC, Atlanta, "COMINFIL SCLC, IS–C," 4 October 1965, 100–438794–684; SAC, New York to Director, "COMINFIL SCLC, IS–C," 12 October 1965, 100–438794–738; Director (by Phillips) to SAC, New York, "COMINFIL SCLC, IS–C," 21 October 1965, 100–438794–738; SAC, New York to Director, "COMINFIL SCLC, IS–C," 8 November 1965, 100–438794–856; SAC, Chicago to Director, "COMINFIL SCLC, IS–C," 9 November 1965, 100–438794–874; and two crucial, unreleased items, Director to SAC, Atlanta, 24 September 1965, and SAC, Atlanta to Director, 8 October 1965, Atlanta serial 100–5718–2008. Other unreleased items concerning Harrison are SAC,

Atlanta (by Alan G. Sentinella) to Director, "COMINFIL SCLC, IS–C," 9, 18, and 19 November 1965, 100–438794–865, 906, and 907. Harrison's own FBI headquarters' file, 134–11126, is not subject to release under the FOIA until Harrison publicly admits his role as a Bureau informant. Years later Harrison claimed to one questioner that he had not been motivated by money, and that his "rationale had mostly to do with whether the Communist Party was manipulating the movement." He did concede that he had answered that question in the negative during his first year with SCLC, and that "I made a mistake" by continuing to work for the Bureau. Both FBI personnel and SCLC staffers believe, however, that Harrison primarily was "motivated by greed." Present-day assertions by some SCLC staffers that they knew or suspected all along that Harrison was an FBI informant are dubious in light of the fact that no one took any action concerning him at that time. Intimations that Harrison began *continuous* work for the FBI in 1964 rather than 1965 are erroneous. See Paul Good, "An Uneasy Life for Man Who Spied on King," and Dallas Lee, "SCLC Had Been Aware of Informants," *Atlanta Journal Constitution,* 16 November 1980, pp. A1, A16. The FBI's Atlanta office also had another informant, a young, itinerant black minister, who on occasion could obtain information from SCLC headquarters that the Bureau needed. His role was never more than minor.

3. See SAC, Chicago to Director, "COMINFIL SCLC, IS–C," 13 October, 27 October, and 22 November 1965, 100–438794–747, 835, and 921; Director to SAC, Chicago, "COMINFIL SCLC, IS–C," 3 November 1965, 100–438794–821; SAC, Chicago to Director, "Martin Luther King, Jr., SM–C," 10 January, 24 January, 2 February, and 8 February 1966, all unserialized in 100–438794; Baumgardner (by R. F. Bates) to Sullivan, "Martin Luther King, Jr., SM–C," 18 February 1966, 100–106670–2306; SAC, Chicago to Director, attn. W. C. Sullivan, "Martin Luther King, Jr., SM–C," 24 February 1966, 100–106670–2330; and David L. Lewis, *King: A Critical Biography* (New York: Praeger, 1970), pp. 332, 340–41. A May 1966 briefing of the pastor of the American Church in Paris, where King was scheduled to preach, also was less than a rousing success. See Legal Attaché, Paris to Director, 9 May 1966, unreleased.

4. SAC, Atlanta to Director, "CIRM, IS–C," 18 Feburary and 11 April 1966, 100–442529–1686 and 1735; Director to SAC, Atlanta, "CIRM, IS–C," 15 April 1966, 100–442529–1734; Baumgardner to Sullivan, "Martin Luther King, Jr., SM–C," 9 May 1966, 100–106670–2521; Director (by R. F. Bates) to SAC, Atlanta, "COMINFIL SCLC, IS–C (COINTELPRO)," 16 Feburary 1966, 100–438794–1162; and Director (by Phil T. Basher) to SACs, Atlanta and Chicago, "COMINFIL SCLC, IS–C," 8 April 1966, 100–438794–1302. Atlanta agents' feelings about Wil-

liams are reflected in SAC, Atlanta to Director, "Unsubs, Unidentified Alabama State Troopers, et al.; Hosea Williams, John Lewis, et al., Victims, CR–EL," 14 April 1965, 100–438794–unserialized.

5. See SAC, New York to Director, "COMINFIL SCLC, IS–C," 3 February 1966, 100–438794–1130; SAC, New York to Director, "COMINFIL SCLC, IS–C," 11 February 1966, 100–438794–1151; SAC, New York to Director, "COMINFIL SCLC, IS–C," 15 February 1966, 100–438794–1171; Director to SAC, New York, 18 March 1966, unreleased; SAC, New York to Director, "COMINFIL SCLC, IS–C," 7 April 1966, 100–438794–1309; Baumgardner (by Phil T. Basher) to Sullivan, "COMINFIL SCLC, IS–C," 15 April 1966, 100–438794–1329; Hoover (by Basher) to Marvin Watson, White House, "SCLC," 18 April 1966, 100–438794–1322; "Dr. King's Group Scores Ky Junta," *New York Times,* 14 April 1966, p. 1; Baumgardner (by Basher) to Sullivan, "COMINFIL SCLC, IS–C," 2 May 1966, 100–438794–1384; SAC, New York to Director, "COMINFIL SCLC, IS–C," 10 May 1966, 100–438794–1401; SAC, New York to Director, "Stanley David Levison, SM–C," 13 May 1966, 100–392452–270; Director to SAC, New York, 18 July 1966, SAC, New York to Director, 15 August 1966, Baumgardner to Sullivan, 31 August 1966, Robert Wick to C. D. DeLoach, 6 September 1966, and SAC, New York to Director, 7 October 1966, all unreleased.

6. SAC, Miami to Director, "Martin Luther King, Jr., SM–C," 23 May 1966, Atlanta serial 100–5586–4532; SAC, Miami to Director, "Martin Luther King, Jr., SM–C," 7 June 1966 and 12 December 1975, 100–106670–2576 and 4008.

7. Hoover to Katzenbach, 28 April 1966, unreleased; Hoover (by M. J. Rozamus), "CIRM (*JUNE*)," 22 June 1966, 100–442529–illegible; SAC Joseph K. Ponder to File 66–293, "ELSUR," 23 June 1966, 100–6670E–106, in House Committee on Assassinations, *Hearings—King,* vol. 6, p. 209; and George C. Moore (by J. J. Dunn) to Sullivan, "Martin Luther King, Jr., SM–C," 19 June 1969, 100–106670–unserialized. The stolen car allegations are detailed in Alex Rosen (by W. A. Frankenfield) to Alan H. Belmont, "Unsubs, Morris Findlay [*sic*], Hosea Williams, Harold Belton Andrews, ITSMV," 18 October 1965, 100–438794–unserialized; Rosen (by Rex I. Shroder) to Belmont, "Harold Belton Andrews, ITSMV," 19 October 1965, and 26 October 1965, both 100–438794–unserialized; Rosen (by J. R. Malley) to Belmont, "Harold Belton Andrews, ITSMV," 1 November 1965, 100–438794–unserialized; and Rosen (by Shroder) to Belmont, "Harold Belton Andrews, et al., ITSMV; ITSP–C," 8 November 1965, 100–438794–887. The Justice Department's reluctance to institute a full investigation raised the ire of Director Hoover, who wrote on one memo,

"These are outrageous restrictions. The moral is, join the SCLC and you are immune to ever being interviewed in alleged crime, much less prosecuted."

8. See SAC, Chicago to Director, "Martin Luther King, Jr., SM–C," 29 March 1966, 100–438794–unserialized; SAC, Chicago to Director, "Martin Luther King, Jr., SM–C," 12 April 1966, 100–438794–unserialized; Director (by Phil T. Basher) to SAC, Chicago, "COMINFIL SCLC, IS–C," 4 May 1966, 100–438794–1369; SAC, Chicago to Director, "Martin Luther King, Jr., SM–C," 17 May and 6 July 1966, both unserialized in 100–438794; SAC, Chicago to Director, "COMINFIL SCLC, IS–C," 8 June 1966, 100–438794–1484; and Director to SAC, Chicago, 21 June 1966, unreleased. Chicago did have a human source, "CG–6905–S," who had some contact with SCLC staffer James Bevel. The informant may well have been a member of the local chapter of the W. E. B. DuBois Club.

9. The reports to the White House were dated 9 September, 4, 17, and 24 October, 2, 7, and 14 November, and 9 December 1966. The almost equally quiet previous part of the year had seen reports go over on 3 and 17 February, 21 and 22 March, and 2 June 1966. All are in the Stegall Files, Johnson Library. Also, the wiretap on Clarence Jones was removed on 29 November 1966.

10. See Baumgardner (by C. D. Brennan) to Sullivan, "Martin Luther King, Jr., SM–C," 27 October 1966, 100–106670–2760; Baumgardner (by Dwight M. Wells) to Sullivan, "Martin Luther King, Jr., SM–C," 24 October 1966, 100–106670–illegible; DeLoach to Tolson, "Martin Luther King; SCLC, Possible Grant of $3,000,000 from Ford Foundation," 26 October 1966, 100–106670–2754; Baumgardner (by Robert L. Shackelford) to Sullivan, "Martin Luther King, Jr., SM–C," 28 October 1966, 100–106670–2779; Baumgardner (by Wells) to Sullivan, "Martin Luther King, Jr., SM–C," 3 November 1966, 100–106670–2782; and Robert E. Wick to DeLoach, "Martin Luther King, Jr., SM–C, Proposed Meeting with James R. Hoffa," 9 November 1966, 100–106670–illegible; all of which are available in House Committee on Assassinations, *Hearings—King*, vol. 6, pp. 239–52, 279–82. Assistant Director Sullivan also had a copy of the 1964 King monograph delivered to the American ambassador to Japan, U. Alexis Johnson, after Sullivan, visiting Tokyo, found the ambassador uninformed about King. Sullivan to DeLoach, "Martin Luther King, Jr., SM–C," 19 December 1966, 100–106670–2807.

11. Charles D. Brennan (by Dwight M. Wells) to Sullivan, "Martin Luther King, Jr., SM–C," 6 January, 8 March, and 21 March 1967, 100–106670–2813, 2867, and 2855; John P. Roche to Lyndon B. Johnson, 5 April 1967, WHCF (CF) Bayard Rustin Name File, Johnson Library. Reports went to the White House on 9, 11, and 18 January and 21 March

1967. C. D. Brennan had succeeded the retiring Fred Baumgardner as chief of the internal security section.

12. *Washington Post,* 6 April 1967; *Life,* 21 April 1967, p. 4. Also see Emmet John Hughes, "A Curse on Confusion," *Newsweek,* 1 May 1967, p. 17; and Senate Select Committee, *Final Report—Book III,* p. 184. The most accurate version of King's February 25 Los Angeles speech, "The Casualties of the War in Vietnam," appears in *Gandhi Marg* 11 (October 1967): 185–94, and the best printing of the 4 April speech, "Beyond Vietnam," is *Freedomways* 7 (Spring 1967): 103–17. The two most controversial remarks in the Riverside speech were a characterization of the U.S. government as "the greatest purveyor of violence in the world today" and a reference to "the concentration camps we call fortified hamlets." King had attacked the war in a 16 January 1966 sermon at Ebenezer Baptist Church, "The Nonconformist," but the remarks were not reported in the press.

13. George Christian to Lyndon B. Johnson, 8 April 1967, WHCF King Name File, Johnson Library; Carl T. Rowan, "Dr. King's Tactical Error," *Cleveland Plain Dealer,* 14 April 1967. Rowan followed that up with "Martin Luther King's Tragic Decision," *Reader's Digest* 91 (September 1967): 37–42, where he stated that King was conceited, Communist-influenced, and "persona non grata to Lyndon Johnson."

14. Charles D. Brennan (by Robert L. Shackelford and Dwight M. Wells) to Sullivan, "CIRM—A Current Analysis," 10 April 1967, 100–442529–illegible, available in House Committee on Assassinations, *Hearings—King,* vol. 7, pp. 78–79; Brennan to Sullivan, "Martin Luther King, Jr., SM–C," 6 April 1967, 100–106670–2881; Hoover to Clark, Rusk, McNamara, White House, and Secret Service, "CIRM," 10 April 1967, 100–442529–2143 through 2146, and 2225; Hoover to Mildred Stegall, "Martin Luther King, Jr., SM–C," 11 and 19 April 1967, 100–106670–2882 and 2895; Brennan to Sullivan, "Martin Luther King, Jr., SM–C," 18 April 1967, 100–106670–2906; Brennan's testimony in *Hearings—King,* vol. 6, p. 296; and George C. Moore to Sullivan, "Martin Luther King, Jr., SM–C," 19 June 1969, 100–106670–3659. Additional reports on King went to the White House on 7, 10, 12, 14, 18, 21, 24, and 25 April 1967. The flow continued at a somewhat reduced pace throughout the summer: 12, 18, and 29 May, 9 and 14 June, and 21, 24, 25, and 31 July 1967. The 25 July one (100–106670–3021) detailed a Levison-Clarence Jones conversation in which both men allegedly made strongly critical remarks about King; the 31 July report (100–106670–3035) alleged that King had had foreknowledge of some planned disturbances in Chicago. Also see SAC, New York to Director, "CIRM, IS–C," 21 July 1967, 100–442529–2278; and Brennan

to Sullivan, "Martin Luther King, Jr., SM–C," 25 July 1967, 100–
106670–3026. Additionally, DeLoach to Tolson, 10 July 1967 (unreleased),
details a conversation DeLoach had had with President Johnson about King.

15. Brennan to Sullivan, "Martin Luther King, Jr., SM–C," 20 April
1967, 100–106670–2913; SAC, New York to Director, "CIRM, IS–C,"
100–442529–2170; Director to SACs, Atlanta, Chicago and New York,
"CPUSA, COINTELPRO, IS–C (Martin Luther King)," 18 May 1967,
100–3–104–34–illegible; SAC, New York to Director, 27 May 1967 (unreleased); SAC, Chicago to Director, "CPUSA, COINTELPRO, IS–C (Martin Luther King)," 1 June 1967, Chicago serial 100–32864–3019; and SAC,
Atlanta to Director, 16 June 1967 (unreleased).

16. Director to SACs, Albany et al., "COINTELPRO Black Nationalist—Hate Groups, IS," 25 August 1967, 100–448006–1, in House Committee on Assassinations, *Hearings—King,* vol. 6, pp. 298–300. Most of
the COINTELPROs are discussed in Senate Select Committee, *Final
Report—Book III,* pp. 1–77, and in Mark Ryter, "COINTELPRO: Corrupting American Institutions," *First Principles* 3 (May 1978): 1–5, and
"COINTELPRO: FBI Lawbreaking and Violence," *First Principles*
3 (June 1978): 1–6. One that is often overlooked is described in Carmen
Gautier et al., "Persecution of the Puerto Rican Independence Movements
and Their Leaders by the COINTELPRO of the U.S. FBI," unpublished
manuscript, 1978, and William Lichtenstein and David Wimhurst, "Red
Alert in Puerto Rico," *Nation* 228 (30 June 1979): 780–82. The Bureau's
extensive efforts against the Socialist Workers party are detailed in Nelson
Blackstock, *COINTELPRO: The FBI's Secret War on Political Freedom*
(New York: Vintage Books, 1976).

Reports on King went to the White House on 9, 14, 21, 29, and 31
August, 21 and 26 September, and 3 and 17 October 1967. By mid-August
King was stating that he would "go all out" in 1968 to defeat Johnson
unless the President moved soon to end the war in Vietnam. See Dick Cun-
ningham, "Dr. King May Oppose LBJ in '68 on Vietnam," *Minneapolis
Tribune,* 18 August 1967; Robert P. Hey, "Dr. King Takes Anti-Johnson
Stand," *Christian Science Monitor,* 19 August 1967; and Walker Lundy,
"King Vows to Oppose LBJ if War Stance Isn't Altered," *Atlanta Journal,*
18 August 1967, p. A8.

17. Moore (by Wells) to Sullivan, "Martin Luther King, Jr., SM–C," 18
October 1967, 100–106670–3129; D. J. Brennan (by W. J. O'Donnell) to
Sullivan, "COMINFIL SCLC, IS–C," 30 October 1967, 100–438794–
unserialized; Moore (by Phil T. Basher) to Sullivan, "Martin Luther King,
Jr., SM–C," 7 November 1967, 100–106670–3138; and Moore (by Wells)
to Sullivan, "Martin Luther King, Jr., SM–C," 29 November 1967, 100–

106670–illegible; all in House Committee on Assassinations, *Hearings— King*, vol. 6, pp. 277–78, 283–87, 291–95. In addition to the report of 8 November, other communications went to the White House on 20, 27, and 30 November and 1, 7, and 20 December 1967.

18. Moore (by Wells) to Sullivan, "SCLC, IS–C, (*JUNE*)," 13 December 1967, 100–438794–2042; Director (by Wells) to SAC, Atlanta, "COMINFIL SCLC, IS–C (*JUNE*)," 14 December 1967, 100–438794–2042; SAC, Atlanta (by Al F. Miller) to Director, "COMINFIL SCLC, IS–C (*JUNE*)," 20 December 1967, 100–438794–2052; Moore (by Wells) to Sullivan, "COMINFIL SCLC (*JUNE*)," 29 December 1967, 100–438794–2053; Hoover (by Wells) to Clark, "COMINFIL, SCLC," 2 January 1968, 100–438794–2052; and Clark to Hoover, "COMINFIL, SCLC," 3 January 1968, 100–438794–2065. Other memos detailing Poor People's Campaign plans include SAC, Atlanta to Director, "COMINFIL SCLC, IS–C," 18 August 1967, 100–438794–1960; Brennan (by Wells) to Sullivan, "Martin Luther King, Jr., SM–C," 28 August 1967, 100–106670–3075; George C. Moore to Sullivan, "Martin Luther King, Jr., SM–C," 6 December 1967, 18 December 1967, and 2 January 1968, 100–106670–3169, 3180, and 3183; and M. A. Jones to T. E. Bishop, "Martin Luther King, Jr., SM–C," 7 January 1968, 100–106670–3182. King initially announced the details of the campaign in a 4 December 1967 press conference at Ebenezer Baptist Church.

19. See SAC, Atlanta (by Alan G. Sentinella) to Director, "CPUSA, COINTELPRO, IS–C," 15 February 1968, 100–3–104–34–1661; SAC, New York to Director, "CPUSA, COINTELPRO, IS–C," 9 February 1968, 100–3–104–34–1663; Charles D. Brennan (by W. G. Shaw) to Sullivan, "CPUSA, COINTELPRO, IS–C," 15 February 1968, 100–3–104–34–1662; George C. Moore to Sullivan, "Martin Luther King, Jr., SM–C," 24 January, 2 February, and 7 February 1968, 100–106670–3191, 3193, and 3196; and Director (by W. G. Shaw) to SAC, New York "CPUSA, COINTELPRO, IS–C," 21 February 1968, 100–3–104–34–illegible. King's 23 February speech, "Honoring Dr. DuBois," and perhaps written by O'Dell, appears in *Freedomways* 8 (Spring 1968): 104–11. The uncertainty within SCLC is discussed in Vincent Harding, "So Much History, So Much Future: Martin Luther King, Jr., and the Second Coming of America," in *Have We Overcome?*, ed. Michael V. Namorato (Jackson: University Press of Mississippi, 1979), pp. 31–78, at 69–72; Thomas E. Offenburger (Katherine Shannon interview, 2 July 1968, Washington, D.C.), Civil Rights Documentation Project Papers, Moorland-Spingarn Research Center, Howard University, pp. 26, 32; Michael Harrington's comments in George Goodman, " 'He Lives, Man!' " *Look* 33 (15 April 1969): 29–31; Tom

Kahn, "Why the Poor People's Campaign Failed," *Commentary* 46 (September 1968): 50–55; and Bayard Rustin's memo of January 1968, which appears in Rustin's *Down The Line* (Chicago: Quadrangle Books, 1971), pp. 202–5.

20. Relevant articles include Jean M. White, "King 'Going for Broke' on April Drive for Poor," *Washington Post,* 28 January 1968, p. A1; White and Robert C. Maynard, "King Keys His Tactics to Response by Hill," *Washington Post,* 8 February 1968, p. A1; Maynard, "Is King's Nonviolence Now Old-Fashioned?" *Washington Post,* 11 February 1968, pp. C1–C2; William Raspberry, "King Acts to Ease Fears of Violence," *Washington Post,* 11 February 1968, p. D1; Walter Rugaber, "Strong Challenge by King," *New York Times,* 11 February 1968, p. E4; Jean M. White, "King Revisits Scenes of Strife, Seeking Aid," *Washington Post,* 17 February 1968, p. A1; Claude Koprowski, "Washington's Business Community Awaits King's March with Unease," *Washington Post,* 1 March 1968, p. D6; Ben A. Franklin, "Dr. King to Start March on the Capital April 22," *New York Times,* 5 March 1968, p. 28; and Jack Nelson, "King Sets New Date for Capital Demonstrations," *Los Angeles Times,* 5 March 1968.

21. Larry Temple to Lyndon B. Johnson, 14 February 1968, WHCF (EX) HU 2, Box 7, Johnson Library; and "Memorandum for Marvin Watson," 2 February 1968, King Name File, Johnson Library.

22. Christopher H. Pyle, "Military Surveillance of Civilian Politics, 1967–1970," Unpublished Ph.D. diss., Columbia University, 1974, pp. 88–93; Jack Anderson, "FBI Used King File in Killer Case," *Washington Post,* 15 August 1970, p. C11, "Boggs Drinking Data Traced to FBI," *Washington Post,* 12 April 1971, p. B11, and "Hoover Floated Hoax Story on King," *Washington Post,* 17 December 1975, p. C18; and John M. Crewdson, "Study of Dr. King's Death Finds No Links to FBI," *New York Times,* 1 January 1976, pp. 1, 6. Also, Hoover to Ramsey Clark, and Hoover to Mildred Stegall, "Martin Luther King, Jr., SM–C," 20 February 1968, 100–106670–3206 and 3209, both unreleased. The former athlete also sent two letters of complaint directly to President Johnson. The woman in question repeatedly has denied that any such relationship existed. The Bureau subsequently investigated her husband as someone supposedly having a motive for arranging Dr. King's assassination, and then leaked the story of having done so to the press.

23. Richard Harwood, "J. Edgar Hoover: A Librarian with a Lifetime Lease," *Washington Post,* 25 February 1968, p. D1; Moore to Sullivan, 29 February 1968 (unreleased); Moore to Sullivan, "Martin Luther King, Jr., SM–C," 4 March and 11 March 1968, 100–106670–3229 and 3526; Moore (by Wells) to Sullivan, "Martin Luther King, Jr., SM–C," 19 March 1968,

100–106670–illegible; and Moore to Sullivan, "Martin Luther King, Jr., SM–C," 19 June 1969, 100–106670–3659. There also existed a longer, thirty-nine–page version of the new report. Other, more brief reports on King went to the White House on 3, 18, and 25 January, 8, 13, 20, 21, and 27 February, and 1 (two) and 5 March 1968. In mid-January the Bureau had refused a request by West Virginia Senator Robert Byrd for material on King for a Senate speech. DeLoach to Tolson, 19 January 1968, unreleased. In early March the CIA intensified its own efforts to collect information on King, efforts that it had resumed in the late summer of 1967 after an apparent two-year pause. A heavily deleted CIA summary report of 7 March 1968, however, contains a number of glaring errors, such as a statement that King took several foreign trips in January 1968, on dates when he actually was in Atlanta. Also, the Agency apparently was unaware of an early 1968 trip that King *did* take, to Acapulco.

24. Director to SACs, Albany et al., "COINTELPRO, Black Nationalist—Hate Groups, RI," 4 March 1968, 100–448006–illegible; SAC Baltimore to Director, "COINTELPRO, BNHG, RI," 8 March 1968, 100–448006–illegible; Director (by T. J. Deakin) to SACs, Atlanta, Baltimore and Chicago, "COINTELPRO, BNHG, RI," 14 March 1968, 100–448006–24; SAC Atlanta (by Alan G. Sentinella) to Director, "COINTELPRO, BNGH, RI," 18 March 1968, 100–448006–40; SAC; Chicago to Director, "COINTELPRO, BNHG, RI," 21 March 1968, 100–448006–39; George C. Moore to SAC, Jackson, "Washington Spring Project, RM," 11 March 1968, 157–8428–363; SAC, Jackson to Director, "COINTELPRO, BNHG, RI," 4 April 1968, 100–448006–72; SAC, Detroit to Director, "COINTELPRO, BNHG, RI," 23 March 1968, 100–448006–84; Director (by T. J. Deakin) to SAC, Detroit, "COINTELPRO, BNHG, RI," 4 April 1968, 100–448006–illegible; SAC, Mobile to Director, 25 March 1968, unreleased; Director (by T. J. Deakin) to SAC, Mobile, "COINTELPRO, BNHG, RI," 2 April 1968, 100–448006–63; Moore (by Deakin) to Sullivan, "COINTELPRO, BNHG, RI," 26 March 1968, 100–448006–illegible; and SAC, Washington Field to Director, "COINTELPRO, BNHG, RI," 4 April 1968, 100–448006–66, most of which are available in House Committee on Assassinations, *Hearings—King*, vol. 6, pp. 301–6, 316–32, 336–42, 369. The letter to Reese apparently was not sent. T. J. Deakin was the Division Five supervisor in charge of the "BNHG" COINTELPRO.

25. See H. Ralph Jackson (James Mosby interview, 10 July 1968, Memphis), Civil Rights Documentation Project, Moorland-Springarn Research Center, Howard University, pp. 12–13; H. Ralph Jackson (Arvil V. Adams interview, 21 July 1969, Memphis); H. Ralph Jackson (Anne Trotter, Bill Thomas, and David Yellin interview, 24 May 1968, Memphis), Mississippi

Valley Collection, Memphis State University, pp. 23–24; James M. Lawson, Jr. (Bill Thomas and David Yellin interview, 1 July 1968, Memphis), MVC, MSU, pp. 2–10; S. B. "Billy" Kyles (Joan Beifuss and Bill Thomas interview, 30 July 1968, Memphis), MVC, MSU, pp. 18–21; Malcolm Blackburn (Tom Beckner and Bill Thomas interview, 2 August 1968, Memphis), MVC, MSU, p. 35; Blackburn (Anne Trotter and David Yellin interview, 24 May 1968, Memphis), MVC, MSU, pp. 34–35; K. W. Cook, "King Urges Work Stoppage by Negroes to Back Strike," *Memphis Commercial Appeal,* 19 March 1968, p. 1, and "King Plans to Return for March," *Memphis Press Scimitar,* 19 March 1968, pp. 1, 8. General accounts of the sanitation strike that are extremely useful include F. Ray Marshall and Arvil V. Adams, "The Memphis Public Employees Strike," in *Racial Conflict and Negotiations,* ed. W. Ellison Chalmers and Gerald W. Cormick (Ann Arbor: Institute of Labor and Industrial Relations, 1971), pp. 71–107; Thomas W. Collins, "An Analysis of the Memphis Garbage Strike of 1968," *Public Affairs Forum* 3 (April 1974): 1–6; Robert E. Bailey, "The 1968 Memphis Sanitation Strike," Unpublished M.A. thesis, Memphis State University, 1974; Richard Lentz, "Sixty-Five Days in Memphis: The *Commercial Appeal,* The *Press-Scimitar* and the 1968 Garbage Strike," Unpublished M.A. thesis, Southern Illinois University, 1976, which is an excellent analysis of the antistrike bias exhibited by the two local papers; Earl Green, Jr., "Labor in the South: A Case Study of Memphis—The 1968 Sanitation Strike and Its Effects on an Urban Community," Unpublished Ph.D. diss., New York University, 1980; and Selma S. Lewis, "Social Religion and the Memphis Sanitation Strike," Unpublished Ph.D. diss., Memphis State University, 1976. Two books by David M. Tucker are essential for understanding Memphis at the time of the strike: *Black Pastors and Leaders: Memphis, 1819–1972* (Memphis: Memphis State University Press, 1975), and *Memphis Since Crump: Bossism, Blacks, and Civic Reformers, 1948–1968* (Knoxville: University of Tennessee Press, 1980).

26. SAC, Memphis to Director, "Sanitation Workers Strike, Memphis, RM," 16 February 1968, 157–9146–X1; SAC, Memphis (by William H. Lawrence) to Director, "Sanitation Workers Strike, Memphis, RM," 23 February 1968, 157–9146–X5; SAC, Memphis (by William H. Lawrence) to Director, "The Invaders, RM," 5 March 1968, 157–8460–2; SAC, Memphis (by Howell S. Lowe) to Director, "COINTELPRO, BNHG, RI," 14 March 1968, 100–448006–25; Director (by C. A. Parkis) to SAC, Memphis, "Sanitation Workers Strike, Memphis, RM," 15 March 1968, 157–9146–X26; and House Committee on Assassinations, *Hearing—King,* vol. 6, pp. 407, 412. Turner and Maxine Smith were primary sources for the 16 February report, and Dr. Vasco Smith for the 23 February one. The Mem-

phis field-office files for the three individuals were 170–46 (Turner), 170–49 (Vasco Smith), and 170–83 (Maxine Smith). The Bureau's "170" file series is labeled "extremist informants."

27. The early history of BOP and the Invaders is detailed in Calvin L. Taylor, Jr. (Bill Thomas and Jerry Viar interview, 17 August 1968, Memphis), MVC, MSU, part I, pp. 6–39 and part II, pp. 8–17. Strikingly similar descriptions of the strategy committee meetings appear in Richard Moon (James Mosby interview, 10 July 1968, Memphis), CRDP Papers, Moorland Spingarn Research Center, Howard, pp. 26, 30; Darrell Doughty (Joan Beifuss and David Yellin interview, 26 June 1968, Memphis), MVC, MSU, part II, pp. 5–6; John Spence (Bill Thomas and David Yellin interview, 16 June 1968, Memphis), MVC, MSU, pp. 21, 26; and Bobby Doctor (Bill Thomas and David Yellin interview, 17 June 1968, Memphis), MVC, MSU, part II, pp. 3–7. Also see Jacques Wilmore (John Britton interview, 26 September 1968, New York), CRDP Papers, MSRC, Howard, pp. 11, 13, 15, 19. The Invaders themselves have testified to having similar feelings. See Taylor, p. 17 of interview cited above ("Cabbage related to us that he was . . . being somewhat left out of the strategy planning"); Charles Ballard (James Mosby interview, 13 July 1968, Memphis), CRDP Papers, MSRC, Howard, p. 10; and Ron Ivy (David Yellin interview, 9 May 1968, Memphis), MVC, MSU, pp. 27–29.

28. Lawson (Joan Beifuss and David Yellin interview, 8 July 1970, Memphis), MVC, MSU, pp. 4–12; Marian Logan to Martin King, "1968 April Demonstrations in Washington, D.C.," 8 March 1968; House Committee on Assassinations, *Hearings—King,* vol. 1, p. 15; and George Favre, "Dr. King's Tour Leaves Wake of Tensions," *Christian Science Monitor,* 30 March 1968, p. 11.

29. S. B. "Billy" Kyles, interview cited in n. 25 above, pp. 27–43; Lawson, interview cited in n. 25 above, part I, pp. 12–18, and part II, pp. 1–27, 37–39, 50; Taylor, interview cited in n. 27 above, part II, pp. 30–37; "Day's Log of Police Calls Traces Racial Disturbance Shock Waves," *Memphis Commercial Appeal,* 29 March 1968, p. 25; Wayne Chastain, "Hint Came Early That March Would Detour from Nonviolence," *Memphis Press-Scimitar,* 29 March 1968, p. 10; James P. Turner to Stephen Pollak, "Memphis Disturbance, March 28, 1968," 1 April 1968, Civil Rights Division, U.S. Justice Department; ASAC C. O. Halter to File 157–1092, "Sanitation Workers Strike, Memphis," 28 March 1968, Memphis serial 157–1092–168; SAC, Atlanta to Director, "Martin Luther King, Jr., SM–C; Sanitation Workers Strike, Memphis, RM," 28 March 1968, 157–9146–1390; Gerold Frank, *An American Death* (Garden City, N.Y.: Doubleday, 1972), pp. 16–27; Bernard Lee (Jim Bishop interview, 5 September 1970,

Atlanta), Friedsam Library, St. Bonaventure University; Malcolm Black-burn, 2 August 1968 interview cited in n. 25 above, pp. 30–31; Baxton Bryant (Joan Beifuss and Tom Beckner interview, 3 August 1968, Nash-ville), MVC, MSU, part II, p. 7; Gerald Fanion (Joan Beifuss and Walter Evans interview, 10 June 1968, Memphis), MVC, MSU, part II, p. 23; Gilbert Patterson (Joan Beifuss and Modeane Thompson interview, 4 June 1968, Memphis), MVC, MSU, p. 23; H. Ralph Jackson, 24 May 1968 interview cited in n. 25 above, part II, pp. 5, 15; and J. Edwin Stanfield, *In Memphis: Tragedy Unaverted* (Atlanta: Southern Regional Council, 3 April 1968). Two other brief SRC reports by Stanfield also are useful:. *In Memphis: More Than a Garbage Strike* (22 March 1968); and *In Memphis: Mirror to America?* (28 April 1968). Concerning the Thursday march, note the statement of the House Committee on Assassinations that "the committee found no basis for a conclusion that the FBI, directly or through its infor-mants, provoked the violence on March 28." *The Final Assassinations Report* (New York: Bantam Books, 1979), p. 541.

30. Howell Raines, *My Soul Is Rested* (New York: G. P. Putnam's Sons, 1977), pp. 464–465; Stanley D. Levison (David L. Lewis interview, November 1968, New York); House Committee on Assassinations, *Hear-ings—King,* vol. 1, pp. 15–17, and vol. 6, pp. 451–52, 512–16; Frank, *An American Death,* pp. 28–33; Thomas BeVier, 'King Disappointed in March—He'll Try Again Next Week," *Memphis Commercial Appeal,* 30 March 1968, p. 1; and Richard N. Billings and John Greenya, *Power to the Public Worker* (Washington: Robert B. Luce, 1974), p. 197.

31. ASAC C. O. Halter to File 157–1092, "Sanitation Workers Strike, Memphis," 28 March 1968, Memphis serial 157–1092–167; George C. Moore (by Theron D. Rushing) to Sullivan, "Sanitation Workers Strike, Memphis, RM," 28 March 1968, 157–9146–38; SAC, Memphis (by Wil-liam H. Lawrence) to Director, "Sanitation Workers Strike, Memphis, RM," 29 March 1968, 157–9146–45; ASAC C. O. Halter to SAC Robert G. Jensen, "Sanitation Workers Strike, Memphis," 29 March 1968, Mem-phis serial 157–1092–173; SAC, Memphis to Director, attn. W. C. Sulli-van, "Sanitation Workers Strike, Memphis, RM," 29 March 1968, 157–9146–47; Moore (by T. J. Deakin) to Sullivan, "COINTELPRO, BNHG, RI," 29 March 1968, 100–448006–illegible; SAC, Memphis (by William H. Lawrence) to Director, "Sanitation Workers Strike, Memphis, RM," 30 March 1968, 157–9146–50; Moore (by Dwight M. Wells) to Sullivan, "COMINFIL SCLC (JUNE)," 29 March 1968, 100–438794–2108; SAC, New York to Director, "Martin Luther King, Jr., SM–C," 1 April 1968, 100–106670–3291; and Hoover (by Wells) to Ramsey Clark, "COMINFIL SCLC," 2 April 1968, 100–438794–2107. Robert G. Jensen, SAC of the

Memphis field office in 1968, emphasized in a 7 July 1976 interview with Justice Department attorneys James F. Walker and Fred G. Folsom that the FBI had conducted no electronic surveillance of any sort of Dr. King in Memphis. A summary of the interview is filed in appendix B of U.S., Department of Justice, *Report of the Department of Justice Task Force to Review the FBI Martin Luther King, Jr., Security and Assassination Investigations,* 11 January 1977. Reports on King went to the White House on 19 and 22 March and 1 April 1968. The latter one (100–106670–3273) detailed a Levison-King phone conversation about the 1968 presidential campaign.

32. Lerone Bennett, Jr., "The Martyrdom of Martin Luther King, Jr.," *Ebony* 23 (May 1968): 174–81, and *What Manner of Man,* 3d ed. (Chicago: Johnson Publishing Co., 1968), pp. 237–38; James Bevel (Katherine Shannon interview, 6 July 1968, Washington, D.C.), CRDP Papers, MSRC, Howard, pp. 9, 16–17; Barbara A. Reynolds, *Jesse Jackson: The Man, The Movement, The Myth* (Chicago: Nelson-Hall, 1975), pp. 82–86; and Harold Middlebrook (Joan Beifuss and Bill Thomas interview, 21 July 1968, Memphis), MVC, MSU, pp. 10–12. Typical of the press commentary in the wake of Thursday's disruption was the *Memphis Commercial Appeal*'s Saturday editorial (30 March 1968, p. 6), "King's Credibility Gap." It asserted that "King's pose as leader of a nonviolent movement has been shattered," that he "fled the melee" and "wrecked his reputation as a leader as he took off at high speed when violence occurred, instead of trying to use his persuasive prestige to stop it." Then, later, it said, King "issued statements attempting to disassociate himself from the violence he had instigated."

33. Taylor, interview cited in n. 27 above, part II, p. 51, and part III, p. 1; Ivy, interview cited in n. 27 above, pp. 23–43, 54–56; "Aura of Tension Slowly Subsides, Ministers' Sermons Ask Restraint," *Memphis Commercial Appeal,* 1 April 1968, p. 1; Jimmie Covington, "Negro Leaders Sifting Rubble for Answers," *Memphis Commercial Appeal,* 1 April 1968, p. 25; SAC, Memphis to Director, "Sanitation Workers Strike, Memphis, RM," 3 April 1968, 157–9146–64; SAC Robert G. Jensen to File 157–1092, "Sanitation Workers Strike, Memphis, RM," 3 April 1968, Memphis serial 157–1092–216 (detailing Harrison's phone call); SAC, Memphis (by William H. Lawrence) to Director, "Sanitation Workers Strike, Memphis, RM," 6 April 1968, 157–9146–9; Walter Bailey (Joan Beifuss, Bill Thomas, and David Yellin interview, 26 June 1968, Memphis), MVC, MSU, pp. 23–34; David Caywood (Anne Trotter and David Yellin interview, 20 May 1968, Memphis), MVC, MSU, part II, pp. 17–18; and Lucius Burch (Joan Beifuss and David Yellin interview, 3 September 1968, Memphis), MVC, MSU, pp. 7–8. Echoing Caywood's statement, Burch recalled that "King made it very clear to me that his *whole* future depended on

having a nonviolent march in Memphis.'' Charles Cabbage detailed BOP's ideas for organizing the black community in a July, 1968, interview with James Mosby, in the CRDP Papers, MSRC, Howard University. McCollough, who remained undercover in the Invaders until early 1969, described his experiences in a 12 July 1976 interview with Justice Department attorneys Fred G. Folsom and James F. Walker, a summary of which is filed in appendix B of the *King Task Force* report, cited in n. 31 above, and in testimony to the House Assassinations Committee, *Hearings —King,* vol. 6, pp. 413–33. Memphis public safety director Frank Holloman emphasized to attorney Walker in a 15 September 1976 telephone interview that McCollough was the only informant that Memphis police had inside the Invaders. A summary of that conversation also appears in appendix B of the *King Task Force* report.

34. Middlebrook, interview cited in n. 32 above, pp. 12–19; S. B. "Billy" Kyles (Joan Beifuss, Bill Thomas, and David Yellin interview, 12 June 1968, Memphis), MVC, MSU, pp. 10–15; Frank, *An American Death,* pp. 48–58; Ivy, interview cited in n. 27 above, pp. 54–56; House Committee on Assassinations, *Hearings—King,* vol. 1, pp. 19–20, and vol. 6, pp. 417, 466–67, 489, 517–19; James M. Lawson, Jr. (Joan Beifuss and David Yellin interview, 25 May 1972, Memphis), MVC, MSU; Lee, interview cited in n. 29 above; Ralph D. Abernathy (Jim Bishop interview, 3 September 1970, Atlanta), Friedsam Library, St. Bonaventure University; Raines, *My Soul is Rested,* pp. 468–69; and Alan F. Westin and Barry Mahoney, *The Trial of Martin Luther King* (New York: Thomas Y. Crowell, 1974), p. 270. The full text of King's April 3 Mason Temple speech is most easily available in Flip Schulke, ed., *Martin Luther King, Jr.: A Documentary . . . Montgomery to Memphis* (New York: W. W. Norton, 1976), pp. 222–24. The developments in court on April 4 are noted in the Caywood, Burch, and Bailey interviews cited in n. 33 above. Also see "Pitch for Unity Made by King," *Memphis Commercial Appeal,* 4 April 1968, p. 11; and Jay Bowles, "King Indicates Disregard of Order to Halt March," *Nashville Tennessean,* 4 April 1968.

35. Hoover (by M. J. Rozamus) to Ramsey Clark, "Electronic Surveillances," 1 May 1968, 66–8160–2978. On the embezzlement, see House Assassinations Committee, *Hearings—King,* vol. 6, p. 71. Harrison was reclassified from a "security" to a "racial" informant in December 1967, and still was functioning as "AT–1387–R" as late as July 1971.

36. Hoover to Dr. Henry Kissinger, "Coretta Scott King," 5 February 1969, 62–108052–42; Hoover to Egil Krogh, Jr., "Coretta Scott King," 26 January 1970, 62–108052–57; and Hoover to Alexander Butterfield, "Coretta Scott King," 1 February 1971, 62–108052–67. Major New York

reports on Levison include ones of 6 May 1970 (100–392452–362) and 9 June 1972 (100–392452–365); New York serial 100–111180–2260, dated 25 August 1971, notes the Security Index listing.

37. SAC, Atlanta (by Al F. Miller) to Director, "COMINFIL SCLC, IS–C (*JUNE*)," 7 February 1969, 100–438794–2525; Director (by C. E. Glass) to SAC, Atlanta, "COMINFIL SCLC, IS–C (*JUNE*)," 14 February 1969, 100–438794–2525; Drew Pearson and Jack Anderson, "Kennedy Ordered King Wiretap," *Washington Post*, 24 May 1968, p. D15; Fred P. Graham, "Drew Pearson Says Robert Kennedy Ordered Wiretap on Phone of Dr. King," *New York Times*, 25 May 1968, p. 17; C. D. DeLoach to Clyde Tolson, "Martin Luther King, (*JUNE*)," 17 May 1968, 100–106670–3458; and DeLoach to Tolson, "Approval of Wiretaps and Microphones by Robert F. Kennedy," 21 May 1968, 100–106670–unserialized. The best available account of SCLC's effort to go forward with the campaign in the wake of King's death is Charles E. Fager, *Uncertain Resurrection: The Poor People's Washington Campaign* (Grand Rapids, Mich.: Eerdmans Publishing Co., 1969).

38. Director to All SACs, "Martin Luther King, Jr., SM–C," 27 March 1969, 100–106670–3581; Milton A. Jones to Thomas E. Bishop, "Senator Hugh Scott, Proposed Bill to Commemorate Martin Luther King, Jr.," 22 May 1968, unserialized; R. W. Smith to William C. Sullivan, "Martin Luther King, Jr., Request by President Johnson for Detailed File," 2 June 1968 (unreleased); Hoover to Mildred Stegall, "Martin Luther King, Jr., SM–C," 3 June 1968, 100–106670–3465; U.S., Department of Justice, *King Task Force*, p. 130; George C. Moore (by T. J. Deakin) to Sullivan, "Martin Luther King, Jr., RM," 17 January 1969, 100–106670–3559; and Hoover (by Deakin) to John N. Mitchell, "Martin Luther King, Jr.," 23 January 1969, 100–106670–3559.

39. See Martin Waldron, "FBI Agent Testifies at Clay Hearing That Bureau Tapped Dr. King's Telephone for Several Years," *New York Times*, 5 June 1969, p. 27; Martin Waldron, "Wiretaps on Dr. King Made after Johnson Ban," *New York Times*, 7 June 1969, p. 29; Martin Waldron, "Clay Case Revises Eavesdrop Image," *New York Times*, 8 June 1969, p. 29; Ronald J. Ostrow and Nicholas C. Chriss, "Didn't OK King Tap, Clark Says," *Washington Post*, 8 June 1969, p. A7; Carl Rowan, "It Is Time for J. Edgar Hoover to Go," *Washington Evening Star*, 15 June 1969, p. E4; Lyle Denniston, "FBI Says Kennedy OKed King Wiretap," *Washington Evening Star*, 18 June 1969, pp. A1, A6; "FBI Says Kennedy Approved Wiretap on Dr. King's Phone," *New York Times*, 19 June 1969, p. 25; Jeremiah O'Leary, "King Wiretap Called RFK's Idea," *Washington Evening Star*, 19 June 1969, A1, A6; "Nixon Supports Hoover On Taps," *New*

York Times, 20 June 1969, p. 18; "Katzenbach Disputes FBI on King Tap," *Washington Post,* 20 June 1969, pp. A1, A12; Lyle Denniston, "King-Wiretapping Dispute Widens," *Washington Evening Star,* 20 June 1969, pp. A1, A6; Carl Rowan, "FBI Won't Talk about Additional Wiretappings," *Washington Evening Star,* 20 June 1969, p. A13; John Herbers, "Clark Suggests Hoover Step Out," *New York Times,* 21 June 1969, p. 11; and John P. MacKenzie, "Clark Says Hoover Should Retire Now," *Washington Post,* 21 June 1969, pp. A1, A14.

6. The Radical Challenge of Martin King

1. See nn. 59, 89, chapter 1, and nn. 34, 30–31, chapter 3.

2. See Victor S. Navasky, *Kennedy Justice* (New York: Atheneum, 1971), pp. 146–47; Athan Theoharis, *Spying on Americans: Political Surveillance from Hoover to the Huston Plan* (Philadelphia: Temple University Press, 1978), p. 173; and Jerry J. Berman, "The FBI's Vendetta against Martin Luther King, Jr.," in Morton H. Halperin et al., *The Lawless State: The Crimes of the U.S. Intelligence Agencies* (New York: Penguin Books, 1976), p. 89. Also see Senate Select Committee, *Final Report—Book III,* p. 85; and the remarks of FBI Assistant Director William A. Sullivan (not to be confused with William C.) in a *Face the Nation* interview, 6 July 1975, vol. 18, pp. 185–91, at 189.

3. Note the language used in two of the memos to Katzenbach, at nn. 53, 64, chapter 3. The relevant files also reflect a gradual transition in FBI reporting practices from "recording" to "forecasting." Most Bureau field communications in the SCLC and related cases before 1965 were reports on what *had occurred* a day or two earlier. By 1966, however, a changeover had taken place, and many field office reports detailed what *was expected to occur* a day or two in the future. Although nowhere near enough files yet are available to judge meaningfully the full import of this apparent shift, it does appear to signal a crucial alteration in Bureau behavior at a time when urban protest and antiwar efforts both were growing in strength.

4. See House Committee on Assassinations, *Hearings—King,* vol. 6, pp. 100–101. This point has been confirmed in a number of personal conversations. Several agents, in fact, became strongly convinced that Levison was no more than a sincere supporter of civil rights and King, despite headquarters' convictions to the contrary.

5. See Senate Select Committee, *Final Report—Book III,* p. 172; and House Committee on Assassinations, *Hearings—King,* vol. 6, p. 71.

6. See nn. 18, 24, 31, chapter 5.

7. Richard Hofstadter, *The Paranoid Style in American Politics* (New York: Alfred A. Knopf, 1965), pp. 3–40; and Frank J. Donner, *The Age of Surveillance* (New York: Alfred A. Knopf, 1980). Almost a decade before Hofstadter wrote, the sociologist Edward A. Shils had voiced some of the same observations Hofstadter later made. See *The Torment of Secrecy: The Background and Consequences of American Security Policies* (New York: Free Press, 1956), pp. 15, 32, 45–46, 77–98.

8. James Q. Wilson, *The Investigators: Managing FBI and Narcotics Agents* (New York: Basic Books, 1978), p. 179. For strong implicit support of Wilson's point, see Samuel A. Stouffer, *Communism, Conformity, and Civil Liberties* (New York: John Wiley, 1955), pp. 39–46, 156–219; and Clyde Z. Nunn, Harry J. Crockett, Jr., and J. Allen Williams, Jr., *Tolerance for Nonconformity* (San Francisco: Jossey-Bass, 1978), pp. 37–38, 41–43, 65, 95. The Bureau was indeed a "representative bureaucracy," but not in the way usually connoted by specialists' use of that phrase. On the standard concept, see Samuel Krislov, *Representative Bureaucracy* (Englewood Cliffs, N.J.: Prentice-Hall, 1974).

9. This further was magnified by the internal homogeneity of the Bureau discussed in the afterword. As two social psychologists have observed, "The more homogeneous the belief-systems of the ingroup members, the more homogeneously hostile towards outgroups will be these members." Donald T. Campbell and Robert A. LeVine, "Ethnocentrism and Intergroup Relations," in *Theories of Cognitive Consistency: A Sourcebook,* ed. Robert P. Abelson et al. (Chicago: Rand McNally, 1968), pp. 551–64, at 559.

10. Hofstadter, *The Paranoid Style,* pp. 14, 29. Also see Shils, *The Torment of Secrecy,* pp. 15, 32; and James Jacobs, "An Overview of National Political Intelligence," *University of Detroit Journal of Urban Law* 55 (1978): 853–75, at 858.

11. See Paul Boyer and Stephen Nissenbaum, *Salem Possessed: The Social Origins of Witchcraft* (Cambridge: Harvard University Press, 1974), pp. 189–216; Thomas J. Curran, *Xenophobia and Immigration, 1820–1930* (Boston: G. K. Hall & Co., 1975), pp. 21, 148; and especially Shils, *The Torment of Secrecy,* pp. 45–46, 77–98. An excellent compendium of exhibits that reflect this recurring response is David B. Davis, ed., *The Fear of Conspiracy* (Ithaca: Cornell University Press, 1971), esp. pp. xviii, 362. Also see Campbell and LeVine, "Ethnocentrism and Intergroup Relations," cited in n. 9 above, and LeVine and Campbell, *Ethnocentrism* (New York: John Wiley, 1972).

12. Donner, *The Age of Surveillance,* pp. xiii–xiv, 9–11, 13–15, 17–19, 119–20. Note in particular his observation that "in the view of intelligence,

subversion is a disease that is hereditary, chronic, incurable—and contagious. The subject, however remote his original subversive connection, taints all the groups and causes to which he subsequently becomes attached.'' The truth of this comment is striking to anyone who has had long exposure to FBI files, and the characterization systems that they employ.

13. Hofstadter, *The Paranoid Style,* pp. 14, 31–32. Hofstadter's suggestion that such a reaction largely is an act of projection is likely correct, but supporting evidence, of course, is difficult to acquire.

14. Donner, *The Age of Surveillance,* pp. 16, 121, 213–14. Also see Donner, ''Oedipus Cowed,'' *Nation* 229 (20 October 1979): 373–76, at 375; and Sandra Salmans, ''Tales of the FBI,'' *Newsweek,* 1 December 1975, pp. 35–36. The Bureau's conduct toward actress Jean Seberg also reflected this theme.

15. William C. Sullivan to Senator Walter F. Mondale, 17 April 1976; and Sullivan, *The Bureau: My Thirty Years in Hoover's FBI* (New York: W. W. Norton, 1979), pp. 138–39.

16. Senate Select Committee, *Final Report—Book III,* pp. 3, 27; and Senate Select Committee, *Hearings—FBI,* vol. 6, p. 42. As James Jacobs has noted, ''The assumptions that guide the operation of a political intelligence process are very closely associated with the dominant political culture of the particular political system.'' ''An Overview of National Political Intelligence,'' p. 855. Also see Frank M. Sorrentino, ''Bureaucratic Ideology: The Case Study of the Federal Bureau of Investigation,'' Unpublished Ph.D. diss., New York University, 1978, p. 139.

17. For excellent evidence depicting those popular beliefs and fears, and how congruent they appear to be with those reflected by the Bureau, see Stouffer, *Communism, Conformity, and Civil Liberties;* and Nunn, Crockett and Williams, *Tolerance for Nonconformity,* both cited in n. 8 above.

18. See n. 32, chapter 3, and n. 11, chapter 5.

19. See n. 17, chapter 5.

20. Donner, *The Age of Surveillance,* p. 3. Also see Sorrentino, ''Bureaucratic Ideology,'' p. 96, who observed, ''The New Left must be destroyed not because it is violent or because it is controlled by hostile powers, but because its ideas and values are unacceptable to the Federal Bureau of Investigation.''

21. Hofstadter, *The Paranoid Style,* p. 39. Note also Hofstadter's telling observation (p. 37) that representatives of the paranoid style laboriously gather mounds of facts that they believe document their claims, but that rarely prove anything and serve only to give ostensible support to conclusions previously arrived at.

22. ''King's Widow Says Americans Should Think about Dismantling the

FBI," *Durham* (N.C.) *Sun,* 30 May 1978, p. A11. Also see Morton Halperin, "The FBI and the Civil Rights Movement," *First Principles* 4 (September 1978): 15–16.

23. See Donner, *The Age of Surveillance,* pp. 126, 146, 154–55, 177, 183, 241, and "Hoover's Legacy," *Nation* 218 (1 June 1974): 678–99, at 698; Robert Wall, "Special Agent for the FBI," *New York Review of Books* 17 (27 January 1972): 12–18, at 18; and Senate Select Committee, *Final Report—Book III,* p. 7.

24. This analysis should not be misinterpreted as saying that the Bureau's actions against King were in any way justified or proper; they of course were not. Few of the eulogies and appraisals that appeared in the immediate aftermath of King's death indicated any appreciation of this more radical King. Two that did are Richard Hammer, "The Life and Death of Martin Luther King," *Midstream* 14 (May 1968): 3–16, at 5 and 14; and Mulford Q. Sibley, "Martin King and the Future," *Liberation* 13 (April 1968): 7–9. Also see Sibley, "Negro Revolution and Nonviolent Action: Martin Luther King," *Political Science Review* 9 (January–June 1970): 173–93, at 184–85, 187, 191.

25. Reverend J. Pius Barbour, perhaps King's closest friend during his three years (1948–51) at Pennsylvania's Crozer Theological Seminary, argued strongly in a September 1968 interview with David L. Lewis that King "was economically a Marxist. . . . He thought the capitalistic system was predicated on exploitation and prejudice, poverty, and that we wouldn't solve these problems until we got a new social order." Barbour added that King "believed that Marx had analyzed the economic side of capitalism right." Barbour is now deceased. See Lewis, *King: A Critical Biography* (New York: Praeger, 1970), p. 354.

26. See Martin Luther King, Jr., "An Autobiography of Religious Development," n.d. [circa 1950], p. 1, King Papers, Boston University. The handwritten essay is reproduced in full in Mervyn A. Warren, "A Rhetorical Study of the Preaching of Dr. Martin Luther King, Jr., Pastor and Pulpit Orator," Unpublished Ph.D. diss., Michigan State University, 1966, pp. 269–84.

27. Examples of King's dialectical criticisms of capitalism and communism can be seen in "Paul's Letter to American Christians," a 4 November 1956 sermon preached at Montgomery's Dexter Avenue Baptist Church, King Papers, BU, Drawer 1; and "At the Threshold of Integration," a 24 April 1957 speech in New York, which is reprinted in *Economic Justice* 25 (June–July 1957): 1, 7–8. Also see *Strength To Love* (New York: Harper & Row, 1963), pp. 10, 18, 88, esp. 98–99; and *Where Do We Go from Here: Chaos or Community* (New York: Harper & Row, 1967), pp. 186–

87. King's tendency to rely on the Hegelian dialectic is noted in Bennie E. Goodwin, "Martin Luther King, Jr.: American Social Educator," Unpublished Ph.D. diss., University of Pittsburgh, 1974, pp. 66–67, 132; Ira G. Zepp, Jr., "The Intellectual Sources of the Ethical Thought of Martin Luther King, Jr.," Unpublished Ph.D. diss., St. Mary's Seminary, 1971, pp. 272, 278; and, most importantly, L. Harold DeWolf, "Martin Luther King, Jr., As Theologian," *Journal of the Interdenominational Theological Center* 4 (Spring 1977): 1–11, at 7–8.

28. See especially King, "The Un-Christian Christian," *Ebony* 20 (August 1965): 77–80, at 79, where King remarked that "Southerners are making the Marxist analysis of history more accurate than the Christian hope that men can be persuaded through teaching and preaching to live a new and better life. In the South, businessmen act much more quickly from economic considerations than do churchmen from moral considerations."

29. See "To Charter Our Course for the Future," an eighteen-page unpublished transcript of King's remarks to an SCLC staff retreat in late May 1967, at Frogmore, South Carolina, at pp. 4–5; King, "A Testament of Hope," *Playboy* 16 (January 1969): 175, 194, 231–34, 236, at 194; King's statements in Jose Yglesias, "Dr. King's March on Washington, Part II," *New York Times Magazine,* 31 March 1968, pp. 30–31, 57–70, at 57; and a ten-page unpublished transcript of King's remarks at a 16 February 1968 mass meeting in Selma, Alabama. Also see King, "President's Address to the 10th Anniversary Convention of the SCLC," (16 August 1967, Atlanta), which appears in full in *The Rhetoric of Black Power,* ed. Robert L. Scott and Wayne Brockriede (New York: Harper & Row, 1969), pp. 146–65, where King mused that "maybe Marx didn't follow Hegel enough. He took his dialectics but he left out his idealism and his spiritualism" and substituted in its place Feuerbach's materialism.

30. The principal influence, of course, was Walter Rauschenbusch, author of *Christianity and the Social Crisis* (1907); *Christianizing the Social Order* (1912); and *A Theology for the Social Gospel* (1917). The effect of social gospel thought on King is most competently discussed in Kenneth L. Smith and Ira G. Zepp, Jr., *Search for the Beloved Community: The Thinking of Martin Luther King, Jr.* (Valley Forge, Pa.: Judson Press, 1974), pp. 33–45. King himself, in the 1950–51 "Autobiography" essay cited in n. 26 above, had an additional explanation as well: "It is quite easy for me to lean more toward optimism than pessimism about human nature mainly because of my childhood experiences."

31. Niebuhr's conflict with social gospel optimism is best seen in *Moral Man and Immoral Society* (New York: Charles Scribner's Sons, 1932), esp. pp. 81, 163, 210, and "Walter Rauschenbusch in Historical Perspective,"

Religion in Life 27 (Autumn 1958): 527–36, at 532–33. King's own increasing movement toward Niebuhrian realism and away from the influence of Rauschenbusch is detailed in Kenneth L. Smith, "Martin Luther King, Jr.: Reflections of a Former Teacher," *Bulletin of Crozer Theological Seminary* 57 (April 1965): 2–3; Smith and Ira G. Zepp, Jr., "Martin Luther King's Vision of the Beloved Community," *Christian Century* 91 (3 April 1974): 361–63, at 361; and Smith and Zepp, *Search for the Beloved Community,* pp. 74–86, 136–38. Two other excellent articles that discuss this maturation are Otis Turner, "Nonviolence and the Politics of Liberation," *Journal of the Interdenominational Theological Center* 4 (Spring 1977): 49–60, at 59–60; and George E. Carter, "Martin Luther King: Incipient Transcendentalist," *Phylon* 40 (December 1979): 318–24, at 321. Also see Paul R. Garber, "Black Theology: The Latter Day Legacy of Martin Luther King, Jr.," *Journal of the Interdenominational Theological Center* 2 (Spring 1975): 100–113, at 100–101; and Joseph L. Roberts, Jr., "The Black Church in the South: A Few Challenges of the '70s," *Black Church* 1 (2d Quarter 1972): 17–36, at 19 and 23.

32. The quotation is from a transcript of "Some Friends of Martin Luther King," a CBS television program broadcast 7 April 1968, which featured Hosea Williams, Andrew Young, and Harry Belafonte, among others. Also see Andrew Young's comments in Jean Stein, *American Journey: The Times of Robert Kennedy* (New York: Harcourt Brace Jovanovich, 1970), pp. 252–53; Peter R. Range, "Interview with Andrew Young," *Playboy* 24 (July 1977): 61–83, at 73–74; and Young's statements in George Goodman, " 'He Lives, Man!' " *Look* 33 (15 April 1969): 29–31, as well as Roger Wilkins, "Remembering Martin Luther King," *Washington Post,* 4 April 1972, p. A18; and William R. Miller, "Gandhi and King: Trail Blazers in Nonviolence," *Fellowship* 35 (January 1969): 5–8, at 6.

33. See Julius Lester, "The Martin Luther King I Remember," *Evergreen Review* 74 (January 1970): 16–21, 70, at 20–21 and 70; and the detailed remarks of Reverend J. Pius Barbour—explicitly quoting King—to David L. Lewis in September 1968.

34. Levison, from a 21 November 1969 interview with Jean Stein vanden Heuvel, which appears in Stein, *American Journey,* pp. 108–9. Also see very similar remarks in Coretta Scott King, *My Life with Martin Luther King, Jr.* (New York: Holt, Rinehart & Winston, 1969), pp. 61–62, 160, 171, 179, 274; and a tribute published under the names of Harry Belafonte and Levison, "Martin Luther King, Jr., 1929–1968," *Encyclopedia Yearbook 1968* (New York: Grolier, 1969), p. 160, which also appears in King, *My Life,* pp. 334–36.

35. Among others, Andrew Young often has noted the intense pace of the

last year and the seeming "war on sleep" that possessed King. See "Remembering Dr. King," in *The Sixties,* ed. Lynda R. Obst (New York: Random House, 1977), pp. 232, 236; Leon Howell, "An Interview with Andrew Young," *Christianity & Crisis* 36 (16 February 1976): 14–20, at 20; and Howell Raines, *My Soul Is Rested* (New York: G. P. Putnam's Sons, 1977), pp. 430–31. Also see Gerold Frank, *An American Death* (Garden City, N.Y.: Doubleday, 1972), pp. 41–42.

36. The same striking peroration appears in numerous sermons, including "But, If Not. . . ," 5 November 1967, Ebenezer Baptist Church, Atlanta; "The Meaning of Hope," 10 December 1967, Dexter Avenue Baptist Church, Montgomery; and "A Knock at Midnight," 24 March 1968, Canaan Baptist Church, New York. None of the three has been published.

37. As the events of January 1965, indicated (see n. 48, chapter 3), the Bureau's activities did indeed distress King very greatly, despite subsequent indications by other people to the contrary. As one 1976 Justice Department review accurately concluded, "the FBI files show that the campaign against King did succeed to the point of causing him serious and prolonged mental anguish." J. Stanley Pottinger to Edward H. Levi, "Martin Luther King Report," 9 April 1976, p. 9.

38. The blend of responses to the FBI's activities are noted by Andrew Young in Raines, *My Soul Is Rested,* pp. 427–28 and 430; in Howell, "An Interview with Andrew Young," pp. 15, 19–20; and by Bayard Rustin in a 30 June 1969 interview with T. H. Baker for the Johnson Library, Austin, pp. 4–6. Also see Samuel D. Cook, "Is Martin Luther King, Jr., Irrelevant?" *New South* 26 (Spring 1971): 2–14, at 4; and Haynes Johnson, "A Dreamer: Eloquence, Conviction—and Frustration," *Washington Post,* 2 April 1978, p. A3. King's only public reference that this author knows of came in an ill-received address to the New Politics Convention at Chicago's Palmer House on 31 August 1967, entitled "The Three Evils of Society." King stated (p. 12) that "we say to our nation tonight, we say to our government, we even say to our FBI, we will not be harassed."

39. See particularly "The Prodigal Son," 4 September 1966, Ebenezer Baptist Church, Atlanta, p. 4; and "Who Are We?" 5 February 1966, Ebenezer Baptist Church, Atlanta, p. 10. Also see *Strength To Love* (New York: Harper & Row, 1963), p. 36; and "Mastering Our Fears," 10 September 1967, Ebenezer Baptist Church, Atlanta, p. 1, in which King stated that "we often develop inferiority complexes and we stumble through life with a feeling of insecurity, a lack of self-confidence, and a sense of impending failure. A fear of what life may bring encourages some persons to wander aimlessly along the frittering road of excessive drink and sexual promiscuity."

40. "Unfulfilled Dreams," 3 March 1968, Ebenezer Baptist Church, Atlanta, pp. 2–6. This is not to be confused with King's "Drum Major" sermon delivered at Ebenezer on 4 February 1968, excerpts from which were played at King's funeral. Also see "Transforming a Neighborhood into a Brotherhood," an address delivered 11 August 1967 in Atlanta to the National Association of Television and Radio Announcers, p. 19, in which King stated, "I make mistakes tactically. I make mistakes morally and get on my knees and confess it and ask God to forgive me."

Afterword—"Reforming" the FBI

1. Christopher H. Pyle, in an untitled review of Athan Theoharis, *Spying on Americans: Political Surveillance from Hoover to the Huston Plan* (Philadelphia: Temple University Press, 1978), in *Political Science Quarterly* 94 (Fall 1979): 542–44, at 542.

2. Former Attorney General Nicholas deB. Katzenbach, in U.S., Congress, Senate, Select Committee to Study Governmental Operations with Respect to Intelligence Activities, *Hearings—Federal Bureau of Investigation,* vol. 6, 94th Cong., 1st sess., 1976, p. 212.

3. See, for example, the comments in U.S., Department of Justice, *Report of the Department of Justice Task Force to Review the FBI Martin Luther King, Jr., Security and Assassination Investigations,* 11 January 1977, pp. 140, 146; and House Committee on Assassinations, *The Final Assassinations Report* (New York: Bantam, 1979), p. 570.

4. See the testimony of Cartha D. "Deke" DeLoach in U.S., Congress, House of Representatives, Select Committee on Assassinations, *Hearings on Investigation of the Assassination of Martin Luther King, Jr.,* 95th Cong., 2d sess., 1978, vol. 7, pp. 45–47, 51–52, who stated that "we had to follow his orders or else we would not stay in our positions"; and the remarks of William C. Sullivan, *The Bureau: My Thirty Years in Hoover's FBI* (New York: W. W. Norton, 1979), pp. 138–39. Two excellent articles by Richard G. Powers detail the emergence of Hoover as a popular symbol: "J. Edgar Hoover and the Detective Hero," *Journal of Popular Culture* 9 (Fall 1975): 257–78; and "One G–Man's Family: Popular Entertainment Formulas and J. Edgar Hoover's FBI," *American Quarterly* 30 (Fall 1978): 471–92.

5. The highest quality examples of this are Theoharis, *Spying on Americans,* cited in n. 1 above, and three relatively early articles by Frank J. Donner, "Hoover's Legacy," *Nation* 218 (1 June 1974): 678–99; "Elec-

tronic Surveillance: The National Security Game," *Civil Liberties Review* 2 (Summer 1975): 15–47; and "How J. Edgar Hoover Created His Intelligence Powers," *Civil Liberties Review* 3 (February–March 1977): 34–51.

6. Early-twentieth-century American political science and history exhibited just such a "formal legal" approach, and it is from criticisms of that work that this label has been borrowed. See Bernard Crick, *The American Science of Politics* (Berkeley: University of California Press, 1960), pp. 95–107; and Albert Somit and Joseph Tanenhaus, *The Development of American Political Science* (Boston: Allyn & Bacon, 1967).

7. Anyone seeking a thorough understanding of the details of this debate should peruse two important General Accounting Office studies of changes in the Bureau's handling of its vastly reduced domestic intelligence case load as of the mid-1970s before proceeding with the additional works cited directly below. See U.S., Comptroller General, *FBI Domestic Intelligence Operations—Their Purpose and Scope: Issues That Need to Be Resolved* (#76–50) (Washington: GAO, 24 February 1976); and *FBI Domestic Intelligence Operations: An Uncertain Future* (#78–10) (Washington: GAO, 9 November 1977). These two documents provide a detailed account of just how drastic a cutback took place in FBI intelligence activities in the mid-1970s, though they do not describe the effective liquidation of what had been FBI Division Five, Domestic Intelligence. Also see U.S., Congress, Senate, Committee on the Judiciary, *FBI Statutory Charter—Hearings before the Subcommittee on Administrative Practice and Procedure*, 95th Cong., 2d sess., 1978, part 2, pp. 92–129, 177–243.

8. See the collection of essays published as "Chartering the FBI," *Nation* 229 (6 October 1979): 294–301, which, with one exception, represent this viewpoint. Note in particular those by John Shattuck et al.; Ramsey Clark; and Aryeh Neier. Also see Jerry J. Berman, "FBI Charter Legislation: The Case for Prohibiting Domestic Intelligence Investigations," *University of Detroit Journal of Urban Law* 55 (1978): 1041–77, as well as two articles by Athan Theoharis: "The Attorney General and the FBI: A Problem of Oversight," *USA Today,* May 1979, pp. 61–62, and "Why the Proposed FBI Charter Is a Threat to Our Civil Liberties," *The Judges' Journal* 18 (Fall 1979): 8–11, 54–56.

9. See John T. Elliff, *The Reform of FBI Intelligence Operations* (Princeton: Princeton University Press, 1979), and "The FBI and Domestic Intelligence," in *Surveillance and Espionage in a Free Society,* ed. Richard H. Blum (New York: Praeger, 1972), pp. 20–45; and the essay by Sanford J. Ungar in "Chartering the FBI," pp. 297–98, cited in n. 8 above.

10. See Richard E. Morgan, *Domestic Intelligence: Monitoring Dissent in America* (Austin: University of Texas Press, 1980), esp. pp. 14, 43, 124,

146–49, 153, 164–67, and, even more strongly, Arnold Beichman, "Can Counterintelligence Come in from the Cold?," *Policy Review* 15 (Winter 1981): 93–101. Some trenchant criticisms appear in Frank Donner, "The Terrorist As Scapegoat," *Nation* 226 (20 May 1978): 590–94.

11. Harry Howe Ransom has noted that this deficiency is almost as great for the CIA as it is for the FBI, and that "political science badly needs better knowledge of the intelligence structure and process." See "Being Intelligent about Secret Intelligence Agencies," *American Political Science Review* 74 (March 1980): 141–48, at 147. Also see David H. Hunter, "The Evolution of Literature on United States Intelligence," *Armed Forces and Society* 5 (November 1978): 31–52. What is available about the Bureau amounts almost wholly to works by journalists (see Sanford J. Ungar, *FBI* [Boston: Little, Brown, 1975] for the best of these) or autobiographical accounts by former agents and executives. The ones by former field agents tend to stress either humor (see Joseph L. Schott, *No Left Turns: The FBI in Peace and War* [New York: Praeger, 1975]; and Bernard F. Conners, *Don't Embarrass the Bureau* [Indianapolis: Bobbs-Merrill, 1972]), or idiosyncratic personal experiences (see William W. Turner, "I Was a Burglar, Wiretapper, Bugger, and Spy for the FBI," *Ramparts* 5 [November 1966]: 51–55, and *Hoover's FBI: The Men and the Myth* [New York: Dell, 1971]; and Cril Payne, *Deep Cover* [New York: Newsweek Books, 1979]). Books by former FBI executives include Sullivan, *The Bureau,* cited in n. 4 above, and W. Mark Felt, *The FBI Pyramid* (New York: G. P. Putnam's Sons, 1979). In addition to Ungar's book, serious students should consult Pat Watters and Stephen Gillers, eds., *Investigating the FBI* (Garden City, N.Y.: Doubleday, 1973); and Ovid Demaris, *The Director: An Oral Biography of J. Edgar Hoover* (New York: Harper's Magazine Press, 1975).

12. James Q. Wilson, *The Investigators: Managing FBI and Narcotics Agents* (New York: Basic Books, 1978).

13. Christopher H. Pyle, "Military Surveillance of Civilian Politics, 1967–1970," Unpublished Ph.D. diss., Columbia University, 1974.

14. Wilson, *The Investigators,* pp. 165–66, 169–70. Another work that perceptively notes this point is Eugene Lewis, *Public Entrepreneurship: Toward a Theory of Bureaucratic Political Power* (Bloomington: Indiana University Press, 1980), esp. pp. 9–11, 18, 19–20, 104, 150. Also see Pyle, "Military Surveillance," p. 415; Senate Select Committee, *Final Report—Book II, Intelligence Activities and the Rights of Americans,* 94th Cong., 2d sess., 1976, p. 271; and James D. Thompson, *Organizations in Action* (New York: McGraw Hill, 1967), pp. 20–24.

15. For confirmation of these observations, see Wilson, *The Investigators,* pp. 90–91, 146, 171, 182, 200–201, 203. Also see Wilson, "The

Changing FBI: The Road to Abscam,'' *Public Interest* 59 (Spring 1980): 3–14, at 4; Senate Select Committee, *Final Report—Book II,* p. 266; Anthony Downs, *Inside Bureaucracy* (Boston: Little, Brown, 1967), pp. 56–57; and the insightful comments of Francis E. Rourke, "Bureaucratic Autonomy and the Public Interest," *American Behavioral Scientist* 22 (May–June 1979): 537–46. One also should note Wilson's important observation that the Bureau remains a means-oriented rather than goal-oriented bureaucracy. See *The Investigators,* p. 124.

16. Ungar, *FBI,* pp. 325–27, 329–31, and 336–38, presents an extremely powerful description of these characteristics. Also see the comments of former agent Arthur L. Murtagh, in House Committee on Assassinations, *Hearings—King,* vol. 6, pp. 114–17.

17. Downs, *Inside Bureaucracy,* pp. 228–35. Downs further observes, "The process of personnel selection implicitly involves four steps: 1. Determining the characteristics to be sought in new members. 2. Developing means of identifying those characteristics in potential recruits. 3. Applying those means to the overall population to identify desirable prospects. 4. Persuading prospects to join the bureau."

18. Charles D. Brennan, former assistant director for domestic intelligence, in House Committee on Assassinations, *Hearings—King,* vol. 6, p. 356. Also see Sanford J. Ungar, "An Agenda for Rebuilding the FBI," *Washington Post,* 21 August 1977, pp. C1–C2: and Wilson, *The Investigators,* p. 106. Wilson notes that anyone seeking advancement had to make themselves "a creature of headquarters," and particularly of the powerful administrative division.

19. William C. Sullivan, "Personal Observations and Recommendations on Privacy," in *Privacy in A Free Society,* ed. Theodore I. Koskoff (Cambridge, Mass.: Roscoe Pound American Trial Lawyers Foundation, 1974), pp. 93–99, at 94–95. Note too the remarks of former Division Five section chief George C. Moore, who called it "a rather small Division in a way and closely confined," in House Committee on Assassinations, *Hearings—King,* vol. 6, p. 365. Also see Irving L. Janis, *Victims of Groupthink* (Boston: Houghton Mifflin, 1972), p. 197.

20. See Charles D. Brennan's remarks in House Committee on Assassinations, *Hearings—King,* pp. 355–56.

21. Wilson, *The Investigators,* p. 108.

22. See Pyle, "Military Surveillance," pp. 355–64.

23. See Wilson, "The Changing FBI," p. 4.

Index